Gender in Policy and Practice

Gender in Policy and Practice

PERSPECTIVES ON SINGLE-SEX AND COEDUCATIONAL SCHOOLING

Edited by

Amanda Datnow *and*
Lea Hubbard

RoutledgeFalmer
Taylor & Francis Group

Published in 2002 by
RoutledgeFalmer
29 West 35th Street
New York, NY 10001
www.routledge-ny.com

Published in Great Britain by
RoutledgeFalmer
11 New Fetter Lane
London EC4P 4EE
www.routledgefalmer.com

10 9 8 7 6 5 4 3 2 1

Library of Congress Cataloging-in-Publication Data

Gender in policy and practice : perspectives on single-sex and coeducational schooling / edited by Amanda Datnow and Lea Hubbard.
    p. cm.
Includes bibliographical references and index.
ISBN 0–415–93270–X — ISBN 0–415–93271–8 (pbk.)
    1. Single-sex schools. 2. Coeducation. 3. Gender identity in education. 4. Sex differences in education. 5. Educational equalization. I. Datnow, Amanda. II. Hubbard, Lea, 1946–

LB3067.3 .G46 2002
371.822—dc21   2002069886

CONTENTS

Section One

INTRODUCTION AND BACKGROUND

CHAPTER 1

Introduction

Amanda Datnow and Lea Hubbard

This volume on single-sex and coeducational schooling grew out of a special meeting at the annual conference of the Research on Women in Education Special Interest Group of the American Educational Research Association, held at Hofstra University in New York in 1998. A group of us who had conducted or were currently conducting studies of single-sex and coeducation schooling were brought together by Patricia Schmuck, a longtime scholar in the field of gender and education. The goal of this meeting was to discuss what we know about single-sex and coeducational schooling and consider the questions that remain unanswered. We shared our research and discussed the commonalities and differences that we saw emerging from our data. Alan Sadovnik, who was also present at the meeting, shared his research and suggested that we put together an edited volume, which he offered to consider for his RoutledgeFalmer book series. Most of the individuals who were present at that meeting contributed chapters to this volume, and additional authors were solicited as the book was developed in order to include a more comprehensive rendering of the subject.

This volume—and indeed the meeting that led to it—comes at an important and interesting historical moment in education in general and for single-sex and coeducational schooling in particular. It is a time when there are persistent calls for the improvement of the American public education system, as well as educational systems throughout other Western countries and elsewhere. The push for improvement has resulted in a plethora of reform agendas, movements for nationally driven standards and increased accountability, a common curriculum, and comprehensive school reform, to name a few. There are also efforts by some to expand school choice both outside and within the public school system.

There also have been concerns on the part of some about gender equity in schooling, as many studies over the past twenty-five years have documented gender bias against females in coeducational classrooms both at the K–12 and higher education levels. (See AAUW, 1992; 1998b for reviews.) Females have historically received less teacher attention than boys, feel less comfortable speaking out in class, and face threats of sexual harassment in school (AAUW, 1993; Sadker and Sadker, 1994). Although the achievement gaps between boys and girls are closing some areas, girls' achievement still lags behind boys in math and science, and most significantly in computer science and technology majors and careers (AAUW, 1998b, 2000). There is also concern that gender equity solutions have reached girls of different ethnic groups unequally. For example, Latinas perform less well than other racial and ethnic groups of girls in several key measures of educational achievement (Ginorio and Huston, 2001).

Although gender equity has long been discussed in terms of remedies designed to raise girls' achievement, more recently, some scholars have begun to ask, "What about the boys?" (Gurian, 1998; Pollack, 1998). Public discourse has centered on a "crisis" for boys, focusing on their lower reading and language test scores and higher rates of special education referrals as compared to girls (Kleinfeld, 1999), as well as boys' greater propensity to be involved in violent crimes (Gilbert and Gilbert, 1998). All boys are seen as at risk of these problems, but most notably boys of color. Increasing rates of dropout and higher rates of incarceration are particularly salient for African-American boys and men (Leake and Leake, 1992).

Some scholars argue that this shift in focus toward boys is the result of social backlash against feminism as well as a "zero-sum" perspective that reforms cannot improve the outcomes of schooling for girls without negatively affecting the outcomes for boys (Gipps, 1996; Yates, 1997), and many feminist researchers believe that gender equity is still problematic for girls. As these debates suggest, gender bias can no longer be seen as an isolated problem, but is now understood as representative of larger systems of oppression, which include race, class, and sexuality. Gender bias is now seen as affecting both girls and boys, because neither group is immune to societal pressures and expectations. Reform efforts are thus more complex than simply eliminating sexist language or curricula, but rather require educators to strive to implement alternative pedagogies that challenge the unequal power relations inherent in traditional education and society (Murphy and Gipps, 1996).

Public schools in at least fifteen U.S. states have recently responded to calls for the improvement of education more generally, or to gender equity concerns, through experiments with single-sex education, most often in the form of separate math or science classes for girls (Streitmatter, 1999). Other manifestations of public single-gender schooling include Afrocentric academies for boys in Detroit, Baltimore, and Milwaukee, California's single-gender academies, and the Young Women's Leadership schools in Harlem and

Chicago. Although some of these experiments have been found in violation of Title IX and have been forced to close or become coed, others continue. Over the past few years, in an effort to loosen Title IX's control, Senator Kay Bailey Hutchison (Republican, Texas) has attempted to pass a Senate bill to allow public school districts to experiment with federally funded single-sex education (Hutchison, 1999; Richards, 2000).

Significantly, as of May 2002, there are new federal regulations which provide more flexibility for, encourage, and help support single-sex public schools. Most instances of single-sex schooling still occur in the private sector in the United States. Recent years have seen a rise in the number of single-sex private schools for girls as well as an increase in applications to girls' schools. A 1998 survey by the National Coalition of Girls Schools of their member schools found that enrollment at girls' schools had increased 18.7 percent since the organization's founding in 1991, and applications to girls schools increased 32 percent over the same period (http://www.ncgs.org/Pages/news.htm). The Coalition reported in 2001 that in the second half of the 1990s, thirty-two new all-girls' schools were founded in the United States (http://www.ncgs.org/Pages/tenyears.htm). The organization describes girls' schools as experiencing a "renaissance."

At the same time, there have been developments with regard to single-sex and coeducational schooling in the higher education sector. Whereas in the 1970s and 1980s numerous women's and men's colleges made the decision to become coeducational, in the 1990s there began to be a renewed interested in women's colleges (Riordan, 1990; chapter 8 of this volume). However, this renewed interest has not yet translated into increases in the number of women's colleges, as we have seen in the K–12 sector. Why the interest in single-sex public schooling? Advocates point to studies of Catholic single-sex and coeducational schools that find academic achievement benefits for girls and low-income and minority boys attending single-sex schools (e.g., Lee and Bryk, 1986; Riordan, 1990). Research on gender in the 1980s (Belenky et al., 1986; Gilligan, 1982), arguing that women learn differently than men, also has helped to provide justification for all-female schooling. Proponents of single-sex education also argue that the separation of the sexes is the most effective way to manage classroom behavior by eliminating distractions and peer pressures for both boys and girls (Pollard, 1998) and providing leadership and character development opportunities for each group. All-boys' classes or schools are looked upon by some educators and policymakers as ways to improve literacy achievement and discipline (Gilbert and Gilbert, 1998).

Advocates of all-male Afrocentric academies in public schools argue that the presence of African-American role models and a focus on multicultural curricula can be beneficial in developing leadership skills and improving achievement for African-American boys (Hopkins, 1997). Clearly, the reasons behind the recent establishment of single-sex schools are no longer simple; they represent efforts to address not only gender bias, but also racial and cultural issues as well.

Single-sex education, however, also has its critics. The National Organization of Women and other feminist groups argue that segregating students leaves the inequities of the public school system intact. Some studies have questioned the academic and social advantages offered by single-sex schooling, arguing that school factors contribute more to positive outcomes than gender separation (Lee, 1997). Other researchers also argue that single-gender educational settings promote stereotypical gender roles and attitudes toward the opposite sex (AAUW, 1998a; Lee, Marks, and Byrd, 1994). A significant limitation is that most studies of single-sex schooling have been conducted in the private sector and therefore may not generalize to public schools. (See Mael, 1998, for a review.) This raises important concerns for the validity and relevance of research findings. As Pamela Haag asks, "Do students achieve because of a school's sex composition or because the schools draw from economically and educationally privileged populations?" (AAUW, 1998a, p. 15).

Our goal in this book is to expose the complexity of single-sex schooling, as well as contribute new insight on how gender operates in policy and practice in education. The chapters in this volume examine a wide range of contexts in which single-sex and coeducational schooling exist. The chapters deal with K–12 and higher education, public and private schools, U.S. and international contexts, and the schooling experiences of both young women and men. Particularly novel issues that receive attention in this volume include public single-sex schooling, the transition between single-sex and coeducation, the voices and experiences of males in addition to females, and qualitative studies of single-sex and coeducational schooling. All of the chapters in this book include implications for policy and/or practice. This is the first volume of its kind; no prior edited collections have examined a diversity of studies on single-sex and coeducational schooling, much less in this breadth or depth.

The authors in this volume approach the topics of single-sex and coeducational schooling from a variety of methodological and theoretical perspectives, including historical, sociological, psychological, legal, and qualitative and quantitative, sometimes using a feminist approach. In general, this book marks a shift away from prior notions of viewing single-sex schools as merely a way to organize students. Instead, in many chapters, single-sex and coeducational schools are examined within a framework that embodies institutional and ideological notions of gender as a principle of social differentiation. Engagement of this critical perspective hopefully will allow our audience to understand the way schooling shapes and is shaped by the social construction of gender in historical and contemporary society.

An important note about language bears mentioning here. Typically, the terms "sex" and "gender" refer to the biological and social characteristics, respectively, of being male and female. As Pamela Haag notes, "Schools with all girls are not necessarily single 'gender' because they may include students with both 'masculine' and 'feminine' identities" (AAUW, 1998a, p. 36). Single-

"sex," therefore, is a more accurate characterization of an all-male or all-female school; however, some of the authors in this volume, ourselves included, often refer to schools as single "gender" because that is the way they were referred to in their local contexts. Hence, in some chapters, the authors refer to single-"sex" education whereas others refer to single- "gender" education.

ORGANIZATION OF THE BOOK

Section One is intended to introduce the reader to the major findings and debates in research and the law related to single-sex schooling. The chapter by Riordan provides a summary of empirical findings on the effectiveness of private single-sex schooling at the K–12 level, finding support for the practice under certain conditions and discussing implications for public schools. Conversely, the chapter by Campbell and Sanders questions the assumptions and findings about single-sex schooling at the K–12 and college levels, particularly with respect to the goal of gender equity. The final chapter in this section, by Salomone, considers in detail the historical and legal issues surrounding single-sex schooling, arguing for "a lifting of the legal cloud" over single-sex schooling in order to allow for more experimentation in the public sector.

Section Two is devoted to the topic of single-sex public schooling in a changing policy environment, examining both U.S. and Canadian contexts. The chapter by Herr and Arms discusses how competing pressures and multiple innovations skewed the implementation of what was touted as primarily a single-gender education reform at one California public middle school. In the next chapter, Sanford and Blair draw on case studies of three schools to discuss how the advent of single-sex public schooling in Western Canada is changing the nature of classroom practice with respect to gender equity. The third chapter in this section, by Hubbard and Datnow, examines some of the conditions facilitating and constraining the sustainability of public single-sex schooling, drawing on findings from our study of single-gender public schools in California and elsewhere.

Section Three focuses on the transitions from single-sex education to coeducation. Sadovnik and Semel discuss the history of Wheaton College, as it moved from being an all-women's institution to "conscious" coeducation in 1998. Next, Miller-Bernal examines the history of coordinate liberal arts colleges for women (i.e., those affiliated with and sharing some resources with men's colleges, but retaining a separate identity), comparing several instantiations of coordinate colleges and concluding with their implications for coeducation. Diamond and Kimmel's chapter explores the integration of women into two military institutions, the United States Military Academy at West Point, and the Virginia Military Institute, providing the perspectives of both female and male cadets from the first coeducational classes. In the final chapter in this section, Schmuck, Nagel, and Brody summarize their findings from a study of the role of gender consciousness and privilege in three Catholic secondary schools in transition from single-sex to coeducation.

Section Four illuminates the experiences and outcomes for students in single-sex and coeducation from both quantitative and qualitative perspectives. First, Streitmatter describes how girls and boys see single-gender schooling in an urban public middle school rather differently, with girls deriving more empowerment and community building from the experience than boys. In the next chapter, Gilson compares the academic experiences and attitudes of girls toward mathematics in single-sex and coeducational independent schools. Ainley and Daly examine how girls' and boys' participation levels in science courses in Australia and elsewhere are affected by whether they attend single-sex or coeducational schools.

Section Five focuses specifically on constructions of gender in single-sex schooling. Although many of the chapters in this volume speak to the issue of "doing gender," the chapters in this section focus directly on how gender is socially constructed from a number of different angles. First, Gallagher considers how gender constructions and perceptions of judgment shifted for girls who participated in the drama in a racially diverse, Catholic single-sex school in Canada. This chapter is novel for its investigation of the arts and single-sex education because most prior work has focused on core academic subjects. Second, Woody illuminates how definitions of masculinity are constructed in public single-gender academies in the United States, illuminating boys' voices as well as those of their teachers and female peers. Finally, the chapter by Heather examines how parents' constructions of gender influence their choice of a single-sex school for their daughters.

COMMON THEMES

Numerous common themes emerge from the findings that are presented across the chapters, and we believe they are worth mentioning here. First, and perhaps most important, many of the authors find that both single-sex and coeducational schooling can provide possibilities or constraints to students' achievement or future opportunities, and these outcomes depend to a great degree on how these forms of schooling are implemented. As Kruse states: "Sex-segregated education can be used for emancipation or oppression. As a method, it does not guarantee an outcome. The intentions, the understanding of people and their gender, the pedagogical attitudes and practices, are crucial, as in all pedagogical work" (1996, p. 189). The same is true for coeducation.

Second, and on a related note, numerous studies reported in this volume find that a commitment to gender equity must be explicit in an organization's practices for it to be realized. In other words, it is not enough to have a philosophical commitment to gender equity, although that is, of course, important, but a school or university's curriculum, instructional strategies, and organization must support this goal or policy. Achieving gender equity means not only providing equal opportunity to both genders but also acknowledging the power differences that exist between men and women in society and looking for ways that educational institutions can alter these taken-for-granted patterns that often place women on unequal footing to men and lead to restrictive notions of masculinity and femininity. Consideration also must be given to how males and females of varied races and ethnicities might be favored differentially in society and educational institutions, and what can be done to create equity in this regard as well.

Next, a number of the chapters in this volume document the ways in which sexism in the larger society undermines institutional efforts to foster gender equity. That is, even when schools, universities, or particular individuals in these settings attempted to create gender equitable environments in which young women and men could thrive, these efforts often conflict with societal beliefs in some communities regarding more traditional roles for men and women. Both within educational institutions and the contexts in which they were embedded, researchers often came across dichotomous understandings of gender wherein males and females were thought to be polar opposites. Often, these definitions of gender served to limit possibilities for males and females in single-sex and coeducational settings.

A final common theme that appears in numerous chapters in the volume is the struggle to make sense of what many see as conflicting evidence regarding the effectiveness of single-sex schooling, as well as the difficulties that institutions themselves face in defining whether and why a particular form of schooling (coed or single-sex) is preferable for whom, and under what conditions. These are thorny questions, which most often result in the answer, "It depends . . ." Although this volume breaks new ground in a number of key areas, further research is still needed into the various contexts in which single-sex and coeducational schooling now exist.

Our hope is that the chapters in this book, taken together, will help inform educators and policymakers about how single-sex schooling is positioned in historical and contemporary perspective; how it operates in the public education landscape, as well as in private and higher education; how it impacts the schooling experiences of young women and men; compares to coeducation; and how it contributes to the reproduction or resistance of constructions of gender and gendered relations of power. With new federal support for single-sex public education, and with single-sex schools proliferating in some areas and provoking considerable debate, this collection provides timely information on an important topic.

REFERENCES

American Association of University Women. (2000). *Tech-Savvy: Educating Girls in the New Computer Age.* Washington, D.C.: The American Association of University Women Educational Foundation.

———. (1998a). *Separated by Sex: A Critical Look at Single Sex Education for Girls*. Washington, D.C.: The American Association of University Women Educational Foundation.

———. (1998b). *Gender Gaps: Where Schools Still Fail Our Children*. Washington, D.C.: Author.

———. (1993). *Hostile Hallways: The AAUW Survey on Sexual Harassment in America's Schools*. Harris Scholastic Research. Washington, D.C.: Author.

———. (1992). *How Schools Shortchange Girls*. Washington, D.C.: Author.

Belenky, M. F., et al. (1986). *Women's Ways of Knowing: The Development of Self, Voice and Mind*. New York: Basic Books.

Gilbert, R., and Gilbert, P. (1998). *Masculinity Goes to School*. London: Routledge.

Gilligan, C. (1982). *In a Different Voice*. Cambridge, MA: Harvard University Press.

Gipps. C. (1996). "Introduction." In P. F. Murphy and C. V. Gibbs (Eds.), *Equity in the Classroom: Towards Effective Pedagogy for Girls and Boys*. London: Falmer Press, 1–6.

Ginorio, A. M., and Huston, M. (2001). *Sí, We Puede! Yes, We Can: Latinas in School*. Washington, D.C.: American Association of University Women Educational Foundation.

Gurian, M. (1998). *A Fine Young Man: What Parents, Mentors, and Educators Can Do to Shape Adolescent Boys into Exceptional Men*. New York: Putnam.

Hopkins, R. (1997). *Educating Black Males: Critical Lessons in Schooling, Community, and Power*. Albany: SUNY Press.

Hutchison, K. B. (1999, October 6). Senate floor speech on single-sex classrooms amendment. Proceedings and debates of the 106th congress, first session. *http://www.senate.gov/hutchison/speech11.htm*

Leake, D., and Leake, B. (1992). "Islands of Hope: Milwaukee's African American Immersion Schools." *Journal of Negro Education* 61(1): 24–29.

Lee, V. E. (1997). "Gender Equity and the Organization of Schools." In B. Bank and P. M. Hall (Eds.), *Gender, Equity, and Schooling* (pp. 135–158). New York: Garland.

Lee, V., and Bryk, A. S. (1986). "Effects of Single-Sex Schools on Student Achievement and Attitudes." *Journal of Educational Psychology* 78: 381–395.

Lee, V., Marks, H. M., and Byrd, T. (1994). "Sexism in Single-Sex and Coeducational Independent Secondary School Classrooms." *Sociology of Education* 67: 92–120.

Kleinfeld, J. (1999). "Student Performance: Males Versus Females." *The Public Interest* 134: 3–20.

Kruse, A. M. (1996). "Single Sex Settings: Pedagogies for Girls and Boys in Danish Schools." In P. Murphy and G. Gipps (Eds.), *Equity in the Classroom: Towards Effective Pedagogy for Girls and Boys*. London: Falmer, 173–191.

Mael, F. (1998). "Single Sex and Coeducational Schooling: Relationships to Socioemotional and Academic Development." *Review of Educational Research* 68: 101–129.

Murphy, P., and Gipps, G. (Eds.) (1996). *Equity in the Classroom: Towards Effective Pedagogy for Girls and Boys*. London: Falmer.

Pollack, W. (1998). *Real Boys: Rescuing Our Sons from the Myths of Boyhood*. New York: Random House.

Pollard, D. S. (1998). "The Contexts of Single Sex Classes." In *Separated by Sex: A Critical Look at Singl Sex Education for Girls*. Washington, D.C.: AAUW.

Richards, C. (2000, November 15). "Public Funds for Experimental Single-Sex Ed?" *Women's News*. *http://www.womensenews.org/article.cfm?aid=160&context=archive*.

Riordan, N. (1990). *Girls and Boys in School: Together or Separate?* New York: Teachers College Press.

Sadker, M., and Sadker, D. (1994). *Failing at Fairness*. New York: Touchstone.

Sadovnik, A., and Semel, S. (Chapter 8 of this volume). "The Transition to Coeducation at Wheaton College: Conscious Coeducation and Gender Equity in Higher Education."

Streitmatter, J. L. (1999). *For Girls Only: Making a Case for Single Sex Schooling*. Albany, NY: SUNY Press.

Yates, L. (1997). "Gender Equity and the Boys Debate: What Sort of Challenge Is It?" *British Journal of Sociology of Education*, 18(3): 337–347.

CHAPTER 2

What Do We Know about the Effects of Single-Sex Schools in the Private Sector?: Implications for Public Schools

Cornelius Riordan

INTRODUCTION

Most Americans take coeducation for granted. Typically, their own school-ing has been coeducational; often, they have little awareness of single-sex schools. Our political culture reinforces the taken-for-granted character of American coeducation. It implies that schools reflecting the variety of soci-ety exemplify what is best about democratic societies. Many people also take for granted that coeducation provides equality of educational opportunity for women. Like racial and ethnic minorities, women have long been excluded from the educational process. Thus, many people regard coeduca-tion as a major milestone in the pursuit of gender equality. Single-sex edu-cation, by contrast, appears regressive.

Coeducation began not because of any firm belief in its sound educa-tional effect, but rather because of financial constraints (Riordan, 1990). Historically, mixed-sex schools were economically more efficient. In America, boys and girls have usually attended the same public schools. This practice originated with the "common" school. Of course, at one time in our society only boys received an education. At other times the only education for either boys or girls was single-sex schooling, either public or private. Once mass and state-supported public education had been established, how-ever, it was clearly the exception for boys and girls to attend separate schools. By the end of the nineteenth century, coeducation was all but universal in American elementary and secondary public schools (Bureau of Education,

An earlier version of this chapter was presented at a symposium entitled Single-Sex and Coeducational Schools and Classrooms: Implications for Public Schools at the annual meet-ing of the American Educational Research Association (April 12, 2000). Several sections of the chapter were published originally by The Brookings Institution Press (1999) and the American Association for University Women Educational Foundation (1998).

1883; Butler, 1910; Kolesnick, l969). Although single-sex schooling remains as an option in private secondary schools, it declines with each decade (Lee and Marks, 1992).

Men's and women's colleges also became coeducational largely as a result of economic forces. This continues to be true today as enrollments dwindle in women's colleges. Thus, coeducation has evolved as a commonplace norm, not because of educational concerns as much as other forces. Women's colleges were established within a context of exclusion in the nineteenth century. And within this context, the underlying assumption, widely held both then and now, was that women's colleges were a temporary, short-term solution on the road to the eventual achievement of coeducation (Tidball et al., 1999).

This historical background has provided a protective halo around coeducation as an institution. Historically, this mode of school organization was never subjected to systematic research. Currently, this protective halo affects the research strategy and logic for comparing single-sex and mixed-sex schools. This "assumptive world" is so deeply ingrained that people often acknowledge the academic superiority of single-sex schools without realizing the aspersion implied for coeducation. A cursory sample of interviews will reveal that most people view single-sex schools as academically tougher, more rigorous, although perhaps less enjoyable than coeducational schools.

The salience of this problem was pointed up with the publication of the report, "How Schools Shortchange Women," commissioned by the American Association of University Women Educational Foundation (1992). (For an update of this study, see AAUW, 1998a.) This study examined more than one thousand publications about girls and education and concluded that bias against females remained widespread in coeducational schools, and was the cause of lasting damage to both educational achievement and self-development. Given these findings, one might think that the burden of proof would shift to coeducational schools, to demonstrate first that they are free of gender bias, and second, that they are at least as effective as single-sex schools in terms of achievement and gender equity. This would replace the current practice, which requires single-sex schools to show greater effectiveness.

A landmark study using expectation states theory was conducted by Elizabeth Cohen and her colleagues at Stanford University (1972). In Cohen's study, and several replications, it was found that simply placing African-American and white students in what appeared to be an equal-status problem-solving situation was *insufficient* to guarantee equal-status outcomes. In fact, the studies have documented and reported relatively extreme manifestations of racism; that is, white dominance in these types of situations. Moreover, in these studies, extensive efforts were made to alter the interaction pattern of white dominance with little success, except under one condition in which the African-American students were literally allocated to a dominant role vis-à-vis the white students, who were allocated a submissive role. These results led Cohen and Roper to the conclusion that:

> The oft made assumption that one has only to join blacks and whites on an officially "equal" footing in the same building for "equal status" relations to develop is not sound. . . . Belief systems concerning race and other status characteristics are so powerful that they will likely reinforce rather than damage stereotypical beliefs. (1972, pp. 645, 657)

Research has shown that small task groups, such as those characterized by classrooms, exhibit status hierarchies where some group members are more active, influential, and powerful than others (Berger and Zelditch, 1985). These unequal status positions occur in groups in which participants have been carefully matched according to various irrelevant status characteristics such as race, gender, age, height, educational level, and occupational attainment. This process has been termed "status generalization" (Berger, Conner, and Fisck, 1974). Whenever members of a social group are performing lower on average than another group, as is the case regarding boys and girls on many educational outcome measures, sound research suggests that some form of prior "treatment" for the disadvantaged group is helpful before engaging in mixed-group interaction or learning (Cohen and Roper, 1972; Lockheed, 1985). Thus, it is incorrect to conclude that coeducational schooling is best, especially when there are existing inequalities.

If dominance and inequality emerge in groups of people who are otherwise equal in societal status, it is not surprising to learn that this occurs even more predictably when group members differ in status characteristics that are viewed as unequal. Thus, because gender and race have historically been defined as unequal, expectation states theory predicts that higher status actors will assume high status positions in classrooms. In the case of race, whites are more likely to be dominant. In the case of gender, it can go both ways depending on the particular skill being evaluated (Lee, Chen, and Smerdon, 1995; Riordan, 2000; U.S. Department of Education, 2000).

In addition, students typically hold unequal standing in the classroom based on previous academic performance. Students hold relatively clear expectations for each other as to academic competence at various tasks (Cohen, 1994, 2000; Rosenholtz, 1985; Tammivaara, 1982). Furthermore, the research demonstrates that group members who assume and are accorded high status in one area of expertise are expected to be more competent and influential in other nonrelated tasks as well, academic and nonacademic. What this means for classrooms is that some students who are seen as performing pecific tasks well, such as reading, are also accorded higher status in performing most other tasks, however unrelated they may be (Rosenholtz, 1985). Specifically, it means that females may be accorded higher status on all academic skills based on their reading ability or that males might be accorded higher status based on their mathematical ability.

Within the context of these introductory remarks, I wish to address four key issues in the remainder of the chapter:

1. What does research in the private sector tell us about single-sex schooling?
2. Why are single-sex schools more effective than coeducational schools?
3. What are the implications of private school research for single-sex public schools?
4. What does all of this mean in terms of educational policy?

WHAT IS KNOWN REGARDING THE EFFECTS OF SINGLE-SEX SCHOOLS IN THE PRIVATE SECTOR?

Surprisingly, there are very few formal reviews of the relative effects of single-sex and coeducational schools or classrooms. Of course, all researchers have conducted their own literature reviews, but these are often incomplete. However, we can effectively draw upon the two exhaustive reviews of research. The first of these was conducted by Moore, Piper, and Schaefer for a U.S. Department of Education report. This review concluded that "there is sufficient evidence to support the proposition that single-sex schools may produce positive outcomes for young women, and that the countervailing evidence to reject that proposition is not sufficiently convincing" (1992, p. 42). In a more recent and fully exhaustive review, Mael concluded that "the predominance of research certainly shows a role for single-sex schools (as an option if not a norm)" (1998, p. 121). Despite the widespread attention given to the AAUW report, *Separated by Sex* (1998b), it is inappropriate to rely on it or the media stories that followed it as a definitive interpretation in light of the independent reviews of the research that are available.

I argue that the research is "exceedingly persuasive" in demonstrating that single-sex schools are effective in terms of providing both greater equality and greater achievement, especially for low-income and working-class students, most particularly for African-American and Hispanic-American boys *and* girls. I believe that the data are both consistent and persistent when several specifications are made. Note first that I exclude single-sex classes from my contention for exceedingly persuasive positive effects. My argument centers on the notion of an academic culture that is endemic to single-sex schools and cannot be produced in one or two classrooms within an otherwise coeducational school. Note that I draw these conclusions almost entirely from research that has been done on private rather than public schools. I begin with two general findings that rest on sound sociological and educational theory and research.

First, the academic and developmental consequences of attending one type of school versus another are typically insignificant for middle-class or otherwise advantaged students. By contrast, the consequences are significant only for students who are historically or traditionally disadvantaged—minorities and/or lower-class and working-class youth (students at risk). Furthermore, these significant effects for at-risk students are small in comparison with the much larger effects of socioeconomic status and type of curriculum in a given school (for a full review of studies, see Riordan, 1997). This basic social science finding has been shown to be true since first identified in the famous Coleman Report (Coleman et al., 1966, see especially tables 3.221.1 and 3.221.2 on p. 229). Over the past three decades, the data persistently confirm this educational fact, which is fully consistent with the following points. We need to understand that all the hollering about types of schools (single-sex or otherwise) applies mostly to these students.

Second, single-sex schools work to improve student achievement (Lee, 1997; Lee and Bryk, 1986, 1989; Lee and Marks, 1990; Mael, 1998; Riordan, 1990, 1994a). They work for girls and boys, women and men, whites and nonwhites, *but* this effect is limited to students of lower socioeconomic status and/or students who are disadvantaged historically—females and racial/ethnic/religious minorities (both males and females). The major factor that conditions the strength of single-sex effects is social class, and since class and race are inextricably linked, the effects are also conditioned by race and sometimes by gender.

Specifically, disadvantaged students in single-sex schools, compared to their counterparts in coeducational schools, have been shown to have higher achievement outcomes on standardized tests of mathematics, reading, science, and civics. They show higher levels of leadership behavior in school, do more homework, take a stronger course load, and have higher educational expectations. They also manifest higher levels of environmental control, more favorable attitudes toward school, and less sex-role stereotyping. They acknowledge that their schools have higher levels of discipline and order and, not surprisingly, they have a less satisfactory social life than students in coeducational schools. In the long term, women who attended a girls' school continue to have higher test scores than women who attended coeducational schools (see preceeding citations). In drawing these conclusions, I do not include two studies by Marsh (1989, 1991), which included many variables such as student expectations, which I argue in the following are inappropriate to use as controls. Bryk, Lee, and Holland (1989) also rejected Marsh's analysis on this and other grounds. The preceeding citations are generally confined to American studies only.

It is important to note, however, that single-sex school effects are fairly robust even when social class or race is not partitioned. In their Catholic school study, Lee and Bryk (1989) analyzed the data by statistically controlling for social class, race, and other background characteristics and applied the results to students generally (assuming that there were no differences in

FIGURE 2.1

EFFECT SIZES OF SINGLE-SEX SCHOOLING (LEE AND BRYK 1989)

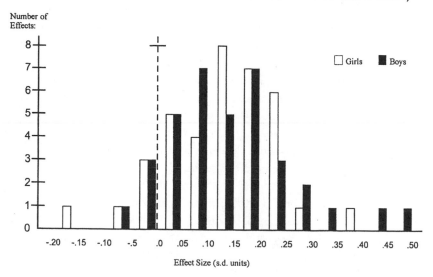

social class, race, or background variables). They found sixty-five of seventy-four separate dependent variable effects to be in favor of single-sex schools. Thirty of seventy-four effects obtained an effect size (ES) of .18 or higher, favoring single-sex schools, equally distributed among boys and girls and the mean effect size was .13, favoring single-sex schools. These results are depicted in figure 2.1.

The results for students attending women's colleges parallel and substantiate the secondary school results. They manifest higher levels of environmental control, greater satisfaction with school (although not social life), and higher occupational success despite the fact that there is no difference in educational achievement when compared to women who attended a coeducational college (Miller-Bernal, 2000; Riordan, 1990, 1994b). This latter finding strongly suggests that their schooling has been of a higher quality, because ultimately they have the same level of educational achievement as women attending coeducational schools. Amazingly, women who attend a women's college for even a single year and then transfer obtain a significant gain in occupational success (Riordan, 1994b).

However, these positive effects, are not universal. In a cross national study of four countries (Belgium, New Zealand, Thailand, and Japan), Baker, Riordan, and Schaub (1995) showed that single-sex schools do not have uniform and consistent effects. The effects appear to be limited to those national educational systems in which single-sex schools are relatively rare. We argue that the rarity of a school type may enhance single-sex effects under certain conditions. When single-sex schools are rare in a country, the proacademic choice-making by parents and students results in a more selective student body that brings with it a heightened degree of academic demands. In turn, we believe that rare school types are better able to *supply* the quality of schooling *demanded* by these more selective students. Being less normative, these schools are likely to possess greater autonomy.

I wish to address another related matter that is quite important: How should we control for the distinct possibility of "selection bias" in studies of single-sex and mixed-sex schools? All researchers acknowledge that students attending each type of school vary in a number of ways, including socioeconomic status, previous academic achievement, family structure, and the like. And everyone agrees that we need to statistically control (and thereby equate) these preexisting characteristics if we are to sort out the effects of the school from the effect of the home. I part company from those who believe that the appropriate strategy is to control or equate exhaustively. If we do, we end up controlling on some of the very characteristics that I maintain drives the entire success of single-sex schools; making a proacademic choice. Hence, my view is that we need to control for factors that pertain to home background resources (e.g., socioeconomic status) and prior academic achievement (e.g., test scores). But not much else, and certainly not educational expectations or similar variables, which measure and may distinguish students in terms of the value they place on academics. (See figure 2.4 and the discussion.) In fact, having controlled for social class and academic achievement, students in single-sex schools may still have higher educational expectations than students in coeducational schools (Lee and Bryk, 1986; Lee and Marks, 1990). It is worth a moment to consider the irony of refusing to allow such students to attend a school that will help them to achieve their high educational expectations, especially when the students are desperate, poor, and powerless.

During the 1970s and 1980s, female students benefited from single-sex schools regardless of their social class position because they were historically and traditionally disadvantaged in school. Sometime during the 1980s, and clearly by 1990, this historical disadvantage for females in schools had been remediated (Riordan, 1998, 2000; U.S. Department of Education, 2000; Willingham and Cole, 1997). As a result of this transformation, I now argue that only females of low socioeconomic status are likely to show significant gains (along with boys) in single-sex schools.

Recent research (LePore and Warren, 1997) in the 1990s found that females in Catholic single-sex schools do not outperform their counterparts in coeducational schools. This is contrary to the results obtained by Bryk, Lee, and Holland (1993) and Riordan (1990) for Catholic school students in the 1970s and 1980s. This now seems completely consistent because students in these schools have become increasingly affluent from 1980 to 1992. Figure 2.2 shows that Catholic single-sex schools for girls have undergone a

FIGURE 2.2

SOCIOECONOMIC COMPOSITION (PERCENT HIGHEST QUARTILES) OF CATHOLIC AND PUBLIC SCHOOLS)

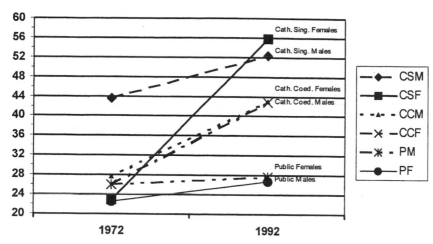

metamorphosis regarding the socioeconomic composition of their student bodies. In 1972, students attending Catholic single-sex schools for girls were approximately equal to public school students in their socioeconomic background. From 1972 to 1992, their socioeconomic status underwent a meteoritic rise. (See Baker and Riordan, 1998, for an elaboration on this phenomenon.) Given the propositions in the preceding, no school effects would be predicted under these demographic conditions.

Lee (1997) also found no differences in educational achievement between students in single-sex and mixed-sex elite independent schools. Thus, it appears that from 1972 to 1982 (and probably earlier) girls in Catholic single-sex schools outperformed girls in Catholic coeducational schools, and their achievements also closed the gender gap in comparison with coeducational males. In the late 1980s and the 1990s, however, the single-sex advantage for girls in "elite" Catholic schools was greatly diminished. Girls in coeducational schools increased their achievement curve surpassing their counterparts in single-sex schools (Riordan, 1998). Thus, we need to note very carefully that the findings from the 1970s to the early 1980s cannot and should not be generalized straightforwardly to the 1990s and beyond. As Catholic single-sex schools received positive media and academic attention in the 1980s, students attending these schools in the 1990s increasingly came from more affluent homes (Baker and Riordan, 1998). And for this reason, the single-sex schooling effects in Catholic schools were attenuated as per the preceding discussion.

However, what is bad for the goose is not always bad for the gander. This troubling news for Catholic schools is not a problem for the potential of single-sex schools in public schools. If single-sex schools are established to serve disadvantaged students, there are always ample numbers of socioeconomically disadvantaged, at-risk youth available in the public sector. Single-sex schools will be effective in the public sector so long as they are earmarked for disadvantaged students. On the other hand, if public schools were to establish single-sex schools and then allow more advantaged students to attend, the single-sex school effect would dissipate. To repeat (perhaps ad nauseam): Single-sex schools do not greatly influence the academic achievement of affluent or advantaged students, but they do for poor disadvantaged students.

It is important to emphasize that white middle-class (or affluent) boys and girls do not suffer any loss by attending a single-sex school. (They are not better off in coeducational schools.) At worse, they realize a neutral outcome, which is the general school effect finding for this subgroup across any two types of schools, as noted. Moreover, there exists the possibility that they do acquire small gains that are undetectable.

WHY ARE SINGLE-SEX SCHOOLS MORE EFFECTIVE THAN COEDUCATIONAL SCHOOLS?

There are at least a dozen theoretical rationales that provide support for the contention that single-sex schools are more effective academically and developmentally than mixed-sex schools, especially for minorities and at-risk students. Each of these rationales is less applicable when the schools and the students are mostly from high socioeconomic home backgrounds, and/or if single-sex schools are normative in the society or a subculture. Note carefully that all of these conceptual rationales are derived and/or linked to Expectation States Theory, as described in the Introduction to this chapter. These rationales are depicted in figure 2.3.

The last four items on this list (9 through 12) draw on the work of Valerie Lee and colleagues (1997), who identified several structural and organizational features of schools that generate increased academic achievement as well as increased equity among the students (a decrease in the gap between racial and social class groups).

Single-sex schools provide more successful same-sex teacher and student role models, more leadership opportunities, greater order and discipline, fewer social distractions to academic matters, and the choice of a single-sex school is a proacademic choice. (For an elaboration of rationales 1 through 8, see Riordan, 1990, 1994.) Females also gain advantages because of significant reductions in gender bias in both teaching and peer interaction, and via access to the entire curriculum; the reverse may be true for African-American males. The schools are typically smaller and provide the academic climate features (9 through 12) noted by Lee (1997). Lee also argues (1997, p. 156) that these organizational differences explain the greater effectiveness of single-sex schools. Obviously I agree. But these explanatory variables are set into motion because of an independent vari-

FIGURE 2.3

THEORETICAL RATIONALES FOR POSITIVE EFFECTS OF
SINGLE-SEX SCHOOLS

1. The diminished strength of youth culture values

2. A greater degree of order and control

3. The provision of more successful role models

4. A reduction of sex differences in curriculum and opportunities

5. A reduction of sex bias in teacher-student interaction

6. A reduction of sex stereotypes in peer interaction

7. The provision of a greater number of leadership opportunities

8. *Single-gender schools require a proacademic parent/student choice*

9. Smaller school size

10. A core curriculum emphasizing academic subjects taken by all students (organization of the curriculum)

11. Positive relationships among teachers, parents, and students that lead to a shared value community with an emphasis on academics and equity (school social organization)

12. Active and constructivist teaching and learning (organization of instruction)

able, which is "school type" (single-sex or coeducational). You cannot just assume that the explanatory variables can be easily operationalized by well-intended educational policymakers and/or administrators.

Single-sex schools are places where students go to learn; not to play, not to hassle teachers and other students, and not primarily to meet their friends and have fun. Aside from affluent middle-class communities and private and alternative schools, coeducational schools are not all about academics. This has been noted often with alarm by respected and distinguished investigators across a variety of disciplines using a variety of methodologies (Devine, 1996; Goodlad, 1984; Powell, Farrar, and Cohen, 1985; Sedlack, Wheeler, Pullin, and Cusick, 1986; Steinberg, Brown, and Dornbusch, 1996; Willis, 1981).

WHAT ARE THE IMPLICATIONS OF PRIVATE SCHOOL RESEARCH FOR SINGLE-SEX PUBLIC SCHOOLS?

Over the course of time, I have come to see the proacademic choice that is made by parents and students as the key explanatory variable. This choice sets into motion a set of relationships among teachers, parents, and students that emphasize academics and deemphasize youth culture values, which as I have suggested, dominate coeducational schools. I want to be absolutely clear about this point. The choice is not at all about sex and romance nor is it about exclusion. It is about the rejection of antiacademic values that predominates in our culture and schools. Moreover, this rejection comes from the bottom up rather than the top down. In my view, it drives all that follows.

Single-sex schools, of course, provide a set of structural norms conducive to academic learning, as shown in figure 2.3. This proacademic single-sex school environment operates in concert and harmony with the choice-making process made by students who attend single-sex schools. In this regard, it is entirely different from a set of structures or programs that are put into place by educators. In single-sex schools, the academic environment is normative in a true sociological sense. It is a set of rules established by the subjective reality (definitions) of participants that takes on an objective reality as a set of social structural norms (Berger and Luckman, 1967). This idea is similar to that proposed by Bryk, Lee, and Holland (1993) of a "voluntary community" for public school policy, which would resemble Catholic schools in every respect except for religion.

Figure 2.4 depicts this reciprocal relationship between organizational structures and student affirmations of those structures. Moreover, as I have indicated, these academic definitions of school contradict the nonacademic definitions that students otherwise bring to school and that come to constitute a youth culture. In effect, single-sex schools mitigate the single largest obstacle that stands in the way of effective and equitable schooling by using a fundamental sociological principle about how real social structures are created. Structures that are imposed and that contradict deeply cherished beliefs (regardless of how wrong-headed and problematic) will be rejected out of hand by any group with substantial power in numbers, such as students in schools.

By contrast, we can consider some alternatives that have been suggested for creating a proacademic environment in coeducational schools or schools generally. Specifically, we should consider the previously mentioned organizational features of effective schools from Lee (1997). In this 1995 study for AAUW, she reported several cautionary findings regarding the effect of this set of school climate variables on the gender gap. For example, the same set of school level variables emphasizing academics (as in numbers 9 through 12 in figure 2.3) increased mathematics, science, social studies, and reading achievement, but these same variables often did not reduce the gender gap favoring either males or females in these subject area tests.

In some cases, these positive school level variables actually made matters worse—greater parental involvement increased the gender gap, favoring males in mathematics achievement, and a whole set of positive academic school

FIGURE 2.4

A THEORETICAL MODEL OF SINGLE-SEX SCHOOL TYPE EFFECTS

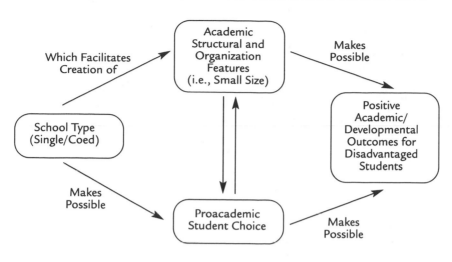

variables (e.g., positive student-teacher relations and an academic learning environment) increased the gender gap in social studies. In fact, aside from decreasing the gender gap in school engagement (which favors females), the school variables either had no effect or negative effects on the gender gap. Lee, Chen, and Smerdon (1995) demonstrate convincingly that a whole range of positive school climate variables will increase student achievement and engagement with school, but these same variables have either null or negative effects on increasing gender equity for these same measures.

The challenge of effective and equitable schooling in the next century is to overcome the resistance and recalcitrance of youth cultures in and out of school (Devine, 1996; Goodlad, 1984; Steinberg, Brown, and Dornbusch, 1996; Willis, 1981). This is not a new problem and undoubtedly predates the modern school. However, the intensity and complexity of the problem are new and represent the most important obstacles in schools today. It is not just about youthful anti-intellectualism, antisocial behavior, athletics and rock concerts, sexual harassment, heterosexual attraction and subsequent distraction, and the contentiousness that comes from increased diversity in the schools; it is about all these things and more.

How do schools get to be small or how do they develop communal relationships, authentic instruction, and/or a core academic curriculum? How can schools provide more successful academic role models and reduce the strength of antiacademic youth culture values? In essence, this requires reconstruction of schools. It requires a proacademic choice on the part of administrators, teachers, parents, and students (see figure 2.4). Of these, I argue that students are the key stakeholders. In contrast to private schools, public schools often serve poor, disadvantaged, lower-class and working-class youth who are often racially stigmatized as well. These are the children and young adults who can benefit most from single-sex schools.

SINGLE-SEX PUBLIC SCHOOLS

One of the interesting by-products of the questionable legal status of single-sex schools and classes has been that it has provided a backdrop for *Profiles in Courage* among public school principals (borrowing the term from John Kennedy's book by that name). During the 1990s, in various public schools across the country, principals were asked (or in some cases they did the asking) to allow teachers to establish single-sex classes. In view of the questionable legal status of single-sex schools and/or classes (see chapter 4 of this volume and Salomone, 1999), most principals were reluctant to venture away from anything but business as usual (carrying out the bureaucratic ethos). Not many were sufficiently courageous as to take on single-sex schooling. Yet, as a result of the problems in coeducational schools for both boys and girls, and the potential offered by single-sex schools (as per the preceding discussion), a variety of efforts were made throughout the 1990s to establish single-sex public schools for disadvantaged students. Some of these experiments were successful, whereas others were stymied by opponents of single-sex schools or other factors described in the following. In the examples that follow, the reader should note that only the California single-sex school experiment and the Young Women's Leadership School in New York City have been subjected to systematic and independent evaluations.

Several Unsuccessful Examples

In 1989, the principal of Martin Luther King Jr. Elementary School in Rochester, New York, heeding the advice of several of her teachers, established a set of single-sex classrooms for both males and females. Students (and their parents) could choose between a single-sex or coeducational classroom in each grade. From the outset, her administrative decision was viewed with criticism from the central office, even though she had full and enthusiastic teacher, parental, student, and community support.

At the time (1989), the school had been identified as the thirteenth worst school in the state of New York as judged by performance standards. It is an inner city school attended predominantly by very poor Hispanic-American and African-American students. During the years 1989 to 1993, school records indicate that the students in the single-sex classrooms showed greater NCE gains on the reading and mathematics tests, higher attendance rates, lower suspension rates, and higher parental participation rates than students in the coeducational classes. Perhaps most remarkably, in one all-male class of African-American and Hispanic-American students, twenty-one of twenty-four *fathers* attended monthly parent-teacher meetings on a regular basis during the time that the program was intact (Riordan, 1993).

During the course of the 1989 to 1993 time period, Anita Boggs received no praise nor support for her work. Rather, she and her staff were pressured by the American Civil Liberties Union (ACLU) and National Organization for Women (NOW) to justify this organizational form of schooling. In 1993, she was abruptly transferred to another school. Single-sex schooling was shut down at Martin Luther King Jr. Elementary School. However, during 1989 to 1993, Boggs increased achievement and equality, she energized a group of teachers by simply supporting and organizing and making possible their pedagogical desires, and she brought forth social capital from the home by the involvement of African-American and Hispanic-American fathers and mothers in the schooling of their children. She utilized educational research to organize her school and for this she was banished to the suburbs where her efforts were not even needed.

Similar examples occurred throughout the 1990s. In 1991, Detroit school officials proposed three all-male academies for African-American boys that were ruled in violation of Title IX; in 1993, school officials in Ventura, California, attempted for several years to experiment with single-sex classes but they too were destroyed by a set of legal challenges, and in 1994 again a courageous principal attempted to establish single-sex classes (see Richardson, 1995; Walsh, 1996). Anthony Palone, Principal of Myrtle Avenue School in Irvington, New Jersey, established single-sex classes for several years. Students flourished and parents were satisfied until the same antisingle-sex school forces that had appeared in other cities moved into action in Irvington. Like Anita Boggs, Anthony Palone was shortly forced to abandon his efforts (Walsh, 1996).

Hubbard and Datnow (chapter 7 of this volume) describe a large experimental effort in the state of California to open single-sex schools for both boys and girls. Here I will only note that Governor Pete Wilson established these schools in 1997 by offering grants as incentives to districts to open schools for both boys and girls. In 1997, money was available for twenty schools (ten for boys and ten for girls) to be opened across the state. As of fall 2000, only one set of these schools (one boys' and one girls' school) remains in operation and each has a different story to tell, as you will discover in chapter 7.

Many of the schools in the California single-gender experiment violated a basic assumption of key theoretical rationales that have been identified in the preceding: namely, that principals and teachers in a single-sex school must believe in the basic philosophy of this kind of school organization, and not simply be in it for the grant money provided to the school. The downfall of the California single-sex school experiment was not pressure by political forces against single-sex schooling, but rather the result of a failure of the experiment itself to assure that principals and teachers minimally embraced the proacademic single-sex school concept. Hubbard and Datnow suggest that these schools could have been sustainable and successful if some of the fundamental components were in place.

Several Successful Examples

Some schools have been successful in warding off the opponents of single-sex schools. They have obtained the services of principals and teachers who fully embrace the potential value of single-sex schooling (the major flaw in the California single-sex school experiment). In 1995, philanthropist and former journalist Ann Rubenstein-Tish, together with her husband Andrew Tish, initiated plans to open what has come to be called the Young Women's Leadership School in New York City. Tish secured the help of a legal team as well as the consulting services of this author and opened the school in fall 1996 as a regular public (not a charter) school in Community School District 4 of New York City. The school was designed to provide both a middle school (grades seven and eight) and upper school (grades nine through twelve) with a demanding college preparatory course of study. Funding for the school is the same as any of the other schools in District 4. Priority for admission to the school is given to students residing in District 4, which is a predominantly poor African-American and Hispanic-American East Harlem community in New York City.

Currently, the school serves about 310 students in grades seven to twelve. The school curriculum focuses on mathematics, science, technology, humanities, and leadership. The student population is diverse: 59 percent are Hispanic-American, 40 percent are African-American, and 67 percent fall below the poverty line, therefore qualifying for a free or reduced-price school lunch. Test scores for reading and mathematics are 30 percent higher than average for New York City coeducational schools. Although initially "only 40 percent [of the students] could read and do math at grade level, by the end of the year, 70 percent could read at or above grade level and 65 percent could meet the standard in math" (*New York Post*, 1997). Remarkably, 100 percent of this year's first graduating class are bound for college.

Following the New York City model, a group of prominent professional women in business, law, the arts, and philanthropy formed an advisory council and developed plans to open a school for girls in Chicago. In fall 2000, the Young Women's Leadership Charter School of Chicago opened its doors to 150 sixth-grade and ninth-grade students for girls only. The school focuses on math, science, technology, and leadership for girls and is located on the campus of the Illinois Institute of Technology. Students are selected by a lottery, and in the first draw 80 percent of the girls qualified for free or reduced-price lunch and 73 percent were African American. At full enrollment, the school will house 525 girls in grades six to twelve. Students are required to be residents of Chicago and in good academic standing.

Finally, brief mention should be made of several other public single-sex schools currently in operation. The Philadelphia School for Girls has existed since 1848, and although it was ordered to admit boys in a 1983 court decision, it remains today as a public all-girl magnet school by default. The school serves fifteen hundred students who come from predominantly poor families. Admission standards are rigorous, and the school was cited for excellence by the U.S. Department of Education in 1987. The school has a 98 percent college acceptance rate.

Western High School in Baltimore, Maryland, was founded in 1844 and remains today as a thriving all-girls' school. The school enrolls 1,250 students, and over 75 percent of these girls attend four-year colleges. The school is 80 percent African-American, and 38 percent of the students qualify for a free or reduced-price lunch. In the 1998 to 1999 academic year, 96 percent of the eleventh-grade students passed the Maryland state exams in reading, mathematics, writing, and citizenship.

In Hartford, Connecticut, the Lewis Fox Middle School houses the Benjamin E. Mays Institute for Boys and its sister program, the Mary M. Bethune Institute for Girls. Approximately eight hundred students attend this school, which is physically divided into separate clusters for boys and girls as well as for mixed-sex classes (schools within the school). About two hundred boys and girls attend classes separated by sex. The institutes share classes for physical education, but all other classes are conducted in separate areas as well as the lunch period. This school was established in 1996 and serves predominantly poor students (89 percent qualify for a free or reduced-price lunch). According to Judith Glover (2001), a school guidance counselor, students in the single-sex classes always excel in the Hartford citywide testing program in comparison with students in mixed-sex classes.

And finally, the New York State Board of Regents has approved a proposal to open two single-sex charter schools. The Brighter Choice Charter School for Boys and the Brighter Choice Charter School for Girls will open in fall 2002 in Albany, New York. Both schools target economically disadvantaged at-risk youth (largely African-American and Hispanic-American), which are precisely the groups most likely to benefit from single-sex schools. In fact, the school will admit only students who qualify for a federal free lunch. It even comes with a guarantee. Any student who is there for three years is guaranteed to pass the state exams in math, reading, and science. Those who do not will be given a private scholarship to any other public or private school (*Wall Street Journal*, 2000).

It is interesting to note that three strategies have been used by these schools to defend against legal attacks from opponents. In New York, Chicago, and Albany, the schools utilized the services of legal consultants and social scientists to develop the school charters. In the California schools, the entire initiative was made available to both boys and girls with exactly equal resources for each school, down to the number of pencils and desks provided. In the case of the Philadelphia and Baltimore schools, the ACLU and other opponent organizations have been unable to find a boy willing to attend the school; moreover, the mayor of Baltimore has literally challenged the ACLU to take the schools to court. Because the school has enjoyed great success and is extremely popular with the citizenry of the city, local officials simply rely on community support to legitimatize the school.

EDUCATIONAL RESEARCH, POLITICS, AND POLICY

Data alone will not save single-sex schools; nor will data alone be sufficient to change the persistent problems that exist for both boys and girls in coeducational schools. This is not to say that research is not important, but only that ultimately the politics of education dictates the future of single-sex schools. It is useful to contrast educational research and educational policy about single-sex schools and the use of uniforms in schools. There exists a substantial degree of empirical research, which contrasts the relative effects of single-sex and mixed-sex schooling. Moreover, that base is both theoretical and empirical. And, although it is not entirely consistent, there is a preponderance of evidence supporting the positive value of single-sex education (under the conditions I have noted). Now, regarding the relative effects of wearing or not wearing uniforms in schools, we know next to nothing. There are all sorts of anecdotal reports and small sample studies, but there are very little hard data, although there is some good theory.

It is instructive to observe how easy it can be for an educational practice such as requiring uniforms to become educational policy without any educational research. Just a short time ago (February 24, 1995), President Clinton instructed the U.S. Department of Education to distribute manuals to all the school districts in the nation advising them how they can legally enforce a policy of uniforms in public schools. With this and several other speeches, the movement toward a national policy of school uniforms is racing ahead full speed, despite the fact that no one knows whether this educational policy will produce any positive educational results by and of itself, including the reduction of violence in the schools, which is the major claim of its proponents.

If you think about this for a moment, you can actually experience what it must have been like when the movement toward coeducation began to take hold about a century ago. In fact, coeducation (as a form of school organization) was institutionalized with little regard for educational research or educational or sociological theory. Just as coeducation was (and continues to be) politically correct, so too are school uniforms. Thus, political correctness can and often does override educational research and sociological theory in the formation of educational policy. Rosemary Salomone (1996) identified this as the perils of ideology.

Single-sex schools are politically incorrect; they are downright politically threatening to many people, and many of these people are in fact educational researchers, policymakers, and special interest stakeholder groups such as the AAUW Educational Foundation. This is not a very inspiring thought, but it is important to realize that this is the nature of what we are working with. It is not just about which type of school works best. It is about what most people think is politically expedient. In the long haul, however, I submit that educational politics may offer a deceiving foundation for educational policy in the absence of educational research and theory.

We desperately need more research on single-sex schools and less attention to educational politics and the formation of educational policy. One of the central problems is that single-sex schools cannot remain in place sufficiently long to develop a systematic long-term plan of action and a viable set of single-sex organizational norms, as I have outlined in this chapter. In all of the public school examples described herein, the period of existence for the schools has been too short to merit a valid evaluation. However, beyond the central question of which type of school works best in terms of achievement and gender equity, there are other questions that researchers have not even attempted to address.

For example, no one in the world has a clue as to the relative effects of single-sex and coeducational schools on identity formation (which is not at all the same as self-esteem). However, we do know from the work of Maccoby and Jacklin (1987; see also, Jacklin and Maccoby, 1978) that young children (two years of age and older) manifest a strong proclivity and greater compatibility in same-sex pairs, that girls exhibit more assertive behavior in same-sex groups, and that these facts remain true despite the efforts of adults to structure mixed-sex groups in such a way as to obtain equal status interaction (Lockheed, 1985; Lockheed and Harris, 1984).

Some people still think the gender gap is a one-way street, with males enjoying all the advantages. Beyond the schoolhouse door, this may still be true; but in elementary and secondary schools, it is not true and perhaps never was. Thus, issues of equity in coeducational schools can no longer be jump started by the phrase "when we shortchange girls, we shortchange America." Recent reports have now confirmed that both boys *and* girls are on the unfavorable side of the gender gap in education and developmental matters (Hedges and Nowell, 1995; Lee, Chen, and Smerdon, 1995; Linn and Hyde, 1989; Nowell, 1997; Riordan, 1998, 2000; U.S. Department of Education, 2000; Willingham and Cole, 1997). Lee, Chen, and Smerdon (1995) suggest that a more balanced approach to the study of gender equity is in order. What is becoming increasingly clear is that coeducational schools will have to provide special attention to boys in reading and writing and engagement, and this is going to complicate the entire equation for creating equity in coeducational schools.

CONCLUSIONS
Single-sex schools remain an effective form of school organization for disadvantaged students. The schools provide a structure that is conducive to learning, as I have detailed in this chapter. In selecting a single-sex school

with its structure in place, students reject the antiacademic norms that permeate most public coeducational schools attended by at-risk youth. They make a proacademic choice. I have no illusions that students do this gleefully and go off to school dancing in the streets. Of course, for most students the choice is made by parents for their children. The point is this: An effective school requires a minimal level of compliance (even if it is begrudging) on the part of the students to the academic norms of the school.

Specifically, in order for a school to provide high levels of achievement and equity for students, it should provide a challenging academic program to all students; the teaching style should be active and constructive; the relationships among teachers, administrators, parents, and students should be communal; and the school should be small. Youth culture and antiacademic values should be minimized, order and control should prevail, successful student role models should be abundant, sex (and race) bias in peer and student-teacher interaction should be nonexistent, and leadership and educational opportunities should be free of sex (and race) bias.

One can try to set this up by instituting rules and regulations and structures and norms from the desks of either superintendents and/or principals. In lieu of any other alternative, this is how it will be done. But institutions simply do not work very well that way, especially when the clients are youth who understandably and justifiably want a stake in the creation of social organizations that ultimately control their behavior. Single-sex schools provide an avenue for students to make a proacademic choice, thereby affirming their intrinsic agreement to work in the kind of environment we identify as effective and equitable. Single-sex schools should not be expected to correct the gender equity problems that exist in society and in coeducational schools. Nor should anyone fear that their existence would detract in any way from efforts that should be made to provide greater gender equity in public coeducational schools.

REFERENCES

American Association of University Women (AAUW). (1998a). *Gender Gaps*. Commissioned and researched by the American Institute for Research, Washington, D.C.: The American Association of University Women Educational Foundation.
———. (1992). *How Schools Shortchange Girls*. Commissioned and researched by S. Bailey. Wellesley, MA: Wellesley College Center for Research on Women.
———. (1998b). *Separated by Sex*. Washington, D.C.: The American Association of University Women Educational Foundation.
Baker, D. P. and Riordan, C. (1998). "The 'Eliting' of the Common American Catholic School and the National Educational Crisis." *Phi Delta Kappan*. September: 16–23.
Baker, D. P., Riordan, C., and Schaub, M. (1995). "The Effects of Sex-Grouped Schooling on Achievement: The Role of National Context." *Comparative Education Review* 39: 468–481.
Berger, J., Conner, T. L., and Fisek, M. H. (Eds.). (1974). *Expectation States Theory*. Cambridge, MA: Winthrop Publishers.
Berger, J. and Zelditch, Jr., M. (eds.). (1985). *Status, Rewards, and Influence*. San Francisco: Jossey-Bass.
Berger, P. L., and Luckman, T. (1967). *The Social Construction of Reality*. Garden City, NY: Doubleday-Anchor.

Bryk, A. S., Lee, V. E., and Holland, P. B. (1993). *Catholic Schools and the Common Good.* Cambridge, MA: Harvard University Press.

Bureau of Education. (1883). *Co-education of the Sexes in the Public Schools of the U.S.A.* Washington, D.C.: United States Government Printing Office.

Butler, N. M. (Ed.). (1910). *Education in the United States.* New York: American Book Company.

Cohen, E. G. (1994). *Designing Groupwork: Strategies for the Heterogeneous Classroom* (2nd ed.). New York: Teachers College Press.

Cohen, E. G. (2000). "Equitable classrooms in a changing society." In M. Hallinan (Ed.), *Handbook of the Sociology of Education.* New York: Kluwer Academic Publishers.

Cohen, E. G., and Roper, S. S. (1972). "Modification of Interaction Disability: An Application of Status Characteristics Theory." *American Sociological Review* 37: 643–657.

Coleman, J. S., Campbell, E. Q., Hobson, C. J., McPartland, J., Mood, A. M., Weinfeld, F. D., et. al. (1966). *Equality of Educational Opportunity.* Washington, D.C.: U.S. Government Printing Office.

Devine, J. (1996). *Maximum Security: The Culture of Violence in Inner-City Schools.* Chicago: University of Chicago Press.

Glover, J. (2001). Personal telephone conversation on August 2, 2001.

Goodlad, J. (1984). *A Place Called School.* New York: McGraw-Hill.

Hedges, L. V., and Nowell, A. (1995, July). "Sex Differences in Mental Test Scores, Variability, and Numbers of High-Scoring Individuals." *Science* 269: 41– 45.

Jacklin, C. N. and Maccoby, E. E. (1978). "Social Behavior at Thirty-Three Months in Same-Sex and Mixed-Sex Dyads." *Child Development* 49: 557–569.

Kolesnik, W. B. (1969). *Co-education: Sex Differences and the Schools.* New York: Vantage Press.

Lee, V. E. (1997). "Gender Equity and the Organization of Schools." In B. J. Bank and P. M. Hall (Eds.), *Gender, Equity, and Schooling.* New York: Garland Publishing.

Lee, V. E., and Bryk, A. S. (1986). "Effects of Single-Sex Secondary Schools on Students Achievement and Attitudes." *Journal of Educational Psychology* 78: 381–395.

———. (1989). "Effects of Single-Sex Schools: Response to March." *Journal of Educational Psychology* 81(4): 647–650.

Lee, V. E., Chen, X., and Smerdon, B.A. (1995). *The Influence of School Climate on Gender Differences in Achievement and Engagement of Young Adolescents.* Washington, D.C.: Paper commissioned by the American Association of University Women, 1995.

Lee, V. E., and Marks, H. M. (1990). "Sustained Effects of the Single-Sex Secondary School Experience on Student Achievement and Attitudes." *Journal of Educational Psychology* 82(3): 378–392.

———. (1992). "Who Goes Where? Choice of Single-Sex and Coeducational Independent Secondary Schools." *Sociology of Education* 65: 226–253.

LePore, P. C., and Warren, J. R. (1997). "A Comparison of Single-Sex and Coeducational Catholic Secondary Schooling: Evidence from the National Educational Longitudinal Study of 1988." *American Educational Research Journal* 34: 485–511.

Linn, M. C., and Hyde, J. S. (1989). "Gender, Mathematics, and Science." *Educational Researcher* 18: 17–27.

Lockheed, M. E. (1985). "Sex and Social Influence: A Meta-Analysis Guided by Theory." In J. Berger, and M. Zelditch Jr. (Eds.), *Status, Rewards, and Influence.* San Francisco: Jossey-Bass, 406–427.

Lockheed, M. E., and Harris, A. M. (1984). "Cross-Sex Collaborative Learning in Elementary Classrooms." *American Educational Research Journal* 21: 275–294.

Maccoby, E. E., and Jacklin, C. N. (1987). "Gender Segregation in Childhood." *Advances in Child Development and Behavior* 20: 239–287.

Mael, F. A. (1998). "Single-Sex and Coeducational Schooling: Relationships to Socioemotional and Academic Development." *Review of Educational Research* 68: 101–129.

———. (1989). "Effects of Attending Single-Sex and Coeducational High Schools on Achievement, Attitudes, Behavior, and Sex Differences." *Journal of Educational Psychology* 81(1): 70–85.

Marsh, H. W. (1991). "Public, Catholic Single-Sex, and Catholic Coeducational High Schools: Effects on Achievement, Affect, and Behaviors." *American Journal of Education* 11: 320–356.

Miller-Bernal, L. (2000). *Separate by Degree: Women Students' Experiences in Single and Coeducational Colleges.* New York: Peter Lang.

Moore, M., Piper, V., and Schaefer, E. (Mathematica Policy Research, Inc.). (1992). "Single-Sex Schooling and Educational Effectiveness: A Research Overview." In *Single-Sex Schooling: Perspectives from Practice and Research. A Special Report from the Office of Educational Research and Improvement.* Washington, D.C.: U.S. Department of Education.

New York Post. (September 19, 1997).

Nowell, A. (1997). "Trends in Gender Differences in Academic Achievement from 1960 to 1994." Paper read at the annual meeting of the American Educational Research Association.

Powell, A. G., Farrar, E., &. Cohen, D. K. (1985). *The Shopping Mall High School: Winners and Losers in the Educational Marketplace.* Boston: Houghton Mifflin Company.

Richardson, J. (1995). "Troubled N.J. School Turns to Single-Sex Classes." *Education Week,* 14(24): 1, 10.

Riordan, C. (1997). *Equality and Achievement: An Introduction to the Sociology of Education.* New York: Addison-Wesley Longman.

——. (1990). *Girls and Boys in School: Together or Separate?* New York: Teachers College Press.

——. (1993). Personal observations, interviews, correspondence, and research regarding the Martin Luther King, Jr. Elementary School, Rochester, New York.

——. (1994a). "Single-Gender Schools: Outcomes for African and Hispanic Americans." *Research in Sociology of Education and Socialization* 10: 177–205.

——. (2000). "Student Experiences in Home and School: Gender Gap Comparisons among 1990 Sophomores in the National Educational Longitudinal Study." Paper read at the annual meeting of the American Sociological Association.

——. (1998). "Student Outcomes in Public and Catholic Secondary Schools: Gender Gap Comparisons from 1972 to 1992." Paper read at the annual meeting of the American Sociological Association.

——. (1994). "The Value of Attending a Women's College." *Journal of Higher Education,* 65(4): 486–510.

Rosenholtz, S. J. (1985). "Modifying Status Expectations in the Traditional Classroom." In J. Berger, and M. Zelditch, Jr. (Eds.), *Status, Rewards, and Influence.* San Francisco: Jossey-Bass, 445–470.

Salomone, R. (1996). "Rich Girls, Poor Girls, and the Perils of Ideology." Keynote Address given at the Annual Leadership Conference of the Connecticut Chapter of the American Association of University Women, Wesleyan University.

——. (1999). "Single-Sex Schooling: Law, Policy, and Research." In D. Ravitch, (Ed.), *Brookings Papers on Education Policy.* Washington, D.C.: Brookings Institution Press.

Sedlak, M. W., Wheeler, C. W., Pullin, D. C., and Cusick, P. A. (1986). *Selling Students Short: Classroom Bargains and Academic Reform in the American High School.* New York: Teachers College Press.

Steinberg, L. B., Brown, B., and Dornbusch, S. M. (1996). *Beyond the Classroom.* New York: Simon & Schuster.

Tammivaara, J. (1982). "The Effects of Task Structure on Beliefs about Competence and Participation in Small Groups." *Sociology of Education* 55: 212–222.

Tidball, M. E., Smith, D. G., Tidball, C. S., and Wolf-Wendel, L. E. (1999). *Taking Women Seriously: Lessons and Legacies for Educating the Majority.* Phoenix, AZ: The American Council on Education and The Oryx Press.

U.S. Department of Education. (1992). *Single-Sex Schooling: Perspectives from Practice and Research* (vol. I). Washington, D.C.: Office of Educational Research and Improvement.

U.S. Department of Education. (2000). *Trends in Educational Equity of Girls and Women.* Written and researched by Y. Bae, S. Choy, C. Geddes, J. Sable, and T. Snyder. Washington, D.C.: Office of Educational Research and Improvement, NCES, 2000–03.

Wall Street Journal. (December 26, 2000). "A Brighter Idea." A-10.

Walsh, M. (1996). "Educators Debate Impact of Ruling on Single-Sex Classes." *Education Week* 15(40): 1, 31.

Willingham, W. W., and Cole, N. S. (1997). *Gender and Fair Assessment.* Mahwah, NJ: Lawrence Erlbaum Associates.

Willis, P. (1981). *Learning to Labor: How Working-Class Kinds Get Working Class Jobs.* New York: Columbia University Press.

CHAPTER 3

Challenging the System: Assumptions and Data behind the Push for Single-Sex Schooling

Patricia B. Campbell and Jo Sanders

"It's kind of nice not to have guys here."
—FOURTEEN-YEAR-OLD STUDENT AT A GIRLS' SCHOOL
(*WASHINGTON TIMES*, JUNE 2, 1999)

The girls in the all-girls algebra class "are in a risk-free environment, supportive rather than competitive."
—CURRICULUM DIRECTOR (*PHILADELPHIA INQUIRER*, OCTOBER 14, 1998)

"If [my daughter] wants to be president of the country, who am I to ruin her chances by having her overshadowed by some boy?"
—MOTHER OF A KINDERGARTENER IN A GIRLS' SCHOOL
(*NEW YORK TIMES*, APRIL 11, 1999)

For decades, coeducation has been the norm for K–12 public education in the United States. Beginning in the 1980s, however, well-publicized reports that girls were being shortchanged in schools and that coeducation provides a "chilly climate" for women and girls (Bailey et al., 1992; Hall and Sandler, 1982) and popular books such as *Reviving Ophelia* (Pipher, 1994) and *Failing at Fairness* (Sadker and Sadker, 1994) began to refuel an interest in the education girls were receiving. The reports and books called for reducing the impact of gender bias and stereotyping in education and improving the education of girls and boys.

However, many who read about gender issues in schools and reflected on their own and their daughters' education appeared to conclude that healthy coeducation for girls was extremely difficult to achieve, and that single-sex education was a much more feasible solution. A 1998 survey of the National Coalition of Girls' Schools found applicants to their member schools increased by a third in the previous seven years, and enrollments increased by nearly a fifth (NCGS, 1998).

As part of this trend, new girls only schools have been established, including the Julia Morgan Middle School for Girls in Oakland, California, which opened its doors in 1999, the Young Women's Leadership Charter School in Chicago in 2000, and the Seattle Girls' School in 2001, the latter two focusing on math, science, and technology.

Underlying this increased interest in single-sex education for girls have been a variety of claims for the superiority of single-sex education over coeducation for girls. There are claims for girls' superior academic achievement, participation in math, science, and technology, happiness, and better careers resulting from the single-sex environment. Are the claims valid? This chapter casts a critical look at the assumptions and research behind the view of single-sex schooling as the answer to girls' educational problems. In so doing, we consider public and private schooling from kindergarten through college.

WHAT DO RESEARCHERS SAY?[1]

There has been no national comprehensive controlled study of academic performance for U.S. students in public and private K–12 single-sex and coed schooling. Such a study has been conducted, however, at the college level. Looking at U.S. colleges and universities, Astin (1993) found that whether a college was coed, single-sex female, or predominantly male[2] had no meaningful effect on a variety of areas including standardized measures of general knowledge, communication skills, or professional knowledge. Neither were there differences in terms of critical thinking, analytic or problem-solving skills, writing skills, foreign language skills, public speaking ability, job skills, or preparation for professional or graduate school.

Having a greater proportion of women administrators or faculty members in a college did have a positive impact on women's education (Astin, 1993), as did having a learning environment, which validated women's scholarship and women's issues (Sax, 1994). Indeed, such a positive learning environment had a stronger effect on women's achievement than having more women or a greater proportion of female students in a major (Sax, 1994).

At the precollege level in the United States, no work has been done with a nationally representative public school sample because there are very few public single-sex environments—either classes or schools, because of Title IX and other possible legal constraints.[3] However, some studies examining individual schools or other single-sex educational environments have been done in the United States as well as in Australia and Great Britain. The results of these studies are not consistent. For example, in studies of achievement and continuation in math and science course taking, one study found no differences in girls' subsequent math and science course taking based on whether they have been in single-sex or coed classes (Wood, Bonnie, and Brown, 1997), whereas another found short-term but not long-term gain (Leder and Forgasz, 1994). No differences in grades or SAT scores between girls in single-sex math classes and those in coed classes were reported by some researchers (Gilson, 1999; Wood, Bonnie, and Brown, 1997), while other researchers found single-sex groupings had little effect on the achievement scores of either males or females (Leder and Forgasz, 1994; Parker, 1985). Still another study (Smith, 1986) identified short-term but not long-term achievement gains for girls in single-sex classes over girls in coed classes (Campbell and Wahl, 1998b).

Using national data sets, there has been research done across representative samples of Catholic and other private schools in the United States, where there are enough single-sex institutions to make the analysis valid. Using a national sample of Catholic schools, studies done by Valerie Lee and her colleagues (Lee and Bryk, 1986, 1989; Lee and Marks, 1990) documented benefits for girls in single-sex schooling, but generally found few differences in the relative benefits of single-sex and coeducational schooling for boys (Lee, 1998, p. 43). LePore and Warren (1996), however, found that single-sex Catholic secondary schools were not particularly advantageous academic settings compared to coed Catholic secondary schools and that the few observed advantages of attending Catholic single-sex schools benefited boys more than girls.

When Lee and her colleagues replicated her work on Catholic secondary schools using a national sample of independent (private, not Catholic) high schools (Lee and Marks, 1992; Lee, Marks, and Byrd, 1994), they found "no consistent pattern of effects for attending either single-sex or coeducational independent schools for either girls or boys" (Lee, 1998, p. 43). Based on his earlier work on Catholic secondary schools, Riordan (1990) concluded that the relative impact of single-sex and coeducational schools was "virtually zero for middle-class or otherwise advantaged students" but was significant for at-risk students, although these effects are "small in comparison with the much larger effects of home background and type of curriculum in a given school" (Riordan, 1998, p. 54).

Riordan's conclusion about the size of the effect owing to the single-sex versus coed nature of the school points out a problem with much of the research on single-sex education and provides one explanation as to why the results are inconsistent. Many of the studies of single-sex education do not control for such important variables as the curriculum, student self-selection, or even the teacher. For example, when single-sex classes taught by one or more teachers are compared to coed classes taught by different teachers, there is no way of telling what proportion of any difference found is owing to the teacher and how much results from the sex composition of the class. This is an especially important caveat in view of the research on the importance of the teacher's role in the classroom, and how much the quality and experience of teachers is related to their students' achievement (Wenglinsky, 2000).

The content, practice, and organization of an educational setting matter greatly when student achievement is being assessed, as do the climate and culture; therefore, it is curious that these factors have been secondary considerations in the research when they have been addressed at all. Yet too much of the literature and discussion compares schools providing different levels of content and pedagogy, and yet concludes that differences result from the schools' sex composition (Campbell and Wahl, 1998a).

As the U.S. Department of Education's 1993 special report on single-sex schools reminded readers that "all single-gender schools are not equal in providing a productive learning environment and many factors contributing to the success to effective single-gender schools are fundamental to effective schools regardless of their gender policy—a small student body, strong emphasis on academics and commitment to the schools' mission and value" (Hollinger, 1993, p. 11). Gill agrees, feeling that

> [a]ll of the research around the topic of single-sex schooling compared with coeducation skirts some highly significant issues to do with what actually happens in one or the other type of schooling. The issue of gender difference in learning outcomes appears more as a question of classroom treatments and teacher expertise than of school gender context per se. (1996, p. 16)

As Campbell and Wahl pointed out:

> While the question "Are single-sex classes better than coed classes?" may sound logical, it makes little sense when there is no consideration of what goes on in the classes, the pedagogy and practices of the teachers, or anything about the students other than their sex. Yet the public, media, educators, and even some researchers compare classes and attribute outcomes to this single factor of whether the class is all girls, all boys, or girls and boys together. Imagine how parents would respond if asked if they would prefer that their child attend a good single-sex math class or a bad coed math class, versus a bad single-sex math class or a good coed one. Basically, single-sex schooling and coeducational schooling can each be highly effective, ineffective, or somewhere in the middle. (1998b, p. 63)

That said, there can be much to learn from highly effective all-girl schools, at least in terms of girls' attitudes toward schooling. In a survey of over four thousand graduates of girls' schools in the United States (National Coalition of Girls' Schools, 2000), 85 percent rated their schools as very good or excellent. Something positive is going on there and it would be worth our while to learn what that might be.

WHAT DEFINES SINGLE-SEX SCHOOLING?

The degree to which confounding variables are accounted for is one reason for unclear and often contradictory results in research on single-sex education, but another equally important reason is that although we may think we know what the phrase "single-sex schooling" means, the phrase signifies several mutually contradictory things to different people.

"Single-sex schooling has been seen, simultaneously, as both conservative and progressive, and as both oppressive and empowering" (Parker and Rennie, 1996, p. 1). Supporting single-sex education are conservatives such as columnists John Leo and George Will, educators such as Diane Ravitch and even the *Wall Street Journal*. Also supporting it are feminists and feminist organizations such as columnist and lawyer Susan Estrich, researcher Catherine Krupnick, and Girls Incorporated.

Feminists supporting single-sex schooling often see it as the best means for girls and boys to achieve equal educational outcomes and find it an appropriate response to perceived different learning styles and maturation rates of boys and girls. They also feel it can provide young people with an environment free from the distractions and harassment often posed by the presence of the opposite sex. Conservatives, meanwhile, often support single-sex education as the best strategy for maintaining essential differences between girls and boys. To them, education should be linked to preserving different roles based on gender (Campbell and Wahl, 1998a; Parker and Rennie, 1996).[4]

The range of definitions of and justifications for single-sex education should not be surprising. Traditionally, single-sex environments have been established for a variety of reasons, ranging from ultrafeminist to ultraconservative. Some colleges, such as Smith College and Mount Holyoke College, were established with the specific mission of empowering women and advancing their careers, and they continue to adhere to this mission. Many of the newly established all-girls grade schools have also been set up with overtly feminist missions.

We must not forget, though, that other single-sex environments have been established with quite different goals in mind. Some, such as some women's clubs and societies, were established with educational, political, social, health, and/or special interest (e.g., gardening) goals and do not deal with gender issues. Other single-sex organizations, such as ladies' auxiliaries, have as their goal the support of their men's activities. Still other all-female environments, such as purdah, have as their goal to keep women "pure" and guard men from "temptation" by keeping women separate and secluded.

That single-sex environments, particularly single-sex education, can mean different things to different people is emphasized by the recent experience of California's single-sex academies. In 1997, the State of California funded six pairs of public single-sex schools, intended as "magnet schools for at-risk students" (Bennett, 1997). To address legal concerns, particularly those raised by Title IX, each pair of schools was required to offer the same resources and opportunities to students. In a recent report, Datnow and her colleagues learned, based on hundreds of interviews with people involved in the academies, that participation in single-sex schooling was not a means to either a feminist or conservative education, but was for most administrators a source of available cash for the purpose of "meeting at-risk students' needs" (Datnow, Hubbard, and Woody, 2001, p. 5). There was no attention to gender bias and teachers did not receive professional development on gender-equitable educational practices. As a perhaps predictable result, "traditional gender stereotypes were often reinforced" (Datnow, Hubbard, and Woody, 2001, p. 7).

It may just be, as Heather Johnson Nicholson has pointed out, that "whether a separate, or single-sex, setting for girls is especially positive for girls or promotes gender equity depends very much on the environment, values and relationships established there" (1992, p. 42).

WHY IS SINGLE-SEX SCHOOLING SO OFTEN SEEN AS THE ANSWER?

With ambiguous and contradictory research results about single-sex and coeducational schooling, increasing acknowledgment of the many variables that have an impact on girls' and boys' educational experiences and the variety of often conflicting goals for single-sex education, the question now becomes: "Why is single-sex schooling so often seen as the answer?" The following provides an overview of some of the answers to that question as well as an exploration of related research and justifications for each.

Assumption #1: Girls and boys are viewed as having different skills, interests, and learning styles; thus, they are better served by single-sex schooling.

This rationale for single-sex education is popular but not accurate. Most of us—educators or not—tend to assume that girls and boys are different, that they are indeed "opposite sexes."[5] In this dichotomous view we see girls as one way, boys as another, as in "boys are competitive, girls are cooperative." There is great diversity among girls and boys. Indeed, other than primary sex characteristics, differences *within* girls as a group and within boys as a group are much, much larger than differences *between* girls as a group and boys as a group[6] (Maccoby and Jacklin, 1974; Willingham and Cole, 1997). "Knowing that a person is female does not tell us if her athletic ability is closer to the Williams sisters or a couch potato. Knowing that a person is male tells us nothing about whether his math skills reflect those of an Einstein or a 'mathphobe'" (Sanders and Campbell, 2001).

Researchers have known for many years that the differences among boys and among girls are far greater than any differences between an "average" girl and an "average" boy (Bailey et al., 1992; Willingham and Cole, 1997). Analyses of thousands of studies have found that gender differences in cognitive and affective areas are actually quite small. For example, the degree of overlap in girls' and boys' math skills has been found to be between 98 and 99 percent, whereas in verbal skills the degree of overlap has been found to be about 96 percent (Hyde, Fennema, and Lamon, 1990; Hyde and Linn, 1988). As the press release headlined about a recent book on gender and assessment, there are "more gender similarities than differences in educational performance" (Educational Testing Service, 1997, p. 1). There are many boys who learn better in the cooperative, relational styles commonly associated with girls, and many girls who learn better in the competitive individualistic style often associated with boys (Campbell and Wahl, 1998a).

Assumption #2: Our efforts to reduce the gender gaps in subjects such as math and science, or in promoting coed environments that serve both boys and girls, have not been successful. Thus, single-sex classes are the only option left for addressing the inequities.

In the past twenty years there have been major advances in girls' math and science achievement and course taking. There are now minimal differences in girls' and boys' average science and math scores on the fourth-, eighth-, and twelfth-grade National Assessment of Educational Progress tests (NAEP) (National Science Foundation, 1999). Girls are now taking upper-level math and science courses needed to enter college majors in these areas in about the same numbers as boys. Today, over 40 percent of high-school physics and calculus students are girls; although girls remain dramatically underrepresented in Advanced Placement Physics and Computer Science courses (American College Testing, 1998; National Science Foundation, 1999).

Women have the ability and the basic academic background needed to continue on in science, engineering, and technology equal to men but they are not going into those fields in anywhere near the numbers men are (National Science Foundation, 2000; Thom, 2001). For many girls, *interest* in these areas is not there. By eighth grade, in all racial and ethnic groups, twice as many boys as girls say they are interested in careers in the physical sciences, engineering, and technology. Girls were found to have less interest in math than boys and less confidence in their math abilities, even though they do not lag behind boys in grades or test scores (Catsambis, 1995).[7]

Studies of graduates of women's colleges found these students were more likely than women from coed colleges to continue on in the natural sciences (Tidball and Kistiakowsky, 1976). However, reanalysis of those data, controlling for variables such as socioeconomic status, found that attending a women's college had minimal impact on whether a female student continued on in the sciences (Cosby et al., 1994). Other studies carried out on women students enrolled in college after Title IX was implemented, when almost all colleges and universities were open to women, have tended not to find career differences between women in women's colleges and those in coed colleges (Astin, 1993), although Riordan (1992) found women from women's colleges more apt to be in "higher prestige jobs."

It is instructive to see what happened when a private boys' school and a private girls' school in the western United States both recently decided to go coed but remain separate. Before coeducation, the girls' school offered a variety of mathematics courses at the lower end of the curriculum, whereas the boys' school offered more upper-division mathematics. As the authors explained, after coeducation the faculty members of the boys' school "did not change the academic or the extra-curricular programs when females entered the school because they believed they already had the best curriculum." However, as males entered Grove High School (a pseudonym for the former girls' school) "many changes occurred in the academic programs, curriculum, and extra-curricular offerings." Grove administrators even changed its name, originally St. Theresa of the Grove (again a pseudonym), because it was felt that such a feminine name would not be attractive to boys. "As a school originally designed for girls, Grove was *not* good enough for boys." (Brody et al., 2000, pp. 88–89 and 100. Emphasis in the original.)

Coeducation has successfully reduced gender gaps in math and science achievement and course participation but not in interest in the subjects or continuation into related careers. However, it is not clear that single-sex education would do any better.

Assumption #3: Single-sex schooling provides girls with leadership opportunities they would not get in coed environments.

All-girl schools are seen as guaranteeing leadership opportunities that are presumed to go to males in coed schools. There are some data to support this assumption. In coed schools many more girls than boys *participate* in student government and most other extracurricular activities, with the exception of athletics (Dwyer and Johnson, 1997; National Center for Education Statistics, 2000, table 147).

However, the pattern is different when it comes to *leadership positions* in these activities. Even though girls are much more likely to be in honor societies, music groups, service organizations, and academic groups (e.g., art, computer, debate), boys are somewhat more apt to be in leadership positions within the organizations. Girls are more apt to be in leadership positions in literary activities (e.g., yearbook, newspaper) and slightly more apt to be leaders in career groups (e.g., future teachers, future farmers) and student government (Dwyer and Johnson, 1997). Leadership opportunities are apparently opening up to girls in coed schools.

Assumption #4: Single-sex schooling is not about money; money is spent equally on girls' and boys' schools.

Money and the resources it buys have always been an issue in single-sex education. "Separate but equal" has always been a myth in American education.

At the college level, the lack of equitable or equivalent resources between the all-male and the all-female colleges was a major reason for the United States Supreme Court's decision that women must be admitted into the Virginia Military Academy (VMI) (United States, 1997). Expert witness analysis of VMI and its sister school, Mary Baldwin College, and of the Citadel in South Carolina and its sister school, Converse College, by the first coauthor, found major differences in the all-male and all-female institutions. The men of VMI and the Citadel had many more resources and hence opportunities than did the women of Mary Baldwin and Converse, including more sports, athletic facilities, academic majors, computers, and even library books. The resources and opportunities that were offered were stereotyped, as well as unequal. For example, the Citadel offered degrees in engineering and had a sports stadium seating over 22,000 people. Converse offered degrees in music and art and had a concert hall seating fifteen hundred (Campbell, 1995). Such differences are not limited to these four schools. Smith College recently became the first and still the only women's college in the country to have an engineering department and offer an engineering degree (Smith College, 2000).

There are similar examples at the precollege level. For example, research on single-sex Catholic schools found that per-pupil expenditures at boys' schools were 25 percent higher than those at girls' schools, and 30 percent higher than those at coed schools (Riordan, 1990, p. 63).

Money is an issue in other ways as well. All-girl classes in coed schools can be a "cheap fix." Using existing teachers and resources incurs little if any costs but shows that schools and administrators are doing something about the "girl problem" in math and the sciences. Money can also be a motivation, as it was in the California public school single-sex experiment mentioned in the preceding, where some of the districts that applied were motivated by the money rather than a belief in the value of single-sex education (Datnow, Hubbard, and Woody, 2001). As in so many other areas, money is an issue in single-sex schooling.

Assumption #5: Nothing can be done to stop boys from disrespecting girls and creating a difficult environment, so girls are safer and more comfortable in single-sex schools.

Studies have found that boys are more apt to cause classroom disruptions than girls, and also that boys receive both more negative and more positive attention in classrooms (Bailey et al., 1992). Indeed, one study found that teachers were surprised at the extent to which the dominant and harassing behavior of boys was impeding girls' educational progress (Parker and Rennie, 1996). However, it has also been found that girls were not the only ones whose education was negatively affected. The same study found that although girls in single-sex classes received the least harassment from other students, boys in single-sex classes received the most (Parker and Rennie, 1996).

Moreover, sexism occurs in all forms of schooling—single-sex female, single-sex male, and coed. Although the quantity of sexist incidents (comments and behaviors) across different types of schools were the same, the types were different. In the single-sex female schools, sexist incidents were more apt to be in the form of allowing and/or reinforcing gender stereotypes by encouraging dependent behavior by girls and by less-than-rigorous instruction. Sexist incidents of explicit sexuality, defined as "the treatment of males or females as sexual objects," were found only in all-boys' schools; and the most prevalent form of sexism in coed schools was boys' domination of girls (Lee, Marks, and Byrd, 1994, pp. 103–104).

As a number of reports have noted, including AAUW's 1993 *Hostile Hallways* and its 2001 update, the hallways and classrooms of many of our schools are hostile to girls *and* boys. The obvious difficulty with sex segregation as a solution to this hostility is that the *real* problems are simply avoided. A teacher who permits a student to ridicule another student on the basis of sex or any other characteristic is actively preventing not only the second student from learning but also intimidates other students. Many of the problems we attribute to students are actually teachers' failures to control the learning environment in their classrooms.

By removing the girls rather than dealing with the issues of classroom misbehavior and disrespect that are creating the problem in the first place, we are assuming a stereotyped view of girls as gentle, weak creatures who cannot handle the rough environment of the real world. Moreover, we are implicitly accepting these beliefs:

- Boys' behavior is naturally incorrigible.
- The acceptable standard of classroom behavior is set by the most aggressive boys.
- It is acceptable for aggressive boys to prey on weaker boys and disrupt their learning.
- The appropriate female response to male aggression is not to fight back or to go to an authority, but to leave; that appropriate "girl behavior" is to be passive.

Assumption #6: Sexual tension between girls and boys and the desire to impress each other is a distraction to learning that can be eliminated by single-sex schooling.

Separating girls and boys is seen as a way of reducing sexual distraction; however, for homosexual and bisexual youth, single-sex education hardly eliminates sexual tensions. The assumption that it does denies the existence of these youth and ignores their stresses. Moreover, aggressions in all-boy schools are particularly an issue for boys who do not fit the ideal masculine stereotype (Datnow, Hubbard, and Woody, 2001).

It is true that in many coed middle school and high school classes, students and teachers report that girls distract boys and boys distract girls. It is felt that girls are discouraged from speaking up and taking initiative because they are concerned about appearing either stupid to the boys, or on the contrary, too smart. Boys are felt to act up more than they otherwise would in order to impress girls (Durost, 1996; Parker and Rennie, 1996). We cannot assume that all classroom tensions and distractions are sexual. Girls want to impress each other too, and the same goes for boys. And everyone wants to impress the most popular students. Gangs, cliques, even clothing all create distractions. Indeed, student uniforms are also touted as a way of decreasing distractions.

As indicated, the obvious difficulty with sex segregation as a solution to classroom climate issues, whether they are student misbehavior or student distractions, is that the *real* problems are behavioral and controllable. As adults and educators, it is our responsibility to create a school climate that is safe and appropriate for girls and boys, gays, lesbians, bisexuals, straights, African Americans, Asian Americans, Hispanic Americans, Native Americans, and whites. "School is a place where everyone can learn" must be more than a slogan.

One reason for teachers' failure to ensure respect in the classroom is the failure of the teacher education establishment and the education profession as a whole to emphasize the role of gender in learning (Sanders, 1997; Sanders and Campbell, 2001). Teachers who do not understand gender issues are ill-prepared to deal with those issues in their classes.

Assumption #7 : The existence of single-sex schooling for few girls does no harm to coed education for the many.

A major reason for the existence of girls' schools is in response to the well-documented failures of coeducation to provide an equitable learning environment (Bailey et al., 1992; Tyack and Hansot, 1990). An unintended result of single-sex schooling as a solution to girls' education dilemmas can be to serve as a pressure valve to release coeducation to deal with gender issues in education. Parents who are concerned enough about the quality of education their daughters are receiving to place them in girls' schools are no longer available to exert equity pressure on their neighborhood coed public schools. In the best of educational situations, parents are actively involved in their children's educations, but only in those schools their children attend. When they take their daughters out of the neighborhood school, that school loses access to the parents' voice and influence on the issue that concerns them so greatly: the education of girls. In the same way, coed public schools that choose to set up single-sex math or science classes—and the number of such schools that have done and are doing this is not negligible—are essentially removing any incentive for their normal math and science classes to change.

Assumption #8: Single-sex schooling provides girls with the best education.

Before we can even begin to determine if single-sex schooling has the potential to provide girls with the best education, we must first attempt to answer these questions:

- What *is* a good education?
- Does a good education differ for girls and boys?
- Do *all* girls and *all* boys need different things to get a good education?
- Does a good education differ if it is within a single-sex male, single-sex female, or coeducational environment?

We as educators and feminists have thought long and hard about these questions and have our own answers. Our goals for education center around the ability of students, both female and male, to develop the skills and capacity to control their own lives and develop compassion and concern for others, along with the skills and capacity to take action on that compassion and concern. We believe that individuals need different things in order to receive that good education; however, to define what students need based on group membership rather than individual characteristics is inappropriate as well as inaccurate.

We also believe that these questions must be answered individually and collectively by educators and others. Unless it is clear what a good education is, it makes little sense to design and implement strategies to move us toward a good education. It is clear to us that few definitions of good education would be achieved by simply separating girls and boys.

CONCLUSION

It is a disservice to frame the current discussion about the efficacy of single-sex education and coeducation as an either/or debate, with individuals on one side or the other. The debate needs to be reshaped into a thoughtful conversation, with an acknowledgment that our shared goal is schooling that fully educates *each* girl and *each* boy. That job is far from done, and that is where we need to dedicate our efforts (Campbell and Wahl, 1998a).

There is a parable about babies in the river.

Once upon a time there were three people walking next to the Hudson River. Looking over, they saw the river was full of babies. One of the three jumped into the river and started throwing babies out to the shore; the second jumped into the river and started teaching the babies to swim while the third started running upstream. "What are you doing?" cried the two in the water to the third. "There are babies drowning in the river!" "I know," said the third, "I'm going to find out who's throwing babies into the river and make them stop." (Campbell and Hoey, 1999)

To save all the babies we need to focus on what is needed to make the coeducational classroom fully equitable, promoting excellent outcomes for both girls and boys, in environments of high expectations. Well-funded, small-scale efforts in single-sex or coed schools will help save some babies, one by one, and even teach a few to swim. But without our best efforts directed toward *all* forms of education—coed, single-sex, private, public, home-schooled—the babies will keep coming down the river. We should be able to do better than this.

NOTES

1. This is in no way intended to be a comprehensive look at the research. More comprehensive examinations can be found in, for example, Haag (1998) and Levit (1999).

2. Because there are so few single-sex male colleges and universities, Astin (1993) included institutions whose enrollment was 90 percent or more male as predominantly male.

3. The United States General Accounting Office (1996, pp. 6–7) concluded in a report to the U.S. House of Representatives that restricting enrollment in a public school by sex violated Title IX of the Education Amendments of 1972, and may also violate the equal protection clauses of the U.S. constitution and different state constitutions.

4. It should be noted that there is a similar range in the political beliefs of those who support coeducation. Some support coeducation because boys benefit from the purported "civilizing influence" that girls bring to the classroom but still receive the larger share of resources and attention (Gill, 1996, p. 3). Others see coeducation as offering the best hope for reframing schooling so that it is not determined by gender (Gill, 1996, p. 5), whereas still others are concerned that prolonged exposure to single-sex education can lead to a "deficit approach" to girls' education, implying that girls are lacking in some ways compared to boys (Campbell and Wahl, 1998a).

5. If we are to understand girls and boys, we must look at the complexities of who they are, which includes their sex but is not limited to it. Race/ethnicity, poverty level, and disability are just three of the demographic characteristics that interact with a child's sex to influence his or her life.

6. Darrell Huff's 1954 *How to Lie with Statistics* (New York: W. W. Norton) provides an informative and entertaining overview of the problems with using "average" differences.

7. This argument is adapted from Campbell, P. B., and Hoey, L. (1999). *Saving Babies and the Future of SMET in America*. Washington, D.C.: United States Congress's Commission on the Advancement of Women and Minorities in Science, Engineering, and Technology Development (CAWMSET).

REFERENCES

The authors of this chapter chose to include entire first names, counter to standard academic style of first and middle initials only, to provide information on the sex of the authors and ensure that authors' sex is not presumed male by default.

American Association of University Women (AAUW). (1993). *Hostile Hallways: AAUW's Survey on Sexual Harassment in America's Schools*. Washington, D.C.: The American Association of University Women Educational Foundation.

American College Testing. (1998). *Are America's Students Taking More Science and Mathematics Course Work?* ACT Research Report Series 98.2 [online]. Available: *http://www.act.org/research/briefs/98–2.html*

Astin, Alexander. (1993). *What Matters in College: Four Critical Years Revisited*. San Francisco: Jossey Bass.

Bailey, Susan; Burbidge, Lynn; Campbell, Patricia B.; Jackson, Barbara; Marx, Fern; and McIntosh, Peggy. (1992). *The AAUW Report: How Schools Shortchange Girls*. Washington, D.C.: AAUW Educational Foundation and National Education Association.

Bennett, Susan M. (1997). "California's Single-Gender Academies Pilot Program." Paper presented at the National Dropout Prevention Conference, New Orleans.

Brody, Celeste M.; Fuller, Kasi Allen; Gosetti, Penny Poplin; Moscato, Susan, and Nagel, Nancy Gail. (2000). *Gender Consciousness and Privilege*. New York: Falmer Press.

Campbell, Patricia B. (1995). "A Comparison of the Citadel and VMI to Converse College and Mary Baldwin." Unpublished manuscript.

Campbell, Patricia B. and Hoey, Lesli. (1999). *Saving Babies and the Future of SMET in America*. Washington, D.C.: United States Congress' Commission on the Advancement of Women and Minorities in Science, Engineering, and Technology Development.

Campbell, Patricia B., and Wahl, Ellen. (1998a). "Of Two Minds: Single-Sex Education, Coeducation, and the Search for Gender Equity in K-12 Public Schooling." *New York Law School Journal of Human Rights* XIV(1), 289–310.

———. (1998b) "What's Sex Got to Do with It? Simplistic Questions, Complex Answers." In *Separated by Sex: A Critical Look at Single-Sex Education for Girls*. Washington, D.C.: AAUW Educational Foundation, pp. 63–74.

Catsambis, Sophia (1995). "Gender, Race, Ethnicity, and Science Education in the Middle Grades." *Journal of Research in Science Teaching* 32(3): 243–257.

Cosby, Faye, Alen, B., Culberton, T., Wally, C., Monty, J., Hall, R., and Nures, S. (1994). "Taking Selectivity into Account: How Much Does Gender Composition Matter? A Reanalysis of M.E. Tidball's Research. *NWSA Journal* 6: 107–111.

Datnow, Amanda; Hubbard, Lea; and Woody, Elisabeth. (2001). "Is Single-Gender Schooling Viable in the Public Sector? Lessons from California's Pilot Program." Toronto: Ontario Institute for Studies in Education.

Durost, Richard A. (1996). "Single-Sex Math Classes: What and for Whom? One School's Experiences." *NASSP Bulletin* (February, 27–31).

Dwyer, Carole, and Johnson, Linda M. (1997). "Grades, Accomplishments and Correlates." In Warren Willingham and Nancy Cole (Eds.), *Gender and Fair Assessment*. Englewood, NJ: Lawrence Erlbaum Press.

Educational Testing Service. (May 6, 1997). "ETS Study Finds More Gender Similarities than Differences in Educational Performance." Princeton, NJ: Educational Testing Service.

Gill, Judith. (1996). "Different Contexts: Similar Outcomes." A paper presented to the annual meeting of the American Educational Research Association, New York.

Gilson, Judith E. (1999). "Single-Gender Education Versus Coeducation for Girls: A Study of Mathematics Achievement and Attitudes toward Mathematics of Middle-School Students." Paper presented at the annual meeting of the American Educational Research Association, Montreal.

Haag, Pamela. (1998). "Single-Sex Education in Grades K-12. What Does the Research Tell Us?" In *Separated by Sex: A Critical Look at Single-Sex Education for Girls*. Washington, D.C.: AAUW Educational Foundation.

Hall, Roberta M. and Sandler, Bernice R. (1982). *The Classroom Climate: A Chilly One for Women?* Washington, D.C.: Association of American Colleges.

Hollinger, Debra K. (1993). *Single-Sex Schooling: Perspectives from Practice and Research*. Vol. I and II. *Special Report*. Washington, D.C.: Office of Educational Research and Improvement, U.S. Department of Education.

Huff, Darrell. (1954). *How to Lie with Statistics*. New York: W. W. Norton and Company.

Hyde, Janet S.; Fennema, Elizabeth; and Lamon, Susan J. (1990). "Gender Differences in Mathematics Performance: A Meta-Analysis." *Psychological Bulletin* 107(2): 139–155.

Hyde, Janet S. and Linn, Marcia. (1988). "Gender Differences in Verbal Ability: A Meta-Analysis" *Psychological Bulletin* 104: 53–69.

Leder, Gilah; and Forgasz, Helen. (1994). "Single-Sex Mathematics Classes in a Coeducational

Setting." Paper presented to the annual meeting of the American Educational Research Association, Chicago.

Lee, Valerie. (1998). "Is Single-Sex Schooling a Solution to the Problem of Gender Inequity?" In *Separated by Sex: A Critical Look at Single-Sex Education for Girls*. Washington, D.C.: AAUW Educational Foundation, 41-52.

Lee, Valerie E.; and Bryk, Anthony S. (1989). "Effects of Single-Sex Schools: Response to Marsh." *Journal of Educational Psychology* 81(4): 647-650.

———. (1986). "Effects of Single-Sex Secondary Schools on Student Achievement and Attitudes." *Journal of Educational Psychology* 78(5): 381-395.

Lee, Valerie E.; and Marks, Helen M. (1990). "Sustained Effects of the Single-Sex Secondary School Experience on Attitudes, Behaviors, and Values in College." *Journal of Educational Psychology* 82(3): 578-592.

———. (1992). "Who Goes Where? Choice of Single-Sex and Coeducational Independent Secondary Schools." *Sociology of Education* 65: 226-253.

Lee, Valerie E.; Marks, Helen M.; and Byrd, Tina. (1994). "Sexism in Single-Sex and Coeducational Independent Secondary School Classrooms." *Sociology of Education* 67: 92-120.

LePore, Paul C.; and Warren, Robert (1996). "The Advantages of Single-Sex Catholic Secondary Schooling: Selection Effects, School Effects, or 'Much Ado About Nothing?'" Paper presented at the annual meeting of the American Educational Research Association, New York.

Levit, Nancy (1999) "Separating Equals: Educational Research and the Long-Term Consequences of Sex Segregation." *The George Washington Law Review* 67(3): 451-526.

Maccoby, Eleanor E., and Jacklin, Carol. (1974). *The Psychology of Sex Differences*. Stanford, CA: Stanford University Press.

National Center for Education Statistics. (2000). *The Digest of Education Statistics, 1999*. Washington, D.C.: U.S. Department of Education, NCES 2000-031.

National Coalition of Girls' Schools. (2000). *Girls' Schools Alumnae Research: Executive Summary*. Concord, MA: Author.

———. (November 1998). "Parents, Students Opting for All-Girl Education: Rising Enrollment Shows Girls' Schools in Renaissance." *http://www.ncgs.org/Pages/news.htm#*

National Science Foundation. (2000). *Women, Minorities and People with Disabilities in Science and Engineering, 2000*. Arlington, VA: Author (NSF 00-327).

———. (1999). *Women, Minorities and People with Disabilities in Science and Engineering 1998*. Arlington, VA: Author (NSF 99-97).

Nicholson, Heather Johnson. (1992). "Gender Issues in Youth Development Programs." Washington, D.C.: Carnegie Council on Adolescent Development.

Parker, Leslie. (1985). *A Strategy for Optimizing the Success of Girls in Mathematics: Report of a Project of National Significance*. Canberra: Commonwealth Schools Commission.

Parker, Leslie, and Rennie, Leonie. (1996). "Single-Sex Grouping: Issues for School Administrators." Paper presented at the American Educational Research Association annual meeting, New York.

Pipher, Susan. (1994). *Reviving Ophelia: Saving the Selves of Adolescent Girls*. New York: Grosset/Putnam.

Riordan, Cornelius. (1998). "The Future of Single-Sex Schools." In *Separated by Sex: A Critical Look at Single-Sex Education for Girls*. Washington, D.C.: AAUW Educational Foundation, 53-62.

———. (1992). "Single and Mixed Gender Colleges for Women: Educational Attitudes and Occupational Outcomes." *Review of Higher Education* 327: 336-345.

———. (1990). *Girls and Boys in School: Together or Separate?* New York: Teachers College Press.

Sadker, M. and Sadker, D. (1994). Failing at Fairness: How American Schools Treat Girls. New York: Touchstone Press.

Sanders, Jo. (1997). "Teacher Education and Gender Equity." *ERIC Digest* 96(3).

Sanders, Jo; and Campbell, Patricia B. (2001, May). "Making It Happen: The Role of Teacher Education in Ensuring Gender Equity." *Policy Perspectives*. American Association of Colleges for Teacher Education, Vol. 2, No. 4, 1-5.

Sax, Linda. (1994). "Challenging Tokenism: The Impact of Major Sex-Composition on College Student Achievement." A paper presented to the annual meeting of the American Educational Research Association, New Orleans.

Smith College. (2000). News from Smith College: *http://www.smith.edu/newsoffice/Releases/00–094.html*

Smith, S. (1986). *Separate Tables? An Investigation into Single-Sex Settings in Mathematics.* London: Her Majesty's Stationery Office.

Thom, Mary. (2001). *Balancing the Equation: Where Are the Girls in Science, Engineering and Technology?* New York: National Council on Research on Women.

Tidball, Elizabeth; and Kistiakowsky, Vera. (1976). "Baccalaureate Origins of American Scientists and Scholars." *Science*: 646, 648, 652.

Tyack, David.; and Hansot, Elizabeth. (1990). *Learning Together: A History of Coeducation in American Schools.* New Haven: Yale University Press.

United States General Accounting Office. (1996). *Public Education Issues Involving Single-Gender Schools and Programs: A Report to the Chairman, Committee on the Budget.* House of Representatives GAO/HEHS, 96-122. Washington, D.C.: General Accounting Office.

United States vs. Virginia et al. Nos. 94-1941 and 94-2107, 1997.

Wenglinsky, Harold. (2000). *How Teaching Matters: Bringing the Classroom Back into Discussions of Teacher Quality.* Princeton, NJ: Educational Testing Service.

Willingham, Warren, and Cole, Nancy. (1997). *Gender and Fair Assessment.* Englewood, NJ: Lawrence Erlbaum Press.

Wood, Bonnie S.; and Brown, Lorrie A. (1997). "Participation in an All-Female Algebra I Class: Effects on High School Math and Science Course Selection." *Journal of Women and Minorities in Science and Engineering* 3(4): 265-278.

CHAPTER 4

The Legality of Single-Sex Education in the United States: Sometimes "Equal" Means "Different"

Rosemary Salomone

INTRODUCTION

Over the past decade, the subject of publicly supported single-sex education has generated considerable debate in legal and policy circles. Since 1996, much of this debate has centered on the Supreme Court's decision in the Virginia Military Institute case and how the Court's ruling intersects with Title IX of the Education Amendments of 1972. In *VMI*, Justice Ruth Bader Ginsburg, speaking for the Court, stated that gender classifications must have "an exceedingly persuasive justification" in order to pass muster under the Fourteenth Amendment equal protection clause of the U.S. Constitution. In subsequent years, *VMI* has become a key factor in determining the legality of efforts by school districts to establish single-sex schools and classes. At the same time, active federal enforcement under Title IX against these programs in recent decades has created continued confusion and uncertainty in school districts interested in establishing single-sex schools and classes for the social and educational benefits they promise girls and minority boys. School officials now find themselves in a legal bind. The *VMI* standard begs for evidence that such programs effectively meet permissible goals while the federal Office for Civil Rights prohibits schools from establishing the very programs critical to producing that evidence.

In this chapter, I underscore three points in response to this dilemma: first, that *VMI* in fact offers support for single-sex programs within certain parameters; second, that *VMI* and other Supreme Court decisions command clarification in the Title IX regulations; and third, that school districts should more actively explore the potential of single-sex programs as another avenue for providing appropriate education, particularly—although not exclusively—to disadvantaged students.

However, as Justice Ginsburg clearly demonstrated in her lengthy *VMI* opinion, the legal analysis does not occur in isolation. It involves a complex weaving together of factual data and research from other disciplines, including the history of women's education and the denial of access, the sociology of gender sameness and difference, philosophical notions of equality, and public policy considerations. Therefore, I digress briefly to these matters before turning to the legal issues.

DEFINING THE POLICY DEBATE

Since 1991, applications to private all-girls schools have grown by 40 percent and enrollments by 29 percent. Some schools have experienced a capacity enrollment increase by as much as 79 percent. Since the mid-1990s alone, nineteen new schools have opened their doors (National Coalition of Girls' Schools, 2000, 2001). Obviously, parents with the financial resources to exercise real choice see something positive in single-sex education for their daughters. In the meantime, public school systems from New York to California have increasingly defied the canon of coeducation in the name of gender equity for girls and equal opportunity for minority students both male and female. From the Young Women's Leadership School in East Harlem, to dual academies in Long Beach, California, to all-girls math and technology classes in Presque Isle, Maine and Olympia, Washington, publicly supported single-sex education has become a hotly contested issue. In fact, on the scale of educational controversy it is probably surpassed only by school vouchers. Then again, both challenge the conventional wisdom of public schooling.

A 1998 report from the American Association of University Women has fanned the flames of this debate (AAUW, 1998). According to the report, the research findings supporting single-sex schooling are simply inconclusive. In releasing its findings to the public, the group called on educators to address gender inequities throughout the system of coeducational schools. However, even prior to the AAUW report, the National Organization for Women and the American Civil Liberties Union had begun to lead the charge against single-sex schooling of any nature. Both groups have persistently argued that public single-sex programs are unconstitutional and that they violate the letter and spirit of Title IX, which prohibits sex discrimination in federally funded education programs. The Supreme Court's *VMI* decision has added more fuel to the fire.

Hovering over the controversy is the Office for Civil Rights (OCR) within the U.S. Department of Education, the federal agency charged with enforcing Title IX. In the past, OCR officials took a hard stand against single-sex programs. Now with new leadership, an administration that supports family choice, and a congressional mandate to issue guidelines on single-sex programs, the agency is faced with the challenge of reconciling the Title IX regulations with the *VMI* decision—and doing so in light of changing demographics, popular opinion, and social realities. Energizing the debate is the school choice movement in its varied forms, not the least of which is the burgeoning world of charter schools, which now number more than two thousand nationwide. Families more than ever, and particularly in the inner city, are looking to exercise more voice in the education of their children. No matter where one stands on the choice question, it is undeniable that the one-size-fits-all neighborhood school is slowly yielding to a new consumer-oriented model.

Given this complex set of political and legal circumstances, it is not hard to understand why this seemingly benign approach evokes visceral responses from educators, policymakers, and scholars who continue to shout at each other across a huge ideological divide. Supporters push for experimental programs that address a range of educational and social problems, including lower self-esteem among adolescent girls; lower standardized test scores, particularly in math and science, among female students; peer sexual harassment in the schools; gender inequities in the classroom; high rates of teenage pregnancy among minority girls; school violence; and high dropout, drug abuse, and crime rates among young African-American men in urban areas. Some suggest that beneath coeducation lies a "hidden curriculum"—a subtle but nonetheless harmful institutionalized program of male dominance in classroom interactions, uneven teacher expectations, and attitudes that prepare students for gender-specific roles in society. They argue that coeducation fails to adequately recognize the range of learning styles and emotional needs that girls and boys bring to school and the differential pace at which they develop various skills.

Proponents point to an adolescent subculture fostered by coeducation—one that promotes popularity rather than academic achievement—what the sociologist James Coleman in *The Adolescent Society* called the "cruel jungle of rating and dating" (1961). From a broader policy perspective, they argue that single-sex schooling provides educational options to parents and children who lack the economic means to purchase them in the private market. What is good for rich kids should be good for poor kids. Obviously, not all supporters embrace the preceding arguments. Some look to compensate girls and minority boys for social conditions and attitudes that have prevented them from succeeding academically. Others look to promote diversity as an end in itself.

Opponents present equally passionate arguments. They argue that single-sex programs smack of benevolent sexism, and deny young women and men the interpersonal skills to relate to each other in the real world. Their worst fear is the return to a pre-Title IX world where gender-segregated public schools and vocational classes shortchanged girls of educational resources and tracked them into a fixed set of low-paying jobs and careers. As a matter of law, opponents argue that separating students by gender violates the "separate is inherently unequal" principle of *Brown v. Board of*

Education (1954). More immediately, they question how any publicly supported single-sex school can survive the *VMI* decision. They view single-sex education, at best, as a short-term political fix that ignores pervasive gender and racial inequities in the schools. At worst, they see it as a dangerous mechanism for reinforcing persistent gender and racial stereotypes. As a matter of policy, they interpret the diversity arguments that support the concept as a wedge in the door of school choice on a larger scale and a potential threat to public schooling.

GENDER, ADOLESCENCE, AND DIFFERENCE

The current interest in single-sex schooling has centered primarily on girls and secondarily on minority boys, although a recent wave of popular literature on boys in general has broadened and deepened that discussion (Gurian, 1997, 1999; Kindlon and Thompson, 1999; Pollack, 1998). What exactly has brought about this change in sentiment, particularly among many but certainly not all women's advocates? And why have some local and national leaders within the African-American community embraced the idea, while others have vehemently opposed it? Obviously something happened as the 1980s turned into the 1990s. In the case of girls, it had all to do with research on women's adolescent development and the reported failure of coeducation to meet the needs of girls at that age. In the case of minority girls and especially boys, evidence mounted that they were falling behind at record speed both academically and socially and that the current system of schooling was doing little to reverse the cycle. Here the data on violence, dropout rates, teenage parenthood, and other indicia of academic failure and social dysfunction were staggering. Both lines of inquiry converged on the question of whether coeducation could effectively deliver on the promise of equal educational opportunity, so integral to the civil rights agenda. Both raised distinct as well as similar legal and policy issues.

First, consider the girl question. Throughout the 1970s, feminists sought gender equality in a formal sense. Girls and boys as a group were identical in intelligence and abilities, they argued. Any differences in interests were purely the result of social conditioning, not biology. Their views were premised on an assimilationist model that called for fairness. They fought to make schools gender neutral. However, by the end of the decade, some feminist scholars and writers began to view sex differences through a new lens. Here the discussion turned to the different experiences of women and men, which have resulted in a different moral and psychological perspective (Belenky et al., 1986; Chodorow, 1978; Noddings, 1984). Some argued that schools reinforced male hegemony and epistemology and marginalized female voices (Tyack and Hansot, 1990).

Carol Gilligan's book, *In a Different Voice* (1982), is considered the seminal work in this genre. Although her work has come under attack in recent years, she undeniably inspired much of the subsequent research on female adolescent development, gender differences, and the effects of schooling. Gilligan challenged classic psychological theory that attached a positive value to certain characteristics culturally defined as "masculine"—separation, detachment, subordination of relationships, and abstract thinking—while negating other characteristics culturally defined as "feminine"—attachment, caring, and interdependence. Among men she found an "ethic of justice" as contrasted with women's "ethic of care." She claimed that both are elements of the human condition and should be equally valued. In her later research on students at the Emma Willard School, Gilligan underscored adolescence as a critical period in the lives of women. She called it a "watershed in female development, a time when girls are in danger of drowning or disappearing" (1990, p. 10). She found that between the ages of twelve and thirteen (the age, she noted, when dropping out of school becomes more common in the inner city), girls' knowledge seems to be buried (p. 14). Gilligan did not intend for her work to support gender separation. She made that point clear more than a decade later in an *amicus curiae* brief submitted to the Court in the *VMI* case (1994). Nevertheless, her conclusions on difference lent theoretical support to the empirical findings of educational researchers examining gender equity in the schools over the following decade.

What ultimately sparked an intense look at coeducational schools were the observational studies of Myra and David Sadker and their now-controversial book, *Failing at Fairness* (1994). The Sadkers found that boys dominated classroom discussion and were more likely to be praised, corrected, helped, and criticized by teachers—all reactions that foster student achievement, so they argued. As the Sadkers were reporting their findings in academic journals and at professional conferences, a series of reports on how schools shortchanged girls unintentionally gave new currency to the percolating debate over single-sex education. Through the early to mid-1990s, the American Association of University Women reported that girls disproportionately lost self-esteem and interest in math and science as they approached adolescence (1991); that women were underrepresented in the school curriculum, teacher behavior and tests tended to favor boys, and girls lagged seriously behind boys in math and science (1992); that girls experienced widespread sexual harassment in public schools (1993); and that they faced social and institutional challenges as they formed identities and negotiated the middle-school environment (1996).

Gilligan, the Sadkers, and the AAUW together painted a painful portrait of growing up as a female in America. Although their methodology, findings, and conclusions have since become the subject of sharp criticism and vigorous scholarly debate (Kleinfeld, 1998, 1999; Sommers, 1994, 2000), their reported findings indisputably touched off a national discussion among educators, psychologists, and feminists. The impact soon began to reach the admissions offices of private all-girls schools where enrollments increased for the first time in a decade—by almost two thousand—between the 1995 and 1996 school years. Between 1997 and 1998, that figure grew by another three thousand (National Association of Independent Schools, 1999). The data also generated a flurry of activity in school districts around the country with single-sex math and science classes suddenly gaining favor.

INNER CITY MINORITY BOYS

Now consider the minority boy question. As interest in single-sex education for girls seemed to explode, inner-city school systems were experiencing a simultaneous movement for boys. This propelled the single-sex debate into another dimension where race and gender became conflated. The focus here was to reverse the downward educational and social spiral of minority students, particularly African-American males. And the primary mechanisms were the all-boys' class and the Afrocentric academy.

Proponents of these programs pointed to the failure of the civil rights agenda to improve the lives of poor inner-city residents. Neither compensatory programs nor court-ordered racial integration had proven successful in raising the achievement of low-income minority students. African-American men, in particular, were becoming reduced to a dismal statistic. As they became increasingly swallowed up in substance abuse and crime, African-American boys suffered from the absence of positive role models in their lives (Holland, 1987). The rationale underlying Afrocentric school programs borrowed many of the gender-based features advanced by the proponents of single-sex schooling for girls—same sex (and race) role models and mentors, greater leadership opportunities, and higher academic standards and expectations. Added to these was an Afrocentric curriculum to enhance self-esteem and develop positive identity.

The issue came to a head in the case of Detroit where the school board proposed to open three all-male Afrocentric academies on an experimental basis. The racial segregation, in effect, would have been more symbolic than real. The public school enrollment in Detroit was approximately 90 percent African American and admission to the academies technically would be open to males of all races. Nevertheless, the very concept of officially created racially identified schools sent shock waves throughout the civil rights community. It also brought to the surface competing desires for integration and segregation that have alternately tugged at the African-American community since the introduction of slavery almost four centuries ago. As one commentator noted, this was a "desperate remedy for desperate times," one that reflected the "grim state of American race relations" four decades after *Brown v. Board of Education* (Cuban, 1991). Kenneth Clark, whose research had guided the Court in *Brown*, called the schools "academic child abuse" and a "flagrant . . . violation of [the decision]" (Wilson, 1992). The NAACP, at its annual convention in 1991, adopted a policy proclaiming its "historical opposition to school segregation of any kind" (1990).

The NOW Legal Defense and Education Fund and the ACLU took school officials to court. However, although the policy debate within the African-American community focused on racial segregation, the civil rights groups focused on gender discrimination in their legal action. They based their chief arguments in the equal protection clause of the Fourteenth Amendment and Title IX, charging that the school district was failing to meet the equally pressing needs of girl students. In *Garrett v. Board of Education* (1991), the district court concluded that the plaintiffs were likely to prevail on most of their claims and granted them a preliminary injunction. The statistics on "at-risk" males simply did not convince the court that the exclusion of girls was substantially related to the program's objectives. Nor could the court find sufficient evidence that the system was failing males because of the presence of females. In fact, there was clear evidence that the system was also failing females. School officials agreed to open the school to girls rather than risk the cost of additional litigation. Similar efforts in New York, Baltimore, and Milwaukee to establish programs for African-American boys were either stalled at the start or eventually discontinued as school districts buckled under a real or perceived threat of litigation from civil rights groups or Title IX enforcement action by the Office for Civil Rights.

FROM *BROWN* TO *VMI*: IS SEPARATE INHERENTLY UNEQUAL?

As the Detroit case demonstrates, there are two key legal arguments raised against single-sex programs: the first is constitutional, based in the equal protection clause; the second is statutory, grounded in Title IX. At some point, the two arguments intersect.

The constitutional argument takes on several casts—that separating girls from boys in public schooling is inherently unequal and therefore unconstitutional and, the less absolutist argument, that offering a particular type of education, that is, single-sex, to one group while denying it to the other violates the constitutional rights of the group denied. A variation of this second argument is that offering certain benefits to one group in the form of single-sex education demands that "comparable" or "substantially equal" benefits be offered to the other, but not necessarily in a single-sex school.

The equality principle draws from *Brown v. Board of Education* (1954). As the controversy over the Afrocentric academies demonstrates, the principle that "separate is inherently unequal" articulated in *Brown* is deeply ingrained in the American psyche. It is not surprising, therefore, that civil rights advocates have invoked that principle in their legal opposition to single-sex schooling. *Brown* tells us that when government policy forces a historically disadvantaged group to remain separate from the dominant group, it stigmatizes the former and conveys the message that its members are of lesser intrinsic worth than the latter.

Over the past three decades, the Supreme Court has applied the equality principle to a number of cases where sex, and not race, was the classifying factor. However, the Court has spoken directly only twice on single-sex education. The first occasion was in 1982 when the Court struck down the all-female admissions policy of the Mississippi University for Women's School of Nursing. In *Mississippi University for Women v. Hogan* (1982) the issue was not gender separation per se but comparability. Joe Hogan had applied to that particular school expressly because he resided in the same city. The state maintained no other nursing program within reasonable traveling distance from his home. The harm he suffered was that the state was constructively denying him an educational benefit available to women.

The state argued that this was essentially "educational affirmative action" to compensate for discrimination against women. Yet Justice Sandra Day O'Connor, speaking for a narrow Court majority, found that women in fact dominated the nursing profession; therefore, the program merely perpetuated the stereotype of nursing as a career for women and not men. The Court, however, left open the possibility that states could provide single-sex education at least for compensatory purposes as long as the intent and effect were not to promote archaic and stereotypic views on the roles and abilities of females and males.

The second time the Court looked at the issue was a decade later, when it struck down the all-male admissions policy of the Virginia Military Institute. That decade had witnessed an unanticipated turn of events. Some school districts, particularly in urban areas, had become passionate defenders of single-sex programs, and they were doing so with the support of some segments of the women's rights community and with increasing affirmation from African Americans. Suddenly single-sex education was no longer the violation but rather a remedy to denial of equal educational access. Therefore, the *VMI* case, with very little in common with this new compensatory model, became caught up in the larger debate over single-sex schooling.

Just as an aside, the *VMI* litigation marched through the federal courts in tandem with the more visible case against the Citadel in South Carolina (*Faulkner v. Jones*, 1995). There we followed the painful efforts of Shannon Faulkner to gain entry despite the determined resistance of school officials, the vocal opposition of alumni, and the cruel hostility of cadets (Manegold, 2000). Both the Citadel and VMI had a male-only policy that remained from a time when women were considered unfit for higher education and particularly unfit for military service and leadership. Unlike the federal military academies, which prepare cadets for service in the armed forces, both the Citadel and VMI primarily train their students for leadership roles in the corporate world and government.

The Citadel presented a live plaintiff at whom the public could direct its sympathy or outrage. VMI, on the other hand, was taken into court by the Department of Justice on the complaint of a rejected female applicant who forever remained nameless and faceless. The Citadel grounded its defense in institutional autonomy and lack of student demand. VMI took a different approach, placing great weight on its "adversative model" as a justification for excluding women. Throughout the litigation, VMI attorneys argued with remarkable certitude that women were simply unfit for this demanding instructional method whose key features include "physical rigor, mental stress, absolute equal treatment, absence of privacy, minute regulation of behavior, and indoctrination in desirable values" (*VMI*, 1991, p. 1421). They claimed that VMI would have to modify the rigors of this method in order to accommodate female cadets, which would destroy the success of the program.

In the course of the litigation, the appeals court found that the VMI program did, in fact, violate the equal protection clause. The court offered the state three options to remedy the violation. VMI could admit women, establish parallel institutions or parallel programs, or forgo state support and pursue its own policies as a private institution (*VMI*, 1992). In response, the state proposed a separate all-female program, the Virginia Women's Institute for Leadership (VWIL). The Institute would be supported with state funds at Mary Baldwin College, a private liberal arts college for women. However, the experience for the women enrolled in the parallel program would stand in sharp contrast to the experience of the cadets at VMI. At Mary Baldwin, the Corps of Cadets would be little more than ceremonial, with an ROTC program providing the main military experience. The women would not live in barracks, wear uniforms on a daily basis, and eat all meals together. In lieu of the adversative approach, students would engage in cooperative learning. It was also clear that the programs would not be comparable in other tangible factors. Only 68 percent of Mary Baldwin's faculty held Ph.D.s as compared with 86 percent at VMI, its course offerings in math and science were less extensive, and its alumni network and endowment did not come close to VMI's. Nor was there any realistic comparison between the facilities of the two campuses, especially in athletics.

Justice Ginsburg, speaking for the Court in *VMI*, presented a carefully and forcefully crafted opinion that stressed the narrowness of the decision and unique facts of the case. She restated and applied with bite the standard used in prior gender discrimination cases, particularly in *Hogan*—that classifications by sex must be "substantially related" to an "important governmental interest" and must be backed by an "exceedingly persuasive justification." However, the opinion appears to add more teeth to that standard. It talks about courts applying "skeptical scrutiny," taking a "hard look," at "generalizations and tendencies" based on gender. Once a violation is found, the remedy must closely fit it, placing the claimants in "the position they would have occupied in the absence of [discrimination]" (*VMI*, 1996, p. 554).

The state of Virginia offered two justifications for excluding women from VMI—to provide diversity in an otherwise coeducational state system, and to preserve the educational benefits of VMI's "adversative approach." On the diversity question, the Court recognized the "state's prerogative evenhandedly to support diverse educational opportunities." But here the state's actions were anything but "evenhanded." It effectively had denied women a unique educational opportunity available solely at the "premier military institute." Justice Ginsburg recounted in detail the history of higher education, replete with pervasive exclusionary policies against women even into the recent past. She counseled that the all-male college, set against that backdrop, is very likely to be a device for "preserving tacit assumptions of male superiority." She warned that even "benign" justifications offered in defense of categorical exclusions were not automatically acceptable (*VMI*, 1996, pp. 543–536). Despite the claims of VMI officials, to her it was clear from the institution's history that diversity had not driven the decision of its founders, nor had it played a part in continuing to exclude women.

The Court roundly dismissed Virginia's arguments supporting the second justification—to preserve the benefits of the adversative method. At trial, expert testimony had established that some women "are capable of the individual activities required of VMI cadets" (*VMI*, 1991, p. 1412). The district court had recognized that "some women . . . would want to attend [VMI] if they had the opportunity" (p. 1414). Citing *Hogan*, the Court warned that "[s]tate actors controlling gates to opportunity . . . may not exclude qualified individuals based on 'fixed notions concerning the roles and abilities of males and females'" (*VMI*, 1996, p. 541).

The Court in *VMI* stopped short of renouncing all gender-based classifications, leaving open the door to single-sex programs under certain conditions. Nor did it claim that men and women must be treated completely the same under all circumstances. Here we see Justice Ginsburg cautiously navigating a middle course between the competing visions of absolute gender equality or equal treatment, on the one hand, and the recognition that women should be compensated for socially imposed disabilities or accommodated for different educational needs on the other. She tells us that the "inherent differences, between men and women" are "cause for celebration, but not for the denigration of members of either sex or for artificial constraints on an individual's opportunity." Gender classifications are permissible where they "advance the full development of the talent and capacities of our nation's people," but not where they are used "to create or perpetuate the legal, social, and economic inferiority of women" (1996, p. 533). In other words, in some contexts, "equal" means "different."

At first glance, this last reference to "women" suggests a particular solicitude toward females. A careful reading, however, more specifically suggests a particular apprehension of discrimination against women in view of single-sex education's dark history. This reference must be read together with the more inclusive language preceding it referring to "members of either sex" and the potential limits on an "individual's opportunity." This broader reference negates the suggestion that the Court would only recognize sex classifications that advance the full development of women and not men. Taken as a whole, it reasonably could be interpreted as an oblique bow to single-sex schools for inner city minority students, both female and male. In fact, to absolutely deny such programs to boys as a group where they can be offered to girls would violate the decision's principle of evenhandedness.

The Court also suggested that equality must be measured by both tangibles and intangibles. In this case, the state had failed to show "substantial equality." The program at Mary Baldwin was but a "pale shadow of VMI" in terms of curricular and extracurricular choices, the stature of the faculty, funding, prestige, library resources, and alumni support and influence" (*VMI*, 1996, pp. 551–552). Although the Court mentioned in passing that the two programs were not "comparable," contrary to the findings of the lower courts, the Court emphasized the language of "equality" rather than the "comparability" standard proposed by Virginia officials. Equality suggests more of an objective inputs standard of some magnitude even if not palpable and measurable with a degree of accuracy. Comparability, on the other hand, suggests a more subjective amorphous standard with less clearly defined guidelines, one that would allow the institution greater discretion, but also lend itself to greater abuse.

VMI was indeed a landmark case in the quest for gender equity. It was also typical of cases where the Court strains to reconcile complicated legal issues that bear on conflicting social norms and understandings. In that sense, it left a trail of unanswered questions. Those questions raise issues of compensatory purposes and affirmative action, gender differences and stereotypes, girls' versus boys' programs, the inherent limitations of "comparability," the meaning of "substantial equality," and the permissible bounds of Title IX.

THE TITLE IX LAW AND OFFICE FOR CIVIL RIGHTS INTERPRETATION

That leads specifically to the approach taken by the Office for Civil Rights with regard to single-sex programs. Title IX prohibits discrimination on the basis of sex in educational programs or activities that receive federal financial assistance. The legal debate over single-sex programs and Title IX has involved two issues—the admissions policies of single-sex schools, and permissibility of single-sex classes in coeducational schools.

First, consider single-sex schools, a concept that has provoked heated controversy in urban school districts across the country. With regard to admissions, the statute applies "only to institutions of vocational education, professional education, and graduate higher education, and to public institutions of undergraduate higher education" (§1681(a)(1)). It expressly exempts admissions to religious educational institutions whose tenets are inconsistent with the law, military training schools (such as the Citadel and VMI), and undergraduate public institutions of higher education that traditionally and continually had a policy of admitting only students of one sex at the time that the statute was enacted. The statute is silent on admissions to private undergraduate colleges (such as Smith and Wellesley) as well as to public and private elementary and secondary schools other than vocational schools. In 1975 OCR adopted regulations that reflect these inclusions, exclusions, and omissions.

From the legislative language and subsequent history of Title IX, we can reasonably conclude that both the statute and the regulations exclude the admissions policies of public elementary and secondary schools. However, the Title IX regulations place a critical restriction on that exclusion and that restriction lends itself to a range of interpretations. According to what is commonly known as the "comparability" requirement, a local school district cannot exclude any student from admission to a school unless it makes available to the student, "pursuant to the same policies and criteria of admission, . . . courses, services, and facilities [that are] comparable" (§106.35). This requirement applies only to public school districts, an understandable accommodation to the numerous single-sex schools that existed in the private sector at the time the regulations were adopted.

For those who have most vocally opposed single-sex schooling, particularly the ACLU and NOW, it appears that comparability implies "sameness." If a school district opens a single-sex school for girls, it must open a corresponding school for boys. Yet the comparability requirement neither mandates expressly nor suggests that courses, services, and facilities must be provided to the excluded group in a single-sex setting. It merely requires that the two programs follow the same admissions policies and criteria. That suggests an alternate interpretation. Where a school district opens a single-sex school for girls, comparable educational opportunities could be offered to boys in a coed setting, such as a comprehensive high school or a magnet school, as long as the admissions criteria (e.g., grades, achievement test scores, residency) are the same and the educational offerings and facilities are of comparable substance and quality.

The second issue that has arisen involves course offerings. Here the interpretation turns not on the statute but on the regulations which explicitly distinguish between admissions and course access. As to admissions, the regulations repeat the language of the statute and expressly limit Title IX coverage "only to institutions of vocational education, professional education, graduate higher education, and public institutions of undergraduate higher education" (§106.15(d)). As to course offerings, the regulations seem to present a broad prohibition. A public school cannot "provide any course or otherwise carry out any of its education program or activity separately on the basis of sex, or require or refuse participation therein by any of its students on such basis" (§106.34).

The regulations, however, incorporate certain exceptions that recognize gender differences in the interest of maintaining privacy and safety. Schools can maintain separate teams for contact sports, group students in physical education activities by ability level assessed on the basis of individual performance, conduct separate portions of classes that extensively address human sexuality, and organize separate choral groups based on a particular vocal range or quality (§106.34(b–f)). School districts can also establish separate programs for pregnant students as long as participation is voluntary and the program is comparable to the program offered to nonpregnant students (§106.40(a)(3)). These narrow exceptions do not cover any of the core academic subjects such as math, science, and computers, all of which have been the focus of many of the recent single-sex class initiatives particularly for girls. Yet the fact that OCR has incorporated certain exceptions into the regulations demonstrates that the Title IX statute does not preclude the agency from expanding the list to include other types of single-sex classes for other compelling educational and social purposes.

Nevertheless, the seemingly blanket prohibition on single-sex classes with few enumerated exceptions may or may not be mitigated, depending on one's view, by another provision that supports single-sex programs within certain guidelines. The regulations permit schools to take "affirmative action" to "overcome the effects of conditions which resulted in limited participation . . . by persons of a particular sex" even where there are no formal findings of discrimination. School districts can undertake remedial programs of this sort even where neither the Department of Education nor a court has made formal findings that the school or district has engaged in sex discrimination (§106.3(b)). Here the concept of compensation or remediation comes into play. However, the regulations are unclear as to whether this provision applies to single-sex schools, elementary schools (arguably unnecessary because the statute impliedly exempts admissions policies), or single-sex classes (arguably contradictory to the broad mandatory language on "access to course offerings" with explicit exceptions). It suggests, however, that single-sex programs of some nature might be permissible for certain populations if justified by a compensatory or remedial purpose. The argument can be made that socially and environmentally imposed conditions have impeded the academic advancement of certain groups of students, for example, inner city minorities—and perhaps single-sex programs can compensate for those conditions.

Of course, this reasoning raises the question as to whether single-sex classes can be initiated only for remedial purposes. Beyond minority boys and girls in general, where does this line of thinking leave nonminority boys? Can schools establish all-boys' classes in language arts or foreign languages, two areas where the data show that boys lag behind girls in interest and achievement? What are the so-called "conditions" that have limited their participation in these subjects? Have boys as well as girls been the victims of social stereotyping and cultural pressures that have limited their vision and life options? Recent attention to the "boy question" seems to point in this direction. Yet the regulations, adopted in the mid-1970s to specifically although not expressly address discrimination against girls, offer no guidance on these more current concerns regarding the educational needs of boys.

RECONCILING TITLE IX WITH THE *VMI*

The underlying question is whether publicly supported single-sex programs are legally permissible, and if so, under what circumstances. The answer, at the national level, lies in reconciling the Title IX regulations with the Title IX statute and with the constitutional parameters that the Court set forth in *VMI*. Obviously the Title IX regulations lend themselves to differing interpretations, assuming that we accept them as a given; however, the analysis goes further. As a matter of constitutional and administrative law, the regulations must conform with congressional intent and they must be reasonable (*Chevron*, 1984). Title IX puts into operation the equal protection clause of the Fourteenth Amendment. The Supreme Court has made clear in recent years that Congress merely sets the remedy or devises ways to prevent an injury for a violation that the Court has defined in the first instance.

Given these ground rules, it is clear that the Court's decision in *VMI* compels a fresh look to determine if the regulations fall within constitutional bounds. This is no easy task. Reading the *VMI* decision and its potential impact is somewhat akin to reading tea leaves. It demands carefully parsing the sweeping and at times opaque language of the decision to distinguish among the limitations set by the holding, the guideposts offered in the dicta, and the interpretive space left open by the unanswered questions. Within that interpretive space, the question remains as to whether changed circumstances now impel federal officials to reinterpret the Title IX regulations or completely rewrite certain provisions. Depending on how you look at it, VMI offers OCR a challenge or an opportunity. If the latter, then OCR now has the legal and political justification to develop a clear position on Title IX that responds to current social conditions, recent research findings on adolescent development, and contemporary directions in school reform that promote local flexibility and family choice.

One issue, however, is crystal clear from the *VMI* decision. Despite protests of some civil rights groups to the contrary, in the context of gender "separate" is not "inherently unequal." All single-sex programs are not per se unconstitutional. The opposite is also true. All single-sex programs are not per se nor presumptively constitutional. From *VMI* we can rightly conclude that coeducation is still the norm in public schooling. Nevertheless, school districts may deviate from the norm as long as they have an "important governmental interest" in mind, the program is "substantially related" to that purpose, and the overall justification is "exceedingly persuasive." The Court suggested that a sufficiently "important" governmental interest might be to develop "the talent and capacities" of students provided the program does not perpetuate gender stereotypes or limit opportunities.

One has to read between the lines and behind the historical pages of the Court's decision to figure out how this all plays into the contemporary interest in single-sex schooling. Actually, the case has little in common with recent efforts among public school districts. *VMI* was more analogous to the first generation of single-sex programs that denied women entrance based on stereotypical notions of their capabilities. Here the Court concluded that VMI, in doing so, was perpetuating the "inferiority of women" and the superiority of men. The more recent vintage of second-generation single-sex programs has just the opposite intent and projected effect. This new crop of public school initiatives, for both females and minority males, focus not on the "inherent" deficiencies of the categorically excluded sex, as was the case with VMI, but on the specific educational needs of the included sex. These programs aim to level the playing field rather than exclude on the basis of negative stereotypes.

But if single-sex programs cannot be based in "fixed notions concerning the roles and capabilities of males and females," are programs that focus on math, science, and technology for girls permissible? Are they not based in stereotypes about girls' underachievement? Do they suggest that girls are deficient in some way, that perhaps as a group they lack the spatial abilities needed to succeed in math, for example? Do they imply that girls lack a math or science gene? I suggest that the response, at least partially, turns on the underlying purpose of the program and the way that school officials present it. I do not deny that these programs are based in certain generalizations about females and males. However, they are not necessarily based in a generalized conclusion about intrinsic ability levels. They merely are designed to address a generalized observation about achievement and participation levels, and the greater willingness of some girls to take intellectual risks in the absence of boys. This is not a generalization intended to exclude girls but one intended ultimately to mainstream them into the fabric of society without restricting opportunities for men. It all boils down to context.

If the program is designed to expand opportunities and not limit them, then the justification becomes more persuasive; however, the effect must also support the intent. No matter how benign the intent, a program cannot perpetuate a sense of inferiority among its beneficiaries or in the eyes of the general public. School officials have to exercise extreme diligence in monitoring the program's explicit and implicit messages and assessing its cognitive and affective outcomes on an ongoing basis. Of course, participation must be voluntary.

Given the directives that seem to emerge from *VMI* and other Court decisions, there remain two provisions within the current Title IX regulations that demand reexamination, specifically the one requiring comparability and the other permitting affirmative action. As to the first, as already noted, *VMI* uses the language of "substantial equality" based on tangibles and intangibles rather than the Title IX term calling for "comparability." Now here it is important to note that the two programs need not be "exactly" but rather "substantially" equal. That distinction rationally flows from the Court's recognition that there exist, in fact, "inherent differences between men and women." As already noted, substantiality, based not only on tangible but also intangible features, puts more teeth into the standard than mere comparability. The significance of this linguistic shift needs to be watched in future cases and in any proposed changes in the Title IX regulations or other federal guidelines.

The question then remains as to whether "substantial equality" can only be met within another single-sex program or within an existing coeducational program. *VMI* does not provide a clear answer. The uniquely "totalistic" approach used at VMI does not lend itself to comparisons with the typical elementary or secondary school. The decision merely indicates that a crucial concern for the Court was that school officials allocate equal resources to both programs and that neither program promotes stereotypical notions of group capabilities or tendencies that might limit life opportunities

The second—and perhaps more controversial—issue relates to affirmative action. The regulations as they are now written may suggest, as some moderate liberals argue, that single-sex programs are only permissible when they have a compensatory purpose. But compensation for what? For limiting conditions imposed by society, or by the school district, or from biological differences? On this count *VMI* offers no direct instruction because compensation was not part of the school's rationale nor its intent. *VMI*, however, requires a *convincing* educational justification and not necessarily a *compensatory* one. Research findings on the technology gap for girls, the compelling social and academic data on inner-city minority students, anecdotal reports on the single-sex experience, and even more recent data on the educational and emotional needs that boys share as a group may prove exceedingly persuasive provided some link can be drawn between the perceived needs and the benefits of single-sex education. The only way to test the truth of that connection is to permit school districts to explore various approaches and gather empirical data. The currently available evidence on single-sex education is mildly suggestive but inconclusive, drawing primarily from schools abroad and Catholic schools in the United States. Yet both of these operate within distinct social and cultural contexts (Salomone, 1999).

Even more pointedly, the affirmative action provision in the Title IX regulations may prove particularly problematic in view of both *VMI* and the general trend in Court thinking. *VMI* speaks in the language of "evenhandedness," which negates the possibility of a true affirmative action approach. School districts cannot bestow benefits on one sex without offering substantially equal benefits to the other. The concept of affirmative action also runs into potential conflict with the Supreme Court's evolving views on the use of group-based classifications as a means to remedy nonspecific discrimination (*Croson*, 1989). Here the school district would bear the burden of proving that it had in fact engaged in sex discrimination, which it hoped to remedy through single-sex schooling. Realistically speaking, how many school officials would move down that perilous road of self-incrimination?

We can effectively and legitimately resolve this apparent conflict by removing single-sex education completely from affirmative action and shifting to an appropriate education paradigm. Affirmative action in the context of job opportunities and college admissions often entails preferential treatment, which is a zero-sum game. The beneficiaries win an important economic advantage, whereas others who have sought the benefit, who arguably have met measurable qualifications, and can also profit from it lose. Single-sex education, on the other hand, only rises to a benefit for those for whom it is educationally appropriate, similar to gifted and talented programs or special educational services. It merely offers a particular approach to education on what we know empirically and experientially about the academic, social, and developmental needs of certain students who fall within group norms. It does not necessarily deny others an appropriate education.

Different treatment does not inevitably imply *preferential* treatment, which lies at the heart of the legal and political opposition to affirmative action. It merely suggests that for some students single-sex programs may provide an environment that is more conducive to learning than coeducation for whatever reason. It does not necessarily evoke negative stereotypes, particularly where participation is voluntary, the resources and opportunities offered to both groups are substantially equal, and the overt and subtle messages convey individual fulfillment rather than group deficiency. The language of "appropriateness" is not only more neutral and less politically polarizing, but also more accurate.

There is, however, one more provision within the Title IX regulations that begs for reconsideration. Here the regulations ban schools from offering a course "separately on the basis of sex." For more than a decade, OCR has consistently interpreted this provision as an outright ban on single-sex classes with few exceptions. On careful reading, however, it appears to conflict with the letter and spirit of *VMI*. It is also difficult to reconcile with Title IX itself. Both the debate surrounding Title IX's enactment and the various exemptions in the statute suggest that Congress did not intend a blanket ban on all single-sex education. The *VMI* decision presents the same view under the equal protection clause so long as programs are voluntary, do not promote gender stereotypes, and provide substantially equal services to both groups. The statute itself implicitly permits a school district to establish an *entire school*, other than a vocational school, that serves students of one sex as long as comparable services are provided to the other group. If single-sex schools are permissible, then it seems inconsistent and unreasonable to preclude a coeducational school from merely offering a *specific class* on the basis of gender.

RECENT DEVELOPMENTS

Federal officials are now struggling to reconcile the Title IX regulations with a reasonable reading of the statute and the Court's decision in *VMI* and related cases. For over two decades, OCR appeared to take an absolutist position on the regulations. Since *VMI*, the agency seems to have quietly stepped back on enforcement. As one former insider noted to me, the single-sex question is probably the most complex gender issue that OCR has faced over the years. Next to women's athletics, it is probably the most politically charged, but OCR's apparent retreat is not simply the result of *VMI*. Urban school districts, in particular, are clamoring for a definitive go-ahead from OCR, whereas the charter school movement is fast creating a fertile field for testing the merits of alternative approaches, including single-sex education.

In February 1999, OCR issued a brief response to concerns raised in a Senate Appropriations Committee report. Here OCR stated that it was "examining whether there is a legal basis for interpreting Title IX to permit single-sex classrooms as well as schools where they are justified on educational grounds *and* do not involve stereotyping or stigmatizing students based on gender *and* where comparable educational opportunities are afforded to students of both sexes" (U.S. Department of Education, 1999). The report estimated that, if changes in the regulations were necessary, a notice of proposed rulemaking would be published in the spring or summer of 1999. That has still not occurred. One significant point should not be overlooked, however. The report made no mention of compensatory purposes or affirmative action.

In May 2000, OCR issued civil rights guidelines for charter schools that included a restatement of the Title IX regulations on single-sex programs. Single-sex schools are permissible as long as the school district offers "comparable courses, services, and facilities" to students of the excluded sex and applies the same admissions policies and criteria. The guidelines permit single-sex classes and programs where they are "necessary to remedy discrimination found by a court or OCR" or where they respond to "conditions that have limited participation by sex" (U.S. Department of Education, 2000). Admittedly, this restatement provides no further interpretation. Nevertheless, it responds to the most extreme oppositionist argument that single-sex programs are impermissible under any conditions. The guidelines also state that the Department was reviewing the Title IX regulations on single-sex programs and schools.

OCR's foot-dragging on the single-sex question did not sit well with some members of Congress, where proposals to make an end run around the Title IX quagmire continued to surface. Over the past several years, Senator Kay Bailey Hutchison of Texas has repeatedly sponsored legislation that would allow school districts to use federal education reform funds for programs that provide "same gender schools and classrooms, if comparable educational opportunities are offered for students of both sexes." The proposal as initially worded met opposition particularly from attorneys at the National Women's Law Center who saw the comparability standard as a marked retreat from *VMI*'s "substantial equality." They feared that it could "open the door to sex-segregated programming based on harmful stereotypes" (National Women's Law Center, 1998). The final and ultimately successful version, proposed as part of the reauthorization of the Elementary and Secondary Education Act, dropped the *comparability* language and explicitly permitted programs that provide "same gender schools and classrooms, *consistent with applicable law.*"

The shift in language proved politically significant in garnering bipartisan congressional support. Senator Edward Kennedy expressly endorsed the proposal. This was a sharp retreat from his firm opposition to legislation proposed by Senator John Danforth back in 1994. The Danforth Amendment would have authorized the Department of Education to waive Title IX enforcement and permit school districts to establish single-sex programs on an experimental basis (*Educational Opportunity Demonstration Program*, 1994). The revised language in the Hutchison proposal removed any potential threat to existing civil rights laws. It also brought in Senator Hillary Clinton, herself a graduate of an all-women's college. Signing on as a cosponsor, she noted how "single-sex schools and classes can help young people, boys and girls, improve their education." Her sweeping endorsement was about as strong as it could get, stating unequivocally that "there should not be any obstacle to providing single-sex choice within the public school system" (*Better Education for Students and Teachers Act*, 2001). Signed into law in January 2002 as a provision within the *No Child Left Behind Act*, the amendment required the Department of Education, within 120 days of the bill's enactment, to issue guidelines to school districts on what is permissible. The Department did so the following May, merely restating the existing Title IX regulations as OCRs past interpretation, policy, and practice. On the same date, however, the Department issues a Notice of Intent to propose regulatory amendments that would provide "more flexibility for educators to extablish single-sex classes and school" (U.S. Department of Education, 2002).

Permitting federal funds for single-sex programs is an important step in the right direction. It places the congressional imprimatur on the core approach, leaving the federal courts to determine the outer bounds of permissibility. It also signals to the Office for Civil Rights that it must end its past aggressive enforcement efforts against these programs. Given the Bush Administration's support for school choice, OCR undoubtedly would have done so even without the new legislation. Nevertheless, in crafting the guidelines for the new federal program, OCR is now faced with the task of amending the Title IX regulations to clarify both the provision covering single-sex schools and the aparent prohibition against singles-sex classes. At the same time, the apparent prohibition against single-sex classes should be revised and replaced with safeguards. The inconsistency between the regulations and the language and intent of the Hutchison proposal now working its way through Congress will confound the federal courts unless the mandated guidelines successfully force the hand of the Department of Education to clarify Title IX once and for all.

WHERE DO WE GO FROM HERE?

What perhaps made sense at least to OCR officials in 1975 when the regulations were adopted, now smack of regulatory "misjudgment," "obsolescence," and even "overkill." At that time, OCR was responding to blatant gender inequities throughout education, widespread gender stereotyping in course offerings, and an all-too-recent memory of prestigious institutions whose doors were closed to women. As a matter of policy, those circumstances seemed to demand a hard line on gender classifications for any purpose. A quarter century down the road, changed realities and understandings now require ongoing reassessment to address more focused inequities and a measure of vigilance to prevent backsliding.

In the meantime, an increasing number of school districts across the country are looking toward single-sex education to address the real and present needs of diverse students. Since the mid-1990s, eleven new public all-girls' schools have opened with several more in the planning stages (National Coalition of Girls' Schools, 2000). Much of the inspiration has come from the Young Women's Leadership School in New York, which successfully graduated its first class in June 2001. The school has shown a stunning record of success, with thirty-one out of thirty-two graduates moving on to college and the remaining one joining the military (*Congressional Record*, 2001). Following New York's lead, in the fall of 2000 a nonprofit group in Chicago, driven by female attorneys and other professionals with the support of the Young Women's Leadership Foundation, opened an all-girls' charter school on the campus of the Illinois Institute of Technology. Drawn on the template of the New York program and with overlapping boards of directors, the Young Women's Leadership Charter School emphasizes math, science, and technology. Beginning with grades six and nine, the school will incrementally expand through the twelfth grade (Cowen, 2000).

Other school districts are exploring alternatives to the New York model. The Jefferson Leadership Academies in Long Beach, California, utilize a dual-academy approach for middle-school girls and boys. The academies are essentially two parallel programs within the same school and utilize the same faculty and curriculum but provide separate classes for academic subjects with extracurricular opportunities for mixed-sex activities. Student test scores have improved and the program has gained enthusiastic support from parents (*LRP Publications*, 1999). Nonetheless, first year findings reveal that inadequate program planning and staff development, along with a failure to consciously address gender issues and gender differences throughout the curriculum, have also led to "missed opportunities" in promoting gender equity (Herr and Arms, 2001). A nonprofit group in Albany is now planning to merge the dual-academy approach with the charter school concept at the elementary school level. The scheduled opening date is fall 2002. And Baltimore and Philadelphia continue to operate historically all-girls' high schools, dating from the 1840s, that are now *de jure* open to boys but remain *de facto* single-sex.

At the same time, more and more coeducational schools are defying past OCR warnings and openly experimenting with single-sex classes, particularly in math, science, and technology, that are primarily geared toward closing the gender gap in these subjects. As the 1998 AAUW report notes, although there is no evidence that these classes improve achievement, participating students tend to have more positive attitudes in these subjects, report that they are less conscious about asking questions and participating in collaborative activities, and tend to enroll in advanced level courses in greater numbers (Hancock and Kalb, 1996; Hudson and Stiles, 1998; Wood and Brown, 1997).

However, regardless of how the Department of Education and specifically the Office for Civil Rights addresses the Title IX regulations, the *VMI* decision still sets the outer bounds for publicly supported single-sex education. The decision's "exceedingly persuasive justification" places school districts under careful scrutiny by the courts and the Department of Justice to assure that single-sex programs meet equal protection standards and avoid the "slippery slope" so feared by gender equity advocates. That slope becomes more real when we consider the unequal resources allotted to all-girls schools in the not-so-distant past. The almost scandalous inequities between Philadelphia's Central High School (for boys) and Girls' High School struck down by a state court less than two decades ago are a vivid reminder of how separation can lend itself to inequalities absent careful monitoring (*Newberg v. Board of Education*, 1983).

Findings from the dual academies established by the State of California in the late 1990s likewise demonstrate how, in a worst-case scenario, single-sex programs can undermine rather than promote gender equity. There researchers found that poor planning, inadequate funding for staff development and monitoring, and a failure to clearly articulate a gender-equity purpose from the state on down to the classroom created an environment where gender stereotypes were actually reinforced in some cases (Datnow et al., 2001). The dual academy approach, in fact, may present unique challenges as first-year findings from the Long Beach program seem to confirm. There, in a drive to maintain compliance with Title IX, teachers have struggled mightily to provide exactly the same curricula, materials, teachers, and resources to both girls and boys. In doing so, they have failed to accommodate the different developmental pace and attitudes of each group, or the larger number of boys identified with special needs. The apparent lesson learned is that the push toward gender equality inherent in this model in fact runs the danger of undermining gender equity (Herr and Arms, 2001).

A recent study from New York City reveals that school systems also must remain vigilant that the vestiges of gender segregated vocational programs no longer remain in schools that are now coeducational under mandate from Title IX. In that case, the National Women's Law Center found that vocational schools were still identifiably and predominantly boys' or girls' schools and clearly reinforced sex-role stereotypes in their course offerings: cosmetology, medical assistance, and fashion for girls, and computer repair, mechanical engineering, and computer electronics for boys. It also found gross disparities between the two types of schools in the number of Advanced Placement classes offered and the range of career opportunities, including the availability of courses in the higher paying fields of technology and engineering. Along with course offerings, recruiting methods and school names sent strong messages to students that certain programs were more appropriate for girls or boys (National Women's Law Center, 2001).

VMI's "exceedingly persuasive" standard begs for compelling research evidence. Yet current research findings on the relative merits of single-sex and coeducation have been inconsistent and the conclusions conflicting. This is not surprising given the diverse objectives, pedagogical approaches, organizational structures, and cultural and political settings of these programs, the various ways in which the studies have measured success, and the inherent limitations of the research enterprise itself. There are significant variables that affect outcomes, not the least of which are socioeconomic background, student motivation and preprogram performance, teaching styles and abilities, class size, school resources, and curriculum materials. Particularly with regard to student selection, legal, ethical, and pedagogical concerns constrain schools from randomly assigning students to single-sex or coeducational treatment groups. With participation essentially voluntary, the problems that arise from self-selection inevitably skew the data and conclusions. However, "inconclusivity" is not "negativity." There is no indication that single-sex programs harm students academically; the assumed long-term social drawbacks are purely speculation.

That being said, the findings of one researcher hold particular relevance for educating disadvantaged students. Based on a study conducted in the 1980s using data from Catholic coed and single-sex schools, sociologist Cornelius Riordan has concluded that the academic effects of single-sex education fall within a hierarchy of low-status characteristics (female, racial minority, low socioeconomic status). The greatest effects, he maintains, are found among poor African-American and Hispanic-American females (race/gender/poverty), slightly diminished effects among poor African-American and Hispanic-American males (race/poverty), smaller effects from white middle-class females (gender), and virtually no differences among affluent students regardless of race or gender (Riordan, 1990, 1994, 1998). These findings support recent efforts by urban school districts to meet the educational needs of poor and minority students through single-sex programs. As these programs slowly increase and expand under various models and at different grade levels, their short-term and long-term results merit close attention.

CONCLUSION

Publicly supported single-sex education is inching its way toward legal certainty and political legitimacy. The Supreme Court's decision in *VMI* leaves much room in the joints for well-designed programs with clearly stated non-biased objectives. Now that the concept has gained bipartisan congressional support, an inevitable executive nod has set the stage for the OCR to resolve the lingering confusion over Title IX. This will permit greater flexibility at the local level and encourage school officials to explore diverse models for appropriately educating a diverse population of students. At the same time, the OCR should continue to play an oversight role to weed out clear cases of gender stereotyping.

I admit that, as a matter of policy, separating students by gender may not be the ideal. Schools must prepare girls and boys for adulthood and the personal and public lives in which they will need to interact in mutual understanding and respect. Then again, this is not an ideal world. For some students and for various social and developmental reasons, perhaps the most effective means to achieve an equitable end is to provide an education separate from the opposite sex, at least for some portion of their school years. Research findings and anecdotal reports suggest that this might prove especially effective for disadvantaged students. Given the fact that more than three decades of federal remediation and court ordered integration have failed to stem the downward spiral of young people growing up in impoverished communities, single-sex programs are an alternative worth consideration. Beyond the critical concerns surrounding the education of the disadvantaged, separate schools or classes may prove beneficial to other students at different periods in their educational experience. More broadly speaking, they also respond to current school reform efforts, including the push for greater local flexibility and educational options and the increasing attention to providing appropriate and not just compensatory education to meet the needs of different student populations.

Perhaps what distinguishes single-sex programs from other pedagogical proposals is not that the research findings are inconclusive, but that we have difficulty uncoupling gender segregation from its tainted history of male privilege and women's subordination and, more importantly, from the shameful legacy of racial segregation. Nevertheless, to argue as many opponents do, that single-sex programs are impermissible because they lack adequate supportive data, which in turn cannot be gathered unless such programs are permitted to exist for a sustained period, obviously represents the most irrational and disingenuous form of circular reasoning. More fundamentally, the argument implies that single-sex programs are inherently harmful, a mere conjecture without grounding in research evidence.

Without the empirical and anecdotal data that such programs can generate over time, the debate over single-sex education will remain mired in political ideology. In the meantime, another generation of poor kids are denied a promising educational option that only the more economically privileged now have the freedom to choose for their children.

ACKNOWLEDGMENTS

The research for this chapter was supported by a fellowship from the Open Society Institute. However, the opinions expressed are solely those of the author and do not represent the policies or positions of the OSI. An earlier version of this chapter appeared in the *Akron Law Review* 34 (1), 200–229 (2000).

REFERENCES

American Association of University Women Educational Foundation. (1991). *Shortchanging Girls, Shortchanging America*. Washington, D.C.

———. (1992). *How Schools Shortchange Girls*. Washington, D.C.

———. (1993). *Hostile Hallways: The AAUW Survey on Sexual Harassment in America's Schools*. Washington, D.C.

———. (1996). *Girls in the Middle: Working to Succeed in School*. Washington, D.C.

———. 1998). *Separated by Sex: A Critical Look at Single-Sex Education for Girls*. Washington, D.C.

Belenky, M. F., Clinchy, B. M., Goldberger, N.R., and Tarule, J. M. (1986). *Women's Ways of Knowing: The Development of Self, Voice, and Mind*. New York: Basic Books.

Better Education for Students and Teachers Act, Chapter 3, Innovative Education Programs, Amendment No. 540 to S. 1, 107th Cong., 1st Sess., 147 *Cong. Rec.* S5943 (June 7, 2000) (statement of Sen. Hutchison).

Better Education for Students and Teachers Act, Chapter 3, Innovative Education Programs, Amendment No. 540 to S. 1, 107th Cong., 1st Sess., 147 *Cong. Rec.* S5943–44 (June 7, 2001) (statement of Sen. Clinton).

Brief Amici Curiae of Professor Carol Gilligan and the Program on Gender, Science and Law, United States v. Virginia, 51 F. 3d 440 (4th Cir. 1995), reprinted in *Women's Law Reporter* (fall 1994), 1–16

Brown v. Board of Education, 347 U.S. 484 (1954).

Chevron U.S.A. Inc. v. Natural Resources Defense Council, Inc., 467 U.S. 837 (1984).

City of Richmond v. J. A. Croson Co., 488 U.S. 469 (1989).

Chodorow, N. J. (1978). *The Reproduction of Mothering.* Berkeley, CA: University of California Press.

Coleman, J. S. (1961). *The Adolescent Society: The Social Life of the Teenager.* New York: Free Press of Glencoe.

Cowen, L. (2000, October 1). "A Class of Their Own: A Girls Charter School Leaves Boys Out of the Equation." *Chicago Tribune Magazine,* 1–17.

Cuban, L. (1991, November 20). "All-Male African-American Public Schools: Desperate Remedies for Desperate Times." *Education Week* 36–37.

Datnow, A., Hubbard, L., and Woody, E. (May 2001). *Is Single-Gender Schooling Viable in the Public Sector? Lessons from California's Pilot Program.* Final Report.

Educational Opportunity Demonstration Program, 103d Cong., 2d Sess., 140 *Cong. Rec.*10163–10172 (August 1, 1994) (statement of Sen. Danforth).

Education Opportunity Demonstration Program, 103d Cong., 2d Sess., 140 *Cong. Rec.* S10169–10172 (August 1, 1994) (statement of Sen. Kennedy).

Faulkner v. Jones, 858 F. Supp. 552 (D. So. Car., 1994), *aff'd,* 51 F. 3d 440 (4th Cir. 1995).

Garrett v. Board of Education, 775 F. Supp. 1004 (E.D. Mich. 1991).

Gilligan, C. (1982). *In a Different Voice: Psychological Theory and Women's Development,* Cambridge, MA: Harvard University Press.

———. (1990). "Preface, Teaching Shakespeare's Sister: Notes from the Underground of Female Adolescence." In Gilligan, C., Lyons, N. P., and Hammer, T. (Eds.), *Making Connections.* Cambridge, MA: Harvard University Press.

Gurian, M. (1997). *The Wonder of Boys.* New York: Tarcher/Putnam.

———. (1999). *A Fine Young Man.* New York: Tarcher/Putnam.

Hancock, L., and Kalb, C. (1996, June 24). "A Room of Their Own." *Newsweek* 76.

Herr, K., and Arms, E. (2001). "The Intersection of Educational Reforms: Single Gender Academies in a Public Middle School."

Holland, S. H. (1987, March 22). "Commentary, A Radical Approach to Educating Young Black Males." *Education Week* 24.

Hudson, K., and Stiles, J. (1998, November). "Single-Sex Classes: A Plus for Preadolescent Girls." *Principal* 78 (2): 57–58.

Kindlon, D., and Thompson, M. (1999). *Raising Cain: Protecting the Emotional Life of Boys.* New York: Ballantine Books.

Kleinfeld, J. (1999, Winter). "Student Performance: Males versus Females." *Public Interest* 134: 3–20.

———. (1998). *The Myth That Schools Shortchange Girls: Social Science in the Service of Deception.* Washington, D.C.: The Women's Freedom Network.

LRP Publications. (1999, October 12). *Your School and the Law* 29: 19.

Manegold, C. S. (2000). *In Glory's Shadow: Shannon Faulkner, The Citadel and a Changing America.* New York: Alfred A. Knopf.

Mississippi University for Women v. Hogan, 458 U.S. 718 (1982).

NAACP Legal Defense and Education Fund. (1990). *Reflections on Proposals for Separate Schools for African-American Male Pupils.* New York.

National Association of Independent Schools. (1999). *Backgrounder.* Washington, D.C.

National Coalition of Girls' Schools. (2000). *Girls' Education in the 90's: All-Girl Schools Founded Since 1995.* Concord, MA.

———. (2001, September). *Bells Ringing, Not Tolling, for Girls' Schools.* Press Release. Concord, MA.

National Women's Law Center. (1998, September 2). Letter from M. Greenberger, copresident and L. Annexstein, senior counsel to Members of the U.S. Senate.

National Women's Law Center. (2001, August 16). Letter from M. Greenberger, copresident, L. Annexstein, senior counsel and K. Keller, counsel to Harold O. Levy, chancellor, New York City Board of Education. Available: *www.nwlc.org*

Newberg v. Board of Education, 26 Pa. D. and C. 3d 682 (1983).

Noddings, N. (1984). *Caring: A Feminine Approach to Ethics and Moral Education*. Berkeley, CA: University of California Press.

Pollack, W. (1998). *Real Boys: Rescuing Our Sons from the Myths of Boyhood*. New York: Random House.

Riordan, C. (1990). *Boys and Girls in School: Together or Separate?* New York: Teachers College Press.

——. (1994). "Single-Gender Schools: Outcomes for African and Hispanic Americans." *Research in Sociology of Education and Socialization 10*: 177–205.

——. (1998). "The Future of Single-Sex Schools." In American Association of University Women. *Separated by Sex: A Critical Look at Single-Sex Education for Girls*. Washington, D.C.

Sadker, M., and Sadker, D. (1994). *Failing at Fairness: How Our Schools Cheat Girls*. New York: Touchstone.

Salomone, R. (1999). "Single-Sex Schooling: Law, Policy, and Research." In D. Ravitch (Ed.), *Brookings Papers on Education Policy*. Washington, D.C.: Brookings Institution Press.

Sommers, C. H. (2000). *The War Against Boys: How Misguided Feminism Is Harming Our Young Men*. New York: Simon and Schuster.

——. (1994). *Who Stole Feminism? How Women Have Betrayed Women*. New York: Touchstone.

Title IX of the Education Amendments of 1972, Discrimination Based on Sex, 20 U.S.C. §1681 et seq. (Supp. 2000).

Title IX of the Education Amendments of 1972, Non Discrimination on the Basis of Sex in Education Programs and Activities Receiving or Benefiting from Federal Financial Assistance, 34 C.F.R. §106.1 et seq. (Supp. 2000).

Tyack, D., and Hansot, S.L. (1990). *Learning Together: A History of Coeducation in American Schools*. New Haven, CT: Yale University Press.

United States v. Virginia, 766 F.Supp.1407 (W.D. Va. 1991), *vacated and remanded*, 976 F.2d 890 (4th Cir. 1992), 852 F. Supp. 471 (W.D. Va. 1994), *aff'd*, 44 F.3d 1229 (4th Cir. 1995), *rehearing en banc denied*, 52 F. 3d 90 (4th Cir. 1995), *rev'd and remanded*, 518 U.S. 515 (1996).

U.S. Department of Education. (1999). *Report to the Senate Appropriations Committee on Review of Title IX Regulations and Policies Regarding single-sex Programs*. Washington, D.C.

U.S. Department of Education, Office for Civil Rights. (2000). *Applying Federal Civil Rights Laws to Public Charter Schools*. Washington, D.C.

U.S. Department of Education, Office for Civil Rights (2002). *Single Sex Classes and Schools: Guidelines on Title IX Requirements: Notice*. Washington D.C.

U.S. Department of Education, Office for Civil Rights (2002). *Nondiscrimination on the Basis of Sex in Education Programs or Activities Receiving Federal Financial Assistance; Proposed Rule*. Washington D.C.

Wilson, J. (1992, February 24). "Expert Dislikes All-Male Schools, Consultant Says They Harm Black Students." *Detroit Free Press*, B1.

Wood, B., and Brown, L. A. (1997). "Participation in an All-Female Algebra I Class: Effects on High School Math and Science Course Selection." *Journal of Women and Minorities in Science and Engineering 3*: 256–277.

Section Two

PUBLIC SINGLE-SEX SCHOOLING IN CHANGING POLICY CONTEXTS

CHAPTER 5

The Intersection of Educational Reforms: Single-Gender Academies in a Public Middle School

Kathryn Herr and Emily Arms

This chapter chronicles how very real pressures and multiple innovations impacted and skewed the implementation of what was touted as primarily a gender reform at one California public middle school. A reconstituted school, boys and girls were divided into separate classes; full inclusion of special education students and blocking of core academic classes were implemented at the same time. These simultaneous innovations, along with the current realities of public schooling—a teaching staff overwhelmingly made up of new teachers, some certified, many on emergency waivers; a student population highly at risk in terms of socioeconomic indicators and past school performance, and a school under great pressure to raise its standardized test scores—diverted time and attention away from the exploration and implementation of gender reform although it had been announced as the school's primary reform effort.

As Tyack and Cuban observe, it is the rare reform that unfolds precisely as planned; some innovations "die on contact with the institutional reality of the school," whereas many "evolve in ways often not foreseen by their proponents" (1995, p. 60). Schools do not get to attempt reforms in a laboratory setting, carefully controlling variables that might impact new practices; instead innovations are implemented within the messy realities of public school life. This chapter explores the messy realities of trying to implement gender reform as one of a number of major reforms in an urban middle school; it documents how the possibilities of the gender reform were virtually engulfed by the demanding realities of multiple innovations. Issues such as accommodating special education students who were previously in contained classrooms and teaching assignments that spanned two or more subject areas competed with, and as some indicated, compounded the difficulty of focusing on gender reforms.

CONSIDERING SINGLE-SEX SCHOOLING

As Mael (1998) points out, Title IX, although perhaps not intending to, has made public single-sex schooling virtually extinct; designed as a corrective to the sex discrimination and inequitable resource allocations found in coeducational institutions, it has also, ironically, curtailed some experiments with gender equity and reform such as public single-sex schooling. Even when some public single-sex sites have been able to demonstrate positive results, the U.S. Department of Education's Office of Civil Rights and the courts have discontinued successful programs on the grounds of sex discrimination (Mael, 1998). By necessity then, given the virtual nonexistence of public single-sex schools in the United States, researchers in this country have predominately studied private, often parochial, schools (chapter 2 of this volume). In addition, much of the research on this topic comes from abroad where single-sex school settings are much more common (Streittmatter, 1999).

Although the single-sex versus coeducational schools debate is beyond the scope of this chapter, it is important to note that research comparing the two has been inconsistent. Singh, Vaught, and Mitchell (1998) observe that although research in this country is limited, it seems to suggest that the effect of an all-female education is positive, whereas the advantage for boys in all-male classes is far less conclusive. Because most of the research in the United States has been in private and parochial schools rather than the public sector, selection bias confounds how the research results can be viewed (Mael, 1998).

Part of the rationale in the United States for single-gender schooling comes from the thinking that adolescents create a culture in school that is at odds with academic performance and achievement; preoccupied with what Mael (1998) refers to as the "rating and dating" culture, students in the coeducational environment are thought to be unnecessarily distracted, concentrating on how they look rather than focusing on academics. Streitmatter, citing Coleman (1961) comments, "Boys and girls together distract each other. Whether this distraction takes the form of dressing to impress the other gender, competition for teacher time and attention, or sexual harassment, there is no question that distractions exist" (1999, p. 36).

Support for single-sex schooling also comes from a general agreement that patterns of unequal support and attention are common in U.S. coeducational classrooms, from the preschool to college levels (Mael, 1998; Sadker and Sadker, 1994) with females being "shortchanged" (AAUW, 1992). Parallels have been drawn between the experience of female students in a coeducational classroom and that of other racial/ethnic minority students; "just as coeducational classrooms have been shown to be hostile in many ways to female students, it has been argued that the coed environment is not optimal for African-American males" (Singh, Vaught, and Mitchell, 1998). Advocates of single-sex education argue that this organizational structure provides a better learning environment not only for girls but also for at-risk urban minority students (Riordan, 1990).

THE CONTEXT FOR GENDER REFORM IN CALIFORNIA

With national and state agendas using the rhetoric of accountability and high-stakes testing, schools increasingly face demands to demonstrate that their students are succeeding. In the quest for quality education, school choice has become a key issue in the educational debate. As a result, magnet schools, charter schools, and voucher programs have been initiated across the country. Although statewide school voucher legislation has been defeated twice in California in the last eight years, once in 1993 and again in 2000, school choice has remained at the forefront of the state's initiatives. It was amid this climate of school choice that former Governor Pete Wilson helped to pass state legislation and funding for the establishment of ten public, single-gender secondary schools in 1997. The goal of the Single-Gender Academies Pilot Program, according to Wilson, was to provide more choice and more options for public school children (Datnow, Hubbard, and Conchas, 2001).

Two years later, a California school district announced that it too would be implementing a single-gender middle school academy in the fall of 1999. The school was not a recipient of state money under the pilot program; instead, it would operate as a magnet school under the auspices of the school district. The district is commonly known as one that is open to and promoting of school reforms. For example, it was one of the first districts to institute mandatory school uniforms in grades K–8; it has also put an end to social promotions. In the district's current school choice program, parents and students may choose to apply to any school within the district. The district offers a variety of magnet schools; the newest ones are the Single-Gender Academy and an Edison elementary school.

According to district officials, the initial conception of the single-gender middle school was different than its final realization. Originally it was conceived of as an all-girls academy in response to the literature of the early 1990s, which reported that girls perform better academically in same-sex settings. When it became clear that this idea might be in violation of Title IX, the idea changed to two single-gender middle schools, one for boys and one for girls. However, lack of physical space for the two academies led to the creation of one coed middle school with all single-gender classes.

The Single-Gender Academy[1] (SGA) would serve both boys and girls, but all classroom instruction would be single gender. District officials explained the purpose of the single-gender magnet as one that would offer their students another school choice as well as one that would "reduce distractions" in the classroom. Designed as a "leadership academy," the school would implement a number of other reforms in addition to single-gender classrooms.

Rather than build a new facility, the district "reconstituted" an existing middle school. Citing poor performance on standardized tests, the district decided to take radical action to improve students' academic performance; in fact, the school was one of the two lowest scoring middle schools in the district. In the reconstitution, the school's administration was replaced with a new team of administrators and teachers were told they would need to reapply to the new Single-Gender academy.

DOCUMENTING THE FIRST YEAR IN A GENDER EXPERIMENT

News that a large, public middle school was going to experiment with single-gender classes began to appear in Los Angeles newspapers in spring 1999. With over a thousand students based on its campus, the very proportions of the experiment made it newsworthy. The fact that the population of the school was particularly diverse—predominantly African-American, Hispanic-American, and Cambodian, as well as economically vulnerable, made the potential results of the innovative experiment even more intriguing. As Singh, Vaught, and Mitchell point out, "creating conditions that improve students' motivation to learn remains a top priority in many urban 'majority-minority' school districts" (1998, p. 157). On the opening day of school, television crews from around the country were on hand to record the beginning of what was seen as an important gender experiment.

As researchers, we too were attracted to witnessing and documenting the single-sex experiment. Arriving separately and from different parts of the country, we did not come into the school as a research team. Maintaining separate research agendas, we quickly discovered that sharing insights derived from our data gathering and analyses cross-fertilized each of our individual research efforts. As outsiders we were both "strangers" to the research site; we found that with our varying research schedules and emphases, we were able to document more of the culture of the school than either of us could have done alone. In addition, just as the teachers were struggling to implement multiple reforms, we were struggling to document and make meaning out of the complexity of the setting; meeting regularly to debrief and analyze what we were seeing allowed us to collaborate across our separate research efforts.

Allowed access to document the experiment, we spent several days each week in the school throughout its first year.[2] This account is based on observations of core classes throughout the school year, interviews with faculty and students as well as student surveys. Field notes were recorded of more informal times in the school—hallway conversations and playground talk with students and faculty. In addition, we sampled other school events— faculty meetings, concerts, assemblies, and sports events and these too were recorded via field notes. Drawing on transcriptions of interviews and field notes as well as the written student surveys, data were coded to identify emergent themes. We were able to meet on an ongoing basis to discuss and compare our separate analyses.

Although the district indicated that a rise in standardized test scores would be proof that the single-gender classes were "working," we were interested in knowing how the reform played out in terms of creating a more gender equitable learning environment for students as well as an improved environment for learning. Sitting in all-girl or all-boy classes day after day, we were able to move a gender lens to the forefront, observing what learning environments were created within all-male and all-female groupings. As others have noted, there are no guarantees that simply separating the sexes creates an equitable learning environment or even one that would be considered "better" in terms of interrupting stereotypical gender relations (Datnow, Hubbard, and Conchas, 2001). What quickly became apparent in the early days of our research was that although gender reform was the prominent and publicized part of the experiment, the many other component parts of the school's reform overshadowed the gender emphasis. For example, a lot of teacher time went to the preparation of the interdisciplinary block classes that was further complicated by teachers commonly having expertise in only one of the two teaching areas. Even experienced teachers with lesson plans that had formerly served them well found that they needed to revamp their classes in line with the new format. There was an air of simply trying to stay afloat, leaving little time to weave in a thoughtful implementation of gender reform.

MAKING WAY FOR GENDER REFORM: RECONSTITUTION

Much as a construction site is leveled to make way for a new building, a school that is reconstituted is dismantled to make way for a new effort. School reforms are often gradual and incremental (Tyack and Cuban, 1995); the reconstitution of a school, however, is at the other end of a continuum of reform, representing one of the more dramatic measures imposed on a setting. Most recently, states have threatened receivership of poorly performing schools and districts have mandated reconstitution for schools singled out as not producing a level of successful performance with their students, most often measured through standardized testing. Although a hierarchical approach to school reform adoption processes is not unusual (Datnow, 2000), the reconstitution of a school leaves a lot of rubble in its wake to be cleared before a new structure can be constructed.

For teachers rooted in this school and this community, the reconstitution "process" hit hard:

> The district came in and announced "this is no longer a school; it's going to be reconstituted and you all have jobs somewhere in the district. Have a nice day." I'm a pretty passive, calm person and even I felt like going over the table, you know, because I put

eight years of my life into this school and wrote grants for it and I have all these relationships with my children, who I love. And it was like "Excuse me?"

By its very definition, a reconstitution of a school is an externally developed reform. In terms of faculty, this both alienates "old" faculty who have been part of an apparently failed effort as well as short circuits input by new faculty who join a reform already fairly conceptualized rather than cocreated with them. Tyack and Cuban make the case that although teachers do not have a monopoly on educational wisdom, "their first-hand perspectives on schools and their responsibility for carrying out official policies argues for their centrality in school reform efforts" (1995, p. 135). We would argue that a reform conceived of without the faculty involved inevitably sets a tone that can haunt a reform effort: It seems to indicate to faculty "your wisdom is not welcome." Without a proactive administrative message assuring teachers otherwise, principals can find themselves in the role of enforcing and developing "their" reform and teachers "are strongly encouraged to go along with the plans" (Datnow, 2000, p. 358).

Of the original teaching staff of the school, two thirds chose to apply to the new academy; the other third asked to be transferred to other schools in the district. Of those reapplying to remain at the school, the commitment seemed to be more to the neighborhood and its constituency of students and parents than necessarily to single-gender reform. Ultimately, of the forty-seven faculty on SGA's staff, only seven were returning faculty from the era prior to the reconstitution. Faculty speculated on why so few original teachers were rehired:

> I don't know the reason why; I'm not sure if they thought tenured teachers would not be easy to change . . . I'm not sure what it was but it started on a negative, unfortunately. So you had people forced out of positions, people who had been here for many years and some really strong teachers in the district.

Those who were chosen to remain felt they were seen as a bit suspect, holdovers from an older era and perhaps impediments to the new vision; at the end of the first year of the Single-Gender Academy, most of them transferred to other schools in the district. This in essence removed the institutional memory from the site of the days prior to establishing the Single-Gender Academy as well as interrupted established neighborhood relationships.

> We have some serious problems in our neighborhoods around here; these kids look at this school as their support system. And they come here and know, knew, that there were many people here where they had a safe place and they cared and they were and *had been here*—whether they were in sixth grade or came back in eleventh grade, they were here. And they knew they could come speak to them or they could walk over from the high school and get help. . . . To pull that whole group from the kids I think is just a travesty.

We have spent time outlining the context that led up to the single-gender experiment because we believe it made the reform effort much more difficult to implement. The reconstitution of a school fairly demolishes any culture of the school, in theory, to allow for more effective student learning. Yet, reconstitution also brings baggage with it that can obstruct the reform process. For example, at SGA, many teachers were wary, having just observed tenured teachers involuntarily displaced from their teaching jobs; in addition, those most responsible for implementing the reform, the teachers (Datnow, 2000), were not part of the planning process to bring gender reform into being. As with many school reform efforts, there was very little time to even thoroughly acquaint let alone prepare teachers for the task of single-gender classes. The removal of the institutional memory also dislodged much of the nitty gritty functioning of the school, things like where to find paper or how to set up field trips. In essence, the task of starting from scratch with little lead time made for a particularly complex undertaking where little within the culture of the school was retained and much had to be created, including a new culture that supported single-gender schooling.

THE SINGLE-GENDER ACADEMY

A new principal for the school was in place by March of the school year prior to the opening of the academy. Her tasks were both conceptual and concrete; she was asked to continue to design the innovative academy and then bring in the staff to implement the vision. The vision for the academy grew beyond single-gender classes to include full inclusion of special education students and blocking of core academic classes (a Humanities Core of Language Arts and Social Studies and a Tech Core of Math, Science, and Technology). A Humanities teacher and a Tech teacher would be paired; efforts were made to have male/female teaching pairs. Although not team teaching, between them the pair was responsible for a class of thirty-five boys and a class of thirty-five girls in the core areas. In addition, an extended homeroom time (twenty-five minutes) with the same students would allow for implementing character and leadership curriculum as well as practice for standardized tests; as much as possible homeroom teachers were matched with students of their same sex, with the idea that this kind of same-sex matching would help foster solid, supportive relationships between the students and their homeroom teacher. Teachers would teach both boys and girls, albeit in separate classes; in addition, they would each offer an elective class as well as an after school club.

It is important to note that much of the preceding description of the plan matches current thinking on "ideal" middle school reforms and recommendations (Beane, 1993; George et al., 1992; Jackson and Davis, 2000). The opportunity for students to change classes and classmates less often, to see the integration of subject areas previously held separate, to have a few key teachers with whom they can hopefully form good relationships, and to learn with special education students previously excluded from their classrooms are all hallmarks of what the literature suggests will make a rich environment for learning in middle school.

At odds with these ideals is the reality that teachers are often trained and certified to teach one subject area and that general and special education are often still separate areas of study in many teacher preparation programs; "out of field" teaching, that is, teachers teaching in areas in which they are not trained nor certified, is of increasing concern in the United States (Ingersoll, 1999). In addition, a national teacher shortage makes it difficult to find certified teachers at all (Weiner, 2000) and schools and classrooms serving the most educationally vulnerable children are more likely to have in their hire teachers who are not yet fully prepared and licensed for their job (National Commission on Teaching and America's Future, 1996, cited in Darling-Hammond, 1997).

In fact, hiring of teachers to replace those who left when the school was reconstituted proved to be a difficult undertaking. Needing to build a faculty virtually from scratch, it was a struggle to find teachers both interested and excited to join the single-gender experiment as well as qualified to teach in the needed combined subject areas. SGA began the school year with an extremely large number of teachers new to the profession, a substantial number of whom were uncertified and teaching on emergency waivers. In addition, because teachers were required to teach more than one subject area in the core blocks, all teachers spent part of the day teaching in an area for which they had not been trained or certified; some reported they were unaware that they would be teaching a core block when they hired on. In addition, virtually none of the teachers, new or experienced, nor the department heads, were trained to teach in a single-sex setting. One department head described the situation as "if not hopeless, disheartening":

> In my department there are fifteen people, ten of which don't have credentials, ten of which are first or less than first year people. Ten of them don't know what they're doing. Ten of them don't know the subject matter. Because it's hard, first of all, to find anybody who knows either subject and when you put both subjects as a requirement [for hiring faculty] you pretty well just cast yourself adrift.

Partly in response to the large number of new teachers, the district allocated four curricular "coaches" to the school site; these are veteran teachers who are "subject matter experts" and serve as department resources in terms of curriculum development. In the case of the SGA, the district located four such coaches on site, a situation the coaches describe as "fairly remarkable" in terms of district allocation of resources. At the SGA, the coaches also served as department heads. Expecting to come in and work on issues of curriculum development and support for teachers, the coaches instead found themselves serving primarily as "the surrogate teacher of teachers, which frankly we're not trained for."

> Not only was I having to do content stuff, which was what I expected, that was what I truly thought I was hiring in for, now I'm working on classroom management; I'm doing discipline. I'm talking about something as elementary as classroom arrangement, where to put the seats, how to keep a roll book, how to make a test—just everything.

They served as substitute teachers, department heads, and quasi-administrators who both helped to support new teachers as well as evaluate them. But the coaches "neither fish nor foul" positions made them suspect in the eyes of faculty; seen as closely aligned to the administration with an evaluative component, it was difficult for them to offer their expertise to faculty who eyed them with suspicion.

> The teachers don't trust us because for us to come in it's kind of like shaking hands with Typhoid Mary; "My god, why are they here? What have I done wrong" On the other hand we're not administrators either, so we just kind of sit over there and talk to ourselves.

As the school year progressed, the coaches were asked to concentrate on four teachers in each of their departments who were struggling and needed extra support. Inevitably this meant that they spent their days with teachers who were struggling to stay afloat; coaches felt both far away from the original job they were hired to do with their expertise in curriculum development and discouraged with the task at hand.

> I often have this sensation—it's like watching a series of automobile accidents. As a matter of fact I had a very vivid dream right before Christmas where all the coaches, all of us were in a car going somewhere, and this huge automobile accident happened in front of us. And we pulled the car over and jumped out and ran over to the first car and the guy was like "Help me! Help me!" But the other coach said, "He's a goner. Let's go on." So it was a really visceral dream; I woke up feeling very physically shaken. That's sort of—obviously the symbolism is very strong, but you know there are days I just feel, whew—it is a little overwhelming.

A number of the coaches did not have middle-school teaching experience and this impacted their credibility in many faculty members' eyes. In addition, they had no specific training or expertise in single-sex education; faculty expressed the sentiment that the single-gender arrangement was so unique that what they yearned for most was a conversation with someone "who has been there." Prior to the start of the school year staff viewed an hour-long video on current research regarding boys and listened to a short talk by the principal of one of the single-gender pilot programs in the state; other than this, there was no opportunity for sustained conversation regarding what the gender reform meant for teachers in the classroom. The yearning expressed by teachers for ongoing discussion and resources highlights the importance of providing staff development and appropriate supports when asking teachers to work on the cutting edge.

BRINGING GENDER REFORM INTO THE CLASSROOM

Despite all the issues described in the preceding section—the effects of reconstituting, difficulty in hiring faculty, and complex arrangement of the school day—the reform effort was first and foremost *named* as a gender reform. We now turn a lens to this issue, trying to bring into focus the gender part of the reform effort.

When creating the Single-Gender Academy, the rationale was very much along the lines of "minimizing distractions"; this became a mantra of sorts, repeated often by faculty and students, easily the most commonly offered explanation for the new configuration of the school.

> When the media came it was almost like we were told the party line. The party line is, no one said it that directly but, it's "we're taking the distractions out of the classroom." I'm the type of person who always looks beyond the surface and I probe within my own mind: "what can that mean?" Can that mean someone would be against us if we were trying to bring up the issue of gender equality? I doubt it but you never know. Would that be frowned upon? Looked down upon by the school district? I don't know but I do know the bottom line, the reason, was the distraction thing.

In scratching beneath the surface, the distraction explanation revealed little thought or teacher preparation in terms of a broader agenda of school reform that addressed gender bias and equity issues. This is not unlike the situation found in the California schools that responded to the state's call for piloting single-gender programs. In their study of these sites, Datnow, Hubbard, and Conchas (2001) found little evidence of single-gender academies designed to address gender bias but rather, for example, that the money connected to the initiative was seen as a unique opportunity to bring goods and services to schools. SGA did not have the monetary incentive to create a single-gender program, but the district was looking for an opportunity to reconfigure a school it saw as not effectively serving students' needs, as measured through their test scores. Although the district did not receive monetary rewards for their initiative, they did reap an incredible amount of positive national publicity, both in print and on television, regarding the innovation.

In the California sites they studied, Datnow, Hubbard, and Conchas also noted a "lack of deep inquiry about gender equity among educators, and an absence of opportunity for discussion about what it meant to be teaching boys and girls in single-gender classrooms" (p. 23). In these schools, as in SGA, educators were essentially left to do the best they could in terms of responding to the single-gender configuration. However, beyond framing the initial initiative around gender, and organizing students' classes around the single-gender concept, there was no evidence of "deep inquiry about gender equity" at SGA other than as teachers chose to develop this individually.

> There really hasn't been much guidance. Um, straight from the principal's mouth, "We took the distractions out of the classroom and that's the bottom line." That's what it's all about, just separating the boys and girls, so they would not distract each other. Anything that is beyond that is just from my own interest, the things that I have learned in my life. It's just an interest of mine, how boys and girls are raised differently in our society; how our society has different norms and expectations for men and women.

Without staff development and ongoing conversations regarding gender, there was nothing to interrupt teachers' gender assumptions and ideologies, no impetus to help them problematize their own understandings or standpoint, no catalyst to try new pedagogical possibilities that might help foster equity.

It was widely believed among educators in the school that the single-gender experiment "was working for the girls." When we as researchers asked to come into their classes to observe, teachers often enthusiastically invited us to see their girls' classes followed by a comment indicating that their male groups were another story altogether. A number of factors were seen by faculty as contributing to the success of the girls' groups: fewer female special education students; a general perception that the girls performed at a higher level academically, particularly in reading; and that in general they had a better sense of how to play school. They were also seen as knowing how to work cooperatively and develop a sense of comradery among themselves. One teacher, in thinking about her girls' group, reflected that one thing she liked about the girls:

> is that they know how to be students. If they can get channeled into doing things, they know stuff. They can do work . . . if I can get them on task and can get them interested and engaged . . . if I can do that, they're *great!* . . . They understand, they remember stuff they've learned from other years. They put it together. They have opinions. So, I like that about them.

There was also a sense that this reform was generally designed with the girls in mind:

> All of this was intended originally to allow them [the girls] to be free of the male influence. To either not worry about being too smart or not worry about being too dumb on the other hand.

Although many teachers were generally pleased with their girls' classes, two ironies emerged. In observing multiple classes of girls and interviewing the teachers, we were unable to discover much inquiry or curiosity on the part of teachers in terms of what classroom pedagogies might foster gender equity, particularly as it might relate to an all-girls' class. We saw fairly typical classrooms, with girls performing much as we have come to expect them to in school. As we mentioned, it is not automatic that just by creating single-gender classes that stereotypical behaviors are interrupted or interrogated. For example, we consistently saw outspoken girls dominate classroom talk time and garner teacher attention, a dynamic not unlike that described in observations of coed classrooms, where boys overshadow girls (Sadker and Sadker, 1994); the cast of characters had changed but the dynamic was reproduced, albeit with an all-female cast.

To echo Datnow, Hubbard, and Conchas, we saw "evidence of how teachers' ideologies about gender and the interactions between teachers and students in the classroom mediated the implementation of single-gender public schooling" (2001, p. 23). For example, teachers remained convinced that the girls were functioning at a higher academic level than the boys, even in the face of information that might muddy this conclusion; for example, there were more girls than boys in the developmental reading classes, a class designed to bring students up to grade level in their reading skills. One curriculum coach speculated that teachers may not register girls' demonstrated academic needs because the girls "have been well-behaved and appear to be students" and that placement in developmental reading may represent the first intervention that these girls have experienced in the school system. In other cases, because the girls' groups did not exhibit the same kind of challenging discipline issues that many boys' groups did, teachers were able to get more done more quickly, but this too created a dilemma for teachers; in an attempt to keep the classes moving at the same pace, teachers reported that they sometimes did not move ahead as quickly with the girls as they might have had they not been concerned with keeping things "equal." The concern seemed to be in keeping things the same between the boys' and girls' classes, confusing issues of equality with equity. In addition, teachers seemed to offer less to the girls in terms of being proactive or creative with them; teachers explained this in reference to anticipating the energies that the boys' classes would take or in recovering from already having had the boys that day.

The second irony we observed is probably connected to the first. Because the boys were so challenging, and because teachers perceived that, by comparison, things were going smoothly with the girls, the talk among teachers outside of the classroom was overwhelmingly in reference to the question, "What do we do about the boys?" By apparently doing well, girls ceded attention to the boys, much like they do in coeducational classrooms.

It was commonly expressed that in separating the boys from the girls, a "tempering" effect on the boys had been removed, shifting all the pressure to teachers to "control" them. Where at one point teachers might have been able to count on the help of girls via their good behavior in the classroom, now the teachers were on their own, as were the boys.

> The boys are free to be just as good or bad as they want to be . . . but in many cases they are going to wind up being just as bad as they want to be. Because before, let's say that theoretically you have half the class in the disruptive male influence, now you've got the entire class as the disruptive male influence. They bounce off of each other in many cases. So for the teachers they have thirty-five kids potentially cutting up as opposed to fifteen or whatever they had before.

In discussing the struggles they were having with the boys, teachers cited: the larger number of boys in special education who were now included in their classrooms; the range of learning levels in the room; the fact that the boys were less likely to hand in homework and perform the roles of a school boy; and the incredible "energy" they seemed to bring to a classroom. In discussing her boys' class, a teacher reflected:

> I love them dearly. There's so much energy, just this strength in the room—and not that the girls aren't strong but it's a different kind of strength—it's like this radiating energy. You can almost feel the vibes when they're in here and it's so electrical. And there's so much going on—I mean they are just constantly on the move, making things or pencils going or hand movements and it's obvious that they really need like kinesthetic learning.

Even when the boys' classes were going well, with few exceptions it was generally agreed upon that a teacher "can never let up" or they will get "out of control." (See Woody, chapter 16 of this volume, for an analogous discussion of the pervasive "bad" behavior of boys.) Teachers, experienced or not, generally expressed a belief that the boys demanded a lot of attention and were difficult to keep engaged and on task. One curriculum coach, in observing a veteran teacher whose boys' classroom appeared to work like clockwork, commented:

> He has ridden those kids hard from day one. He never lets up. You talk to him and his comment is that he never once relaxes; he is unable to relax. Well then you get some guy off the street, or some sweet little thing off the street, and put them in there because every teacher's got a boys' and a girls' group and they eat them up; they spit them up. It's pretty bad. Pretty bad. And of course the kids aren't smart enough, because they're twelve, thirteen, and fourteen years old, to realize they're killing themselves. That they're the ultimate losers. So that's, that for me is the real tragedy—the kids are losing.

DISCUSSION

As researchers interested in the single-gender reform we were struck by the fact that what was conceived of as a gendered reform was not about gender at all. Issues of creating a single-gender school, gender equity and teacher education on gender issues were left unexamined as the school shifted its focus to one main goal: improving standardized test scores. Meetings, discussions, and prepackaged curricula designed to enhance student performance on test taking all had as their focus the raising of test scores. Single-gender classes were seen merely as a way to organize classrooms, an end rather than a means to further gender reforms. With "distractions minimized," the school essentially went about business as usual, albeit now in a race to raise standardized test scores. Despite the great potential of single-gender classes to be sites where gender equity is interrogated, the school district's and new administration's main goals for SGA were to focus on learning as it relates to raising standardized test scores.

SGA is not unusual in its singular focus on test scores. Changing political tides in many states have pushed schools to show quick and dramatic results on standardized tests (Oakes et al., 2000), and improvement in standardized testing is commonly employed to demonstrate the success of a school's particular reform. Teachers and the administration at SGA were cognizant that the single-gender reform would be viewed as a success if standardized test scores went up at the end of the first year. Staff were aware that the goal for their school year was to raise scores by sixteen points. However, as Tyack and Cuban point out, one of the problems with defining "success" as meeting predetermined goals such as raising standardized test scores, "is that some of the most significant dimensions of actual programs, both positive and negative, may not be captured by the measured outcomes" (1995, p. 62).

We would add that some potentially significant dimensions of programs are not even developed or given much focus in light of the emphasis in raising standardized test scores. In the case of SGA, test scores were higher at the end of their first single-gender year but the larger potential of the single-gender experiment, possible gender equity, remained largely unexplored. We see the rise in test scores as a direct result of devoting so much curricular and teaching time to "teaching to the test." As McNeil (2000) has pointed out, this emphasis on preparation for standardized measures comes at the expense of innovative curriculum and teaching, reducing the quality of educational instruction that might significantly benefit historically disenfranchised students. In the case of SGA, the emphasis on test preparation completely overshadowed any schoolwide discussions or thinking about the potential for single-gender schooling. We were struck that throughout the year, issues or possibilities created by the single-gender arrangement were virtually never discussed in faculty meetings; the single-gender classes were simply the context or backdrop for the emphasis on standardized testing.

Although conceived of as a gender reform, gender equity was a concept only briefly touched on at the first faculty meeting before the school year began. Much of this early discussion was framed in terms of compliance with Title IX, and, as discussed in this chapter, recent rulings and interpretations of Title IX do have implications in terms of single-gender reform efforts. As explained to the faculty, boys and girls in the school needed to receive the exact same content and curriculum, as demonstrated through daily lesson plans to be in compliance. Much as "reducing distractions" minimized the possibilities of the single-gender reform, a concern with gender equality or sameness narrowed what faculty and administration saw as possibilities for gender equity.

Lack of deep inquiry into gender equity as well as a dearth of teacher preparation and development meant that SGA teachers were forced to grapple with gender and the single-gender classes on their own. Many were simply struggling to survive in a complex teaching situation—full inclusion and blocked core academic classes, for example—and thinking about gender was often not high on the list of teachers' concerns as reported to us.

Because teachers received very little guidance on gender, gender issues, and single-gender schooling, they were left to their own notions of gender and gender differences to make sense of what they were encountering in the single-gender classrooms. This meant that some teachers held very stereotypical and rigid ideas about gender differences, whereas others offered a more fluid notion of gender. Teachers' beliefs and ideologies played out in the classroom in varying ways, but the larger issue is that there was nothing structurally to foster teachers' growth and development in terms of interrogating their own beliefs and pedagogy as they relate to gender. These findings are consistent with those of Datnow, Hubbard, and Conchas (2001).

The story of SGA's first year of single-gender reform is primarily one of missed opportunities. The multiple innovations, the short lead time in terms of implementation, and the reconstitution of the whole school and its culture, all overshadowed initial and any ongoing thinking regarding the possibilities of gender reform. On its own terms—that of raising standardized test scores—the school was a success. Yet viewed through the lens of contributing to what we can learn about gender equity, the missed opportunity emerges as the biggest story to be told. This is particularly worrisome given the population of the school; its student constituency is one of the most underserved through the educational status quo. It is, of course, the first year in a complex reform effort. Still, without institutional support and space to discuss what it means to teach in single-gender classes, as well as relevant faculty development, the school is left without structures that would help it move into the multiple realities of gender reform.

NOTES

1. A pseudonym.
2. Emily has continued her research into the second year of the school's experiment.

REFERENCES

American Association of University Women. (1992). *How Schools Shortchange Girls.* Washington, D.C.

Beane, J. A. (1993). *A Middle-School Curriculum: From Rhetoric to Reality.* Columbus, OH: National Middle School Association.

Darling-Hammond, L. (1997). *The Right to Learn: A Blueprint for Creating Schools that Work.* San Francisco: Jossey-Bass.

Datnow, A. (2000). "Power and politics in the adoption of school reform models." *Educational Evaluation and Policy Analysis* 22(4): 357–374.

Datnow, A., Hubbard, L., and Conchas, G. (2001). "How Context Mediates Policy: The Implementation of Single-Gender Public Schooling in California." *Teachers College Record* 103 (2): 184–206.

George, P., Stevenson, C., Thomason, J., and Beane, J. A. (1992). *The Middle School and Beyond.* Alexandria, VA: Association for Supervision and Curriculum Development.

Ingersoll, R. M. (1999). "The Problem of Underqualified Teachers in American Secondary Schools." *Educational Researcher* 28 (2), 26–37.

Jackson, A.W., and Davis, G. A. (2000). *Turning Points 2000: Educating Adolescents in the Twenty-first Century.* New York: Teachers College Press.

Mael, F. (1998). "Single-Sex and Coeducational Schooling: Relationships to Socioemotional and Academic Development." *Review of Educational Research* 68 (2): 101–129.

Oakes, J., Quartz, K. H., Ryan, S., and Lipton, M. (2000). *Becoming Good American Schools: The Struggle for Civic Virtue in Education Reform.* San Francisco: Jossey-Bass.

Riordan, C. (1990). *Girls and Boys in School: Together or Separate?* New York: Teachers College Press.

Sadker, M., and Sadker, D. (1994). *Failing at Fairness: How America's Schools Cheat Girls.* New York: Charles Scribners' Sons.

Singh, K., Vaught, C., and Mitchell, E. (1998). "Single-Sex Classes and Academic Achievement in Two Inner-City Schools." *The Journal of Negro Education* 67 (2): 157–167.

Streitmatter, J. L. (1999). *For Girls Only: Making a Case for Single-Sex Schooling.* Albany, NY: SUNY Press.

Tyack, D., and Cuban, L. (1995). *Tinkering toward Utopia: A Century of Public School Reform.* Cambridge, MA: Harvard University Press.

Weiner, L. (2000). "Research in the '90s: Implications for Urban Teacher Preparation." *Review of Educational Research* 70 (3): 369–406.

Woody, E. L. "Constructions of Masculinity in California's Single-Gender Academies." Chapter 16 of this volume.

CHAPTER 6

Engendering Public Education: Single-Sex Schooling in Western Canada

Kathy Sanford and Heather Blair

INTRODUCTION

In Canadian schools there is a continuing concern about issues of gender, the inequities between boys and girls (Canadian Council of Ministers of Education, 1994, 1995, 1998; Canadian Teachers' Federation, 1990a; Rice and Russell, 1995), the gendered nature of school harassment (Canadian Teachers' Federation, 1990b; Kaufman, 1993, 1997; Larkin, 1994a, 1997; Larkin and Staton, 1993; Ontario Secondary School Teachers' Federation, 1994; Staton and Larkin, 1998), the need for discussions of gender in curriculum and pedagogy (Ellis, 1993; Robertson, 1992; Rogers, 1985, 1997), and the gendered nature of literacy (Blair, 1998; Blair and Sanford, 1999; Cherland, 1994; Gambell and Hunter, 1999; Ricker-Wilson, 1999; Wason-Ellam, 1997). Yet in spite of the advances and the contributions of the feminist movement, of men's movements, research, and teacher development, issues of gender inequity continue to surface in public education. In this chapter we discuss schools as one context in the lives of adolescents where they are "doing gender" (Thorne, 1993), and schools involved in rearticulating what school, curriculum, and pedagogy could be for girls and boys. These are single-sex programs in Canadian public schools.

It was generally recognized during the late 1980s and early 1990s that North American schools were not reaching full potential for all students and, in particular, girls (AAUW, 1992; Canadian Teachers Federation, 1990a; Sadker and Sadker, 1994). Many provinces and school districts in Canada adopted policy initiatives in the area of gender equity. There was a growing public awareness about gender equity and at the same time a continuing concern as to its meaning. Gender equity was recognized to be not just about hiring and promoting women or improving girls' participation in math and science; it was a more far-reaching issue that included curriculum and pedagogy, relations between boys and girls, expectations, classroom climate, sexual harassment, and equality of learning opportunity.

Although our study has focused on three single-sex programs, many other schools across western Canada in the mid-1990s experimented with alternative gendered classroom constructions. These programs were only known about in their local areas, and often the experiments lasted only a year or two. It is our contention in this chapter that single-sex programs can provide an important way of increasing gender awareness and sensitivity in schools for adolescents, especially girls. However, a lack of gender equity policies and a lack of conceptualization of boys' programs have led to insufficient support and direction to new programs, thus undermining the impact of single-sex programs on education as a whole.

In our classroom observations, it appears that issues of gender for children are easily overlooked in policy and practice as teachers focus on individual identity rather than gendered identity. Our research has suggested that it is during early adolescence that students' gender and sex become visible characteristics for teachers to recognize. When teachers do become aware of gender issues, they think they face intractable patterns that have been firmly fixed outside of school. Two popular explanations of gendering are those of: (a) the sociobiological view that behavior springs from the biological nature of humans, coded in the genes and a result of hormones; and (b) the internalization of gender roles following broad cultural expectations for men and women. From this perspective schools are believed to be conduits for societywide norms, and children are passive recipients of socialization (Connell, 1996, p. 212).

Gender is firmly embedded in the institutional arrangements of schools, and creates a "gender regime." This regime can clearly be identified in four ways:

1. Power relations, including supervision and authority among teachers and patterns of dominance, harassment, and control over resources among pupils
2. Division of labor, work specialization among teachers such as women in humanities and men in sciences, and informal specializations among pupils
3. Patterns of emotion, often associated with specific school roles such as "tough" administrators, and a prohibition on homosexuality
4. Symbolization, such as dress and language codes (Connell, 1996, p. 215)

The practices of the single-sex schools discussed in this chapter have addressed this gender regime in a variety of ways. These include hiring practices, development of role models that challenge traditional stereotypes, encouraging attitudes for acceptance of diversity, and examining appearance and discourse among staff and students. Examples of challenges to the gender regime described by Connell, in the form of single-sex programs, are described later in the chapter.

In our work on single-sex programs over the past five years, separation by gender, or biological sex, has raised and made explicit issues such as these. In this chapter we use both of the terms *gender* and *sex*, recognizing the limitations and essentialness of the categories of male and female, a classification based primarily on biology. We use the term gender to represent the social construction of a gendered identity. Among teachers and administrators in single-sex settings, we are seeing a growing awareness of curriculum needs, pedagogical concerns, and concerns over relations of power. There is also, especially in these settings, a recognition of the gendered nature of schools, the social construction of gender, and the implications for a deeper understanding of gender for equity of outcomes. In single-sex schools and programs, gender, by virtue of its prominence, is changing the nature of these schools.

HISTORICAL FRAME

According to the public media, single-sex classrooms and programs in public schools emerged in western Canada in the mid-1990s (Chatelaine, 1996; Krueger, 1998). This marks a shift because coeducational schooling based on the premise that the same means equal for both genders has been the norm in public education in Canada as in the United States for most of this century (Riordan, 1990; Tyack and Hansot, 1990). Public school policies and practices have been such that few parents, teachers, or administrators considered that a return to the single-sex schooling of the prior century had much educational value to offer their children. Until recently, most single-sex programs in Canada fell within the jurisdiction of private schools.

In 1995 there were fifteen private girls' schools in Canada (Cannon, 1995). The longstanding and traditional girls schools such as Balmoral Hall in Winnipeg (established in 1901), the Sacred Heart School of Halifax (established in 1849) and Montreal (established in 1861), as well as the Study in Montreal (established in 1915), have histories of providing exceptional educational opportunities where girls are empowered to be both learners and leaders. Each of these schools sets out to provide excellent academic preparation for their girls as well as a curriculum that includes the contributions of women. These schools have provided for the daughters of the Canadian elite what many parents want for their daughters. As a testimony to their academic success, the graduates of these schools have produced an inordinate number of women in leadership roles in both the public and private sectors in Canada (*www.bss.inforamp.net*). The more recently established Linden School in Toronto, established in 1993, as Canada's first self-proclaimed "woman-centered school" (Cannon, 1995, p. 20) has emerged in a very different time and to a parent "generation weaned on the glories of equal education for all" (Cannon, 1995, p. 21). Linden School administration has put women, feminism, and equity on top of the agenda for their program.

Boys-only programs such as Upper Canada College in Toronto (established in 1829), Selwyn House in Montreal (established in 1908), and St. George's School in Vancouver (established in 1931), focus on scholarship and rigorous athletics, and provide a university-preparatory education for boys. Schools such as St. John's School for Boys in Alberta (established in 1957) focus on character building and discipline. Military programs also exist, such as the Robert Land Academy in Ontario (established in 1978), that prepare boys for life in the military.

The establishment of single-sex programming for girls in public schools, established at approximately the same time as the Linden School, demonstrates a new phenomenon and awareness among a growing number of parents and educators in Canada that coeducational schooling might not be truly equitable, particularly for girls. At the time of their emergence, educational research suggested the need to provide a different kind of education for girls. There was a view that girls needed more math, science, and technology to make their education equal to that of boys. Canadian girls, it appeared by reviewing test score results, were lagging behind the boys in these critical areas (Erickson and Farkas, 1991; Haggerty, 1991; Randhawa, 1991; Randhawa and Gupta, 2000).

In the mid-1990s, several school jurisdictions in western Canada instituted girls' and boys' separated classes at the junior-high level in order to improve the girls' performance in these areas. Included in this initiative were the school sites reported in the case studies described later in this chapter. These sites were established by interest groups such as school administrators, staff, and parents, and were established for a variety of different, often conflicting purposes. Although parental concern for educational equity was one impetus for considering single-sex schooling, there were other reasons for considering single-sex schools, including school district interest in bolstering falling school enrollments in communities with declining school-age populations, a heightened public profile for some schools, an interest in financial support from industry for developing partnerships, and a concern to save public education. The mid-1990s was a time when schools had become increasingly concerned with accountability and there was a strong interest in privatization of public education (*Western Report*, 1996). These programs came about in a neoconservative political climate, as Staton and Larkin suggest, a time when "there has been a return to the 'equal opportunity' or 'let's treat everyone the same' thinking about equality, and a move away from the more political concept of 'equity'" (1998, p. 1).

With increased pressure for publicly funded independent schools, the province of Alberta moved slowly toward legislation to allow charter schools. Framed as "educational reform," legislation to allow publicly funded independent schools was passed in 1994. By 2000 there were ten charter schools in the province (*www.charterschools.ca/acs.html*). In response to this growing demand, some school districts opened options for "schools of choice" within public education. It is within these parameters that single-sex programs emerged.

In western Canada we found that single-sex programs emerged at the junior-high and middle-school levels. There was some consensus that schools at these levels begin to fail girls. Adolescence is a critical time for the construction of gender identity, and often academic success can be jeopardized. It is at this point that many girls begin to lose confidence in themselves as learners (Barbieri, 1995; Gilligan, 1982, 1993a, b) and question their own knowledge and authority. As we looked at the research on early adolescent girls, it became obvious that there were many questions of equity for girls that single-sex programs could address.

Boys' programs were later to emerge and are still more scarce. Issues for boys, such as literacy and the declining interest in school, appeared in the press. The popular press highlighted selected issues for boys, such as literacy achievement, exam results, and concerns over their continuation to higher education, and made little mention of issues of gender such as masculinity or abuse of power. The boys-only programs, and programs created to stimulate and maintain an interest in school, often through physical activities (such as hockey schools[1]), may deflect and/or disguise issues of gender equity by creating alternative foci.

Certainly another reason for the development of single-sex programs was parental motivation for the improvement of educational opportunities for their adolescent children by offering a broadened set of learning opportunities, safety from harassment, and elimination of distractions, (i.e., the "opposite" sex). These fledgling single-sex initiatives came in a variety of configurations and contexts. Those taking leadership roles in developing these programs had few models to follow and found themselves facing many new and challenging questions. The case studies reported in this chapter show concern for all of these issues. Before describing these cases, we discuss the AICE Model of Equal Opportunity, which serves as the theoretical framework of our study.

AICE MODEL OF EQUAL OPPORTUNITY

Equality of opportunity and equity have fundamentally different characteristics and results, and, as we explain, the failure to explicitly articulate the difference between the two created confusion and difficulty for the single-sex schools discussed in this chapter. As Staton and Larkin point out, "Equity is concerned with the elimination of systemic barriers and the development of policies and practices that will support equal outcomes. The 'equal opportunity' notion of sameness overlooks structural inequities and focuses on transforming individuals to fit the dominant mold" (p. 1). The lack of understanding of the differences between equity and equality on the part of program developers, administrators, and other interest groups, and the implications of these differences for schools, was one reason that single-sex programs were created without supporting foundational theory or policy.

Staton and Larkin (1993) have framed gender equity in Canadian schools in terms of access, inclusion, climate, and empowerment (AICE), a framework that we have found useful in examining the single-sex programs described in this chapter. The AICE Model of Equal Opportunity is a comprehensive and inclusive look at equity initiatives in schools.

- ACCESS: Encouraging equal opportunity in instruction, particularly in fields related to nontraditional jobs; enabling young people to choose from a range of careers
- INCLUSION: Looking at gender bias in teaching and learning materials both in terms of inclusive language and content
- CLIMATE: Creating an educational atmosphere that is safe and supports equity; dealing with sexual harassment and violence against women and those of alternative sexual orientations; looking at what goes on the walls [and] what goes on in the halls
- EMPOWERMENT: Creating a space within the school where young women can develop a sense of solidarity; providing an antidote to counter the negative messages young women receive both within and beyond their schools

Staton and Larkin suggested that, to be effective, programs of equal opportunity must give equal weight to all four components. "It's a lot like baking a cake; you can't leave out the eggs or the flour. Similarly, if an equal opportunity program doesn't include all the essential ingredients, it won't be very effective" (1993, p. 152). Staton and Larkin also suggested that through a comprehensive approach such as the AICE Model of Equal Opportunity, educators tackle specific problems such as sexual harassment in a wider context of gender inequity. Examining single-sex programs from this framework may give us a way to examine existing policy and practice and a way to understand the role these can play in the transformation of current policy and practice.

RESEARCH METHODS

Through observations, interviews, and document analyses, we investigated a range of single-sex programs in western Canada during a four-year period from 1996 to 2000. We focused on three programs having both similar and unique features, as described in the case studies that follow. These programs were identified through public media and subsequent invitations from school administration to visit the school sites. Our research was qualitative in nature and our goals included:

1. The exploration of the students' perceptions of gendered issues in single-sex programs.
2. The examination of the pedagogical and curricular practices of teachers in single-sex classrooms.
3. The analysis of local and provincial policy in relation to these programs.

Our data-gathering techniques varied somewhat depending on the site, but generally included: participant observations of school and classroom events; interviews with students about their present and past educational experiences to determine any differences that might exist in philosophy and/or teaching strategies because of the single-sex element of their programs; interviews with teachers and administrators as to the nature of the program; and collections of school documents that recorded the histories, policy, stories of success, and challenges of each program as well as the gender equity and related policies within each jurisdiction.

One research site came to our attention through personal involvement with the program; another from a front-page headline in a local newspaper; and another from a connection with a former staff member from the second site. Depending on location of the site, school interest, and opportunities over the years of our research, the interaction between ourselves as researchers and the school participants differed in depth and breadth. Our data analysis included transcribing the interviews of students, teachers, and administrators; and coding the transcripts for themes, document analysis, and triangulation of multiple data sources.

THREE SCHOOLS ENGAGED IN SINGLE-SEX EDUCATION

We used Staton and Larkin's AICE model to examine the practices and policies of these three programs in western Canada to better understand how these single-sex programs have contributed to gender equity for early adolescents and the implications for policy and practice. Single-sex programs provide an important contrast to the more commonly experienced coeducational programs and are one context where gender becomes explicit. It is our contention that these programs are potential sites for a transformation of educational practice that can benefit both boys and girls. However, when applying the AICE gender equity framework to the three sites, it appears that some components are more easily developed in the programs than others. Although access, climate, and empowerment are evident in the programs, inclusion (i.e., examining gender bias in classroom materials and teaching practices), requires more action and conscious commitment on the part of the administrators and staff.

Northpark Elementary/Junior High School is a K–8 school located in a small northern Canadian city populated largely by people connected to the oil industry. The oil industry attracts workers from across the country, and some families stay only as long as there is work; others who are involved in management are often well-established residents. The school is located in a residential area of the town some distance from the downtown core. The single-sex program was established in 1996 for the all of the grade-seven and eight-students, consisting of two classes of each grade. The school offered separate girls' and boys' classes for math, science, and physical education, and coed classes for language arts, social studies, and optional classes. The student body was comprised of approximately 120 students, the majority of whom were of European descent.

The program was initiated by the vice principal and supported by the principal, who felt it important to address the educational inequities and opportunities for girls in the areas of mathematics and science. The reorganization involved all the students attending the school and no additional recruitment was attempted. Parents of the students were informed of the change and the rationale for the change through public meetings. Rationale given by the administrative team involved research evidence indicating improvements for girls' grades in the areas of math and science.

The girls' classes were staffed by women, and the boys' classes were staffed by men; same-sex modeling was seen as an important aspect of the program. The teachers of both the boys' and girls' classes worked closely together to plan and develop curriculum materials, thus offering the same content to all of the students. Parents and students were surveyed regularly regarding their satisfaction with the program, and, as reported by the school administrators and teachers, overwhelmingly reported their enthusiasm for the single-sex classes. The students moved to a grades nine-to-twelve high school after their eighth grade year, and the teachers of the high school reported a noticeable strength of the girls in their coed mathematics classes.

The teachers, interviewed after two years of involvement in the program, expressed a desire to continue the program; their only concern was the lack of focus on courses not segregated by sex (i.e., language arts, social studies, and options). From our own observations, there seemed to be a less positive atmosphere in the coeducational classes than in the single-sex classrooms; students arriving from a single-sex class to a coeducational class spent considerable time in interacting with class members of the opposite sex, gaining their attention by calling out remarks and gesturing.

In relation to Staton and Larkin's gender equity model, there was clearly greater *access* to a wider range of educational opportunities in all areas, especially for girls. Science and mathematics was the focus of the program, ensuring that girls had increased access and encouragement. A female math and science teacher provided the girls with a model of genuine interest and expertise in these more traditionally male subjects. However, the same access was not considered for the boys in terms of literacy or humanities. As mentioned, the educational atmosphere in the coeducational language arts and social studies classes was less focused and more disruptive. There was not the same emphasis on literacy needs for boys and less recognition of the gendered needs of boys.

The *climate* in the single-sex classes was one of comfort and security; in our classroom visits we observed math and science that were taught through examples from the students' own personal (and gendered) experiences, which enabled students to ask more questions and relate concepts to their own previous understandings. Teachers of the same sex were assigned to the boys' and girls' classes, providing a further element of trust and communication. Spaces were created within the school for a sense of *empowerment* to be generated, again in the sciences, math, and in physical education through the single-sex settings. As reported by the teachers in this school and the receiving high school, students, especially females, entered their high school with a heightened sense of confidence in their abilities in traditionally male subjects.

Inclusion was acknowledged in classrooms, more through teachers' comments and examples rather than an examination or change of materials being used, for example, textbooks and worksheets. One of the teachers acknowledged possibilities of the gendered nature of her practice, for example, the collaborative, dialogic nature of students' work that was evident in her classes, but stressed the fact that the girls and boys received the same subject content as she coplanned with her male counterpart. The content of both math and science classes has been traditionally viewed as "male" and resource materials such as textbooks reinforce the male bias. However, these teachers, through their gendered personalizing of the content, attempted to connect the content to students' previous personal knowledge and experiences.

NANCY MAJOR ALL-GIRLS JUNIOR HIGH SCHOOL

Nancy Major All-Girls Junior High is an alternative program of choice in a large western Canadian city initiated in the fall of 1995 by local parents who wanted an option for academic achievement and leadership possibilities for their early adolescent girls. The parents' council of the school was very active in the support and development of this program. There is no boys-only counterpart to the program. Nancy Major All-Girls Junior High School consists of a program located in three school sites within one school jurisdiction. The first is located in a working-class inner-city neighborhood very close to the downtown district. It is a multicultural neighborhood, but the students are not primarily neighborhood youth. They come to the program from all areas of the city and parents are responsible for their daughters' transportation. Some students take public transit and others are driven, whereas a few of the students who live in the vicinity walk to school.

In the first year, 1995, when the program operated at the first site, there were eighty girls, 160 in the second year, and 225 in the third. Although the students are predominantly of white, middle-class backgrounds, there is a small percentage of students of Asian descent (10 percent). Apart from the students who live locally in this working-class neighborhood, they are predominantly from middle-class families. There are presently (in 2002) three classes at each grade level, grades seven to nine, with 220 girls in the program at the original site.

After three years of operation, the program expanded to a second site that now includes another two hundred junior high girls. This site is situated in a middle-class neighborhood in another district of the city, but also draws students from across the city, and includes similar racial and socioeconomic mixes as the first site. The third site was developed at the request of local parents who did not want their daughters bused across the city to participate in the program. It is located in an area of more transient, working-class families and draws more from local areas than do the other two sites. Currently the third site has sixty-eight girls and plans to expand to include seventy girls in the 2001 to 2002 school year.

At all three sites, parents and their daughters apply for admission to all three locations and in some years there have been waiting lists for entry. Student selection is made on a first-come first-serve basis on application to the specific program site. In the spring of each year, local elementary schools are visited with presentations about the program to acquaint students with the program option, and an open house event is held at each school site for interested parents and students.

The program's focus on science has won the school awards in recent years such as the selection of two ninth-grade students to go to the Canada-wide science fair. It is rare that two students from one local school are selected, and in 1999 they were the only two students selected from the entire city. One student won a gold medal. The performance was repeated in 2000, with two eighth-grade girls winning silver medals. Other program innovations include communication and writers' events as well as a focus on opportunities for the girls to bridge classroom learning to the outside community and world.

The Nancy Major programs explicitly emphasize equal opportunity in all fields, and their teachers are exemplary role models, particularly in the areas of mathematics and science, demonstrating their expertise and personal interest in science and mathematics. These teachers themselves have excelled in their field, and are able to demonstrate their knowledge to the students. One of the teachers orchestrated an extended ninth-grade science experience at the Bamford Marine Station on the west coast of Vancouver Island, which provides an intensive marine biology fieldwork opportunity. The success of the trip has relied, in part, on her expertise as a biologist. The field trip is challenging both intellectually and physically, and is viewed as one of the highlights of the program. Students and their parents do extensive fund-raising throughout the year in order to finance this trip, which is available to all of the students. Applying the AICE model, we find that students in the Nancy Major programs have *access* to knowledge about many types of careers, through guest speakers and field trips to workplaces. Women in engineering, science, and the military have been invited to speak, as well as artists, writers, and those in other nontraditional careers. The climate in these programs is clearly different from that of coeducational programs. Students commented about the class and school *climate* more than any other aspect of their single-sex programming. Some of the girls' comments included: "I feel like I can say more things, talk out loud more than I could before. Last year the boys were usually all the class clowns and everything, and they got most of the attention. And the teachers usually spent more time with them. We get more attention right now this year." This supportive climate *empowers* the students to envision their futures differently. They have worked with local professionals and charity organizations and volunteered at hospices, retirement homes, and environmental groups. They successfully undertake real-world problem-solving ventures, develop their own research projects, provide plans to visit research sites unaccompanied, and conduct and present their own research. Students become more willing and able to take risks and assert their own voices.

Inclusion is an important component of this single-sex program. Although existing traditional textbooks and examinations are still used, teachers have explicitly made changes to their teaching practices and learning materials. Students have considerable choice in areas of study, and voice in the decisions made both in the classroom and school as a whole. They have implemented a weekly program that involves integrating the curriculum in the community. Students develop projects that involve local organizations, research in archives and libraries throughout the city, and community events. They are expected to demonstrate collaboration and individual initiative in developing their own learning experiences. Female author studies are included in the language arts curriculum; writers' workshops are led by local women authors; and units of study on women in media and advertising are developed.

WOOD HARBOUR JUNIOR HIGH SCHOOL

Wood Harbour Junior High is situated in a suburban satellite community, largely white and middle class, adjacent to a large Canadian city. It has a student body of 550 students, with seven classes of each grade level. This single-sex program began in the fall of 1997 as an initiative of the school guidance counselor and principal. The counselor was new to the district and had come from a school where some single-sex programming had been implemented. She thought the idea had merit, read some research suggesting the strengths of single-sex programs for girls, and wanted to offer this alternative to the students at her new school. As a counselor, she had become very aware that many of the students' difficulties were issues related to gender, and thought that single-sex classes would be beneficial to some students. In addition to the counselor's observations that students have difficulties with the opposite sex in junior high years, there was research suggesting curriculum benefits for girls regarding math and science. The principal and counselor discussed the possibilities with the school parents' council and teachers, and a decision was made that a single-sex program might benefit both boys and girls, although the benefits for boys were not articulated in the same way that they were for girls.

Students from the elementary schools in the area were recruited to this single-sex alternative. An open house was held for interested parents. The students were designated to the single-sex classes based on the parents' and students' choice, similar to the way that children were placed in the French immersion strand at this school. During its first year, there were five single-sex classrooms in the school, one girls' class for each of grades seven to nine, and one boys' class in grades seven and eight. In the second year, the program was reduced to girls' only at the seventh and eighth grades. The entire program was abandoned after two years, as we explain below. We studied the program in the spring before it was first implemented until its finish two and a half years later.

In this program the students had single-sex core classes—math, science, English language arts, and social studies—and then combined in coeducational classes for their optional courses. During the first year most of the teachers felt that the program was more successful for the girls than for the boys, based on the relationships they developed with the students, the relationships the girls developed with each other, the behavior of the students, and the grades of the students at the end of the year. At the end of the year a decision was made to have only the girls' component for the second year. As reported by one teacher, "It's been a really positive experience for a lot of the students; a lot of them will help each other. One girl that gets really high marks says that she will help the other girls, they'll phone her on the weekend and she'll help—she's *volunteered* to help the class." The girls' math teacher also reported her observations: "I know a few girls, when we did problem solving, they wouldn't even attempt it. They'd look at the question, they'd read the question and say, 'I don't get it,' where now there is a little more—they realize that maybe they *can*, and they might have to pull out a manipulative to do it, but they *can* figure it out. So it seems to be more risk-taking."

During the second year, although no major curriculum changes or special events were planned for the single-sex programs, teachers started to talk about the selection of the material and the way they related to the girls and boys in the classes. One teacher commented, "I will approach issues in a way that is more gender-oriented sometimes. I think in terms of relationships, I can ask the boys, 'What do you think the girls' point of view is here?' . . . And so if there's a gender issue, we are going to have an interesting input of what may not come out if that gender was in the classroom." For the third year, the school planned to reinstate the boys' program at the seventh grade and to look at ways in which the boys' program would be more tailored to the need of boys. The teachers were hoping to increase the time for the physical education and outdoor education component of their program, after recognizing some of the boys' needs: "Grade seven boys are very physical, they see things physically; they see solving problems physically as the way to go at this point." The English language arts teacher was also redesigning her language arts curriculum in order to address issues of literacy for boys, examining both topics and genre in her selection of literature, the range of their media literacy, and methodological considerations to build the reader-writer connection.

However, because of lack of interest on the part of the boys and their parents, and lack of support for the staff, these plans did not materialize and the entire single-sex program was discontinued. As one boy in the single-sex class reported, "My mom doesn't care if I'm in the single-sex class or not; she just thought she'd try it to see if anything would change." Although a small group of teachers on staff was committed to the concept of single-sex classes, there was considerable disinterest or opposition from other members of staff. One such teacher involved in teaching a girls' class expressed her skepticism: "In the coed class they meet the boy challenges all the time, and they just have to learn to put up with them if they're being teased or whatever; they're going to be right back in it next year, so what good did this experience do them?" Timetabling of a large junior high school was problematic in involving all of the interested teachers, and excluding all of the teachers who were disinterested. Therefore the commitment of some of the teachers did not exist and served to undermine the intent of the program. Additionally, the program was implemented quickly without a strong theoretical foundation, and when problems arose, responses were not immediately apparent.

Nevertheless, during the two years of this single-sex program's existence, there was an obvious change in the educational climate, as noted by the girls: "It's nice because you don't get teased a lot, because they say that boys are two years behind girls in maturity, psychologically and everything, but we're all at the same level pretty much in this class, so it's nicer that way."

"You're not really as embarrassed in the classes and stuff. The classes are pretty loud sometimes, but that's just because we're having friendly conversations—we're not like we don't get our work done."

The boys commented: "Nobody is really mad or angry at anyone we are all just doing our own thing and stuff like that."

"I like being around boys who aren't trying to influence girls to like them, because then they do bad stuff too."

"You get treated differently . . . you get more respect from your friends, other people in your class, because there is no girls around, you get a little more respect from the teacher because he doesn't have to worry about all of those other kids."

When viewed in light of the AICE framework, we find that the change in classroom *climate* in the single-sex program influenced the *access* teachers offered their students to alternative perspectives, foci, and content. Because of the obvious element of gender in these classes, the teachers began to consider their choices in material and in their teaching strategies. The language arts teacher redesigned her curriculum in order to address issues of literacy for boys. She looked at both topic and genre in her selection of literature, the range of their media literacy, and methodological considerations to build the reader-writer connection. The social studies teacher described a difference in her class discussions:

> We've just been talking about World War II and Japan's role in the war and the American dropping of the atomic bomb, and almost unanimously the boys said that they should have dropped the bomb. The girls unanimously said "no." Some people say that we're socialized differently as boys and girls, and that how we perceive what's just and right comes from quite different perspectives.

The introduction of acceptable alternative views and interests *empowered* the students to speak up and voice their opinions, as well as accept other perspectives. One teacher commented: "What is different in these classes is that I have all the girls' hands up. Every time an issue comes about, we have a lot of eagerness. Everybody has a story to tell, right? And that is also true of the boys. So there is a lot more discussion, particularly with the girls' classes." At the beginning of this program, teachers made a deliberate choice not to change their curriculum or teaching strategies. At the end of the second year, some teachers had begun to consider changes to the materials used in classes and imagine a greater range of perspectives, but change in practice was not considered in any depth. Although *inclusion* was not explicitly considered in the two years of the program, owing in part to the initial decision deliberately *not* to make any changes to the materials or methods of teaching, by the end of the second year teachers were considering changes to their approaches and resources.

DISCUSSION AND IMPLICATIONS: CONTRIBUTIONS TO GENDER EQUITY

As the three programs developed and teachers reflected on the realities of having student groups of only one sex in their core subject areas, they began to examine their own educational practices and pedagogy. These programs increased the teachers' awareness of issues of gender both in education and society, such as what is valued, what is encouraged, what is ignored, and for whom. Our investigation created a window of understanding for ourselves as teachers and teacher-educators, and for the teachers with whom we worked.

The Model of Equal Opportunity presented by Staton and Larkin offered a way to examine four critical aspects of single-sex programs: access, inclusion, climate, and empowerment. Using these criteria as lenses, we have examined these three western Canadian programs. *Climate* is clearly the aspect of single-sex programs that changes most quickly and most dramatically. Comfort, security, and trust are key elements of single-sex programs continually remarked on by students, teachers, and parents. This positive and safe climate provides spaces within schools and classrooms that *empower* adolescents to recognize and believe in themselves, which then affords them greater *access* to alternative careers and lifestyles. The aspect of *inclusion*, however, is a greater challenge to educators and administrators. Lack of supportive gender equity policy does not enable a recognition of the need for new materials, spaces in which to examine teaching practices, and examination of existing configurations of adolescents in classrooms and schools. It is this area that demands the greatest effort, and perhaps will be the aspect that determines the success or demise of single-sex programs in western Canada.

The AICE model has enabled us to recognize the positive effects of single-sex programs in terms of access, climate, and empowerment, while making us aware of the need to push further with policy development, research, and teaching practice to make inclusion a reality. Inclusion will require teachers and administrators to examine their own beliefs and practices in more depth and "necessitates the asking of questions which may bring discomfort and in some cases, disharmony" (Larkin and Staton, 1998). Moreover, although premised on the needs of girls, the AICE may also have some applicability to boys. However, it is our contention that the boys' programs we studied are underconceptualized in terms of addressing issues of gender for boys and need to clarify and focus their goals and efforts.

The purposes and objectives of each of the three programs we investigated were varied, depending on the perceived needs and desires of each community and school. Underlying the inception of each of the programs was a belief in the need to address issues of gender for adolescents. Although two of the programs offered boys-only classes as well as classes for girls, the impetus for the shift has been an increasing focus on equality of educational opportunities for girls. The policies and practices in each of these programs have been driven by the overall program goals, some of which have been more clearly defined than others. Several goals for single-sex education in relation to girls have been identified. The programs all list among their objectives increased confidence on the part of the girls. They want the girls to believe in their own capability (empowerment). The programs all explicitly delineated their attempt to increase opportunities for girls in math, science, and technology, the traditionally "male" subjects (access). Safety in the classroom and school and freedom from bullying, violence, and intimidation were mentioned as important (climate). Parents clearly wanted to see a greater focus on schoolwork for their daughters via a removal of distractions caused by boys in the class.

The objectives for boys were less clear, but included, again, greater focus on schoolwork and increased literacy skills and interests. Results of the 1994, 1995, and 1998 Council of Ministers of Education in Canada literacy study indicate that girls score better than boys in terms of literacy assessment. This is not to disregard the seriousness of the gender inequities in schools for girls, but rather to recognize that there may well be just as serious issues for boys when it comes to literacy. Numerous questions remain as to how Canadian schools may be shortchanging or failing boys and what role literacy plays.

Similarly, educational research in Great Britain has indicated concerns for boys in educational settings—for example, boys do not view education positively, they do not like to read, and some do not read very well—and a growing percentage of boys are "failing" at school (Millard, 1997). Phillips (1998) described how British boys are faced with many pressures as they enter and progress through school. She suggested that there are few acceptable gender positions for males, and that boys are expected to be tough, competitive, and independent. Application of the AICE model to boys-only classes enables us to recognize and more clearly articulate goals and objectives for boys as well as girls.

In terms of practice, there were both strengths and problems in the three single-sex programs described. There were shifts taking place in practices in these single-sex schools, some more obvious than others. Even the fact that there were discussions of gender in some of these schools was a major step. Teachers were coming to understand the implicit gendered nature of schooling and explore the ways to celebrate and extend learning for both girls and boys. These teachers began to look at the gendered nature of their curricula and change some of the resources and materials they had been using. However, there were still problems. The fact that these discussions occurred in relative isolation remained a concern. These teachers had few places to go to discuss their common recognitions, experiences, issues, and problems. In some cases this was even true of their own staff. The hiring of staff, commitment among appointed staff, and recruitment were not easy in times of school financing cutbacks. School administrators found themselves looking for competent teachers from within their school division with little opportunity for hiring based on discussions of issues of gender. The logistics of timetabling remained a major factor and problem, in both large and small schools. With limited staff resources, administrators juggled to balance essential resources.

In terms of policy, we think that it is fair to say that these programs were developed and continue to operate, not on established policy, but rather on local working policies. It is important to note that the Canadian context is different from the United States in that there is no legislation comparable to Title IX that would challenge the establishment of these programs. Canada does have human rights legislation, but single-sex programs in public education have not been challenged at any level of jurisprudence. In the western Canadian province in which this research was done, there is no school division policy or province wide policy to impede or to support these single-sex initiatives. Provincial policy makes limited reference to gender equity with regard to issues of stereotyping, resources, inclusive language, and career counseling (*www.teachers.ab.ca/policy*, 1999). Local school board policy makes brief reference to gender: "Students shall show respect for ethnic, racial, religious, and gender differences" (*www.epsb.edmonton.ab.ca*, 1998), but makes no mention of gender equity.

One local school district we studied offers a variety of gender-suggestive alternative programs, such as a cadet/ballet academy and a "sports alternative" program. These very different programs, although suggestive of strong gender interest, are indicative of the lack of consistent board vision or policy, and demonstrate a lack of explicit focus on gender issues. Absence of policy in the school jurisdictions where the research occurred demonstrates lack of any explicit support for these gender equity alternatives. Few school districts in western Canada have a comprehensive gender-equity policy that encompass equity for students, and even fewer have any in-depth plan for implementation of equity initiatives. In the absence of policy and planning, these programs are carving out their own place in terms of policy development.

In conclusion, we want to reiterate that the single-sex programs we studied *are* changing the nature of their schools and educators' conversations about gender equity, albeit slowly. It is important that teachers, students, and administrators are beginning to acknowledge that gender matters in school. In western Canada these programs are taking place in public schools and are looking at gender issues for both boys and girls. We acknowledge that there has been little research to support what is happening in these programs and that we have a long way yet to go, especially with the lack of support and direction of gender equity policies at provincial and national levels, to ensure that access, inclusion, climate, and empowerment are realized for all the youth in our schools regardless of their construction of gender.

NOTE
1. Alternative gender-suggestive programs:
   - Vimy Ridge Academy (focusing on Canadian history and military history, world history, and Canadian geography and politics, with a number of specialized complementary courses including courses in drill, pipes and drums, and outdoor pursuits)
   - Ballet Academy (internationally recognized for its outstanding dance program)
   - Sports alternative programs (balancing schoolwork and competitive sport, especially hockey and soccer, and geared toward young athletes with the potential to compete at the provincial and national levels)

REFERENCES

Alberta's Charter Schools (September, 2000). Canadian Charter Schools Centre. Available: http://www.charterschools.ca/acs.html [2001, May 28].

Charter Schools in Canada: What Are Charter Schools? Canadian Charter Schools Centre. Available: http://www.charterschools.ca/wacs.html [2001, May 28].

"Edmonton's Public School Board Gives Ground (Nellie McClung Junior High, A School for Girls in Edmonton)." (1996). *Western Report 11* (33): 42.

"Where the Girls Are: All-Female Classes in Public Schools Are Catching on." (1996). *Chatelaine 69* (4): 30.

American Association of University Women. (1992). *How Schools Shortchange Girls.* Washington, D.C.: American Association of University Women Educational Foundation.

——. (1998). *Separated by Sex: A Critical Look at Single-Sex Education for Girls.* Washington, D.C.: American Association of University Women Educational Foundation.

Barbieri, M. (1995). *Sounds of the Heart: Learning to Listen to Girls.* Portsmouth, NH: Heinemann Educational Books.

Blair, H. (1998). "They Left Their Genderprints: The Voice of Girls in Text." *Language Arts 75* (1), 11–18.

Blair, H., and Sanford, K. (1999). "TV and Zines: Media and the Construction of Gender for Early Adolescents." *Alberta Journal of Educational Research 45* (1): 103–105.

Canadian Council of Ministers of Education. (1994). *School Achievement Indicators Program: 1994 Reading and Writing Assessment.* Toronto: Author.

——. (1998). *School Achievement Indicators Program: 1998. Reading and Writing Assessment.* Toronto: Author.

Canadian Teachers' Federation. (1990a). *The A Cappella Papers of the Canadian Teachers' Federation.* Ottawa: Author.

——. (1990b). *Thumbs Down: A Classroom Response to Violence Towards Women.* Ottawa: Author.

Cannon, M. (1995). "No Boys Allowed: Liberating Our Daughters Used to Mean Getting Them into Boys' Schools, but Girls' Schools are Bastions of Women's Liberation? Right on, Sister (Linden School, Toronto)." *Saturday Night 110*(1): 18–24.

Cherland, M. (1994). *Private Practices: Girls Reading Fiction and Constructing Identity.* Bristol, PA: Taylor and Francis.

Connell, R. W. (1996). "Teaching the Boys: New Research on Masculinity, and Gender Strategies for Schools." *Teachers College Record 98* (2): 206–235.

Ellis, J. (1993). "If I Were a Boy . . . : Constructing Knowledge about Gender Issues in Teacher Education." *Curriculum Inquiry 23*(4): 367–393.

Erickson, G., and Farkas, S. (1991). "Prior Experiences and Gender Differences in Science Achievement." *Alberta Journal of Educational Research 37*(3): 225–239.

Gambell, T. J., and Hunter, D. M. (1999). "Rethinking Gender Differences in Literacy." *Canadian Journal of Education 24*(1): 1–16.

Gilligan, C. (1982). *In a Different Voice: Psychological Theory and Women's Development.* Cambridge, MA: Harvard University Press.

Gilligan, C. (1993a). "Joining the Resistance: Psychology, Politics, Girls, and Women." In L. Weis, and M. Fine (Eds.), *Beyond Silenced Voices: Class, Race, and Gender in United States Schools.* Albany: SUNY Press.

Gilligan, C. (1993b). *Meeting at the Crossroads*. New York: Ballantine Books.

Haggerty, S. M. (1991). "Gender and School Science: Achievement and Participation in Canada." *Alberta Journal of Educational Research* 37(3): 195–208.

Kaufman, M. (1993). *Cracking the Armour: Power, Pain, and the Lives of Men*. Toronto: Penguin Books.

———. (1997). "Working with Young Men to End Sexism." *Orbit* 28(1): 16–18.

Krueger, L. (1998). "Gender Contenders: Closing the Learning Gap between Boys and Girls." *Today's Parent* 15(5): 31–34.

Larkin, J. (1994a). *Sexual Harassment: High School Girls Speak Out*. Toronto: Second Story Press.

Larkin, J. (1994b). "Walking through Walls: The Sexual Harassment of High School Girls." *Gender and Education* 6(3): 263–280.

Larkin, J. (1997). "Confronting Sexual Harassment in Schools." *Orbit* 28(1): 14–15.

Larkin, J., and Staton, P. (1998). "If We Can't Get Equal, We'll Get Even: A Transformative Model of Gender Equity." *Canadian Woman Studies* 17(4): 16–22.

Millard, E. (1997). *Differently Literate: Boys, Girls, and the Schooling of Literacy*. London: Falmer Press.

Phillips, A. (1998). "It's Just so Unfair." *Times Educational Supplement* 14–15.

Ontario Secondary School Teachers' Federation. (1994). *Student to Student Sexual Harassment*. Toronto: Author.

Randhawa, B. S. (1991). "Gender Differences in Academic Achievement: A Closer Look at Mathematics." *Alberta Journal of Educational Research* 37(3): 241–257.

Randhawa, B. S., and Gupta, A. (2000). "Cross-National Gender Differences in Mathematics Achievement, Attitudes, and Self-Efficacy within a Common Intrinsic Structure." *Canadian Journal of School Psychology* 15(2): 51–66.

Rice, C., and Russell, V. (1995). "Embodying Equity: Putting Body and Soul into Equity Education, Part II: Strategies for Change." *Our Schools/Ourselves* 7(2): 42–54.

Ricker-Wilson, C. (1999). "Busting Textual Bodices: Gender, Reading, and the Popular Romance." *English Journal* 88(3): 57–63.

Riordan, C. (1990). *Girls and Boys in School: Together or Separate?* New York: Teachers College Press.

Robertson, H.-J. (1992). *The Better Idea Book: A Resource Book on Gender, Culture, Science, and Schools*. Ottawa: Canadian Teachers' Federation.

———. (1997). "Changing Women or Changing Mathematics? A Mathematician's Story." *Orbit* 28(1): 30–33.

Rogers, P. (1985). "Overcoming another Barrier: Real Women Don't Do Math—with Good Reason!" *Canadian Women's Studies Journal* 6(4): 82–84.

Sadker, M., and Sadker, D. (1994). *Failing at Fairness: How America's Schools Cheat Girls*. Toronto: Maxwell Macmillan International.

Staton, P., and Larkin, J. (1993). *Sexual Harassment: We Can Do Something About It*. Toronto: Green Dragon Press.

Thorne, B. (1993). *Gender Play: Girls and Boys in Schools*. New Brunswick, NJ: Rutgers University Press.

Tyack, D., and Hansot, E. (1990). *Learning Together: A History of Coeducation in American Schools*. New York: Russell Sage Foundation.

Wason-Ellam, L. (1997). "If Only I Was Like Barbie." *Language Arts* 74(6): 430–437.

CHAPTER 7

Are Single-Sex Schools Sustainable in the Public Sector?

Lea Hubbard and Amanda Datnow

Single-gender public schools in the United States represent efforts at expanding choice in the public school sector, responding to academic inequities across gender, and/or building on a successful model in the private schools. Schools and districts in a number of states have experimented with Afrocentric educational programs for boys, single-sex classes in math and science for girls, and leadership academies for girls (Pollard, 1998). There have also been attempts over the years by Senator Kay Bailey Hutchison (Republican, Texas) to pass a Senate bill to allow public school districts to experiment with federally funded single-gender education (Hutchison, 1999; Richards, 2000). As of May 2002, the federal government has issued new regulations providing more flexibility for experimentation with single-sex public schooling. Prior to this significant move, in 1998, California became the first state to experiment with single-gender public education on a large scale. Six districts opened single-gender academies (both boys and girls) as a result of former California Governor Pete Wilson's legislation and funding for a single-gender academies pilot program in the public school system.

Despite some success with this single-gender schooling experiment (see Datnow, Hubbard, and Woody, 2001, for an extensive review of these findings), within two to three years, only one district's academies remained open. The relatively quick demise of these single-gender public schools encourages us to question, are single-sex schools sustainable in the public sector in the United States? We address this question using data from a qualitative case study of the California single-gender academies program.

SUSTAINABILITY OF EDUCATIONAL INNOVATIONS
Very few studies have actually examined the sustainability of educational innovations over long period of times, in part because most reforms do not last (Anderson and Stiegelbauer, 1994; Cuban, 1986, 1992; Kirst and

Meister, 1985; Tyack and Cuban, 1995). However, there are a few notable exceptions. Cuban's research (1992, 1998) has focused on how the kindergarten and junior-high-school innovations were institutionalized in the American school system over time. Other researchers have focused on how externally developed educational reforms (Berman and McLaughlin, 1978; Datnow, 2001; Yonezawa and Stringfield, 2000) or restructuring efforts (Anderson and Stiegelbauer, 1994) have sustained over time.

There is a significant gap in the research, however, on the sustainability of newly formed public schools that have been developed specifically for the purpose of expanding school choice, such as charter schools, alternative schools, and in this case, single-gender public schools. We know from some research that new charter schools, for example, face a host of difficulties in terms of resources, support, and staffing. A study by RPP International found "that newly created schools typically confront all of the start problems by those starting a new business" (1998, p. 5). These issues might also affect the schools' longevity over time.

Our interest in looking at the sustainability of single-gender public schools as an interrelated set of forces has foundations in prior research and theorizing on the topic. Most researchers argue that institutionalization involves a multilevel process of embedding an innovation in the structure and norms of the organization. For example, Curry (1991) describes the conditions for institutionalization as *structural* (innovation reflected in a concrete fashion throughout the organization), *procedural* (activities associated with innovation become standard operating procedure), and *cultural* (norms and values associated with innovation are embraced by members of the organization). Similarly, Yonezawa and Stringfield (2000) found that schools sustained reform when there was political support, alignment of the "cultural logic" of the reform design and that of the local reformers, and when reform was structured into the daily lives of the school community. Schools that simultaneously attended to these change processes—and more importantly, the interaction between them—were able to sustain reforms over eight years or more.

We agree that it is the *interaction* of multiple elements—what we term culture, structure, and agency—that impact reform sustainability (Datnow, Hubbard, and Mehan, 2002). In this chapter we provide a careful investigation of the multiplicity of factors that contribute to the sustainability of six single-gender public schools. Single-gender schools are a somewhat unique case among educational innovations because they deal explicitly with the issue of *gender*. We argue that it is by looking at the interplay among structural factors, cultural norms and ideologies, and the actions of the participants that we can best understand the sustainability of these public schools.

The agency of individuals is key in sustaining an educational innovation. We know that the actions taken by educators can support or undermine reform efforts. Little is known, however, about the way in which these actions are embedded within a context of cultural beliefs. Bringing new ideas and new ways of implementing old structures creates excitement for some, opportunity and challenge for others, and outright resistance and fear for many because responses are intimately connected to people's ideologies. Even the best innovations suffer without adequate support or "buy-in" from administration and faculties. For reform to be successful, educators must interpret the goals of the reform as matching their own. Buy-in demands that there is a genuine interest in change (Anderson and Stiegelbauer, 1994; Moffet, 2000) but frequently norms and values exist that oppose change efforts. Good leadership can inspire this support (Anderson and Steigelbauer, 1994; Fullan, 1991), yet all individuals are influenced by their interests, ideology and information, past experiences, education and training. The sustainability of the single-gender schools in our study was clearly impacted by the agency of those involved. Importantly, their actions were inextricably intertwined with cultural beliefs.

Hargreaves (1994) points out that educational reform requires the "reculturing" of a school. And Fullan (2001) explains that "you need to respect the existing culture and then open it up for a new culture." As we explain, educators involved with the single-gender schools in our study brought a new way of educating students to districts with their own culture and way of doing school.

We know from the literature on school change that structural constraints also impact reform sustainability. A challenge in sustaining reforms involves not just harnessing the agency of educators for initial buy-in and start-up, but also "building an internal collective capacity" among key agents (Fullan, 2001). Yet educators' actions are constrained by the "practical circumstances" of school life. Fullan suggests it often requires "re-timing" (Fullan, 2001). Hargreaves and Fink (2000, p. 7) point out that such seemingly mundane issues as time to implement, conduct staff recruitment, address retention issues, accommodate to the size of the institution, understand district and policy changes, and deal with any detrimental relations that may occur within the community can inhibit or enhance the sustainability of reform. In fact, these issues turn out not to be mundane at all.

Because the schools in our study were newly staffed, and in many cases, teachers were hired quite hurriedly, and moreover, they experienced tremendous teacher turnover, we questioned not only to what extent the faculty was supportive of the single-gender arrangement, but also whether they had time for adequate training and the opportunity to construct support systems that would allow the schools to survive.

Structural considerations impose both opportunity and constraints to reform sustainability and encourage us to also look beyond school boundaries and issues of time. Although researchers have argued that building an infrastructure at the state, district, and community level that will support reform is important to successful implementation and sustainability

(Anderson and Stiegelbauer, 1994; Bodilly, 1998; Datnow, 2001; Moffet, 2000), most research on reform sustainability or institutionalization has not dealt with issues outside the school in an in-depth fashion.

There are some important exceptions. Lusi (1997) found in her case study of Kentucky and Vermont that states play a pivotal role in the implementation of school reform. State accountability mechanisms are important features of states' roles in sustaining or hindering innovation. So too, Hubbard and Mehan (1999) found that state fiscal support contributed significantly to the strength of the Advancement Via Individual Determination (AVID) program, an educational innovation designed to assist low-income and minority students achieve academically and go onto college. When state support was withdrawn, schools wishing to continue with the program were forced to scramble for funds, ultimately threatening the continuation of the reform. State and district imperatives impose heavily on decisions to maintain support for an innovation, especially, we might argue in the case of single-gender education, which although successful in the private sector has not been adequately tested nor supported in the public sector (Mael, 1998). This chapter both complements and complicates the relationship between structural constraints and educational innovation by including a careful look at the role of the district and state in school reform.

By looking at the intersection of culture, structure, and agency within the context of the California single-gender public schools experiment, we expand our knowledge of reform sustainability. Structural constraints at the state level, most evident in the power and politics that existed there, interacted with the ideologies and beliefs of those at the district and school level around the merits of single-gender schooling. Economic constraints imposed by the state or district competed with the motivations and aspirations of all participants and shaped ensuing decisions and practices that undermined the sustainability of the single-gender public schools.

METHODOLOGY

From 1998 to 2000, we were engaged in a longitudinal study of California's single-gender academies. The six districts that operated single-gender academies were located across the state of California in a variety of urban, suburban, and rural contexts. The academies served student populations that were diverse in terms of race, ethnicity, socioeconomic, and linguistic background. Four of the districts operated a total of eight paired single-gender academies at the middle-school level, and two operated a total of four paired single-gender academies at the high school level. Table 7.1 includes a description of each district's single-gender academies. For the purposes of confidentiality, pseudonyms are used in this report for all names of persons and places.

TABLE 7.1

CHARACTERISTICS OF THE SINGLE-GENDER ACADEMIES,
1997–1998

District	Location	Grades Served/Type	Student Population	Approximate Ethnic Distribution[a]
Palm	Urban	Grades 7–12 Self-contained alternative schools	60 boys; 30 girls Students had a history of truancy, gang violence, or substance abuse.	80% Hispanic American 12% Asian 8% White
Evergreen	Rural	Grades 7–8 Schools within a K–8 school; 2/3 of middle-school students were in academies	28 boys; 30 girls Students were very low income. Most relied on public assistance.	88% White 9% Hispanic American 3% Native American
Cactus	Suburban	Grades 7–8 Schools within a K–8 school; 1/2 of middle-school students were in academies	36 boys; 50 girls Students were a mix of upper-middle, middle, and low income.	65% White 14% African American 9% Asian 8% Hispanic American 3% Pacific Isl.
Birch	Urban	Grade 9 (expanded to grade 10 in 1998–1999) Schools within a high school	18 boys; 22 girls Students were predominantly low income.	32% Hispanic American 27% African American 14% Asian 12% White 10% East Indian 5% Pacific Isl.
Pine	Urban	Grades 5–8 Self-contained schools	90 boys; 50 girls Students were low income and at-risk because of academic, health, and human-service needs.	46% Hispanic American 38% African American 18% Pacific Isl.
Oak	Urban	Grades 6–8 Schools within a middle school	67 girls; 46 boys Students were predominantly low income.	32% Asian 27% African American 16% Hispanic American 13% White 11% Other nonwhite

[a.] Some percentages do not add up to one hundred because of rounding.

Our study relied primarily on qualitative, case study research methods.[1] We chose case study methods for our study because it enables us to examine the process and consequences of single-gender schooling in the real life contexts in which they occur. It allows us to present the perspectives of those actually implementing the single-gender schooling legislation (Yin, 1989).

Three members of our research team visited each of the single-gender academies in California five or six times, for two days each visit. Using semi-structured protocols, we interviewed teachers, principals and/or academy directors, parents, students, and district officials. We interviewed almost all of the teachers in the single-gender academies, and the majority of students enrolled during the 1997 to 1998 and 1998 to 1999 school years. We asked about the origin of the academies and why educators and students chose to participate. We inquired about the professional background of teachers and noted their plans for staff development, teacher collaboration, and curriculum development. We also asked teachers, principals, and academy directors about their perceptions of the benefits and weaknesses of the single-gender academies.

In our visits to schools, we observed academic and elective classes. When there was the opportunity, we also observed coeducational classes, because some single-gender academies were schools-within-a-school. We focused on student-teacher interactions, student-student interactions, and pedagogical strategies. We also interviewed officials at the California Department of Education and the governor's office in order to gather information regarding the single-gender schooling legislation and the process that led to its development.

Four of the six districts we studied closed their single-gender academies in the fall of 1999. The fifth district closed their schools in spring 2000. Only one district continued to operate the single-gender schools through the duration of our study and continues to operate currently. We conducted data collection at all closed sites, including conducting interviews with staff, parents, and students, either in the fall of 1999 or spring 2000, depending on their closure date. This data collection effort proved very useful in learning about teachers' and students' perspectives of their experiences in the single-gender academies and their experiences returning to coeducation.

In order to assess what can be generalized from of our case study findings, we also completed two-day site visits to three other single-gender public schools: (a) an all-girls public high school in the eastern United States that has been open for over one hundred years and serves over twelve hundred students; (b) a comprehensive high school in California that offers single-gender classes (boys and girls) for special education students; and (c) a new middle school in California that offers single-gender education to one thousand students (six hundred girls; four hundred boys). Data collection in these sites has helped us assess whether the findings from our schools are consistent with other single-gender public schooling experiments in different contexts and schools that did not benefit from state start-up grants.

All interviews were taped and transcribed verbatim. We analyzed transcripts from a total of more than three hundred interviews and field notes from school and classroom observations. Our analysis of the data took two primary forms: coding and case report writing. We coded interview data using HyperResearch qualitative data analysis software. We also wrote detailed descriptive and analytic case reports on each set of academies that facilitated cross-site comparisons and helped us identify emergent themes.

THE CALIFORNIA SINGLE-GENDER PUBLIC SCHOOLING EXPERIMENT

In the 1997 to 1998 school year, California's then Governor Wilson pushed for legislation that resulted in the opening of twelve single-gender public academies (six boys, six girls) in six districts. In Wilson's 1996 "State of the State Address" he argued that single-gender academies were a way to provide public school students more options, more choice, and better preparation for real world opportunities (California Department of Education Fact Sheet: Single-Gender Academies Pilot Program, Enclosure A). Later, in a speech at one of the single-gender academies, Wilson stated: "Kids need options . . . and single-gender academies will stimulate competition and give kids opportunities they currently do not have because they are trapped in their schools and they need another approach." Expanding school choice was the key motivation for Wilson's actions. This goal is quite different from the motivating forces (e.g., gender equity, cultural affirmation) behind the single-gender public schooling experiments that were not funded by the state grant mentioned above.

According to sources at the state level, Wilson initially presented a plan for all male academies as magnet schools for at-risk boys and all-female schools focused on math and science. His expectation was that sex separation would allow for the establishment of strong disciplinary climates for boys and more attention for girls in traditionally male-favored subjects. His initial plan for the single-gender academies raised concerns among legal advisors and feminists alike. Wilson's attorneys pointed out that attending to perceived gender differences could violate constitutional law, specifically Title IX. Feminist groups who had long fought for integration and equality saw the separation of the genders as a move toward inequality.

As a result, Wilson's initial vision for different types of academies for boys and girls was compromised in the final legislation. Although his choice plan remained, what changed was that the academies had to be identical for girls and boys. The legislation stated that although single-gender academies would "tailor to the differing needs and learning styles of boys as a group and girls as a group . . . if a particular program or curriculum is available to one gender, it shall also be available to those pupils in the other gender who would benefit from the particular program or curriculum" (Education Code Section 58520–58524). In other words, there must be "equal opportunities at both boys' and girls' academies." These equality provisions were important to ensuring equal access to this new school choice option. After all, the "primary goal" of the legislation was to "increase the diversity of California's public educational offering" (Education Code Section 58520–58524).

The legislation instructed the California Superintendent of Public Instruction to award grants on a competitive basis to "ten applicant school districts for the establishment of one single-gender academy for girls and one single-gender academy for boys, in each of those selected school districts" at the middle or high school levels under the pilot program (Education Code Section 58520–58524). In other words, a district that opened a school for one gender must open a second school for the other. Moreover, both schools had to provide equivalent funding, facilities, staff, books, equipment, curriculum, and extracurricular activities, including sports. Finally, although a single-gender school could be located on the campus of another school, it had to be a complete school, not just a single-gender class or program. These legal guidelines reflected an effort to stem legal challenges against single-gender public schools.

The push for equal opportunity was apparent in the allocation of funds. California's law allowed the school districts to receive $500,000 to operate single-gender academies at the middle- or high-school levels. The grant was to be divided equally between a district's boys' and girls' academies. The funding was intended as a development grant to schools; they would be able to use the money as they wished, but the expectation was that after two years they would fully fund themselves through average daily attendance (ADA) money. The single-gender academies would operate magnet schools pursuant to the California Education Code. The legislation gave the responsibility of oversight of the single-gender academies to the State Department of Education. Management of the program was assigned to the office of educational options. No extra funding was provided by the legislation for the administration of these new schools.

Two experienced staff members at the California Department of Education were charged with writing the Request for Proposals (RFP) based on the legislation and, subsequently, reviewing the proposals that were submitted. Initially, twenty-four districts expressed interest in proposing single-gender academies. Disappointingly, according to one State Department of Education official, there were only eight school districts that submitted proposals for funding. The grant opportunity was apparently not well marketed. The timing of the grant application posed a problem for some potential applicants, because there were only two months between the release of the RFP and the proposal deadline. A state official said that administrators in some districts were also concerned about the legalities of single-gender public schooling, despite assurances from attorneys that the legislation met the standards of Title IX. Of those eight that submitted proposals, one district's proposal was rejected because their design was not appropriate, and a second district pulled out of the review process because of legal concerns. In the end, only six districts in California were funded to start single-gender academies. These districts were not particularly unusual in any way and represented a broad range in terms of demographics, district size, location, and prior success at obtaining grant funding.

For most district and school administrators, single-gender schooling was a vehicle for meeting at-risk students' needs and not an end in itself. Instead of seeing the single-gender academies as primarily an opportunity to address gender inequities for girls or boys (as one might predict), most educators saw the $500,000 state grant as a way to help address the more pressing educational and social problems of low-achieving students. With the grant funding, educators developed social and academic support structures to address the needs of their particular student populations, such as low achievement, truancy, poverty, violence, or geographic isolation. To be sure, all of the educators sought to decrease distractions among boys and girls and many sought to improve students' self-esteem (Datnow, Hubbard, and Conchas, 2001).

Most of the single-gender academies were, by design, not open to all students. The California single-gender academies pilot program was constructed largely as a vehicle for expanding public school choice. However, who attended was largely a matter that was determined by design and target population of each district's single-gender academies. In at least four of the six districts, "at-risk" students of color were recruited to join the single-gender academies. White, average, or high-achieving students were more likely to choose freely to attend. In some districts, the academies operated under capacity owing to insufficient public interest or to difficulties in marketing the single-gender academy option (Datnow, Hubbard, and Woody, 2001).

For most parents, California's single-gender academies were seen as an opportunity for their children to benefit from special resources and reduce distractions from the opposite sex. Parents were attracted by the extra computers, field trips, small class sizes, and special opportunities offered in many of the academies, and the hope that distractions among boys and girls would be decreased. Parents rarely mentioned that they chose to attend the single-gender academies because of their interest in empowerment for their young boys and girls, except for some parents of white girls in a suburban district (Datnow, Hubbard, and Woody, 2001).

The success of California's pilot program was undermined from the beginning by implementation challenges related to the timing of the legislation. Educators were hampered by short timelines to propose and begin operation of the academies. They had very little time to think about and plan for the single-gender academies, engage the support of constituencies, recruit qualified teachers, and advertise the new schooling option for students. These difficulties were compounded by an absence of legislated funding for state-level support and monitoring of the academies' progress. Once the academies were operational, they continued to suffer from implementation difficulties including staff and leadership turnover, a lack of political support, and funding problems. In the sections that follow, we discuss the sustainability of these single-gender academies, demonstrating the interplay of structure, culture, and agency as we foreground each particular factor. We begin by examining the cultural lens.

CULTURAL NORMS: THE INFLUENCE OF IDEOLOGIES AND THEORIES OF SINGLE-GENDER EDUCATION ON SUSTAINABILITY

The establishment of the single-gender schools in this study marked a significant shift in the organization of schooling within the public school sector. Unquestionably, it required that students, parents, and educators examine their own ideological notions of gender. It forced people to reconcile their beliefs about whether boys and girls should be educated differently or the same and whether this education should take place in separate settings. As teachers planned curriculum, they were forced to revisit their own thinking about whether gender differences evolve from biological or social constructions of gender and what that would mean to their pedagogy. Ideological support that weighs heavily on the side of gendered behavior as mostly the result of innate characteristics assumes a static and predetermined notion of gender. For educators this often means that gendered traits are viewed as immutable and that classroom practices must be designed to accommodate them. Conversely, seeing gendered traits as socially constructed, malleable, and changeable might lead to teaching practices that breakdown stereotypical notions of gender and result in gender empowerment, for both genders. No doubt, ideologies stem from experiences in a society that socializes individuals to learn appropriate gender roles early on (Thorne, 1993; Weitzman, 1975), and one in which men occupy positions of higher status and women face constraints because of their gender, in the school and workplace (Acker, 1996; Biklen, 1995; Datnow, 1998; Hubbard and Datnow, 2000). Yet, beliefs about gender are typically conflicting, both across the population and even within an individual. Ideologies about gender clearly shaped educators' views of single-gender education and ultimately the events that followed.

The sustainability of the single-gender schools was undermined by some teachers and district administrators who lacked a clear theory for, and commitment to, single-gender schooling. Although commitment to single-gender education among the original school founders was somewhat shaky to begin with, as many were attracted by the grant resources first and foremost, it was clear the founders wanted the schools to survive. This commitment, however, was generally absent among new administrators, who replaced many of the founders of the schools. Frequent administrator turnover—the result of actions taken by administrators with new belief systems created a culture that did not support the single-gender reform. These newcomers questioned the theoretical foundations behind the single-gender arrangement. Without the time to create a theory and a commitment to single-gender education, they pondered the very reasons for the academies.

Three of the six schools experienced turnover in the principalship during the two-year or three-year operation of the single-gender academies. The Evergreen academies had three principals in three years, and only interim superintendents at the district level during that same time. Palm had a remarkable turnover of six principals in three years. By all accounts, the new administration at Palm could not wait to close the school, disperse the resources to other schools, and assume new administrative positions in schools that were run in a more traditional way. These administrators lacked a commitment to single-gender schooling. As one administrator quipped, "There are bigger fish to fry."

Changes in administration created difficulties for all of the schools, even in those where there was not a principal change. In two of the three schools that had stable principal leadership, the directorship of the single-gender academies changed after the first year of operation. In both cases, the leadership of the academies changed from young white males with some administrative experience, credibility, and a rapport with the staff, to African-American women who were new to the schools and who had not formerly held administrative posts. One district administrator admitted that the new school administrators (as well as himself) were not very committed ideologically to single-gender and supported a return to coeducation:

> Single gender, in and of [itself] . . . from that standpoint, it doesn't fit into my vision. The site fits into my vision of creating magnet schools that are built upon the interest, the orientation and the ability of students. I would like to be able to have sites that appeal to kids based upon "this is what I'm good at, this is what I'm interested in." Great, we have a place for you to go. So from that standpoint it doesn't. From the standpoint of having segregated classes, that doesn't fit into my vision at this point in time.

The "vision" or belief system of these administrators threatened the survival of the single-gender academies. This point became very clear when one teacher explained the turnaround in the culture of the school after their former principal, described as the charismatic leader who had advocated and started the school, left to take another position. When she left, so too did her vision. "If you don't have the same person with the same passion, they don't have the same interest . . . and that's a problem for all of educators, they're not driven by research, they're driven by personalities, by interests." Educators at the site suggested that there was a "paradigm shift" after the principal was replaced. As a result, there was no loyalty, rationale, or understanding as to why the single-gender arrangement was better than any other educational strategy.

The single-gender schools were also plagued by teacher turnover (an agency problem that shows the way in which cultural beliefs are deeply connected to individuals' behaviors), which put the theory or ideological support of the academies on shaky ground. Most of the academies were designed to address a population of students, which in most cases had severe academic and social problems. Attracting and retaining high quality staff was extremely difficult. The reform suffered from an inability to create strong teacher buy-in and an internal collective capacity by which to support the reform. Granted there were a few teachers who saw the single-gender academies as a unique opportunity to address students' needs in a new way. This was particularly true for some of the teachers who had girls-only classes. However, many teachers were concerned about the discipline problems that would arise in all-boys classes, particularly given the "troublesome" male students that many of the schools targeted. (See chapter 16 in this volume for a more comprehensive examination of this issue.)

In some schools, administrators found it difficult to attract veteran teachers to the academies because teachers were scared that accepting a position that was funded by a temporary grant might result in unemployment when the money ran out. The assistant principal at one school explained that experienced teachers often said, "I've been here for twenty-five years. I've seen the funding come in; I've seen it go out. If I go out there on a limb, cut off my knee, what am I going to be doing? I don't think so." In order to be in compliance with the legislation and local teachers' union regulations, teachers could not simply be assigned to teach in the single-gender academies.

Even when schools were fortunate to find well-qualified teachers, they typically did not stay long, often citing personal problems as the reason for leaving. The truth was that in numerous schools, the students, particularly the boys, were challenging to teach. The number of original teachers remaining in the single-gender academies was disappointingly low, as illustrated in Table 7.2.

Teacher turnover created dire consequences for students whose lives were already troubled by instability and it added to students' feelings of confusion and anomie. In some cases, students complained that they never knew who their teacher would be because they frequently had substitutes. Even when they had permanent teachers, they were often new, inexperienced, and frequently unknowledgeable about working with at-risk youth.

TABLE 7.2

SINGLE-GENDER ACADEMIES TEACHER TURNOVER

District	Number of Original Teachers	Number of Original Teachers Remaining by 2nd or 3rd Year of Operation
Palm	5	1
Evergreen	5	3
Cactus	4	1
Birch	7	2
Pine	8	1
Oak	6	2

Several schools placed inexperienced Teach for America candidates who lacked teaching credentials as teachers in the academies. These teachers were not given a choice, and although clearly committed and academically qualified individuals, they often lacked the teaching experience and training to deal effectively with some students. In the absence of expert teachers, some students struggled academically. At one school, administrators sought district approval to offer higher salaries to attract better teachers, but doing so financially impacted their districts and resulted in resentment and disapproval from other schools. Establishing and maintaining a high-quality education for students was a major challenge for these single-gender public schools, and teacher turnover threatened their sustainability. Without a stable teaching staff, schools did not build a culture that sustained an ideological commitment to single-gender public schools.

When we contrast the culture of single-gender public schools with private single-sex schools, we find that private schools often have a mission and purpose that is readily identifiable, unlike their public school counterparts, which commonly do not have a sense of shared mission, purpose, and history (Persell and Cookson, 1985). When educators, parents, and students *do* have a strong theory about the purpose of single-gender education, when the culture of a school and a district support it, single-gender schools are more likely to survive. We did find, however, what we believe was a strong theory guiding education at one all-girls public high school in the eastern United States. This school was founded in the mid-1800s and for over one hundred years has maintained its single-sex status as an all-girls school, as well as its reputation as an excellent public school in an urban district. The school's enormous pride in its traditions continues to shape everyday practices at the school. The school's strong alumni include the principal and many teachers and parents at the school, all of whom help to preserve the mission of single-gender education. As the principal explained, "The tradition, the history, the fact that it has been established for such a long period of time . . . and I would venture to say that if there was a campaign to [become coed] there would be a public outcry against it."

At the same time, she recognized the tenuous existence of single-sex education within the public school system, "While we are advocating that we are unique, at the same time we know that we have to keep a very low profile because we don't want to draw a lot of attention to ourselves." Most students chose the school for its reputation of academic excellence, although several students were encouraged by their mothers, aunts, and grandmothers who had attended the school in the past and valued the opportunity for single-gender education. Irrespective of administrative or teacher turnover and a changing student population, this school's vision is passed onto succeeding generations by all those who attend and by an active alumni group in the community.

Unlike the school described above, the schools in this study were mostly without a strong ideological commitment to single-gender education. There was one important exception to the lack of sustainability among the public single-gender schools in this study that makes the importance of district support and having a theory for implementing single-gender schooling abundantly clear. The Pine Single-Gender Academies continue to operate today in the wake of the closure of the five other schools. Their success can be attributed in large measure to the strong support of Pine's superintendent who was behind the concept of single-gender schools before the California grant was even issued. She had a philosophical belief that this schooling arrangement was important for the students in her district, particularly the boys. She said, "We want boys particularly to know how to be boys. Some of them in this community were having difficulty with that because they were around women a lot; they have no men in the house." She thought that the boys would be better served in an all-male environment taught by male teachers: "They can talk male talk to them. They don't talk like we would talk to them."

Governor Wilson's legislation for the single-gender schools was actually inspired by the efforts of the Pine administrator who paved the way for such schools. He called the superintendent "a distinguished educator," who "helped troubled boys in grades six through eight learn good study habits and the value of discipline." District support in Pine not only helped to inspire the legislation, but also was responsible for sustaining their single-gender schools after the grant funding ended. The superintendent used the single-gender schools as a place to educate most of the district's middle school students who had behavioral or academic problems. This relieved the rest of the schools in the district from the challenges that accompany such students and justified a larger than normal monetary investment in the single-gender academies. Although Pine students benefit from having a district that supports low student-to-teacher ratios, the director admitted that even this generous support is not enough to respond to all of the students' needs. She said they need additional staff on the campus "to really manage the discipline and the safety issues and that's the part that [the Director is] challenged with." Pine continues to struggle for money.

The success of Pine single-gender academy and the high school described in the preceding, as well as the closure of the other five state-funded single-gender schools, emphasize the importance of having a culture supportive of single-gender public schools. Educators must be ideologically in synch and committed to the goals of single-gender schooling. Without such a supporting belief system, we find the problem of high teacher and administrative turnover, which often results in a cultural logic that is absent of a theory that supports the reform. It is in this context that reculturing becomes essential for sustainability. In the next section, we consider the structural constraints that influenced the sustainability of the single-gender public schools in California.

STRUCTURAL CONSTRAINTS: POWER, POLITICS AND RESOURCES

Actions at the state level shaped events that led to the adoption and implementation of the single-gender schools and it played a role in their closure. The state's impact was unequivocally about funding, but it was also from the beginning very much about power and politics. As Blackmore explains, "The state is not a thing, system, or subject, but a significantly unbounded terrain of powers and techniques, an ensemble of discourses, rules, and practices, cohabiting in limited, tension-ridden, often in contradictory relation with each other" (1999, p. 34). According to those who helped write the initial single-gender academies' Request for Proposals (RFP), there was a major flaw in the drafting of the document, which led to some confusion among administrators as to how long the schools would be funded. The state had assumed that schools would institutionalize the program the first year, and then would pay for it in the second year out of their own money using average daily attendance (ADA) funding. School administrators clearly expected the arrangement to be different. In fact, administrators had been told that the two million dollars left over (because only six districts were funded rather than ten) would be divided among them in the second year to support the upkeep of their programs. Faced with no more money, some administrators argued their case in front of the legislature, but the legislature would not grant this additional funding as it was intended for start-up costs.

Additionally, support for single-gender schooling at the state level was always questionable. One state official explained that events were clearly political:

> The Democrats as a caucus opposed it. They'd only bought off on it in '96 because they weren't going to hold up a budget over five million dollars for that. They gave

the governor his little piece. There had never been a legislative hearing on the validity of the program and had it gone through as a straight policy issue.

Whether state politicians were actually worried over best educational practice, equity for all students, and/or responded in a partisan way, single-gender schooling did not have state support. One district superintendent explained:

> The Senate did it [cut the funding] on the basis of an AAUW report that had been printed in the *Sacramento Bee* the day before. And it was a pretty innocuous report. It frankly wasn't opposing gender academies. It was bland, but they used that as the vehicle to cut it out. And I believe the Senate cut it out purely on the basis that it was a governor, a Republican governor's proposal, and that the Democratic senate was not going to let that survive at all because they believed that they were going to win the next governorship, as a Democrat. And they were right. . . . So I considered it to be nothing more than a political partisan cut. That was it.

At the initiation of the single-gender academies experiment, educators and politicians used research to support their position on single-gender schooling. They specifically pointed to *How Schools Shortchange Girls* (AAUW, 1992), a report that suggested that girls are disadvantaged in coeducational settings. Their support occurred despite the fact that there was a conflicting body of evidence surrounding single-gender schooling. Later, when the political climate changed and Wilson was on his way out of office, the legislature complained that they were not interested in continuing the program because "there was no information that showed that it worked," explained a state policymaker. As the superintendent described, they pointed to the newer AAUW (1998a) report, *Separated by Sex*, which they interpreted as providing negative evidence against single-gender schools. According to a state policymaker, those opposed to the academies argued that "there should be more substance behind the program before you start throwing money out to little special things without having any inkling as to whether or not this is a good thing."

Given the power and political actions at the state and district level and without a clear commitment and understanding of single-gender education, schools found themselves without the resources to survive. When funds were not awarded the second year, the situation deteriorated significantly for students. As we explained, the founding of these schools was profoundly impacted by the money. All of the schools in this study were in California, a state where the per-pupil funding level is among the lowest in the United States. Because resources are scarce in public education, educators often behave opportunistically. The educators who applied for the single-gender schooling grant saw it as a way of addressing the needs of students in their district. To accomplish this goal often meant that expenditures went beyond the financial interests and/or willingness of public school district administrators.

The initial state funding gave the schools the capacity to open, but sustaining high-quality programs demanded continuous funding. The state hoped that the schools would use the funding for staff development, materials, and other costs of starting a new program, rather than to pay staff salaries. However, many of the schools used funding for salaries as well. This created a serious dilemma when the state funding ran out. Likewise, low student-to-teacher ratios were costly for districts to sustain without grant funding. The separation of students by gender also demanded space and facilities that were often scarce. Resources such as computers that were purchased with grant funding demanded upkeep, yet the schools lacked the money to pay for their maintenance. The expensive Sylvan reading program operating in one school and providing remedial help to students needing to raise depressed reading scores had to be cut because there were insufficient district dollars to continue.

In this public school climate where everyone was vying for their fair share of limited funds, single-gender schools also lacked support from other educators in their districts who resented what they perceived to be preferential treatment. Non–single-gender school educators often put pressure on district superintendents to reconcile their complaints or justify the continuation of the academies whose existence had not been institutionalized in district plans. One single-gender teacher commented that people in his district thought, "We were spoiled, that we were feeding at the public trough." Although it was pointed out that the technology and other resources at the school were purchased with grant funds, some upset teachers wanted to close the school and redistribute the technology to the "more impoverished institutions," namely, their schools. School boards also demanded that district superintendents justify decisions to continue funding the schools once the grant ended. One superintendent said that his school board was insistent that the single-gender academies not "create a drain on the general fund. That it would be as self-supporting as everything else is or you can't do it. They didn't want it to be another special education drain." In sum, the economic circumstances were in large part informed by power and politics at the state level and are of particular importance to understanding the structural constraints to the sustainability of these single-gender public schools in California.

LEGALITIES INJECT A SPECIAL KIND OF STRUCTURAL CONSTRAINT

The single-gender academies legislation offered a very specific kind of structural opportunity and constraint. The sustainability of the public single-gender academies was threatened by the prospect of Title IX complaints against single-sex public education. Feeling somewhat protected under the grant, administrators began worrying when they no longer had the state defending the existence of their schools. Districts became scared, when the safety umbrella of the legislation ended. As we explained, single-gender schools throughout the country were being challenged on grounds that they were violating Title IX. The California single-gender schools were afraid they would experience similar attacks. Administrators were concerned they were "getting into an area that is a little bit cloudy from a legal perspective" and were reticent to support continued implementation.

Although the schools made every effort to maintain equal funding, resources, and opportunities for boys and girls, there were some real practical constraints that undermined their efforts and left them vulnerable to legal action. As we explained, maintaining equal enrollments of boys and girls demanded by the state of the single-gender schools caused serious concern for all the administrators in this study. In some cases, administrators suggested that they might be interested in continuing one of the academies (boys or girls, whichever seemed to be "working" in a particular context), but they believed that offering single-sex education for only one gender was not constitutionally defensible.

It seems that one solution to avoiding legal challenges was by maintaining a low profile, as we described with the all-girls public high school in the eastern United States. Similarly, a California high school (non–grant-funded) that offers single-gender classes to boys and girls in its special education program has also attempted to keep their program under wraps. By not calling attention to themselves or their agenda, they have not been threatened by closure from district administrators who are genuinely concerned about legal issues. They have been able to operate without attention in part by the fact that they are nestled in among a coeducational setting. They are less obvious than whole schools that are designated as single gender, especially those that are recognized to be receiving special state funds. By keeping the single-gender arrangement quiet, the school has been able to continue to serve their students in a way they feel is advantageous. The special education teachers had strong beliefs that the single-gender classes provided safer, less distracting environments for students in which they could develop maturity and academic and social skills. They worry, however, that over time the district may put an end to their efforts for fear of legal challenges.

These legal concerns notwithstanding, the single-gender schools in this study struggled to survive under circumstances that in many ways are symptomatic of the public educational system in general. Their very existence was the result of political actions at the state and district level. They, like their coeducational school counterparts faced the challenge of educating an at-risk diverse population of students without the resources or commitment from those who could support it. Power and politics dictated the course of events that followed. As long as the experiment brought money into the districts, they thrived, but without it, they faced competing agendas and demands for accountability. In the next section, we analyze how the agency of particular individuals or groups of individuals in districts, schools, and communities also shaped the sustainability of the single-gender public schools.

THE AGENCY OF INDIVIDUALS IN DISTRICTS, SCHOOLS, AND COMMUNITIES

We define *agency* as the capacity to change the existing state of affairs—a capacity that all people have regardless of how they choose to exercise it. The agency of individuals in schools and school districts can take various forms: Some people push or sustain reform efforts, whereas others resist or actively subvert these efforts. Additionally, agency may be passive or active. Therefore, we look carefully at the actions and inactions of individuals in shaping the sustainability of the single-gender schools and assess how some agents have more power than others in determining the shape of things to come. We first look to the agency of district superintendents.

District superintendents, faced with economic constraints of their own and state demands for accountability, took actions that thwarted parents' and students' attempts to keep the schools open. As implied in the preceding examples, district support was key to the survival of the single-gender academies; however, except for the Pine academies, once the grant ended, superintendents did not rally behind the schools. Some superintendents insisted that the schools were ending because there simply was not enough money to continue, but many teachers and parents disagreed with that assessment.

In Evergreen, parents blamed the closure of the schools on the superintendent's lack of commitment to the district in general and the single-gender schools in particular. They described their superintendent as an "outsider" and "someone who throws his title around." The superintendent described the community as "not an enlightened spot" and "very provincial." Clearly there was a lack of mutual respect. The parents saw the superintendent as someone who did not have the interests of their community or their children in mind because he did not support the academies. The superintendent saw the community as in need of his expertise. His support seemed contingent on the extent of districtwide imperatives and not the desires of Evergreen parents. He admitted that his concerns were centered on the district as a whole, not the single-gender schools because the district was "not healthy." Financially, the district was still trying to recover from the costs of building a school torn down because of faulty construction. They had been without a permanent superintendent for over two years and lack of leadership had confounded difficulties across the school system. Test scores were low and students were not meeting standards. In a climate that increasingly privileges accountability as measured by high test scores, this superintendent along with the many others in our study felt pressured to strategize allocation of time and resources.

Educators in the other schools also worried about losing Average Daily Attendance (ADA) funds. Because several of the schools educated a highly truant population of students, low attendance translated into less ADA. It was a formidable task to keep students coming to school. They were also continually challenged in their attempts to enroll new students because parents were concerned about sending their children to school with an identifiable high-risk population of students. Educators in one district claimed that low ADA accounted for the closing of their academies. One district administrator lamented over the inherent financial problem caused by low female attendance in the academies:

> That site has never had the number of girls that they hoped to have. And because of those issues, there's a financial problem, and so the grant has allowed that to work, but when the grant runs out we'll have to . . . look very carefully at whether we can continue to run things under the current format. The data that I have indicates that we can't.

With competing district demands, most superintendents were reticent to offer their support for the single-gender academies and took actions that forced their closure.

Cultural interpretations regarding notions of gender and education in chorus with the power, political, economic, and legal constraints at the state and district levels created varying responses by agents in the single-gender academies. Sometimes it was their actions, but often it was their inactions that most profoundly influenced the sustainability of the schools. Although commitment to reforms related to gender is generally not strong in the public sector (Marshall, 1997), we found pockets of support for the single-gender education from educators, parents, and students. These supporters, however, were ineffectual in retaining their schools because they were forced to challenge the power brokers at the district level. Teachers at the school felt impotent, despite their strong advocacy to keep the schools open. In our final visit to Palm one week before the single-gender school doors were closed, teachers expressed being scared, angry, and sad. One teacher was clearly distraught at the events that led to the final closing of the schools: "I mean it's just been very bad. Like a shipwreck. . . . You don't know what's going to happen with the school . . . and with yourself as well."

Students were very upset. One Palm student told us that she used to hate coming to school until she attended the single-gender academy. She cried as she tried to make sense as to why the administration was doing this to her. Girls at Cactus and boys and girls at Birch wrote letters of protest to district administrators and state legislators when they were told the academies would close. Without exception, students' perspectives were not given voice.

Some parents were outraged too when the decision was made to close their academies, but they felt their voices were silenced. In an interview with a focus group of Evergreen parents, one parent claimed, "It didn't matter what we thought." Similarly, Cactus parents felt they had no voice in the decision. Although they claimed strong support for continuing the girls' academy, they admitted they lacked power. The district superintendent disagreed. He pointed to a low rate of return on a survey that was disseminated to parents to determine interest in returning to the single-gender schools. He cited low attendance by parents at a board meeting that was held to decide the fate of the school. Parents claimed they never really had an opportunity to speak their mind because decisions had already been made to close the schools. District gestures were seen as merely symbolic. The Cactus principal explained that in the face of other competing demands in public education (e.g., literacy, high-stakes accountability), this gender-based reform was simply not a priority for policymakers and administrators, and thus there was little motivation on the part of the district to continue.

The lack of attentiveness to parents' wishes is striking as we compare it to events at a public single-gender middle school in California that was started without the benefit of the state grant. Here, we found that parents had more power and were actually pointed to as the reason for the adoption of a single-gender arrangement. When we visited this school, it was in its second year of implementation and showed no signs of closing. In contrast, the fate of the public single-gender schools founded under the state legislation were at the hands of both state and district officials who were reportedly not responsive to the demands of local parents, and instead acted according to their own political imperatives.

CONCLUSION

It is in the interaction of cultural and structural factors and the agency or actions of the participants involved in the reform that the life of the single-gender public schools can best be understood. First and foremost, it appears that the schools suffered from a lack of support for single-gender schooling. Advocacy for single-gender schooling is particularly difficult in the public sector given that issues of gender are seldom given the level of importance awarded to other district concerns. Clearly, the cultural norms around gender inhibited efforts at sustainability. Some saw no reason for single-gender education and others were diametrically opposed. These newly formed schools suffered from a lack of ideological commitment on the part of many educators, administrators, and policymakers because many of them had joined the schools after its initiation. With an unsupportive culture in which to embed a passion and vision for single-gender public education and given the needs of the students who attended them, support waned among educators.

We found, however, that cultural considerations alone were insufficient to explain the challenges that the single-gender academies faced as they struggled to survive in public education. By looking outside the school at the district and state levels, we found that these schools were plagued by a scarcity of resources, the power and politics of state and local government, and worries over Title IX legal threats. As cultural factors interacted with structural constraints, some parents and students took action only to be trumped by district and state officials who were willing and in many cases anxious to take the necessary actions to close the schools. This gender-based reform, and gender issues more generally, were simply not high priorities for district officials who held decision-making power.

Our findings have led us to make the following policy recommendations regarding single-gender education in the public sector. First, experiments with single-gender public schooling need to be driven by a strong theory of single-gender education. In order to face the challenges that occur at the school, district, and state level, educators need to have a strong sense of why they are doing single-sex schooling, both for girls and boys. We add that the theory for single-gender schooling should be driven by an agenda of gender equity for girls and boys.

Second, leadership stability at the school or district level is important for successful experiments with single-gender public education. District administrations impact the pace, quality, and form of school reform through their stability or instability of leadership (Bodilly, 1998; Desimone, 2000). Reform efforts become very unstable when there is leadership and teacher turnover (Hargreaves and Fink, 2000). The result is that the reform is left without a culture to support it.

Third, innovations that have an inauthentic beginning almost surely will not be sustained. It is understandable that educators will act in entrepreneurial ways in response to funding opportunities connected to school reform because we know that resources are essential to initiating and sustaining reform (Fullan, 1991). Nevertheless, it is important that the goals of the actual reform effort match their intended purposes; otherwise, reform failure is more likely.

Finally, policies for single-gender public schooling need to be more carefully crafted. The policy for single-gender public schooling in California could have better enabled the successful implementation of single-gender public education through expanding the time in which educators' had to prepare applications and hire ideologically committed and qualified staff. At the state level, provisions should have been made for instructional and curriculum development, and for directing educators toward gender-equitable practices. Without the proper infrastructure of support, educational innovations risk termination before they have the time to flourish.

ACKNOWLEDGMENTS

The research described in this chapter was supported by grants from the Spencer Foundation and Ford Foundation. However, any opinions expressed are the authors' own and do not represent the policies or positions of the funders. We wish to thank the participants of our study who kindly invited us into their schools, districts, and state offices and who were very generous with their time. We are also greatly appreciative of Betsey Woody, Gilberto Conchas, Barbara McHugh, and Jennifer Madigan for their research assistance. Our sincere thanks to our advisory board members Patricia Gandara, Peter Hall, Pedro Noguera, and Amy Stuart Wells for their insights throughout the study. An earlier version of this chapter was presented at the annual meeting of the American Educational Research Association, April 13, 2001, Seattle.

NOTE

1. We initially planned to also evaluate student achievement outcomes over the three-year period of our study. However, because most of the sites closed in the first two years, this data collection effort turned out not to yield meaningful results.

REFERENCES

Acker, S. (1996). "Gender and Teachers' Work." In M. Apple, (ed.), *Review of Research in Education*. Washington, D.C.: AERA.

American Association of University Women. (1992). *How Schools Shortchange Girls*. Washington, D.C.: Author.

——. (1998). *Separated by Sex: A Critical Look at Single-Sex Education for Girls*. Washington, D.C.: Author.

Anderson, S.E., and Stiegelbauer, S. (1994) "Institutionalization and Renewal in a Restructured Secondary School." *School Organisation* 14: 279–293.

Berman, P., and McLaughlin, M. W. (1978). *Federal Programs Supporting Educational Change*, vol. VIII. Santa Monica: Rand.

Biklen, S. K. (1995). *School Work: Gender and the Cultural Construction of Teaching*. New York: Teachers College Press.

Blackmore, J. (1999). *Troubling Women: Feminism, Leadership and Educational Change*. Buckingham, UK: Open University Press.

Bodilly, S. (1998). *Lessons from New American Schools' Scale Up Phase*. Santa Monica, CA: RAND.

Cuban, L. (1986). *Teachers and Machines: The Classroom Use of Technology since 1920*. New York: Columbia Teachers College Press.

Cuban, L. (1992). "What Happens to Reforms that Last? The Case of the Junior High School." *American Educational Research Journal* 29(2): 227–251.

——. (1998). "How Schools Change Reforms: Redefining Reform Success and Failure." *Teachers College Record* 99(3): 153–177.

Curry, B. K. (1991). "Institutionalization: The Final Phase of the Organizational Change Process." *Administrator's Notebook* 35(1).

Datnow, A. (1998). *The Gender Politics of Educational Change*. London: Falmer Press.

——. (2001). "The Sustainability of Externally Developed Reforms in Changing District and State Contexts." Paper presented at the annual meeting of the American Educational Research Association, Seattle, WA.

Datnow, A., Hubbard, L., and Conchas, G. (2001). "How Context Mediates Policy: The Implementation of Single Gender Public Schooling in California." *Teachers College Record* 103(2): 184–206.

Datnow, A., Hubbard, L., and Mehan, H. (2002). *Extending Educational Reform: From One School to Many*. London: Routledge Falmer Press.

Datnow, A., Hubbard, L., and Woody, E. (2001). Is *Single-Gender Schooling Viable in the Public Sector? Lessons from California's Pilot Program*. Toronto: Ontario Institute for Studies in Education.

Desimone, L. (2000). *Making Comprehensive School Reform Work*. New York: ERIC Clearinghouse on Urban Education.

Fullan, M. G. (1991). *The New Meaning of Educational Change*. New York: Teachers College Press.

———. (2001). Invitational Address. San Diego City Schools Institute for Learning K–12 Principals Meeting. January 29.

Hargreaves, A. (1994). *Changing Teachers, Changing Times*. New York: Teachers College Press.

Hargreaves, A., and Fink, D. (2000). "Three Dimensions of Educational Reform." *Educational Leadership* 57(7): 30–34.

Hubbard, L. and Datnow, A. (2000). " A Gendered Look at Educational Reform." *Gender and Education* 12(1): 115–130.

Hubbard, L., and Mehan, H. (1999). "Scaling Up an Untracking Program: A Co-constructed Process." *Journal of Education for Students Placed at Risk* 4(1), 83–100.

Hutchison, K. B. (1999, October 6). Senate floor speech on single-sex classrooms amendment. Proceedings and debates of the 106th congress, first session. *http://www.senate.gov/hutchison/speech11.htm*

Kirst, M., and Meister, G. (1985). "Turbulence in American Secondary Schools. What Reforms Last?" *Curriculum Inquiry 15:* 169–186.

Lusi, S. (1997). *The Role of State Departments of Education in Complex School Reform*. New York: Teachers College Press.

Mael, F. (1998). "Single Sex and Coeducational Schooling: Relationships to Socioemotional and Academic Development." *Review of Educational Research* 68: 101–129.

Marshall, C. (1997). *Feminist Critical Policy Analysis: A Perspective from Primary and Secondary Schooling*. London: Falmer.

Moffet, C. A. (2000). "Sustaining Change: The Answers are Blowing in the Wind." *Educational Leadership* 57(7): 35–38.

Persell, C., and Cookson, P. (1985). *Preparing for Power: America's Elite Boarding Schools*. New York: Basic Books.

Pollard, D. S. (1998). "The Contexts of Single Sex Classes." In *Separated by Sex: A Critical Look at single-sex Education for Girls*. Washington, D.C.: AAUW.

Richards, C. (2000, November 15). "Public funds for experimental single-sex ed?" *Women's News. http://www.womensenews.org/article.cfm?aid=160&context=archive*

RPP International (1998). "A National Study of Charter Schools: Second Year Report." Washington, D.C.: U.S. Dept. of Education.

Thorne, B. (1993). *Gender Play: Girls and Boys in School*. Brunswick, NJ: Rutgers University Press.

Tyack, D., and Cuban, L. (1995). *Tinkering toward Utopia*. Cambridge, MA: Harvard University Press.

Weitzman, L. (1975). "Sex Role Socialization." In J. Freeman (Ed.). *Women: A Feminist Perspective*. Palo Alto, CA: Mayfield Publishing.

Yin, R. (1989). *Case Study Research*. Beverly Hills, CA: Sage Publications.

Yonezawa, S., and Stringfield, S. (2000). "Special Strategies for Educating Disadvantaged Students Follow-Up Study: Examining the Sustainability of Research Based School Reforms." Baltimore, MD: Johns Hopkins University CRESPAR.

Section Three

THE TRANSITION FROM SINGLE-SEX EDUCATION TO COEDUCATION

CHAPTER 8

The Transition to Coeducation at Wheaton College: Conscious Coeducation and Gender Equity in Higher Education

Alan R. Sadovnik and Susan F. Semel

In September 1988, after over 150 years as an institution of higher education for women, Wheaton College (Norton, MA) became a coeducational college. After considerable debate and the consideration of complex sociological, philosophical, demographic, and historical factors, the college believed that coeducation was the best course for its future. Given its historical commitment to the education of women, Wheaton College pursued coeducation within a framework dedicated to ensuring that its commitment to women not be lost in the transition. The implementation of coeducation at Wheaton did not simply speak to the maintenance of women's education, but rather developed a unique view of coeducation to educate both men and women to live in a society with significantly more gender equity. Through its philosophy of "conscious coeducation," or what is called "differently coeducational," Wheaton has attempted to create a coeducational institution that links its strengths as a women's college to the education of both men and women. Such an education is grounded in the view that coeducation should help young men and women create a more just world, with men and women equal partners in this quest. The difficult task in this endeavor was how Wheaton would expand its mission and not lose the historical commitment to women characteristic of women's colleges.

The purpose of this chapter is to analyze the transition to coeducation at Wheaton College. Based on archival research; in-depth interviews with faculty, administrators, and students, and (once the college was fully coeducational) participant observation and site visits over six years (1995 to 2001), the chapter examines the factors that led to Wheaton's decision to become coeducational, the ways in which the college made the transition to coeducation, and whether or not Wheaton today—thirteen years after becoming coeducational—remains committed to its philosophy of "conscious coeducation." Moreover, the chapter illustrates the importance of a conscious commitment to gender equity and an administration and faculty committed to it for ensuring that the emphasis on women's education that characterized the college in the decade prior to coeducation continued in a coeducational environment. Finally, we argue that it may be the processes associated with Wheaton's philosophy of conscious coeducation that may be more important than whether it is a single-sex or coeducational institution for ensuring a climate of gender equity.

This chapter addresses the following questions:

1. What were the historical, sociological, organizational, and demographic factors that led to the decision to become coeducational?
2. Once the decision to become coeducational was made, how did the college go about making the transition?
3. What effects did the admission of the first classes of men have on the college in the first years of coeducation and how did the college respond?
4. Has the philosophy of "consciously and differently coeducational" been implemented in curricula and pedagogical reforms?
5. Has the college's past mission as a women's college been incorporated into its new coeducational mission and does Wheaton College today remain committed to the philosophy of "conscious coeducation"?

This chapter chronicles the process by which a college has attempted to broaden its direction without losing its historical sense of mission. Sadovnik (1994) analyzed how a compensatory higher education program evolved in the context of a college's institutional history and identity. He argued that the organizational processes of higher education are central to the success or failure of a higher education reform. Semel (1992), in her study of the transformation of the Dalton School, analyzed the complex interaction between cultural, social, and organizational forces and how they affect an institution's ability to maintain its historical mission. Grant (1988) shows how a secondary school evolved in relation to racial integration. Grant and Riesman (1978), in their insightful study of reform and innovation at American colleges, underscore the important relationship between tradition, philosophy, and innovation. Finally, Lever and Schwartz's (1971) study of the transition to coeducation at Yale suggests that women faced significant dilemmas at Yale as the tradition of male domination did not die easily. Many of the processes of educational innovation and change, resistance and accommodation, and conflict and compromise that are described in the preceding studies appear to have occurred at Wheaton. It is important to explore them historically in order to better understand how and why institutions change and adapt to a number of internal and external forces, as well as their effects on students. In the case of Wheaton, how and why a college committed for 154 years to the education of women made the decision to change, and how it implemented this radical innovation is a fascinating story with profound implications for the education of both men and women.

The ways in which institutions pass on their "collective memory" is an important aspect of this study. Educational stability and change are both related to the ways in which institutions manage to pass along their traditions or erase institutional memory. Semel (1992) documents how the Dalton School radically changed once the collective memory of the Dalton Plan had been sufficiently erased; and also, how the selective use of tradition was often used to legitimate educational innovation and change. In the case of Wheaton College, it is important to examine how the institutional memory of the traditions of a women's college and the transition to coeducation are kept alive as the architects of coeducation retire and new faculty and administrators come to Wheaton. Therefore we pose the following questions: To what degree is Wheaton today a special place, with a keen awareness of its traditions as a women's college, and to what degree has it become like other coeducational institutions? Moreover, how have the Wheaton administration and faculty planned for the inculcation of a collective memory in its faculty and students?

SINGLE-SEX EDUCATION AND COEDUCATION

The advantages and disadvantages of single-sex versus coeducation have been long debated in the sociological and historical literature. Tyack and Hansot's (1991) comprehensive history of coeducation pointed out the complex political and historical factors that have affected educational policies related to the education of women. Miller-Bernal (1989, 1993, 2000, and chapter 9 of this volume) in a study comparing women's colleges to coeducational liberal arts colleges argued that although there are significant differences in the experiences of women students at women's colleges, there was little evidence to link these differences to differences in educational outcomes. Miller-Bernal's study, however, indicated the need to study differences in the education of women in a larger number of campuses. Her historical and sociological study (2000) of Wells (women's college), Middlebury (coeducational), William Smith (coordinate to Hobart), and Kirkland (coordinate to Hamilton), indicates the importance of studying the history of colleges to understand the dynamics of gender relations at the postsecondary level. Wheaton College's transition to coeducation provides an opportunity to examine the ways in which the movement to coeducation has affected the educational experiences and outcomes of both women and men students.

The history of women's colleges in the United States provides an important framework for understanding the history of Wheaton College and its eventual decision to become coeducational. Boas (1935), Faragher and Howe

(1988), Horowitz (1984), Palmieri (1987), Rosenberg (1988), and Solomon (1985) provide detailed analyses of the history of women's education in the United States and the rise, evolution, and transformation of women's colleges and women's higher education from the nineteenth century to the present, although much of the literature on women's colleges examines the nineteenth and early twentieth centuries. Some of the early women's colleges, like Mount Holyoke, often began, as Wheaton College did in 1834, as a seminary. Others, such as the remaining Seven Sisters, were founded as women's colleges. The relationship between Puritan culture, patriarchy, and changing conceptions of the role of women in the nineteenth century is central to understanding the rise and evolution of women's colleges. Women's colleges developed, particularly in the case of the Seven Sisters (Horowitz, 1984), as the acceptable institutions to provide education to the daughters of the privileged.

Although the history of women's higher education and women's colleges in the nineteenth and early twentieth century is too expansive and complicated to explore here, it is important to see their evolution in relation to debates about women's place in society. Palmieri (1987) argues that the expansion of women's higher education must be understood within the context of expanding roles for women, as well as the ongoing debates between nineteenth century feminists (Leach, 1980) and conservatives' reactions to reformers. She divides the history of women's education into three periods: the Romantic Era (1820 to 1860) or the period Linda Kerber calls "Republican Motherhood"; the Reform Era (1860 to 1890), marked by the opening of women's colleges and the emergence of profound debates about higher education for women; and the Progressive Era (1890 to 1920), which includes both the entrance of the first generation of women college graduates into the professions, as well as the conservative reaction to women's higher education. Within this context, women's access to higher education, first in women's colleges, and later in coeducation institutions, evolved historically in relation to changing and liberalized conceptions of women's roles, as well as to conservative reactions to them.

In the twentieth century, the place of women's colleges in an increasingly coeducational system of higher education became an important issue. In 1870, 59 percent of existing colleges were for men only; by 1930, 69 percent were coeducational, with an equal number of male and female single-sex schools; since 1960, the number of women's and men's colleges has declined considerably, with the 268 women's colleges that existed in 1960 reduced to one hundred in 1990 (Riordan, 1990). With the advent of coeducation at the once all-male Ivy League colleges in the 1970s, the pressure for women's colleges to become coeducational dramatically increased. In the 1970s, many formerly women's colleges such as Vassar, Skidmore, and Connecticut College became coeducational, and in the 1980s, others such as Goucher and

Wheaton followed suit. However, since the early 1990s there has been renewed interest in women's colleges and the benefits of women's education (Riordan, 1990; Sadker and Sadker, 1994). Much of this interest comes out of a growing feminist literature on the underside of coeducation (AAUW, 1992; Brown and Gilligan, 1992; Sadker and Sadker, 1994) and the benefits of feminist curriculum and pedagogy (Maher and Tetrault, 1994). The debates about single-sex education versus coeducation for women must be understood in the context of ongoing debates about the effects of women's colleges.

The educational and attitudinal effects of single-sex and coeducational institutions at the secondary and postsecondary levels has received considerable attention over the past two decades, with little consensus about overall effects and differences. Although Tidball's research (1973, 1980, 1985, 1986) has consistently argued that graduates of women's colleges have higher achievement and career aspirations, and are more likely to attend graduate or professional schools than women graduates of coeducational institutions, critics have argued that her research has not adequately controlled for "selection bias," including the social class advantages of many females at women's colleges, as well as the selectivity of many women's colleges in admissions (Oates and Williamson, 1978, 1980). More recent studies (Rice and Hemmings, 1988), which use adequate controls, indicate that graduates of women's colleges achieve at higher rates than graduates of coeducational institutions.

Studies of differences between women who graduate from single-sex versus coeducational secondary schools in the United States and other countries indicate that there are advantages to single-sex education for women in terms of educational outcomes (Astin, 1977; Carpenter and Hayden, 1987; Finn, 1980; Lee and Bryk, 1986; Riordan, 1985, 1990) and self-esteem (Astin, 1977; Carpenter, 1985; Lee and Bryk, 1986). These studies have been summarized elsewhere in this volume. This section concentrates on postsecondary education.

Miller-Bernal (1993) reports that studies of the effects of single-sex versus coeducation on attitudes to the women's movement and school life have not been conclusive. Whereas some studies (Lee and Bryk, 1986; Trickett et al., 1982) suggested that girls in single-sex secondary schools are more supportive of feminist issues and less likely to accept traditional gender role stereotypes, other studies at the postsecondary level (Giele, 1987) found women's college students to be more traditional. Miller-Bernal (1989) did not find significant differences between women at women's colleges and coeducational colleges on measures of gender role attitudes. Her more recent study (Miller-Bernal, 1993, 2000) finds that although women at a single-sex college or a coordinate college have more positive experiences than women at two coeducational colleges in terms of having women faculty as role models, participating in college activities, and perceiving their college experiences as positive, these positive experiences did not have a significant effect on changes in attitudes and goals, except in the area of self-esteem.

The evidence on the effects of single-sex education versus coeducation for women at the postsecondary level is not conclusive. However, both Miller-Bernal (1993, 2000) and Riordan (1990) argue that there is sufficient evidence to conclude that the atmosphere for women at coeducational institutions may be "chilly." Feminist educators such as Sadker and Sadker (1994) and Maher and Tetrault (1994) argue that without a consciously feminist curriculum and pedagogy, women are more likely to be silenced in classroom interactions, experience lower self-esteem, and lower levels of aspirations and achievement. It is within this context that feminist educators have sought to learn from women's colleges about ways to educate women that enhance, not shortchange them. Since the 1970s, in addition to debates about the efficacy of women's colleges in terms of studies of the empirical effects of single-sex education on women students, a literature emerged about the extent to which women's colleges reflected feminist visions and objectives. In the 1970s, a number of disenchanted graduates of women's colleges published popular exposes, which argued that women's colleges (particularly the Seven Sisters) historically reinforced traditional gender roles, encouraged docility, and that coeducation might better serve the causes of gender equality (Baker, 1976; Kendall, 1976). In the 1980s and 1990s, historians of education (Horowitz, 1984; Palmieri, 1987), sociologists of education (Komarovsky, 1985; Miller-Bernal, 2000), and feminist educators (Maher and Tetrault, 1994; Sadker and Sadker, 1994) have provided a more balanced treatment that, in Palmieri's words, "display a new appreciation for the complexity of their subject" (1987, p. 50). These studies have acknowledged both the positive effects of single-sex education, as well as some of the negative ones pointed out by the critics.

Nonetheless, by the 1990s, there had been a renewed interest in the positive effects of single-sex education, ironically at a time when fewer and fewer women's colleges exist (Beard, 1994; Riordan, 1990). A study on the transition to coeducation at Goucher College (Canada and Pringle, 1995) reported that there have been significant changes in classroom interactions at Goucher College since the advent of coeducation in 1987, with these changes having a negative impact on women students. Wheaton College's decision to become coeducational in 1987 came precisely at a time when these debates were taking place. More importantly, Wheaton College in its transition to coeducation understood the possible negative consequences of coeducation for women. Therefore, it consciously and purposely attempted to avoid the kinds of negative effects reported about Goucher College.

Miller-Bernal (2000) concluded that declining enrollments at women's colleges such as Wells may make coeducation inevitable at all but the well-endowed women's colleges such as Wellesley, Bryn Mawr, Smith, and Mount

Holyoke. Given her reluctant and ambivalent conclusion, Miller-Bernal argues that former women's colleges must incorporate the characteristics that have made them special places for women. This is precisely what Wheaton intended to do when it became coeducational in 1988. However, to properly understand and study its transition to coeducation, one must first understand the history of Wheaton College.

WHEATON COLLEGE: 1812 TO 1975

Wheaton College was founded as Wheaton Female Seminary by Judge Laban Wheaton with the assistance of Mary Lyon in 1834, three years before she founded Mount Holyoke. In 1912, it was incorporated as Wheaton College. (See Helmreich, 1985, for a detailed history of the seminary years.) Although it is not possible to recount here its entire history, Wheaton's beginning and evolution as a women's college must be understood in the context of the overall history of the education of women in the nineteenth and twentieth centuries. In the early years, Wheaton Female Seminary was similar to the other seminaries for women founded in the mid-nineteenth century, and was part of a larger movement for women's education, initiated by reformers such as Mary Lyon, Emma Willard, Catherine Beecher, and Zilpah Grant (Boas, 1935; Rosenberg, 1988). In the nineteenth and early twentieth centuries it reflected the changes charted by Palmieri (1987) and, by the time it was incorporated as a college in 1912, because of its location between Providence and Boston and its student body, it was an important alternative to the Seven Sisters. By the early 1960s, Wheaton College, in line with the general expansion of higher education that began in the post–World War II period, doubled its enrollment to twelve hundred women (for a detailed discussion of Wheaton between 1912 and 1957, see Helmreich, 2002).

In the late 1960s and early 1970s, as the Ivy League colleges became coeducational, and as a number of women's colleges, including Vassar, Skidmore, and Connecticut College also became coeducational, Wheaton College began to consider its future as a women's college. With many women who formerly would have gone to women's colleges now electing to attend coeducational colleges, and with many now viewing women's colleges as quaint anachronisms, Wheaton began to have considerable difficulty attracting high-quality women applicants. In 1971, the Wheaton College faculty voted to consider becoming a coeducational institution; however, President William Prentice decided not to make the change at that time.

THE PRELUDE TO COEDUCATION

In 1975, Alice F. Emerson became Wheaton's first woman president and under her leadership the college moved first to strengthen its position as a women's college, and second, to become a coeducational institution. Under Emerson's leadership the college moved to become an explicitly feminist institution. Reflective of the times, Wheaton developed an explicit mission to provide women with a feminist vision of the world. Through its curriculum and the development of feminist pedagogy (Maher and Tetrault, 1994) in many classrooms, Wheaton became committed to women's education.

In 1980, as part of the influence of feminism on higher education, Wheaton began a four-year "balanced curriculum project." This curriculum innovation energized the Wheaton faculty in an institutional effort to infuse gender issues into all facets of the curriculum and campus life. Funded by a FIPSE grant (Fund for the Improvement of Post-Secondary Education), Wheaton faculty and administration made a concerted effort to change the college from a college without men to a women's college; that is, a college with an explicit mission to provide women with a feminist curriculum. For the next four years, the faculty and administration worked arduously toward the creation of a gender-balanced curriculum, the culmination of which was a conference on gender and curriculum and the publication of its proceedings (Spanier, Bloom, and Boroviak, 1984) as a model of women's education. As the college celebrated its Sesquicentennial it seemed to have defined its place as a college committed to the serious and distinctive education of women.

However, in January 1987, faced with ongoing enrollment problems and a continuing decline in the quality of its applicant pool, President Emerson announced to the faculty and students the Board of Trustees' decision to seriously consider becoming a coeducational college. She announced that the college community would explore the options in the spring 1987 semester and make a final decision by the end of the semester for implementation in fall 1988.

Although the faculty appears to have been committed to Wheaton's remaining a women's college, a declining applicant pool, in both numbers and admissions profiles, is cited most often as the precipitating cause of the decision to become coeducational. President Emerson and Board of Trustee Chair, MIT President Paul Gray, however, also stressed changes in the culture at large as a main reason. For Emerson, as feminism dramatically increased women's opportunities, some of the original reasons for separate colleges for women began to become less important. Further, as women were making significant gains in the labor market, Emerson argued that women and men had to learn to work together as equals. Therefore, what was needed was a conscious coeducational philosophy that would allow men and women in colleges to work together to create a more just and gender-balanced world. To educate men and women separately would not provide them with this opportunity. Further, to provide women with a feminist curriculum and gender-balanced environment in a women's college, would not provide men with the opportunity to become socialized toward gender equity. Thus, Emerson argued that what was needed for both men and women was a different type of coeducation.

For Emerson and the board, although they believed the college was in good financial health, demographic trends necessitated measures to strengthen the college in the coming years. As a member of the twelve College Exchange (a cooperative relationship with eleven other New England liberal arts colleges, including Williams, Amherst, Smith, Wellesley, Mount Holyoke, Trinity, Wesleyan, Vassar, Connecticut, Bowdoin, and Dartmouth), Wheaton ranked at or near the bottom on all measures of student admission profiles (SAT, class rank), as well as on measures of institutional health (endowment, library volumes, faculty salaries). Thus, according the president and board, the decision to become coeducational was justified in terms of philosophical, educational, demographic, and economic reasons.

When the board's decision to consider coeducation was announced by President Emerson in January 1987 to an all college assembly in the Chapel, the Wheaton College community reacted with shock, dismay, and, in some cases, outrage. The faculty, many of whom might have been sympathetic to coeducation, felt betrayed by the failure of the administration and board to include them in the decision-making process. Students, some of whom who had come to Wheaton primarily because it was a women's college, and others who once at the college became transformed by its feminist pedagogy and gender-balanced curriculum, reacted angrily to the decision to consider coeducation.

Once President Emerson and Board Chair Gray publicly announced the decision to alumnae through a letter, many alumnae were deeply troubled and angry. The alumnae felt that they had been misled by the Sesquicentennial fund-raising drive, which explicitly was connected to preserving Wheaton as a women's college. Most important in terms of alumnae reaction were the differences in reactions among different generations of alumnae. Although there were supporters and detractors from all groups of alumnae, it was the younger graduates, from the late 1970s through the mid-1980s, who were most vocal in their opposition. Thus, the women who were the products of Emerson's feminist vision, those who had experienced the gender-balanced curriculum and feminist pedagogy, were the ones who most vocally and viscerally attacked the decision and President Emerson. Many alumnae sent letters to President Emerson and Board Chair Gray, the majority opposing coeducation. The emotional tone and thoughtful arguments of most of the letters was a testimony to both the quality of a Wheaton education and the passion that many alumnae felt about Wheaton as a women's college. The following is but one example of such passion:

Dear President Emerson:

I have just received your letter informing me that Wheaton will be admitting men soon. It is late at night and I find myself angry and unable to sleep. . . . I don't know why I am wasting my time here for I know that once again I will be whistling in the wind.

I am a woman who spent three years in a girls' boarding school and three and a half years in a women's college. I am a much stronger person as a result of this experience. I never saw any field as off-limits to me due to my sex. My life and career choices were never defined due to my sex. I was always recognized in the classroom and on the athletic field and in the dorms as strong mentally, physically, and emotionally as anyone else there. This was not the case for women that I know who attended coed colleges.

I spent one semester in a small coed university where girls (and they were *girls*) were totally overshadowed by the presence of boys. I was astounded by the fact that they would not go to class if they had a pimple that couldn't be hidden by several layers of Revlon cosmetics. (God forbid a woman should appear flawed.) I was appalled at the fact that they actually tried to get lower grades than that of the boy on whom they had a crush. This is not the kind of woman that I can be proud of as a person.

It seems to me that there are too many places on this earth where women can be devoured and overshadowed by the male presence. My years in school were the only ones where I could concentrate on my work without having to worry about what I wore or whether I would look too aggressive in the eyes of the BMOC.

Other schools have gone coed in recent years. Soon one is never really aware that there are women on campus. The women, whose field hockey games were the big event on autumn Saturday afternoons, will become cheerleaders for the football games where admission can be charged and a profit made. The women will become the girls. The boys will become the men.

I realize that I may be speaking for a small portion of humanity here. Perhaps most high school girls are now graduating with the courage and conviction that an all female college gave me. However, there still is a group . . . that needs a place like Wheaton desperately. I hate to see this group stranded. I would hate to see a woman with potential be engulfed by a male atmosphere that won't give her a chance because she doesn't fit the stereotype fed to us by Madison Avenue.

It is also my conviction that if an organism has outlived its original purpose, at which it excelled, than perhaps extinction is preferable to homogenization. Wheaton is an excellent all-female institution. If it joins the coed trend, at best it will become another mediocre small college, serving neither male nor female well.

You are the last of a dying breed. If at all possible, give women a chance to enter the world as strong individuals who see the world as their own place, a place where choices are limitless, options are open, and where they create the shadow, not stand in it.

My time at Wheaton meant a great deal to me or why else would I bother to write? If the school had not done such a good job in educating and strengthening me, you would not have to read this letter. This is a compliment. Take it as such. If you persist in this decision to admit men, it will be one of the last compliments you receive from me as well as the last letter. I will have nothing in common with you and therefore will be relieved of caring.

I would find that most unfortunate.

Although President Emerson announced in January that the board was only considering the move and no final decision would be made until June 1987, after a series of hearings with faculty, staff, students, and alumnae, many in the Wheaton community felt that it was a *fait accompli*. Nonetheless, until and after June, when the board announced its decision to admit the first coeducational class in September 1988, many students and alumnae organized to prevent coeducation. Faculty, although still angry about the process resulting in the decision, nonetheless committed themselves to making coeducation work.

Beginning in June 1987, the planning process for coeducation began in earnest. At the same time, the college began the painful process of trying to win over alumnae, some of whom were actively pursuing legal avenues to prevent coeducation. During this period, administrators and faculty traveled the country speaking with alumnae groups. A student group, SOS (Save Our School), and a group of alumnae interveners challenged the college's right to admit men. The interveners sued the college saying that it had raised funds for its Sesquicentennial under false pretenses by indicating the money would be used for the maintenance of Wheaton as a women's college. Another alumnae group TOWEL (The Opportunity for Women's Education is our Legacy) organized a public campaign to reverse the decision.

By the end of the spring 1987 semester, the Board of Trustees voted to change Wheaton to a coeducational college by the following fall. In spring 1988, the college reached an out-of-court settlement, which allowed alumnae to ask for refunds of their gifts (approximately $150,000 of a twenty million dollar campaign was refunded) and permitted Wheaton to proceed with coeducation. Unlike the case of Mills College in California in the 1990s, where the alumnae successfully convinced the Board of Trustees to reverse its decision to become coeducational, the Wheaton protests were unsuccessful.

From January 1987 to the first day of classes in September 1988, when the first men arrived, Wheaton was constantly in the press. At the same time, a careful planning effort, implemented through a number of committees, examined the direction coeducation would take. The planning effort was quite extensive and impressive. President Emerson named a Commission on Coeducation, which included distinguished educators from outside Wheaton to examine the issues. In addition, a Planning Council, including administrators, faculty, staff, students, and alumnae worked diligently both prior to and after September 1988 to plan for coeducation. Other committees on Student Life, Athletics, Facilities and Master Plan, and the

Development of Norton Center, all met regularly and produced detailed reports and recommendations.

The Planning Council grappled with how to make the transition to coeducation without losing Wheaton's heritage as a women's college and its commitment to women's education. The tension between becoming an excellent coeducational institution and remembering its past was a key problem and remains so today. For the more successful a coeducational institution Wheaton would become, the more difficult it might be to retain its sense of history. The final report of the Planning Council, issued in January 1989, indicated Wheaton's vision of different coeducation, in such a way that it would not lose its historical legacy to women:

> From the beginning, coeducation has been viewed not as an end in itself but as a means to achieve a larger agenda. We are mindful that a successful transition to coeducation in the late 1980s requires more than a simple minded recipe to "add men and stir." . . . The more complex and significant issues deal with continuity and change—how the campus will be changed as men enter them, how we can anticipate and shape that change in ways that are consonant with many of the values we held as a women's college and how we can maximize the opportunities inherent in this transition to strengthen and reposition Wheaton nationally.
>
> Wheaton College undertakes the education of women and men together after a distinguished 154 year history as a women's college. And it does so in an era when one of the most fundamental changes within our society has been the altered consciousness about the roles of women in society. In planning for a successful transition to coeducation, we have attempted not only to consider those initiatives that will assure Wheaton's success in the competition for able students but also to consider what distinctive contributions Wheaton will make to the lives of those students and to the wider arena of higher education by approaching coeducation in new and distinctive ways.
>
> Achieving a successful transition to coeducation does not, we believe, imply a new educational mission for Wheaton. Indeed Wheaton's mission is as relevant for the future as it has been for much of our history, as relevant for men as it has been and will continue to be for women. That mission is "to educate young people for successful lives in an increasingly challenging and complex world." (Wheaton College, 1989)

THE TRANSITION TO COEDUCATION

In fall 1988, Wheaton College, after 154 years as an institution for women, admitted its first coeducational class. In the first years of coeducation, both faculty and women students who had come to Wheaton because it was a women's college, expressed concern and, at times, hostility about the decision. Despite its feeling of betrayal, especially about how the decision to become coeducational was reached, the faculty committed itself to translating the balanced curriculum into a "differently coeducational curriculum." Thus, Wheaton College was not going to allow coeducation to destroy its historical commitment to the education of women. Rather, the college would attempt to develop a program committed to gender equity for both men and women. In 1992, the Board of Trustees, at the new President Dale Marshall's inauguration ceremony, urged her to "heed the proud history of Wheaton College recognizing the promise of the future in the strengths of the past." Consistent with this vision of using Wheaton's history as a women's college as the foundation for a gender-balanced and consciously coeducational experience, the male students at the spring 1991 graduation of the last all-women's class at Wheaton, presented the graduates with buttons saying "the legacy will not be lost."

Clearly the presence of men at Wheaton has had considerable short-term and long-term effects. For the first few years of coeducation, given the opposition of a majority of women students who came to Wheaton as a women's college, there were numerous tensions and conflicts between women and men. Additionally, by the second year, women who came to Wheaton because it was coed, or at the very least, with full knowledge that it was coeducational, often resented the way women from the classes of 1989 to 1991 treated the men. These women, especially from the class of 1993, often bonded with the men and felt alienated from their more overtly feminist classmates who preceded them at Wheaton. The women in the 1989 to 1991 classes, the last all-female graduating classes, were sometimes angry at the younger women for their apparent lack of female solidarity and feminist consciousness. Thus, during the first years immediately after coeducation there was significant conflict between both women and men and women and women.

Today, this open hostility and conflict between women and men has disappeared. In 1987, the questions most often asked were, Why would a man come to Wheaton? and, What type of men would apply? Like Vassar, in the 1970s, where the question of what typified the Vassar man was asked, at Wheaton the question of what typified the Wheaton man was constantly asked. Looking at the student population today, the original question needs broadening. In addition to examining what type of man comes to Wheaton (preliminary evidence suggests two types: artsy-intellectual types and jocks, for very different reasons), it is clear that a more important question may be, how have Wheaton women changed?, a question that the planners did not address. Discussions with faculty, administrators, and students indicate that women who come to Wheaton today are significantly different from Wheaton women of the 1970s and 1980s. First, they appear less concerned with women's issues and are less feminist (at least in their first year), reflecting the culture at large, which is less supportive of feminism. Second, they selected Wheaton because it is coeducational. Although not all women came to Wheaton before coeducation because they were committed to women's colleges (some came for geographic reasons, others financial, others because their mothers were Wheaton graduates), they all knew it was for women only, and could have attended coeducational institutions. Wheaton women today consciously choose coeducation.

The Planning Council spent very little time examining curriculum reform for coeducation. According to former Provost Hannah Goldberg, the college believed that the gender-balanced curriculum developed in the early 1980s was an outstanding curriculum for both women and men, and therefore little curriculum reform was necessary. It is ironic, according to Goldberg, that many alumnae she met during the year before coeducation asked how the college was going to change its curriculum in light of the admission of men. "Did Dartmouth explore how to change its curriculum when it admitted women?" Goldberg asked, "If not, why should Wheaton have discussed curriculum change for men? We believed that if our curriculum was good for women it was equally appropriate for men."

The Planning Council also spent little time on the gender composition of the faculty. Well before 1988, because of a conscious hiring policy, Wheaton had an an almost equal number of male and female faculty members. According to Wheaton historian, Paul Helmreich, "This meant that when we went coed, (a) there were men and women relatively equally spread out among rank levels, and (b), that incoming students—taking eight courses in the first year—would almost certainly have faculty of both genders teaching them, and probably several courses with faculty of each gender." According to Helmreich, this equitable gender composition and the faculty's commitment to making coeducation work in a gender equitable manner, was an essential aspect of Wheaton's transition.

It is clear, however, that the issue of gender has continued to permeate the Wheaton community, with relationships between men and women an explicit part of much of its formal and hidden curriculum. Although gender issues and feminist pedagogy do not permeate all classes, they clearly are part of the overall climate of the college. Discussions of gender continue to permeate student life, with freshman orientation, men's and women's groups, a feminist theme house, and other extracurricular activities all incorporating discussions of gender; in fact, so much so that some students by their senior years are frankly sick of gender. One male student told us, "I am so sick of gender. I just want to graduate, get a job, get married, have a family, and never think about gender again." Nevertheless, most of the students we have talked with believe that they are much more aware of gender issues than their friends who have attended other coeducational colleges. What is not entirely clear, however, is how different Wheaton's form of coeducation is from other coeducational colleges, or how different Wheaton is from the remaining women's colleges.

Although there is clearly a recognition of Wheaton's past as a women's college, the tension between past and present is evident. In the years immediately following coeducation, there was a conscious and explicit attempt to honor the past. Today, however, less attention seems to be paid on a daily basis. As the college has moved into its fully coeducational period, it has to walk a finer line between reverence for the past and the reality of the present. Students come to Wheaton today because it is coeducational, and although most of them are aware, certainly by the end of the first year, of Wheaton's heritage as a women's college, their commitment is to coeducation. Nonetheless, the college is solidly committed to not letting the legacy of the past die. At an Alumnae/i Weekend panel discussion of "Women's Lives, Men's Lives," a male alumnus from the second coeducational class, commenting on Wheaton today and current students apparent lack of awareness of the struggles over coeducation, stated, "My Wheaton is dead." In response, two alumnae from the early 1980s stated "What do you mean *your* Wheaton; how do you think we feel?" In response, President Marshall stated, "We will *never* forget our past as a women's college, even as we continue to move successfully into a coeducational college."

The exchange indicated a number of important points. First, the college appears to have made the transition to coeducation in such a way that the conflicts that marked the first years are not central to the daily activities of the campus. Second, as the college becomes more comfortable as a coeducational institution, its relationship to its past becomes more ambiguous and at times tenuous. Finally, the college has maintained its commitment to preserving the past and is struggling with how do best accomplish this. However, recent issues of the Wheaton alumna/i magazine have suggested that conscious coeducation and Wheaton's past as a women's college are becoming less salient. Up to 1996, most issues had a number of articles on both; more recent issues have few if any and appear to be playing down Wheaton's past and presenting a view of the college as another good liberal arts college, stressing its work and learning requirements (through the Filene Center for Work and Learning) as an important feature.

The administration and faculty, especially those who predate coeducation, are concerned with the loss of institutional memory. Former Provost Goldberg expressed concern for what happens when those with ties to Wheaton as a women's college retire. The former provost, perhaps more than anyone at Wheaton, had been the driving force for maintaining institutional memory. She worked diligently to impress all new faculty of the importance of Wheaton's past and its commitment to a different form of coeducation. A core of veteran faculty attempt to formally and informally socialize new faculty to Wheaton's philosophy and practices. Nonetheless, it is not yet clear how successful this will be. Discussions with faculty and students suggest that although Wheaton remains different from many coeducational institutions, in many ways it has become another good coeducational liberal arts college. Our observations indicate that at the surface level, it is difficult to distinguish Wheaton from similar coeducational liberal arts colleges; however, when one looks beneath the surface, Wheaton is different, especially in its emphasis on gender across the curriculum and in student life activities. Whether this continues, remains to be seen.

In fall 1997, Provost Goldberg announced her retirement at the end of the 1997 to 1998 academic year. At the May 1998 graduation ceremonies, Wheaton honored her with an honorary doctorate. After a failed search, Professor of Economics Gordon Weil was appointed Acting Provost for the 1998 to 1999 academic year, when a new search was conducted. A leader in the transition to coeducation, Gordon Weil has been an important link to Wheaton's past. Despite this connection, it remained to be seen whether the memory of Wheaton as a women's college and its conscious coeducational philosophy and practices would continue without Goldberg's vision and leadership.

In spring 1999, Wheaton appointed another woman provost, Susanne Woods, the former Dean of the College at Franklin and Marshall, with a distinguished record in women's studies. Although this appointment appears to indicate an important commitment to linking its future to its past, the next few years will provide the important answers.

Finally, the tension between past and present is reflected in the admissions process. Whereas many veteran faculty believe the college should market its "different coeducation," the admissions director argues "that seventeen-year-olds do not come to college for feminist pedagogy; and that students come to Wheaton today because it is coeducational." Thus, admissions literature plays up Wheaton as an excellent, small, coeducational liberal arts college. There is little mention of its history as a women's college, nor any discussion of "different or conscious coeducation." Discussions with students support this perspective as almost all of the women students we talked to stated they would not have applied to Wheaton had it remained a women's college.

Today, although Wheaton College is an institution still grappling with the effects of coeducation and how to implement its "differently coeducational" philosophy, curriculum, and pedagogy, the transition to coeducation is complete. Wheaton sees itself as a coeducational liberal arts college, but one that has incorporated the best lessons of women's education for both men and women. These include an explicit emphasis on gender equity in the curriculum, pedagogic practices, and student life and government; a respect for the history and traditions of the institution as a women's college; a broadening of the definition of gender equity to include both women and men; a broadening of the definition of diversity to include not only gender, but race, ethnicity, social class, and sexual orientation; and the socialization of new faculty, students, and administration into the ethos of the institution.

In October 1998, Wheaton sponsored a conference on coeducation to celebrate its tenth anniversary of coeducation. A planning committee headed by sociology professor Kersti Yllö and including education professor Frances Maher (coauthor of the *Feminist Classroom*), both leaders of the Wheaton feminist community and concerned with maintaining Wheaton's heritage as a women's college and its feminist vision, organized the program. In Goldberg's view, the purpose of the conference was not only to celebrate Wheaton's transition to coeducation, but to transmit the importance of conscious coeducation to a national audience.

The conference brought over two hundred people to Wheaton and provided an important forum for discussing issues related to single-sex and coeducation. Most participants agreed that the Wheaton story represented an important lesson: that a coeducational college must be committed to gender equity in explicit ways and that it may be the processes of education rather than its structure that are central to the goals of gender equity. That is, coeducation does not have to be "chilly" to women if it is accompanied by a philosophy, curriculum, and pedagogy committed to gender equity.

Wheaton's January 1999 Self Study, prepared for the New England Association of Schools and Colleges (Wheaton College, 1999), places the transition to coeducation squarely at the forefront of its policies during the 1990s:

> The dominant feature of Wheaton's recent history has been the transition to coeducation. The admission of the first coed class in the Fall of 1988 followed two years of careful planning in which we assumed a purposefully literal understanding of "co-education" as signifying the education of men and women learning from, as well as with, one another.

With coeducation, there was a sustained commitment to maintaining the college's commitment to gender:

> Transforming academic program and campus culture to include men, we nevertheless sought to sustain our commitment to a gender-balanced curriculum and our awareness that gender differences in learning styles and behaviors shape student experiences and must inform curricular planning, pedagogy and student life.

In summarizing its transition from women's college to coeducational liberal arts college, the report stated:

> Becoming a coeducational college did not so much change our mission as a liberal arts institution as focus its application on a new student body. Our mission is more clearly and more widely articulated than it was ten years ago because we have had to devote new attention to what we must do to fulfill it in the context of a redefined student market and campus environment. Having repositioned the college, the challenge is now to use our growing popularity to improve our position among leading arts colleges.

Finally, the College's mission statement summarizes its commitment to becoming one of the leading coeducational liberal arts colleges, but one that retains its historical commitment to gender balance:

> The mission of Wheaton College is to provide an excellent liberal arts education in a small, residential coeducational learning community, enabling students to understand and participate in shaping the multicultural, interdependent world of which they are a part. . . . *Wheaton teaches men and women to live and work as equal partners by linking learning, work, and service in a community which values equally the contributions of men and women* [italics added].

In our interview with new Provost Susanne Woods, on May 30, 2001, she stressed the connection between past and present in the ongoing faculty review of Wheaton's curriculum, the first such major revision since the balanced curriculum project in the 1980s. Part of the process includes a reexamination of the place of the gender-balanced curriculum in a now, coeducational college. The Self Study stressed a broader conception of gender as embedded in multicultural and global issues, including race, ethnicity, and social class. Likewise, this curriculum review does not appear to privilege gender issues, but rather seeks to integrate gender as part of a larger multicultural and global thrust.

Based on her experience at other coeducational institutions that were previously men's colleges or universities, Woods argued that Wheaton is a different type of coeducational college because of its history as a women's college. She indicated that if she were to write a comparison of Wheaton to the others, it would be titled "from boot camp to tea party." She has found Wheaton to be "astonishingly collegial compared to other institutions." She added that "the single thing that characterizes the difference is self-consciousness of hierarchy at other institutions and comfort with collaborative modes at Wheaton." Provost Woods indicated that its history as a women's college probably is responsible for these differences. When asked if in 2010 Wheaton were to be described as an excellent coeducational liberal arts college, but with no mention of its history as a women's college, she replied that it would be "unacceptable and impossible to think that the history would be eradicated."

Clearly, Wheaton College is a different place than it was thirteen years ago. Coeducation has resulted in a much healthier financial and enrollment picture. The last three years have brought its largest first-year classes in its history, with the incoming class in 2001 predicted at more than five hundred students. Different does not necessarily mean better or worse. How its differences have affected women and men still need to be determined empirically. One preliminary "finding" that needs to be explored concerns the nature of curriculum, pedagogy, and student life in a "differently" coeducational college. To some degree it may be that it is the type of educational processes that occur at a college, rather than whether the college is single-sex or coeducational that determines the level of "friendliness" or "chilliness" to women students. Central to Wheaton's philosophy of "different or conscious" coeducation is the claim that the college's sensitivity to gender issues and to the continuation of its historical commitment to women will serve both men and women in an equitable manner. Thus, although many coeducational colleges may be "chilly" to women, Wheaton will not be one of them. Based on our observations over the past six years we believe that there is sufficient evidence to suggest credence to the claim.

Just as Wheaton is different today, so too are societal gender relations. The majority of Wheaton students come out of coeducational secondary schools and take coeducation for granted. Although feminism today may be less prevalent than in the period of the balanced curriculum era of the 1980s, nevertheless, the precepts of liberal-feminism appear to be largely accepted by college women at Wheaton, prior to their arrival. Obviously, changes in societal level gender relations have affected Wheaton and its students, just as Wheaton has affected them. The dynamics of this reciprocal relationship, however, remains an empirical question.

Wheaton's philosophy of conscious coeducation was not only concerned with the maintenance gender equity for women; it was also concerned with socializing its new male students. The accreditation report of the New England Association of Schools and Colleges stressed the transformative effects of a Wheaton education on its male students:

> Significant institutional and divisional energies have been devoted to ensuring the successful transition of males into this community. Conversations with male students about their experiences at Wheaton College and their perceptions of the quality of their lives in this community indicate that the Wheaton experience is a transformative one and that they (males) are different individuals at the end of their experience here. This transformation was attributed to the belief that the enduring philosophy of the College was one that still supports the growth of women but fosters the evolving role of men as members of the community. (1999, p. 10)

CONCLUSION

This chapter provides an examination of the transition to coeducation at Wheaton College. It chronicles the complex factors that resulted in the decision to admit men, the conflicts over that decision, the planning for coeducation, and some of the processes that have defined the past thirteen years of coeducation.

Our research indicates a number of lessons to be learned from Wheaton's transition to coeducation:

1. The importance of an explicit institutional philosophy that is committed to gender equity under coeducation.

2. The importance of a careful implementation of this philosophy and a constant assessment and reevaluation of its successes and shortcomings.

3. The importance of maintaining institutional memory with regard to its history as a women's college and the creation of a process to socialize new students, faculty, and administration about this history.

4. The type of gender characteristics of an institution (single-sex or coeducational) may be less important to gender equity than the processes within the institution. That is, coeducational institutions with gender equitable practices do not have to be "chilly" places for women.

Based on our research, we have found Wheaton College to be a place continuing to define its own identity as a coeducational college. It remains institutionally committed to the education of women, but has integrated this historical concern into its own philosophy of coeducation in a larger multicultural and global context. The extent to which its original conception of "conscious coeducation" continues to be part of curriculum and pedagogy, and to what degree it will survive as Wheaton moves further from its past, remains uncertain. What comes through is that Wheaton is a fine coeducational liberal arts college committed to the education of both men and women. Whether or not it is significantly different from other coeducational liberal arts colleges requires further comparative analysis over a prolonged period of time. However, our observations indicate that it probably is. Whether it can successfully balance the tensions between its future as a coeducational college and its past as a women's college remains to be seen. If it cannot, it does not appear that it will be for a lack of trying.

ACKNOWLEDGMENTS

This research has been supported in part by grants from the Spencer Foundation Small Grants Program and the Hofstra University Faculty Grants Program (where Semel was on the faculty from 1994–2001). In addition, Wheaton College has provided in kind contributions of housing for the researchers during site visits. The findings do not reflect the opinions or policies of the Spencer Foundation, Hofstra University, or Wheaton College. We would like to thank the many students, faculty, administrators, trustees and alumnae/i who gave generously of their time, both formally and informally, and without whom this research could not have been completed. In particular, College Archivist Zeph Stickney provided invaluable archival support and assistance, and made our hours of research in Wallace Library anything but a lonely experience; and Wheaton College historian and Professor Emeritus of History, Paul Helmreich, shared generously his rich understanding of the history of Wheaton.

NOTE

The idea for this research began in 1991, when Semel, a Wheaton alumna, returned to the campus and discussed the decision to become coeducational with a group from the last all-female graduating class. Based on these discussions, she asked for permission from the Wheaton administration to study the transition to coeducation. The formal study began in 1995, when Sadovnik spent a half-year sabbatical at Wheaton.

REFERENCES

American Association of University Women (AAUW). (1992). *How Schools Shortchange Girls*. Washington, D.C.: AAUW.

Astin, A. (1977). *Four Critical Years*. San Francisco: Jossey-Bass.

Baker, L. (1976). *I'm Radcliffe; Fly Me: The Seven Sisters and the Failure of Women's Education*. New York: Macmillan.

Beard, P. (1994). "The Fall and Rise of the Seven Sisters." *Town and Country* (November): 159–174.

Boas, L. (1935). *Women's Education Begins: The Rise of the Women's Colleges*. Norton, MA: Wheaton College Press. (Reissued by Arno Press, 1971).

Brown, L. M., and Gilligan, C. (1992). *Meeting at the Crossroads: Women's Psychology and Girls' Development*. Cambridge: Harvard University Press.

Canada, K., and Pringle, R. (1995). "The Role of Gender in College Classroom Interactions: A Social Context Approach." *Sociology of Education* 68 (3): 161–186.

Carpenter, P. (1985). "Single-Sex Schooling and Girls' Academic Achievements." *Australian and New Zealand Journal of Sociology* 21:456–472.

Carpenter, P., and Hayden, M. (1987). "Girls' Academic Achievements: Single-Sex Versus Coeducational Schools in Australia." *Sociology of Education* 60:156–167.

Faragher, J. M., and Howe, F. (1988). *Women and Higher Education in American History: Essays from the Mount Holyoke Sesquicentennial Symposium*. New York: Norton.

Finn, J. (1980). "Sex Differences in Educational Outcomes: A Cross-National Study." *Sex Roles* 6:9–25.

Giele, J. Z (1987). "Coeducation or Women's Education? A Comparison of Alumnae from Two Colleges: 1934–1979." In Carole Lasser (Ed.), *Educating Men and Women Together*. Urbana: University of Illinois Press.

Grant, G. (1988). *The World We Created at Hamilton High*. Cambridge: Harvard University Press.

Grant, G., and Riesman, D. (1978). *The Perpetual Dream: Reform and Experiment in the American College*. Chicago: University of Chicago Press.

Helmreich, P. C. (1985). *Wheaton College, 1834–1912: The Seminary Years*. Norton, MA: Wheaton College.

———. (2002). *Wheaton College, 1834–1957: A Massachusetts Family Affair*. New York and London: Cornwall Books.

Horowitz, H. L. (1984). *Alma Mater: Design and Experience in the Women's Colleges From Their Nineteenth Century Beginnings to the 1930s*. New York: Knopf. (2nd ed. published by University of Massachusetts Press in 1993.)

Kendall, E. (1976). *Peculiar Institutions: An Informal History of the Seven Sister Colleges*. New York: Putnam.

Komarovsky, M. (1985). *Women in College*. New York: Basic Books.

Leach, W. (1980). *True Love and Perfect Union: The Feminist Reform of Sex and Society*. New York: Basic Books.

Lee, V., and Bryk, A. (1986). "Effects of Single-Sex and Coeducational High Schools on Achievement, Attitudes, Behaviors, and Sex Differences." *Journal of Educational Psychology* 78:381–395.

Lever, J. and Schwartz, P. (1971). *Women at Yale: Liberating a College Campus*. Indianapolis: Bobbs-Merrill.

Maher, F., and Tetrault, M. T. (1994). *The Feminist Classroom*. New York: Basic Books.

Miller-Bernal, L. (1989). "College Experiences and Sex-Role Attitudes: Does a Women's College Make a Difference?" *Youth and Society* 20:363–387.

———. (1993). "Single-Sex versus Coeducational Environments: A Comparison of Women Students' Experiences at Four Colleges." *American Journal of Education* 102(1):23–54.

———. (2000). *Separate by Degree: Women Students' Experiences in Single-Sex and Coeducational Institutions*. New York: Peter Lang.

———. (2002). "Conservative Intent, Liberating Outcomes: The History of Coordinate Colleges for Women." Chapter 9 in this volume.

New England Association of Schools and Colleges. (1999). Wheaton College Accreditation Report. Norton, MA: Wheaton College archives.

Oates, M., and Williamson, S. (1978). "Women's Colleges and Women's Achievers." *Signs* 3:795–806.

——. (1980). "Comment on Tidball's Women's Colleges and Women's Achievers Revisited." *Signs* 6:342–345.

Palmieri, P. (1987). "From Republican Motherhood to Race Suicide: Arguments on the Higher Education of Women in the United States, 1820–1920." In Lasser, C. *Educating Men and Women Together, 49–66.* Champaign-Urbana: University of Illinois Press.

Rice, J., and Hemmings, A. (1988). "Women's Colleges and Women's Achievers: An Update." *Signs* 13:546–559.

Riordan, C. (1985). "Public and Catholic Schooling: The Effects of Gender Context Policy." *American Journal of Education* 93:518–540.

——. (1990). *Girls and Boys in School: Together or Separate?* New York: Teachers College Press.

Rosenberg, R. (1988). *The Limits of Access: The History of Coeducation in America.* In J. M. Faragher and F. Howe (Eds.), *Women and Higher Education in American History,* pp. 107–129. New York: W. W. Norton.

Sadker, M., and Sadker, D. (1994). *Failing at Fairness: How America's Schools Cheat Girls.* New York: Scribners.

Sadovnik, A. R. (1994). *Equity and Excellence in Higher Education: The Decline of a Liberal Educational Reform.* New York: Peter Lang.

Semel, S. F. (1992). *The Dalton School: The Transformation of a Progressive School.* New York: Peter Lang.

Solomon, B. M. (1985). *In the Company of Educated Women.* New Haven: Yale University Press.

Spanier, B., Bloom A., and Boroviak, D. (1984). *Toward a Balanced Curriculum.* Cambridge, MA: Schenkman.

Tidball, E. (1973). "Perspectives on Academic Women and Affirmative Action." *Journal of Higher Education* 54:130–135.

——. (1980). "Women's Colleges and Women's Achievers Revisited." *Signs* 5:504–517.

——. (1985). "Baccalaureate Origins of Entrants into American Medical Schools." *Journal of Higher Education* 56:385–402.

——. (1986). "Baccalaureate Origins of Recent Natural Science Doctorates." *Journal of Higher Education* 57:606–620.

Trickett, E., Trickett, P., Castro, J., and Schaffner, P. (1982). "The Independent School Experience: Aspects of Normative Environments of Single-Sex and Coeducational Secondary Schools." *Journal of Educational Psychology* 74:374–381.

Tyack, D,. and Hansot, E. (1991). *Learning Together: A History of Coeducation in America.* New Haven: Yale University Press.

Wheaton College. (1989). *Planning Report on Coeducation.* Norton, MA: Wheaton College archives.

Wheaton College. (1999). *Wheaton College Institutional Self-Study: Prepared for the New England Association of Schools and Colleges.* Norton, MA: Wheaton College archives.

CHAPTER 9

Conservative Intent, Liberating Outcomes: The History of Coordinate Colleges for Women

Leslie Miller-Bernal

Neither single-sex nor coeducational, coordinate colleges are an interesting hybrid that evolved in the late nineteenth century out of women's struggle to gain admission to men's colleges. Rather than taking the more "drastic" step of becoming coeducational, many men's colleges preferred establishing an associated institution for women students in order to maintain the prestige of their all-male institutions. Although coordinate colleges were thus usually established for the conservative purpose of dealing with women's demands for education while avoiding full coeducation, I argue in this chapter that they nonetheless have had advantages for women themselves. I show that women who have attended coordinate colleges have attained some of the same benefits as women who have attended women's college—a supportive environment, leadership opportunities, and women role models among faculty and staff. In other words, women who attend coordinate colleges have not been marginalized to the same degree as women in coeducational institutions. I use my findings about women's experiences in coordinate colleges to suggest ways that coeducational colleges can be changed to promote gender equity.

WHAT ARE COORDINATE COLLEGES?

Coordination is a little known form of higher education in the United States. Many people assume that single-sex and coeducation are the only possible institutional forms, whereas in fact, even the terms themselves are misleading. Today, single-sex education for women is generally coeducational in all respects—faculty, administration, staff, and trustees—except for the student body.[1] Coeducation, especially in the past, is more like a men's college with women, because men typically dominate in every aspect, from the trustees to the student body. Coordination is a third form of higher education that has generally developed when a men's college has established or affiliated with a women's college. The two colleges retain separate identities but share resources to varying degrees. Some coordinate colleges share facilities, faculty, and most of their administration, but have separate admissions, student residences, student governments, and athletics. Other coordinate colleges are more like full-fledged separate colleges whose association occurs mostly through students' being able to cross-register easily in order to take courses on the other campus. Two of the earliest coordinate arrangements represent each type. Radcliffe shared most resources with Harvard, including Harvard's faculty. Barnard, on the other hand, has always had much greater separation from Columbia, including its own faculty and trustees. Although today only about ten coordinate institutions remain in the United States, more coordinate colleges used to exist and even more were contemplated but never established.[2]

METHODS OF STUDY

In order to demonstrate the relative advantages of coordination over coeducation, I mainly discuss three colleges that are or have been coordinate at some point in their history: William Smith College in Geneva, New York, currently a coordinate of Hobart College; Middlebury College in Middlebury, Vermont, which in the first half of the twentieth century had the skeleton of a coordinate college for women for almost twenty years; and Hamilton College in Clinton, New York, which in the late 1960s had a nearly autonomous coordinate college, Kirkland, for about a decade (Miller-Bernal, 2000). My research is based on extensive archival work over a period of five years, from 1994 to 1999, in which I studied many aspects of these colleges' histories, using catalogs, reports to accrediting agencies, presidential papers, minutes of boards of trustee meetings, student newspapers and yearbooks, and where available, oral histories that had been tape-recorded. In addition, I interviewed top administrators and surveyed students at each college (Miller-Bernal, 2000). The key issues I analyzed concerned the experiences of women students at these four colleges—how they had originally been admitted and how the colleges changed as a result. I specifically focused on how supportive the institutions have been for women, for example, what type of housing they provided, and to what degree women's presence was acknowledged in college catalogs; the opportunities for women students to take leadership positions in campus organizations; and how much staffing and curriculum reflected women and their interests.

WILLIAM SMITH AS AN EARLY COORDINATE COLLEGE:
LIMITED AUTONOMY STILL HAS BENEFITS

When William Smith opened in 1908 as a coordinate of Hobart College, coordinate institutions were a recognized feature of the higher education landscape in the United States. Coordination had existed since 1879 when Radcliffe College became an "annex" of Harvard. The country's first coordinate college for women did not develop by conscious design, however, but rather emerged as a compromise. Harvard refused to admit women students; it could only be persuaded, beginning in 1872, to allow women to take examinations. How the women prepared for the examinations was their own responsibility, but if they passed, Harvard gave them a certificate, not a degree. Women and their allies, organized into an association, were determined to go further and enable women to obtain the same education as Harvard's men students. The Society for the Collegiate Instruction of Women was headed by the respected Elizabeth Carey Agassiz, wife of the famous Harvard professor and naturalist, Louis Agassiz. Comprised of women "unsuspected of seeking 'women's rights'" (Morison, 1936/1964), the Society did not want to establish a women's college. Similar to many people of the time, including leading feminists, members of the society thought of women's colleges as inferior, little more than finishing schools (Miller-Bernal, 2000). The Association focused on getting President Eliot of Harvard to agree to allow its faculty to instruct women in rooms rented for this purpose. In 1879, twenty-seven women became the first students of what was informally called the Annex and later became Radcliffe. A more visible presence for women students and changes in the relations between Harvard and Radcliffe developed gradually (Horowitz, 1984). No matter how much money the Association raised, however, it was not able to convince Harvard to give its degrees to women (Morison 1936/1964). In fact, it was not until 1963 that Radcliffe seniors were finally given degrees from Harvard University; in 1971, the Harvard Corporation voted to award retroactive degrees to all surviving Radcliffe alumnae.

Once Radcliffe led the way, other coordinate colleges followed, including Sophie Newcomb (1887), the coordinate of Tulane in New Orleans; Barnard (1889), the coordinate of Columbia in New York City; and Pembroke (1891), the coordinate of Brown in Providence (Woody, 1929/1980). Although Radcliffe's precedent may have made their establishment somewhat easier, proponents of women's education usually had to struggle for women to gain academic privileges, raising money as part of the bargain. Coordination also became a way for coeducational colleges to revert back to being men's colleges because men's colleges were felt to be more prestigious. The University of Rochester may be the most famous instance of such reversion, given women's earlier intense struggle for admission. Susan B. Anthony had even pledged her life insurance in order to raise the final sum the university demanded before women were admitted in 1900. But then in 1912, the president of the University of Rochester, Rush Rhees, citing the precedents of both Radcliffe and Barnard, convinced the trustees to authorize the Women's College, which lasted until 1952 (May, 1977).[3]

Coordination between Hobart and William Smith resulted from a compromise between a man who wanted to establish a spiritualist college for women and the president of a men's college who was eager to have funds to expand and modernize its curriculum. William Smith was a successful, elderly businessman, philanthropist, and spiritualist who began building a spiritualist college for women on his property in Geneva, New York.[4] He had gone as far as choosing a president and trustees and planning the colleges' curriculum, which was to "give special prominence to the 'science of psychology'" to "reveal the powers of the mind" (William Smith file, documents, HWSCA). Ultimately, however, Smith's trustees advised him that the half million dollars he had available for this enterprise was insufficient to establish an independent institution. The president of Hobart College, an older men's college in Geneva loosely affiliated with the Episcopalian Church, approached Mr. Smith to see if he would be interested in using his money to educate women at Hobart College.[5]

Hobart College needed money to be able to offer such programs as biology and psychology that contemporary students were demanding. On his part, William Smith needed to be convinced that his desire to do something for women's education could be met by using the faculty and facilities of Hobart. A major stumbling block in the negotiations was the Episcopalian nature of Hobart College. Mr. Smith required assurance that women students' attendance at religious services would be entirely voluntary and that their chapel would be nondenominational, unlike the situation for the men of Hobart. William Smith also insisted that all of Hobart's courses of study be open to women students, even though men and women students were to be taught separately (Miller-Bernal, 2000).

One of the last issues to be decided concerning the admission of women was whether Hobart should become a coeducational college, or whether it should establish a coordinate college for the women students. William Smith's closest advisor, Anna Botsford Comstock, a widely respected science teacher and celebrated naturalist wood engraver, apparently was the person who made this decision:

> I have always been a firm believer in co-education from the kindergarten through the university but I did not hesitate a moment to decide that a college for women at Hobart should be co-ordinate. I felt that make Hobart co-educational would alienate the alumni and antagonize the undergraduates and, like putting new wine in old bottles, would ruin everything. (Comstock, undated, HWSCA)

Given the time period, it is not surprising that coordination was chosen over coeducation for Hobart and William Smith. The early twentieth century was a period of backlash against coeducation, related to the larger cultural "fears of feminization." Women constituted about one-third of all undergraduates, and their numbers had been increasing at a faster rate than had male undergraduates' (Newcomer, 1959; Palmieri, 1987). Moreover, women students were renowned for excelling academically. The elderly mayor of Geneva, who was himself an alumnus of Hobart, was relieved that his college was not becoming coeducational. At the opening ceremonies for William Smith in 1908, he noted that there was a "strong prejudice against co-education in the mind of the average young person of the male sex . . . accentuated by the fact that the girls have a way of leading their classes and taking the prizes" (1908–1909 Hobart College Bulletin, HWSCA).

From one perspective, the choice of coordination over coeducation can be seen as conservative or reactionary (Fish, 1990). The intention, at Hobart and elsewhere, was to disturb men students and alumni as little as possible while gaining some benefits for the men's institution. Older and richer men's colleges were able to dominate their coordinate partners, as Alice Mary Baldwin recognized in the 1930s in her position as dean of the women's college associated with Duke University (Kerber, 1988). William Smith, for example, was not really a college but rather a department of Hobart. Its enrollment was much lower than Hobart's, and it did not have its own trustees, but rather three representatives (one of whom had to be a woman) on Hobart's board. It was headed by a dean who functioned quite independently but was under Hobart's president. Even more autonomous coordinate colleges, such as Barnard, which had its own trustees and early on, some of its own faculty, were poorer than and subordinate to the men's colleges with which they were affiliated (Gildersleeve, 1954). Moreover, coordinate colleges like William Smith tended to model themselves after women's colleges, which until the 1960s were socially exclusive and concerned not only with their students' academic accomplishments but with their social graces as well.

However, coordination had some benefits for the women students themselves. William Smith students, for example, had their own publications, drama societies, music groups, athletics, student government, and traditions. In all of these groups, women students held the leadership positions. Women also formed clubs to reflect their interests, for example, a suffrage club before World War I. Moreover, buildings on the William Smith campus were named after women, dedicated by women, and contained paintings of women (Miller-Bernal, 2000). Thus it is not surprising that an early student at William Smith later wrote:

> Everything, except the dances, was for William Smith alone. We were a separate college and gloried in that fact. We had our own Dramatic Association, Christian Association, Athletic Association, and Glee Club. (Durfee '17, "William Smith College in the Mid-Teens," 1975, HWSCA)

Thus despite being coordinate to a richer, larger, and dominant men's college, William Smith gave women students a space in which they and their concerns were the institutional focus. William Smith had some of its own buildings, some women administrators and faculty, its own name and college culture. It was subordinate to but not entirely overwhelmed by men students and their activities. One way that the benefits of coordination over coeducation can be seen is by looking at the situation for women at Middlebury, an institution that shifted from being a men's college, to a coeducational college, then to a coordinate arrangement, and finally back to coeducation.

MIDDLEBURY COLLEGE: ADVANTAGES FOR WOMEN DURING A PERIOD OF COORDINATION

Middlebury College opened in 1800 and for more than eighty years, remained a small, struggling, conservative institution that enrolled mainly white Protestant men from nearby towns and farms in Vermont and New York. Women tried to enter the college at least twice. In the early part of the century, the famous educator Emma Hart Willard, tried, and much later, in the 1870s, so did local women. It was not until 1883, however, when Middlebury's enrollment dropped to thirty-eight students, that the trustees finally consented to women's admission. Six women were then admitted as an "experiment" (Miller-Bernal, 2000).

From 1883 on, Middlebury was nominally a coeducational college, but more realistically, a men's college that happened to have some women enrolled. It took over twenty-five years before the college appointed a Dean of Women who was simultaneously the first woman faculty member (Miller-Bernal, 2000). The first women students had to struggle to get the college even to give them a room where they could rest and study, and they themselves had to raise the money to furnish it. Housing was likewise slow in coming, with a small residence for women (inadequate for the numbers enrolled) first provided in 1891. There were only a few clubs for the women students, and when college organizations were mixed sex, as the newspaper and yearbook were, it became institutionalized that the women took the second-in-command position, even when they did the work of the head (Pollard, 1959, MCA). Only in sororities did at least some women students have the opportunity to take leadership positions and to plan activities focused on women's interests.

Reactions to the women students at Middlebury were at first guarded but not very hostile. Men students expressed confidence that they could safeguard "the rights of the masculine element" (*The Undergraduate*, October 1883, MCA). However, as women increased in numbers and took a majority of the academic prizes, men students, as well as many trustees, became alarmed. In 1902, a time when the country at large was expressing fears of feminization, Middlebury applied to the State of Vermont for a charter to establish a coordinate college for women. Although the college had no money for new buildings, the trustees agreed to limit the numbers of women students, and more college exercises became segregated by gender (Stameshkin, 1985).

Middlebury moved more firmly in the direction of coordination in the 1920s. A major impetus was that the college had failed to receive several million dollars from an alumnus trustee's will because it had not established a coordinate college for women, which this trustee believed was appropriate. A College for Women at Middlebury was declared, and architectural plans for a complete campus for the women were drawn up. At the same time, a women's advisory board to Middlebury's board of trustees was reactivated. Although the campus was never built because of the problem of raising funds during the Depression, the college did try to segregate women and men in classes as much as possible. The Women's College of Middlebury existed in this form for nineteen years, from 1931 to 1949 (Miller-Bernal, 2000).

There is no doubt that Middlebury's president and trustees' real reason for wanting a coordinate college for women was their belief that Middlebury would be more prestigious if it reverted to being a men's college. Other more dire arrangements for the women students, such as putting all the women in a new teacher's college or sending first year women students to a campus in the mountains usually used for the summer school, were also contemplated (Miller-Bernal, 2000). Yet in some ways, the women students benefited by the incomplete coordinate arrangement that did get established. In particular, the advisory board meant that for the first time women students' needs (for housing, athletic facilities, etc.) were being presented to the trustees. The Dean of Women, Eleanor Ross, herself a graduate of Middlebury, functioned like a president of the women's college. Working with the advisory board, Dean Ross managed such improvements for women students as getting academic programs that they were particularly interested in (art, social sciences, etc.), a lodge for the women's athletic association (which was the first college building named after a woman), more scholarships for women students, and more women faculty hired (Miller-Bernal, 2000).

When Middlebury returned to coeducation in 1949, women students did not fare well. In fact, in 1965, when NIMH (the National Institute of Mental Health) conducted a study at Middlebury, it concluded that men were dominating campus life, evident by their holding most leadership positions and their writing 80 percent of the letters to the student newspaper (Miller-Bernal, 2000). Some attempts to rectify these inequalities occurred during the student protests of the late 1960s and early 1970s. Not until the late 1980s, however, after a bloodied female mannequin was hung outside a fraternity during a weekend of parties, did Middlebury take problems of gender inequality seriously. Several excellent reports analyzed the situation. Fraternities were disbanded, and a woman trustee donated money so that a house for the women's resource center could be beautifully renovated (Miller-Bernal, 2000).

Middlebury College's history thus shows how a coordinate structure benefits women more than coeducation. The greatest strides for women students occurred in the 1920s and 1930s when the college was attempting to separate women and men students so that the college could achieve the prestige of men's colleges such as Williams and Amherst. Although Middlebury's president and trustees were mostly concerned with men's education, the incomplete coordinate structure that they established led to women students' needs getting more attention than they did when Middlebury was simply coeducational. It remains to be seen whether Middlebury College today can fully implement the recommendations of its own studies of campus gender inequality and thus become a coeducational college in which women receive the same attention and resources as men and are equally represented at all levels of the faculty, staff, and administrative and trustee hierarchies.

KIRKLAND COLLEGE: COORDINATION AT ITS STRONGEST

The early and mid-1960s was a boom period for higher education. Many colleges, including Hamilton College in Clinton, New York, were considering how to handle enrollment growth without destroying the benefits of a small college. In this contex it is not surprising that the idea of coordinate colleges resurfaced.[8] Hamilton had been a conservative men's college with a traditional curriculum for about 150 years; in 1965, for example, it had no courses in the fine arts, and only one course in sociology. Hamilton's president, Robert McEwen, liked the idea of a cluster of small colleges, along the Claremont colleges model, in which each college would be, in essence, a coordinate of Hamilton. Besides retaining the benefits of a small size, President McEwen believed that properly planned, cluster colleges might have a "lively impact" on Hamilton (McEwen memo, 1961, historical documents of Kirkland College, HCA).

Fairly early on in its lengthy planning process, Hamilton decided that the first cluster college would be a women's college, which was eventually named Kirkland after the eighteenth-century Congregational minister who worked among the Iroquois and founded the Hamilton-Oneida Academy (Pilkington, 1962). In looking for a president for Kirkland, a planning group put most emphasis on someone "ready and willing to experiment" (minutes of a July 9, 1964 meeting of the advisory subcommittee, HCA). The choice of Samuel Babbitt was excellent from that perspective. Charismatic and handsome, he also had impeccable academic credentials and progressive political views (Miller-Bernal, 2000). Interestingly, though, the planning documents reveal that many people in the community had quite traditional views of women's roles and that they were more concerned about the benefits to Hamilton College and its men students than they were about women's education. Just like the decision at Hobart sixty years earlier, coordination was seen as preferable to coeducation since it would upset Hamilton's students and alumni less (Miller-Bernal, 2000). A faculty report argued for coordination because a "women's college would strengthen Hamilton where it is weakest—a proper social environment—[but] disturb it the least as far as curricular matters are concerned" (quoted in "Draft, Proposed Units for the Hamilton Cluster," undated, HCA).

Hamilton gave land and an initial one million dollar interest-free loan to the new coordinate college, which opened in an unfinished state in 1968.

The college was planned to be independent of Hamilton, more like Barnard is to Columbia than William Smith is to Hobart, a decision undoubtedly influenced by the person who headed a key planning group—Millicent McIntosh, the former president of Barnard College. Kirkland had its own trustees, president, faculty, buildings, and curriculum; its progressive educational philosophy also strongly differentiated it from traditional Hamilton. Kirkland shared a library with Hamilton, and students at both colleges were free to cross-register with only a few restrictions. This independence of Kirkland also suited the president, Sam Babbitt, who considered William Smith and other similar, less independent coordinate colleges to be "not models of two institutions, but only one and its shadow—hardly worth the hassle" (Babbitt to Musselman, March 1, 1977, HCA).

When Kirkland opened, the second wave of the women's movement was just beginning. Students and faculty at this progressive, experimental college were generally not as concerned about women's issues as they were about other social movements, in particular, the antiwar and civil rights movements. Sexist assumptions about Kirkland students and the college's academic program were therefore not at first challenged. Although Kirkland students were not expected to learn to be hostesses, as students at earlier women's colleges were, they did report that they felt men students were condescending to them. Kirkland's progressive educational philosophy, which stressed students' participation and independence and had evaluations rather than grades, tended to be viewed as inferior by Hamilton faculty, students, and trustees. Kirkland's curriculum was influenced by Hamilton College's needs—for example, it stressed social sciences and the arts—but this was then interpreted as another way in which it was not as rigorous as Hamilton. The new college also faced monetary difficulties almost from the start, and it was prohibited from using Hamilton's alumni for fund-raising (Miller-Bernal, 2000).

Despite hostility from some elements in the Hamilton community (or perhaps even partly because of this treatment), most Kirkland students felt an intense loyalty to their college. As one student later described her experiences, the college felt like a "very, very family kind of thing" (transcript of interview with Connie Strellas by Peggy Farber, April 16, 1978, HCA). Institutional research showed that while almost no women were initially attracted to Kirkland because it was a women's college, by the time they were seniors, more than one-third attached "very much" importance to its single-sex status. Also, almost one-half of the seniors said that Kirkland had helped them develop self-confidence and nearly one-third said that they had become better able to relate to other women (Miller-Bernal, 2000).

Kirkland's end in 1978 made it clear how powerful Hamilton was in comparison to Kirkland. Despite an outpouring of protest over its demise and many eloquent defenses of the benefits of one institution with two different educational approaches, Hamilton made it impossible for Kirkland to continue by refusing to loan the women's college any more money. Negotiations between the two colleges' deans concerning how coordination might be improved were terminated. Probably the most painful part of Hamilton's takeover was the treatment of Kirkland's tenured faculty. They were no longer considered tenured but had to undergo another review at Hamilton.

The new, coeducational Hamilton benefited in many ways from the former Kirkland. It obtained many faculty members who were innovative, committed teachers; a modern campus with an impressive theater; and most importantly for women students, a Kirkland endowment that was committed to supporting programs for women. As Kirkland was coming to an end, one of its students eloquently expressed the coming challenges:

> We will not have the fierce sense of female solidarity, of being a woman's school in conjunction with—and opposed to—a men's college. . . .We will have the larger responsibility of continuing to prove receptive to the specific problems that attend being a woman in a male-oriented culture. (*The Spectator*, Sept. 23, 1977, HCA)

Kirkland's brief existence as perhaps the last purposefully designed coordinate college for women in the country is instructive for a variety of reasons. Coordinate women's colleges are precarious when their design and continued existence depend on an older, richer, and larger men's institution. Moreover, the tenacity and depth of sexism were obvious from the way that Kirkland students, their college's academic program, and the faculty who taught them, were never perceived as equal to Hamilton's students, courses, and faculty. Nonetheless, Kirkland women students benefited from having their own space in a college designed for them. They clearly worried that their interests would not receive the same attention in a coeducational Hamilton. Women students' fierce loyalty to Kirkland and their strong sense of loss with the college's demise reveal how unusual it is for women to feel that they have a "room of their own."

EVALUATION OF COORDINATION AS AN EDUCATIONAL MODEL
In the late nineteenth and early twentieth centuries, coordinate colleges for women developed as a compromise. On the one hand, supporters of men's colleges wanted to maintain the prestige of all-male institutions; on the other hand, women students and their allies believed that progress for women depended on their having access to all-male institutions. Although advocates of women's rights viewed coordination as less desirable than full coeducation, they felt it was preferable to separate women's colleges, which were seen as academically inferior. However, because women students at coordinate colleges were taught separately from men students, albeit usually by the same faculty, women students sometimes became suspicious that they were still not receiving the equal education they so earnestly desired. The Rhode Island Society for Collegiate Education of Women (RISCEW),

which raised money to get a coordinate college for women established at Brown University, even conducted a study for women students to reassure them that their courses had the same academic rigor as the men's (Eisenmann, 1991). William Smith students counted on their men friends at Hobart to fill in the parts of their lectures that men faculty omitted when presenting them to the women students (Miller-Bernal, 2000).

In the latter half of the twentieth century, fewer coordinate colleges for women were established, yet some of the same conservative motivations for avoiding coeducation were still apparent. By then women's colleges were considered at least as prestigious as coeducational colleges, however, which is one reason why Kirkland was set up to be essentially an independent women's college. Yet sexism existed in the way that men's colleges like Hamilton were regarded as superior to women's colleges like Kirkland (Astin and Lee, 1972).

Seldom if ever did the founders of coordinate colleges argue that coordination would provide better education for women students than coeducation would. Yet by avoiding coeducation, women students did not experience all the pernicious effects of what has recently been identified as "chilly climates," whereby men students and their activities receive disproportionate resources, including faculty members' time, and men students dominate college organizations' leadership positions (Hall and Sandler, 1982). Because coordinate colleges are a hybrid form, they do not confer to women all the advantages that attending a women's college does, but they are more beneficial than coeducational colleges. Specifically, coordinate colleges for women generally have a greater proportion of women faculty and women administrators than coeducational colleges, but not as high as women's colleges; women students hold more leadership positions than they do at coeducational colleges, but again not as many as they do at women's colleges; and they also offer their women students a supportive atmosphere, where the women students' concerns, accomplishments, and history are recognized—not as much as at women's colleges but more than is generally true at coeducational colleges (Miller-Bernal, 2000).

Coordination provides a flexible structure. In certain historical periods for example, William Smith has stressed its separation from Hobart, whereas at other times, it has advertised itself as being virtually a coeducational institution. In the 1920s, William Smith's curriculum diverged from Hobart's; women students were offered fewer electives in fields deemed to be masculine, such as physics and chemistry, and more courses in areas deemed appropriate for women, such as the fine arts. Later, as coeducation became more socially acceptable, and the costs of maintaining a dual structure seemed prohibitive and unnecessary, Hobart and William Smith stressed its essentially coeducational nature. As a 1970 student editorial expressed it, "Hobart and William Smith are one college . . . we're friends no longer; we've been lovers for years, it's time we got married" (Miller-Bernal, 2000). More recently, since the second wave of the women's movement, William Smith has again emphasized the advantages of being a women's college in conjunction with a men's college. A dean of William Smith, Rebecca Fox, argued forcefully in 1982 that coordination enabled men and women students to come together "as equals," and was better than coeducation at helping both men and women achieve a "distinct identity" (Miller-Bernal, 2000).

There are risks to such flexibility, however. Given the pressures to economize and the lack of public understanding of what coordination is, the temptation to slip into coeducation is great. Recently, in October, 1999, Radcliffe's final and complete merger with Harvard was effected; Radcliffe now exists only as an institute for advanced study at Harvard. Even at relatively independent coordinate institutions like Barnard, financial difficulties have apparently led on occasion to the temptation to merge with Columbia (*http://Barnard.edu*, Interactive History, McIntosh Years, 1950). At Hobart and William Smith, women students have supported the coordinate structure more than the men students have, at least since the 1970s. Deans of William Smith have also championed and eloquently explained coordination's benefits in many publications. Yet over time, various administrative offices have been combined into one, most recently the admissions offices. A key to maintaining the coordinate structure may be ensuring that men students benefit from it and come to understand the ways that they do (Miller-Bernal, 2000).

Currently, most of the approximately ten coordinate institutions in the United States advertise themselves as providing the "best of both worlds," or even the best of three worlds (a men's college, women's college, and coeducational college), as the Internet homepage of the Colleges of Saint Benedict and its partner, Saint John's, claims. Usually coordination means some single-sex residential and social opportunities in combination with the academic advantages of a larger coeducational context. A structure approximately equivalent to coordination has also evolved in a few instances as separate institutions have affiliated to some degree as a way of reducing costs, offering more programs, and in general, being more attractive to prospective students.[7] Bryn Mawr, a women's college, and Haverford, a formerly men's college that is now coeducational, have some joint academic programs and student clubs. Spelman and Morehouse Colleges are similar in being interrelated, though historically and administratively separate. The deans of Kirkland and Hamilton tried to establish a combination of joint and separate programs in 1977, but given the lack of support for the endeavor at Hamilton, and the financial precariousness of Kirkland, the attempt did not ultimately succeed.

Clearly one of the underlying problems with coordination has been the differences in resources and bargaining position between the women's and their affiliated men's institutions. True coordination would mean a men's institution being seen just as coordinate to women's as women's to men's.

Columbia, in other words, would be seen as a coordinate of Barnard as much as the latter is viewed as a coordinate of Columbia. Such institutional equality is difficult to establish because men's colleges are generally older and wealthier, with richer alumni. It is also difficult given the sexism in society at large, in which anything connected to women is generally seen as inferior to that associated with men. Hard does not mean impossible, however. Today, William Smith students are the numeric majority and so successful academically and in their sports teams that they seem almost able to counter the dominance Hobart men students have traditionally sustained through their fraternities, football, and lacrosse teams. Bryn Mawr and coeducational Haverford are another interesting case. One might expect Bryn Mawr to "need" Haverford more for the coeducational environment it provides than coeducational Haverford would "need" Bryn Mawr, and yet Bryn Mawr is probably a bit better known and more prestigious. A visit to their Internet homepages makes it appear that Haverford stresses its relations to Bryn Mawr more than Bryn Mawr emphasizes these connections. The first page of Haverford's homepage mentions its extensive cooperation with nearby Bryn Mawr, whereas one has to search further on Bryn Mawr's site to discover "bi-college" clubs and literary groups or residence halls.

Despite the risks to coordination or perhaps, more accurately, the difficulties of sustaining true coordination, women have benefited from coordinate education. In coordinate women's colleges, women have not been as overwhelmed by men's dominance as they have at conventionally coeducational institutions. Their presence has been acknowledged, even celebrated, and women students have been provided with the means, through their own publications and through decision-making structures, to have their voices heard. As the 1970 president of the student government association at William Smith College noted when recalling her undergraduate years, coordination provides women students with many leadership opportunities, women role models, and their "own territory," and makes them "part of a community of women" (Connally, Founder's Day Address, 1977, HWSCA).

APPLYING LESSONS FROM COORDINATION TO COEDUCATIONAL INSTITUTIONS

Coordination, to the degree that it approximates "true coordination," or coordination in which both partners are equal in resources, builds gender equity into the heart of the educational institution. It guarantees that women's and men's concerns are brought into all decision-making rather than being assumed to be identical. Because colleges that are currently coeducational probably cannot institute coordination, we need to look for other institutional mechanisms whereby gender equity can be structured into the very fabric of a college or university. Certainly greater numbers of women—at all levels of the faculty, on the boards of trustees, in the higher administrative ranks, and among students—will help, but only if gender equity remains one of their major concerns. Specifically, women and their men allies need to work to attain the following:

- Frequent monitoring of all campus student organizations, and faculty and staff committees, to ensure that women are represented about equally to their proportion in the larger community. Without such monitoring, it may happen that women begin to disappear without people's awareness. A coordinate structure helps to guarantee that the women's "campus" gets represented. Because coeducational colleges lack such an automatic mechanism, some group that has clout needs to be responsible for monitoring gender equity in campus groups annually.
- Faculty and staff training, on an ongoing, institutionalized basis, about "chilly climate" issues and the best ways to handle them. It is naïve to assume that because faculty and staff know that men students tend to dominate, for example, in classroom interactions, that they recognize the problem in specific instances or, more importantly, have developed strategies to counter such dominance. Workshops and discussion groups on gender equity issues, using a variety of imaginative formats, should become a regular feature in academic program calendars.
- Traditions to celebrate women's accomplishments and symbols that recognize women's place in the history of the institution. A special speaker series or award named after the first or most famous woman graduate, such as the Elizabeth Blackwell Award[8] given at Hobart and William Smith Colleges, focuses attention on women's achievements. Paintings, statues, catalog histories of the college—all should be examined to ensure that women's place is given due emphasis.
- An active, well-funded, attractive women's center, where women of all sexual preferences, ethnicities, and races can organize programs, guest lectures, films, and discussions that address their concerns. These centers should have an administrator and/or faculty member to ensure that their needs get represented when programmatic decisions are made.
- A strong women's studies major, with at least some faculty dedicated to it (rather than simply borrowed from other academic major fields). Recently there has been some debate about the wisdom of making "women's" studies "gender" studies; in some institutions, gay, lesbian, bisexual, and transgender groups have worked to establish queer studies, formerly discussed to some degree within women's studies. Such changes and conflicts are probably inevitable and beneficial. What is most important is that the curriculum respond to changes in scholarship that give special attention to historically marginalized groups.

A basic lesson to be learned from coordination is that simply adding women to a formerly men's institution, which is the way coeducation typically has evolved, does not create equality. The weight of the institution's history, as well as sexism in the larger culture, means that women students (and faculty and staff) continue to be disadvantaged. Coordinate colleges have given women "a place at the table." They ensure that women's interests are not marginalized but rather represented, at least to some degree, at the levels at which key decisions are made. Coeducational institutions that are committed to gender equity need to develop similar mechanisms to counteract male privilege, not by denying that it exists but rather by building on the insight that women's concerns may be different from men's. Institutional structures that are sensitive to power differentials have the greatest potential to lessen them.

NOTES

1. The student body of women's colleges is not entirely women, either. The U.S. Department of Education reported that in 1993 approximately ten thousand men attended women's colleges, and about two-fifths of them attended full-time (Harwarth, Maline, and DeBra, 1997).

2. Depending on definitions, in 2001 the following colleges can be considered coordinate colleges:

   Barnard College and Columbia University
   College of Saint Benedict and Saint John's University
   Douglass College and Rutgers University
   Hartford College for Women at the University of Hartford
   Hobart and William Smith Colleges
   Saint Mary's College and Notre Dame University
   Scripps College, one of the consortium institutions at Claremont
   Sophie Newcomb and Tulane University
   Westhampton College and Richmond College
   Stern College and Yeshiva University

3. Woody (1929) mentions other institutions that developed coordinate colleges after they had already been coeducational: Tufts and Wisconsin, and to a lesser extent, Stanford, Chicago, and Cornell. He does not mention Wesleyan, which abandoned coeducation in the early part of the twentieth century. Connecticut College for Women was then established so that the state of Connecticut would have some institution for the higher education of women. Wesleyan did not become coeducational again until the early 1970s. (*http://www.wesleyan.edu/wmst/women.html*).

4. Key beliefs of spiritualism are that individual souls continue to exist after death and that direct communication with disembodied spirits is possible. In the nineteenth century, many spiritualists were simultaneously involved in such social reform movements as temperance, abolition, and women's rights. For all these reasons spiritualists tended to be viewed with suspicion by "respectable" society (Moore, 1977, pp. 70–74).

5. Earlier, in the 1890s, Hobart College trustees had refused a couple of petitions to allow women to take Hobart's examinations or to be admitted (Miller-Bernal, 2000, p. 70)

6. Wells College, a women's college since its founding in 1868, considered establishing a men's coordinate college at about this time (Miller-Bernal, 2000). Yale and Vassar were discussing coordination, and according to John Chandler, former president of Hamilton and Williams Colleges, both Williams and Princeton considered establishing women's coordinate colleges (personal communication, 1998). For Princeton, this would have been the second time, as briefly in the late nineteenth century, Evelyn College was a women's coordinate of Princeton (Graham, 1974).

7. An article in *The Chronicle of Higher Education* (Grassmuck, 1991) discusses various

approaches taken by small, private liberal arts colleges to cut costs and increase their chances for survival. It distinguishes pure mergers, consolidations, transfers of assets, collaborations, and joint educational ventures. Major concerns for the colleges include preserving their identity and retaining their faculty.

8. Elizabeth Blackwell received a medical degree at Geneva Medical College (Hobart was originally called Geneva College) in 1849, the first woman to graduate from a regular or allopathic medical school in the United States (Miller-Bernal, 2000).

ABBREVIATIONS

Archival sources are noted within the text using the following abbreviations: HCA = Hamilton College Archives; HWSCA = Hobart and William Smith College Archives; MCA = Middlebury College Archives.

REFERENCES

Astin, A. W., and Lee, C. B. T. (1972). *The Invisible Colleges: A Profile of Small, Private Colleges with Limited Resources.* New York: McGraw-Hill.

Eisenmann, L. (1991). "'Freedom to be Womanly': The Separate Culture of the Women's College." In P. W. Kaufman (Ed.), *The Search for Equity: Women at Brown University, 1891–1991.* Hanover and London: Brown University Press, 55–85.

Fish, V. K. (1990). "The Struggle over Women's Education in the Nineteenth Century: A Social Movement and Countermovement." In G. West and R. L. Blumberg (Eds.), *Women and Social Protest.* New York: Oxford University Press, 263–276.

Gildersleeve, V. C. (1954). *Many a Good Crusade.* New York: Macmillan.

Graham, P. A. (1974). *Community and Class in American Education, 1865–1918.* New York: John Wiley and Sons.

Grassmuck, K. (1991). "More Small Colleges Merge with Larger Ones but Some Find Process Can Be Painful." *The Chronicle of Higher Education,* September 18.

Hall, R. M., and Sandler, B. R. (1982). "The Classroom Climate: A Chilly One for Women? Project on the Status and Education of Women." Washington, D.C.: Association of American Colleges.

Harwarth, I., Maline, M., and DeBra, E. (1997). *Women's Colleges in the United States.* Washington, D.C.: U.S. Department of Education.

Horowitz, H. L. (1984). *Alma Mater.* Boston: Beacon Press.

Kerber, L. K. (1988). "'Why Should Girls Be Learned and Wise?': Two Centuries of Higher Education for Women as Seen through the Unfinished Work of Alice Mary Baldwin." In J. M. Faragher and F. Howe (Eds.), *Women and Higher Education in American History.* New York: W. W. Norton, 18–42.

May, A. J. (1977). *A History of the University of Rochester 1850–1962.* Rochester, NY: University of Rochester Press.

Miller-Bernal, L. (2000). *Separate by Degree.* New York: Peter Lang.

Moore, R. Laurence. (1977). *In Search of White Crows.* New York: Oxford University Press.

Morison, S. E. (1936/1964). *Three Centuries of Harvard, 1636–1936.* Cambridge, MA: Belknap Press of Harvard University Press.

Newcomer, M. (1959). *A Century of Higher Education for Women.* New York: Harper and Row.

Palmieri, P. A. (1987). "From Republican Motherhood to Race Suicide: Arguments on the Higher Education of Women in the United States, 1820–1920." In C. Lasser (Ed.), *Educating Men and Women Together.* Urbana: University of Illinois Press, 49–64.

Pilkington, W. (1962). *Hamilton College, 1812–1962.* Clinton, NY: Hamilton College.

Stameshkin, D. M. (1985). *The Town's College: Middlebury College, 1800–1915.* Hanover, NH: University Press of New England.

Woody, T. (1929). *A History of Women's Education in the United States.* New York: The Science Press.

CHAPTER 10

Gender Integration at Virginia Military Institute and the United States Military Academy at West Point

Diane Diamond and Michael Kimmel

INTRODUCTION

Under the universal assumption that men alone were humanity, that the world was masculine and for men only, the efforts of the women were met as a deliberate attempt to "unsex" themselves and become men. To be a woman was to be ignorant, uneducated; to be wise, educated, was to be a man. Women were not men, visibly; therefore they could not be educated, and ought not to want to be.
—CHARLOTTE PERKINS GILMAN (1911)

In recent decades, as gender barriers have fallen, women have entered many traditionally male domains. As the doors of opportunity have opened, increasing numbers of women have joined the ranks of lawyers, doctors, and military officers. However, the first women to enter such traditionally male domains typically encounter opposition to their presence. Some question why women would desire admittance into such fields, others question whether women are temperamentally suited to such "masculine" pursuits. Female pioneers have not only had to tackle the task before them (as do their male counterparts), they have also had to strive to fit into a masculine environment, contend with likely opposition to their presence, and survive as one of only a few women in a newly coeducational setting.

This chapter explores the integration of women into one such traditionally masculine environment: the military educational institution. Through a case study of two military schools, the United States Military Academy at West Point and the Virginia Military Institute (VMI), this work examines gender integration, and provides the perspectives of both female and male cadets from the first coeducational classes. Although West Point and VMI share a common identity as military educational institutions initially opposed to coeducation, they differ in significant ways, including their institutional mission, training philosophy, and approach to incorporating women into their corps of cadets. Despite these differences, striking parallels emerged both in the experience of female cadets, and the attitudes of male cadets, in the first coeducational classes at West Point and VMI.

Over four years, 1997 to 2001, we conducted interviews with women cadets at both West Point and at VMI. We interviewed ninety-three present and former cadets. Present cadets and male alumni were volunteers provided by the Office of Public Affairs at West Point and the Office of Public Relations at VMI. West Point alumnae were selected through a snowball sampling technique, asking participants to refer others for interview. At West Point, thirty-five were present or former female cadets; twenty-one were present or former male cadets. All but one of the male alumni were still on active duty in the Army. At VMI, we interviewed fifteen current male cadets and twenty female cadets.[1] (This number of female cadets represents half of all cadets ever enrolled at the school.) These semistructured interviews ranged over a variety of issues, including their motivations for attending a military school, their social and educational experiences, and their perceptions of the barriers to women's full integration.

We argue that gender was, and remains, the most significant issue that structures the experiences of women cadets. As in other male-dominated occupations and institutions (police, firefighting, the military itself, as well as many corporations) women face a constant negotiation between public perceptions of successful femininity and successful performance in the institutional role (Williams, 1989).

To better understand coeducation at VMI and West Point, we begin by providing some background on the circumstances in which they became coeducational, and a description of their distinct institutional cultures. Next, we describe the institutions' approaches to incorporating women into their corps of cadets. Then, we describe the experiences of female cadets in the first coeducational classes at West Point and VMI, tracking changes in the experience of female cadets at West Point over more than two decades of coeducation. Finally, we examine the attitudes of male cadets in the first coeducational classes at West Point and VMI.

HISTORY

In the summer of 1976, the first women entered the United States Military Academy at West Point as cadets. This ended a constitutional debate that had begun two years earlier, as the United States Congress sought to decide whether West Point's all-male Corps of Cadets violated the Fourteenth Amendment of the Constitution. West Point officials had argued that West Point training was inappropriate for women, because it trained men to join the army's infantry in harsh Spartan conditions—conditions that were unsuitable for women. They argued that the costs of modifying the facilities to accommodate female cadets was prohibitive and that women's presence would sap the morale of the men, making impossible the bonding necessary for "unit cohesion." Unconvinced, Congress passed the Stratton Amendment in October 1975, admitting women to all federal service academies. With some resignation, West Point opened its doors to women in the summer of 1976.

Fifteen years later, Virginia Military Institute, a state-supported military educational institution, began a long court battle to preserve its male-only admissions policy. Like West Point before it, VMI argued that the essential character of the institution would change with the admission of women (VMI II, 1995). VMI officials maintained that women were not suited to VMI's "adversative" educational methodology, and that the presence of women would undermine the cohesiveness of the corps. Although the lower court ruled in favor of VMI, the appellate decision reversed the lower court's decision, and remanded the case back to the district court for remediation. VMI then proposed the formation of a separate women's version of VMI, and VMI provided funds to establish the Virginia Women's Institute for Leadership (VWIL) at Mary Baldwin College, a women's college thirty miles from VMI. Although the district and circuit courts agreed with VMI that VWIL would provide women with a comparable educational experience that was suitable to their gender, the Supreme Court was unpersuaded. In June 1996, the Supreme Court followed the path set by the Congress twenty-five years earlier, and ruled seven to one that VWIL did not provide women with the opportunities that would be offered them at VMI and "Virginia Military Institute's all-male admissions policy violated women's constitutional right to equal protection." (Justice Clarence Thomas recused himself because his son was attending VMI at the time.)

Whereas West Point had been compelled to admit women, VMI's Board of Visitors could have voted to relinquish state funding and have VMI become a private institution. Although privatization would have permitted VMI to preserve its all-male admission policy, it was a costly proposition. Cognizant of this fact, on September 21, 1996, VMI's board of trustees voted (by a narrow margin of nine to eight), to admit women into the Institute's corps of cadets. Thus, in 1997, little more than two decades after the first women entered West Point as Plebes, the first women entered VMI as Rats.

INSTITUTIONAL CULTURE

Both West Point and VMI maintain a spartan military environment and regimen where incoming students receive indoctrination aimed at transforming them into cadets. As part of this process, entering Plebes and Rats are given closely cropped haircuts, issued uniforms, and taught the proper way to march, salute, and address those with seniority. Cadets at both schools live by the honor code, "cadets will neither lie, cheat, steal, nor tolerate those who do." They rise early and their days are highly regimented, filled with military, athletic, and cadet activities, in addition to academic classes. A typical day may include marching, military drill, discipline, class, and extracurricular activities. Although both schools employ a military paradigm, their end products differ. Whereas West Point trains its cadets to become U.S. Army officers, VMI trains its cadets to become *citizen-soldiers*. Citizen-soldiers are "prepared both for civilian leadership in their professions and for military leadership in times of national need" (VMI admissions brochure, 1999). Every graduate of West Point incurs a five-year commitment to the army, but only about 35 percent of each graduating class at VMI accept commissions in the armed services (VMI admissions brochure, 1999).

> At West Point the basic unit of leadership . . . is the company, dominated by an offi-
> cer of the United States Army. At VMI the class system, with leadership by cadets, is
> at the core of cadet conduct. . . . The differences between the two schools is logical.
> VMI is a college educating primarily for civilian life. Its students, cadets, pursue
> their academic courses in a regimen of strict military discipline to the end of draw-
> ing out the whole man. . . . The mission of the United States Military Academy, on
> the other hand, being military instruction and organization. The Academy in fact is
> a segment of the U.S. military establishment. (Wise, 1978, p. 422).

Both schools have "rigorous, challenging, stressful, physically demand-ing training programs," but their approaches to training, and the duration of their acute initiation (comparable to boot camp) differ.

A cornerstone of VMI is its Ratline, an adversarial system of verbal abuse and physical stress. During the Ratline, freshmen (Rats) are yelled at, dropped for pushups, placed under constant stress, and learn "about persistence against adversity" (VMI Admissions Brochure, 2000, p. 20). The Ratline typically lasts seven months and ends in February of freshman (Rat) year. West Point's Cadet Basic Training, by comparison, lasts six weeks during the summer before fresh-man (Plebe) year. During Cadet Basic Training "extensive demands are made on new cadets as a test of their emotional stability, perseverance, and ability to organize and perform under stress" (West Point Online Admissions Brochure, 2001). At both schools training is demanding and stressful; however, at West Point the emphasis is on positive leadership, at VMI, it is on adversarial disci-pline. These disparate missions and training paradigms may explain the institu-tions' differing approaches to incorporating women into their corps of cadets.

ASSIMILATION VERSUS INTEGRATION

Prior to the arrival of the first female cadets, each institution needed to deter-mine how women were to be incorporated into its corps of cadets. Whereas West Point chose to "integrate" women into its corps of cadets, VMI chose to "assim-ilate" women into its corps of cadets. This subtle difference in wording reveals a significant difference in institutional approach; whereas *integrate* is "to bring together or incorporate, to unite," *assimilate* is "to bring into conformity, adapt or adjust; to cause to resemble" (*Random House Dictionary of the English Language*, 1967). Thus, whereas West Point sought to incorporate women into the Academy, VMI applied an equality equals sameness paradigm that sought for women to conform to the already existing standards of the Institute. These distinct ideological positions are best illustrated by the institutions' differing approaches to physical fitness standards for women and men.

At the start of integration, West Point developed, and has maintained a system of "equivalent training," which recognized physiological differences between men and women. This is also known as "gender norming." During the first years of integration at West Point "equivalent training" was perceived as establishing lower standards for women and fostered animosity among many male cadets. Project Athena, West Point's self-study of the first four years of coeducation, concluded that:

> many male cadets still do not accept or understand the doctrine of equivalent training. As long as the doctrine is not accepted, men will continue to use physical performance differences as an artificial headwind to the integration of women in physical development (Adams, 1980, p. 140).

Ten years later, male cadets at West Point were still complaining about the dual standards. As one female alumna explained:

> While at West Point, there was always much griping among the males that the physical standards for females were lower than for males. The attitude among many seemed to be that if females wanted to compete with males, then they should also have to meet the same physical fitness standards (numbers of pushups, pullups, etc.) as the males. . . . I am glad that the physiological differences between men and women are recognized. . . . As long as everyone is contributing with their personal strengths, the team is strong (And, how heavy is a rifle, after all?). (WP 2–6)

An alumna from one of the first coeducational classes at the Academy, who returned to West Point as an officer in the early 1990s, expressed her consternation at male cadets' continued lack of understanding about the need for differential standards:

> There's a lot of hype about, "women don't have to do the same athletically as we do." And it's funny, the same people, well, they understand that as you get older, "well we don't expect Schwartzkopf to be able to run the two-mile run." . . . Well you understand that because you understand physiology right? When you age you can't do as much. And the point of the P.T. test is to ensure you're fit. So why don't you understand that men and women are physiologically different? . . . The P.T. test is not a fitness for combat. Simply, we want a fit force. But they don't get that because they don't want to. (WP 1–5)

Today, dissension over West Point's differential physical fitness standards is more muted yet remains a point of protest for some male cadets who question women's place at the Academy.[2] Although some West Point male cadets still do not accept dual physical fitness standards, today, most seem to recognize the need for gender norming.

Whereas West Point adopted a strategy of gender norming, with dual standards for female and male cadets, VMI chose to maintain a single standard (i.e., male standard) for its female and male cadets. Although a single physical fitness standard may appear gender neutral, it is, in fact, based on a standard developed by and for men. As sociologist Joan Acker explains:

> Understanding how the appearance of gender neutrality is maintained in the face of overwhelming evidence of gendered structures is an important part of analyzing gendered institutions. One conceptual mechanism is the positing of an abstract, general human being, individual, or worker who apparently has no gender. On closer examination, that individual almost always has the social characteristics of men but that fact is not noted. (Acker, 1992, p. 568)

Having adopted a policy of assimilation, it was ideologically consistent not to separate VMI cadets based on gendered physiological differences. In concordance with VMI's assimilation policy, a VMI male cadet remarked, "I feel that if a female is going to come here she should be able to pass the fitness test. If she wants to be here that bad she should get in shape and be able to pass it" (VMI 1–1M). Another asserted, "I believe that if they decide to have women here, that they have to perform up to the standards that have been upheld. You don't lower your standard. We don't lower our standard for anybody" (VMI 1–2M).

However, because since the physical fitness standard at VMI is based on the male body, more female cadets than male cadets fail the Virginia Fitness Test (VFT). Although it came as no surprise that VMI male cadets insisted that female cadets meet the "standard" set by the institution, it was somewhat surprising that VMI female cadets were adamant that standards not be changed. VMI male and female cadets alike maintained that women could achieve the goals set for them if they worked hard and put in the extra effort. One VMI female cadet who expressed concern that VMI was considering changing the VFT standards for women provided a rationale shared by many female cadets for preferring a single physical fitness standard:

> They're trying to adjust it to female standards. . . . You do that and that's gonna single us out even more. That's gonna make us look even weaker. And the male cadets are just gonna resent us even more. We don't need that. So you might as well just keep the standard. Keep it straight across the board. (VMI 1–4F)

Thus, it seemed preferable to the women to maintain a single standard even though fewer female cadets would pass the VFT. Given the alternatives—failing the test or being resented by male cadets—female cadets preferred failure. However, as a VMI professor noted, there were consequences for not adopting a policy of gender norming:

> They have not adjusted the VFT . . . and that has caused some problems. You know, women can't pass it. It's geared towards men and the women can't pass it and there-

fore it's a double standard. It's a setup. The women can't pass it and to be respected in the corps you have to pass it and so they don't stand a chance. (VMI Faculty Member)

In 2000, when West Point and VMI cadets were asked whether physical fitness standards should be the same or different for male and female cadets responses varied more by institution than gender. Although the majority of male and female cadets at VMI maintained that PT standards should be the same, and the majority of male and female cadets at West Point asserted that PT standards need to take physiological differences into account. Although this may be partly the result of embracing one's own institutional culture, it may also reflect the different types of demands and pressures that each set of women faced.

SUPPORT SYSTEMS

VMI and West Point are both total institutions, "a place of residence and work where a large number of like individuals, cut off from the wider society for an appreciable period of time, together lead an enclosed, formally administered round of life" (Goffman, 1961, p. 1). Although emotional support and advice are useful in any environment, it is crucial in a total institution, where individuals are immersed in institutional practices from the moment they wake up to the moment they fall asleep, and much is learned outside of official channels.

Support systems have long existed for men at military institutions, providing them with practical information and emotional support. Given women's minority status within these institutions, it is all the more important that they have access to support systems. Two characteristics of VMI culture helped provide support to VMI's first female cadets. The first was VMI's long established formal support system known as the Dyke-Rat system. Through a system of "compulsory fraternization" each Rat (freshman) is assigned a *Dyke*[3] (senior) to whom she or he is expected to turn for succor. Given the adversative nature of the institution, the Rat-Dyke relationship is vital for surviving the Ratline. The women found their Dykes an important means of support. Explained one VMI female cadet, "sometimes you just need a mentor. It's hard to make it by yourself. That's why VMI gives people mentors . . . some people take that job seriously and that's what helps you through this place" (VMI 1–10F).

A second form of support at VMI that helped reduce isolation among female cadets was VMI's housing arrangement. Cadets are housed four to five to a room, which makes for both cramped living quarters and provides other female cadets with whom they could communicate and find support. One VMI female cadet compared her experience with that of the first female cadets at West Point, "[female cadets at West Point] were much more spread out. We're more living together. We always had that. Even though we had nobody older we always had each other" (VMI 1–10F).

West Point's first female cadets recounted fewer support systems than VMI's first female cadets. At West Point, there was no support system comparable to the Dyke-Rat system at VMI. West Point did create a support system especially for the women, the Margaret Corbin Seminar. Established as a forum where female cadets could meet and find support, the Corbin Seminar was belittled by male cadets. Consequently, many female cadets chose not to attend. One alumna from the first coeducational class at West Point explained, "The main stigma attached to the Corbin Seminar was that it was a 'women's' group. We were always made to feel bad about wanting to meet together with other women" (Barkalow, 1992, p. 100). An alumna who did attend the Seminar recalled that the meetings made her feel "re-energized," but, she conceded, "I did not *publicize* my attendance at these meetings to anyone other than close friends and roommates for fear of retribution" (WP 1–8).

West Point's first female cadets were also geographically segregated, spread out throughout the companies. Often a woman's roommate was the only other female cadet in the company. One woman from the first coeducational class at West Point recalled, "we were very isolated in that there was only a room (or at most two) of us [women] in any company (of 120 or so cadets). Unless we were involved in some sort of activity, we didn't have much to do with other women at all. No, the support was totally ineffective. Lots of times the roommate was the problem!!" (WP 1–7F).

One arena where the women at both West Point and VMI were able to meet and find support was sports teams. Recalled a woman from the first coed class at West Point,

> We did a lot of bonding on the team . . . . I found that it was on the gymnastics team [that] we let it hang out. . . . We did more crying on that gymnastics team . . . we'd listen and we'd support each other. That woman would cry and then we'd move on. It was a real release and it was very important. (WP 1–5F)

One VMI female cadet recounted:

> Besides just talking about all the things that have gone on during the day or during the week or how this happened . . . often stories or things that come up where, "oh my gosh, you won't believe what this male cadet did" . . . But it's just something where we can talk and talk and talk about what's going on at VMI and of course it helps cause we can talk about a lot of things. Still, the majority of our conversations do center around things that the males have done that we're upset about. (VMI 1–2F)

Although female cadets at both schools reported that they benefited from participating on team sports, they found that it, too, was often negatively regarded by some male cadets. An alumna from the first coeducational class at West Point described both support and resentment from participating on team sports:

The best deal for woman-to-woman contact was the varsity sports teams. Intramural sports were all coed (not enough women to field a basketball team if there are only four women in a company!). So, us athletes had very good friendship and support from other women. Consequences were mixed and interesting. There was some support for the women's teams, but resentment of course as well. It's always such a mixed bag! (WP 1–7F)

At VMI, male cadets frequently complained that some female cadets joined sports teams in order to get out of (otherwise required) Ratline activities.[4] A VMI female cadet on the cross-country and track team reported that male cadets would stop her on the stoop and declare, "most of you females just come here to get in sports to get out of stuff. . . . Why would you come to our school and then join every sport you can think of or anything you can think of to get out of everything?" (VMI 1–2F).

The first female cadets at both schools encountered male cadets who did not want them to engage in any activity that would set them apart from the men, whether it be attending a seminar expressly created for women or participating in an activity that removed them from Ratline activities. When the women participated in activities that set them apart, they faced resentment by some of the male cadets. Nonetheless, the first female cadets at West Point and VMI benefited greatly from those opportunities where they were able to secure advice and support, either through contact with other women, as on sports teams or with roommates, or through a mentor, such as a Dyke.

Although both schools provided their first female cadets with sports teams and seminars or established support systems, they realized that unlike subsequent classes, these first women would have no same-sex role models within the corps. Role models or mentors have been found to be important to women's success within academia (Chandler, 1996) and some evidence suggests that students prefer mentors of their own gender (Gumbiner, 1998). Both VMI and West Point concluded that the women would benefit from same-sex role models and so each imported women to serve as mentors for their first female cadets.

FEMALE ROLE MODELS

West Point brought in women officers to serve as role models for its first female cadets. However, for several reasons the first female cadets did not find them especially helpful (Barkalow, 1990; Diamond and Kimmel, 1999). First, these women had not attended the academy and did not know what it was like to be a cadet. Second, they were all older single women who had made the military their life. This gave female cadets the impression that military women could not have both professional and personal lives. The female cadets wanted to see military women who were wives and mothers, as well as officers. An alumna from the first coeducational class at West Point recalled a female officer West Point brought in to help the female cadets:

She was a nice woman and she certainly was a woman officer, but she wasn't in a lot of ways a good role model because she was not married. She didn't have children. She didn't have a family. At some point after about November, the women were going, what do we turn into, people who can't have kids? And you're going to just be a single woman your entire life. Is this what I want? Is this who I came here to be? (WP 1–1F)

Many of West Point's first female cadets opted for male role models rather than model themselves after the women officers.

As women progressed through the ranks, as cadets and later as officers, subsequent classes had female upperclassmen and officers to whom they could turn for advice and guidance. In the late 1990s several female cadets described how, on their arrival at the Academy, upper-class female cadets sat them down and explained that they would "be there" if the new female cadets had a problem. "Their door was always open. They didn't treat us any different but they came in and they told us that that support net's there" (WP 3–3). Upper-class female cadets were especially useful early on when the new cadets did not know to whom they should turn for advice. Women described a range of issues for which they might seek the advice of another female cadet rather than someone in their chain-of-command:

When I was a plebe, the upperclass females in the company got us together and said, if you ever have a problem, either harassment, or just like a girl problem, or anything, that we should just go talk to them because they were familiar with the experiences. Guys in our chain of command weren't familiar with those kinds of things so, that was a comforting thing. (WP 3–2)

Female officers at the Academy also served as models of achievement for the female cadets. A female cadet in 1997 described the importance of upper-classmen and female officers as role models to new female cadets (plebes):

Firsties [seniors] here know what West Point is like and they had women before them who experienced it and kind of set the standard that what we have to do. They're like our role models. The majors, the female majors on post . . . you can talk to them. . . . And if it wasn't for those upper-class women, I mean, where would you turn? You're a plebe. You're a freshman. You can't even call anyone by their name, can't even go to the bathroom without asking. (WP 3–1)

Today, women are found at almost all levels at West Point, from plebes to upper-class leaders, and from military trainers to officers and professors. Even if these women do not take on a mentoring role for the female cadets, their presence throughout the ranks sends a message to both male and female cadets that women can achieve in the military. Having females in positions of authority provides female cadets with role models who are women like themselves. The presence of female officers and upperclassmen increases female cadets' sense of belonging and overall satisfaction.

Surmising that VMI's first female cadets would benefit from female role models, VMI invited upper-class female cadets from Texas A&M and Norwich University. Unlike West Point's first female cadets who had lacked exposure to more advanced female cadets, VMI's first female cadets were given role models with whom they could more readily identify, role models who were younger and already cadets. Although these imported mentors would seem to fill a void for the first female cadets, interviews with VMI female cadets suggest that, similar to West Point's first female officers, these role models were not entirely useful. Because each institution has its own unique practices and culture, the female role models from other military institutions could not teach VMI female cadets how to navigate the VMI system. Nor had these imported mentors participated in VMI's arduous rite of passage known as the Ratline. Instead, female cadets turned to male mentors, assigned to them through VMI's Rat-Dyke system. When one of the first women at VMI was asked why she did not seek out these "mentors," she explained:

> Because they were outsiders. They weren't here. . . . How can you tell me how to get through the Ratline when you've never been through it. How can you tell me how to fill out a special if you've never done it, when you haven't done it twenty thousand times before. How can you get me out of trouble when you don't know the right people to go to or all these other things. They were pretty much useless. (VMI 1–10F)

Another felt sorry for the exchange student role models because they did not have a clearly defined role and they were not respected by the corps.

> Actually, looking back I feel kind of bad for those girls. They totally stood out. They wore their uniforms, had long hair, and they weren't sure of their role. The administrators were kind of like, they're supposed to be there in case you need somebody to talk to or whatever, but since we had Dykes we didn't really, you know. I remember talking to a lot of people [who told us] . . . "They're stupid. They don't belong here. They didn't go through the Ratline," this and that. And looking back I feel really bad for those girls cause they wanted to help. (VMI 1–9F)

Nonetheless, female cadets may have benefited from the female role models in other ways: Some evidence suggests that the female exchange students may have served as role models for male cadets acclimating them to the presence of women as upper-class cadets.

> It was more good for the upperclass then it was for the Rats because as Rats our mentality was that these individuals did not go through the Ratline and they have no right to tell us what to do or how to do it. . . . I think it was good for the upperclass because they were a class that just wasn't used to having females around. . . . I think it was good for the upper-class. (VMI 1–6F)

EXTRA ATTENTION IS NEGATIVE ATTENTION

At both schools the first female cadets received a great deal of attention; a major consequence of all the extra attention was resentment by male cadets. During the first four years of coeducation, West Point conducted an extensive study, entitled Project Athena, that followed the progress of the first female cadets at the Academy. Although Project Athena provided valuable insights into the process and progress of coeducation, the study itself had an adverse effect on the women's integration. West Point's first female cadets were frequently released from day-to-day activities in order to participate in interviews and studies for Project Athena. An alumna explained:

> We were removed for discussion periods at points along the way, though a lot of times that was interviews which is something I really . . . feel strongly against, this selecting you out. You know, inevitably it was a time when you should have been doing something else and the repercussions of that were fairly long winded. . . . Any kind of drawing you out of the crowd, for whatever reason, whether it's for interviews, doing weight tests, you know, we had a lot of that done on us. That's always detrimental because it's always perceived as you're getting away with something. You're telling tales or whatever. It's a no-win situation. (WP 1–3)

The female cadets resented being removed from activities for constant interviews and testing, and the male cadets became jealous of the extra attention female cadets were receiving. One male alumni from the first coed class at West Point recalled that "the huge amount of public attention was hard for all to bear: The women didn't want more attention and the men were jealous" (WP 1–9M). Many male cadets perceived the additional attention as confirmation that female cadets were receiving special (i.e., preferential) treatment; as another male alumni from the first coed class recounted:

> I know a lot of us were somewhat disturbed or irritated by all the attention that was shown to the women. . . . From our perspective it was kind of a big deal that we were at West Point and then suddenly that first year the 4,300 men were no longer important. What was important was the 100 women. (WP 1–2M)

By contrast, VMI undertook no comparable study of assimilation. Having studied both military and civilian institutions that became coeducational, VMI officials concluded that no unnecessary attention should be drawn to the female cadets. Explained Colonel Bissell, who was in charge of assimilation at VMI:

> All the lessons learned from every college . . . they all did the same things and did them wrong. They first of all took the women and kept them separate till they got bigger numbers and then they didn't have the same uniforms, in some cases [they had] separate little corps and that polarized it worse. And you know, they had separate meetings with the women. It made the men mad. You could write down the lessons learned and say, don't do it. I mean it didn't take a mental genius to sit down and say we shouldn't repeat things.

Yet, in spite of VMI's efforts to not separate the women from the men, VMI's first female cadets still found themselves the center of attention. Attention came in the form of the press and researchers who interviewed them, and visitors who ogled at them. And as at West Point, male cadets in VMI's first coed classes resented all the extra attention given the females. "The only thing that really gets me . . . [is the] press always coming here asking people . . . questions about women this, women that, all the crap about women, here and there, people always talking about it," commented one male cadet. "It's just ground into people's faces all the time" (VMI 1–7M). Several male cadets recalled with annoyance the time news organizations came to interview the first VMI female cadet to receive a high-ranking position.

> When one of our upper-classmen females was appointed to a high-ranking position I heard that . . . *Good Morning America* came to interview her . . . we had a guy made an even higher spot but why didn't he get interviewed? I heard some dissention about that. Why does the less ranking official get interviewed by *Good Morning America* simply because she's female? (VMI 2–1M)

This extra attention alienated male cadets and created antipathy toward female cadets.

> We have a female that's been appointed to battalion commander position. Well, every magazine, every newspaper . . . made a big deal out of it and a lot of friends that got comparable positions they're just like, "whatever." . . . That creates a lot of animosity. (VMI 2–5M)

Not only did male cadets resent the extra attention given female cadets, female cadets resented it, too. Female cadets experienced negative repercussions from being the center of attention. Asked what was the hardest part about being a female cadet at VMI, a woman from the first coeducational class responded:

> Everybody likes looking at us. . . . Everybody says, "You were with them [researchers]? What did they want to know?" Things like this [our interview] make it very uncomfortable for us to go back in the barracks. Because they probably don't see that you guys are going to be interviewing men too. . . . They just get jealous. They want the attention, too. (VMI 1–1F)

The first female cadets found it impossible to simply blend in and be members of the corps. Instead, they were constantly reminded that they were *female* cadets, not just cadets.

LOSS OF FEMININITY

Like their male counterparts, the first women at West Point and VMI were striving to be good cadets. Unlike their male counterparts, as women, they had the additional burden of striving to fit into a masculine environment. How did the first female cadets negotiate their way as women in a masculine environment? Did they lose their femininity in order to be accepted by the male cadets, or were they able to maintain their femininity in such a pervasively masculine environment?

West Point's Project Athena concluded that, "for women, exposure to the masculine environment did not adversely affect the feminine side of their self-concept" (Adams, 1979, p. 63). In an interview as a senior, an alumna from West Point's first coeducational class remarked, "I never worried about losing my femininity. I thought it was totally ridiculous that anyone even thought that we would lose our femininity" (Adams, 1980, p. 109).

Nor did VMI's first female cadets seem concerned that they were losing their feminine identity. One female cadet remarked:

> I really don't find it that difficult because no matter how you look at it I'm still a girl and I'm still going to be a girl. My roommates are girls and we still have our little girly conversations and we find our times to get away from people and VMI doesn't insist that you be a man. It insists that you be a qualified cadet. (VMI 2-7F)

In her study of female recruits in the Marine Corps, Williams (1989) also found that "women in the marines do not feel that their femininity is threatened when they engage in 'nonfeminine' activities" (Williams, 1989, p. 79). Apprehension over "loss of femininity" prompted both the Marine Corps and West Point (but not VMI) to institute policies to insure that femininity be maintained. The Marine Corps, the only branch of the military that required all women recruits to wear makeup, had its women "take classes on makeup, hair care, poise, and etiquette" (Williams, 1989, p. 63). West Point, fearing that its first female cadets might become masculinized, likewise organized a makeup class for its women. This alienated the female cadets who felt that wearing makeup was a personal decision.

> I personally never wore makeup. I never wore makeup before. I don't wear makeup now.... One minute we were supposed to do bayonet training and the spirit of the bayonet is to kill. And screaming and yelling and you're in camouflage. And then the next half hour later you're cleaned up, over. You're cleaned up well. But then, what's the real woman, what the real girl? We were girls becoming women.... We were girls turning into women and we felt we had choices and makeup was one of them. If that was gonna make us feel better about ourselves, we would make that choice ourselves. This class was an insult because it assumed that we had no idea what we were doing, and that's why we weren't doing it. (WP 1-4)

By the time VMI became coeducational, the number of women in traditionally masculine occupations had increased substantially. There were no longer institutional concerns that women entering such fields would lose their femininity. VMI also learned from other institutions' experiences with incorporating women. Thus, VMI did not institute makeup classes for its women.

DOWNPLAYING FEMININITY

Despite their insistence that they did not risk losing their femininity as cadets, women at both West Point and VMI were certain that successful gender identity was constantly in play. For many, the phrase "female cadet" was an oxymoron: One could not simultaneously be successful as a cadet and a woman (Diamond, Kimmel, and Schroeder, 1997). At West Point, the first female cadets found that femininity was discouraged. "They [male cadets] didn't want us to be the slightest bit feminine" (WP 1–3F), recalled one woman in the first coed class. Project Athena reported that female cadets "avoided culturally feminine behavior, no makeup, short hair" (Adams, 1979, p. 63), yet the female cadets were sent to the barber as soon as their hair began to grow out. Although instructed by the Academy in the fine art of wearing makeup, female cadets were ostracized when they wore it, or their army-issue skirts. Not surprisingly, many of the first female cadets also chose to avoid outward displays of femininity in order to blend in and be accepted by male cadets. An alumna from the fourth coeducational class at West Point described attitudes toward femininity among women in the first coed class and women in her own class:

> They did what they had to do to not . . . stand out, very short haircut, they never wore makeup, they never wore their skirt, anything like that that would make them singled out. Well, our class [class of 1983] comes along and we want to wear makeup, and we want to wear our skirts. And I think to some extent, to some of these women, it bothered them. . . . There was some resentment from the first class. It was like we were doing it on our own terms, they did it on the men's terms, and they sort of, in a way, looked down on us because we wanted to be feminine, wanted to wear our skirts, and we wanted to be seen as women. (WP 1–5)

Yet, almost a decade after the inception of coeducation at West Point, female cadets were still struggling to fit in as women in a highly masculine environment. "Females wanted to be 'one of the guys' sometimes and 'still feminine' at others and that is a hard combination to hold" recalled a West Point alumna (WP 2–1). Even after female cadets had become an established presence at the Academy, they continued to find male resistance to femininity. Femininity could be taken as a sign of weakness.

> Any attempt to be particularly feminine in uniform was scorned, more so at West Point than in the Army. If you wore a skirt to dinner formation, you were chided for dropping out of formation, unable to keep up with the march in high heels. . . . Feminine equals weak, so it was hard to strike the balance. You were encouraged to have a deep, command voice to call cadence and give commands. My other roommate was harassed and made fun of so terribly when she became deputy brigade

commander and gave squeaky, feminine commands. Because her voice was higher, she couldn't do the job as well, or so the males thought. (WP 2–6)

Today, more than twenty years after the first women entered the Academy, female cadets seem more comfortable with being feminine in a masculine environment. An alumna from the class of 1988, who worked at the Academy in the late 1990s, described changes in female cadets' experiences of femininity:

> Women seem more confident and much more feminine than in my day. We all looked like men while we were here . . . afraid to wear makeup or skirts because we were supposed to be soldiers not women. . . . I think they feel like they can look like women and still be cadets at the same time. That took a while for men to accept the women as women and as cadets at the same time. I have talked to some female cadets however and I think they still feel some of the same feelings about not being feminine enough but I have to say the way they look now is ten times better than what we looked like back then. (WP 2–1)

A man from the second coeducational class at West Point who was working at West Point in 2001 concurred:

> When I was a cadet the women cadets almost always tried to blend in as much as possible. This meant wearing trousers and minimal makeup and trying not to be too feminine. This is not true today. The women cadets today do not seem to feel that they have to bury their femininity. (WP 1–9M)

As at West Point, the first female cadets at VMI also struggled to negotiate femininity within a masculine institution. Some VMI female cadets confessed that living in such a pervasively male environment made them yearn all the more for outward displays of femininity.

> A lot of the girls, they want to be more feminine. They want to show their femininity. They want to put the skirt on, the makeup on, and I can see that because there are times here at VMI it just gets so stressful and the guys look at you like, I don't know, they don't look at you like they do other girls in general. They don't look at you like they would a girl that goes to UVA or whatever and I think a lot of it is the stigma attached to women here at VMI. (VMI 1–5F)

One way VMI female cadets chose to display their femininity was through wearing their skirts. Some felt it was an act of defiance; some simply liked wearing them. Others chose not to wear them because they wanted to blend in and/or they did not like wearing skirts. A VMI female cadet who decided to wear her skirt described the first time she wore it.

> Last year when we just got skirts and everybody was making a big deal about it like, "You know you can't wear your skirts. You wanted to come here, you know, you want to be the same as us. You can't wear skirts." I was like, ugh, "Well, I'm going

to wear mine to class." So I wore mine to class and I walked in. I was so scared . . . my heart was pounding and I knew everybody was staring at me. (VMI 1–9F)

Another who chose not to wear her skirt explained, "something you want to do is fit in here as much as possible. I refuse to cut my hair again. I just refuse to do it. So I'm not going to wear a skirt. I'm going to try to fit in as much as possible and plus, I hate skirts." However, she remarked, "One of my roommates was the first girl who wore a skirt on post to class and she just got hammered. . . . The cadets voiced their opinion so I feel bad for her, too. It wasn't right." Asked why she wasn't going to cut her hair to fit in better she replied, "Cause . . . the minute I step off post with a haircut like that I'm a freak. I don't want to look like that" (VMI 1–4F). Keeping their hair short made female cadets look more like male cadets but it made them look different from women outside of VMI. The women had to negotiate a compromise between outward displays of femininity and fitting in through uniformity (i.e., looking and dressing like the men). For some, fitting in took precedence, for others affirming their femininity on occasion was more important, even though that made them vulnerable to criticism from the men.

VMI's assimilation paradigm asked female cadets to conform to the already existing cadet model. Neither the institution nor the male cadets realized that the generic cadet they expected female cadets to become was, in fact, gendered male. Both the institution and male cadets had difficulty accepting female cadets as women.

> As far as skirts go and things like that, they integrated women but they integrated women who looked like men, acted like men. You couldn't tell the difference. Maybe, but barely. You could hardly tell the difference and I think they need to realize now that you can't do that. You have to integrate women. You have to deal with the fact that there are women here and you can't make us look like men. Cause people would say . . . 'Well, you wanted to come here. You have to do this. . . . I think you should have the same haircut as the men.' And I think they tried to do that in the beginning to make us just like the guys but I think that's changing now. (VMI 1–9F)

Many male cadets in the first coeducational classes at both schools resented when female cadets asserted their femininity and they criticized female cadets who aspired to be different in any way. An alumna from the first coeducational class at West Point described the importance placed on women blending in.

> The first hurdle for men seemed to be accepting that women could do the same things they did. Once they got over that their attitude was, "Okay, you women can do what we do, but then that means you're one of us. As long as you blend in, you're okay. But don't stand out as a separate group." There could be no unity without uniformity. (Barkalow, 1990, p. 100)

Many VMI male cadets expressed similar sentiments, stressing that female cadets should not try to be different or stand out. "You may be female but just try and be one of the guys. Do everything they do and don't try and be different or single yourself out and you'll fit in like everyone else" (VMI 1–4M) asserted a VMI male cadet. "Blending in and conforming is a basic part of life at military school," declared another, who then expressed his indignation over female cadets' desire to display their femininity.

> By virtue of being at VMI they have destroyed the fraternal brotherhood that they
> so desperately wanted to be a part of. This is not enough though: now they yearn
> for a greater degree of femininity and individuality. . . . If they were so interested in
> being lady like and expressing themselves, why did they come to a military school
> and an environment that scorns individualism? First earrings, then long hair, and
> skirts. Where do we draw the line?" (*www.mellennj.mellen.com/ed2.htm*)

MALE CADET ATTITUDES

These last comments illustrate our central argument: The greatest obstacle to the acceptance of women at VMI and West Point was, and remains, the behaviors and attitudes of men. Asked to identify the most significant obstacle she had to overcome, an alumna from the first coed class at West Point replied, "the total, complete, entrenched opposition to women" (WP 1–8F). Answered another, "attitudes . . . and knowing you weren't really accepted" (WP 1–5F). VMI female cadets proffered similar answers. "The hardest obstacle?" replied one of VMI's first female cadets, "I think it's just overall acceptance by the guys" (VMI 1–5F). "The guys . . . just have to be willing to accept us because we're going to be here for the rest of history," replied another (VMI 1–7F).

The most common reason offered by male cadets at VMI for opposing coeducation was tradition. One VMI male cadet maintained that other male cadets "just feel they've broken up the tradition that we've had here. You know, so many other schools, why did you have to come specifically here to ruin what they consider a traditional brotherhood" (VMI 1–5M). "The big disadvantage is tradition that was broke[n]" (VMI 1–2M) asserted another. Even VMI male cadets who had never experienced VMI without women still mourned the loss of the all-male tradition: "One thing that I did like was the fact that there was a tradition here and that once I heard that females were gonna be coming there I was like, 'oh man,' you know, 'nothing's held sacred anymore.' I was very upset about that" (VMI 2–2M). Tradition was also among the reasons male cadets in the first coeducational classes at West Point opposed coeducation. Asked how supportive male cadets were of female cadets, an alumnus from the last all-male class at the Academy replied, "generally unsupportive" and then advanced several reasons why West Point male cadets opposed coeducation.

> [F]or many of the reasons, you know, tradition, for the idea that they were being
> treated differently than we were . . . a lot of my contemporaries thought that West

Point should only be producing combat arms officers and since women were not allowed in combat arms they shouldn't be here. Really it was a specious argument because we produced noncombat arms officers but there was a fair amount of Neanderthals who just didn't like the idea of women at West Point. (WP 1–2M)

Even when male cadets did not enter with a bias against female cadets, there were male cadets with seniority who taught them to resent female cadets for invading their domain. At West Point and VMI cadets with seniority had a great deal of influence both in inculcating certain attitudes in the incoming male cadets and in hampering integration of female cadets.

[T]he class that were seniors when I was a freshmen were the last all male class so they obviously had, I don't want to say a chip on their shoulder but they certainly had this feeling of the last. . . . So they had that air about them and I think that they made it very obvious that their last kind of goal . . . it wasn't their goal as a class but certainly certain individuals you know made it very difficult for some of the females because of that. (WP 1–8M)

Although some VMI male cadets came to accept female cadets, many continued to feel that the presence of women had destroyed an essential part of VMI. Remarked one VMI male cadet, "I just think that the friendships and the camaraderie is a really big part of life here and that just by their presence it's just sort of breaks it up a little. I think it's also just a shame, the destruction of a tradition" (VMI 1–5M). Among the fiercest resisters, some male cadets attempted to force women out, blackball them, and treated them as lepers from whom they kept their distance.

I know that there are cadets here that really totally are against women being here and I know of incidents where they've tried to even force them out of here by locking their doors and stuff like that. . . . Doing little stuff continuously. I guess it could get on one's nerve. (VMI 1–2M)

Some male cadets would not talk to female cadets:

The male cadets, they treat them like, sort of like lepers I guess. A lot of the guys do. They're not very well liked just because of the fact that the corps morale has gone down considerably and they're cadets that have been there three or four years. (VMI 2–2M)

VMI's first female cadets encountered resentment from male cadets who questioned why women wanted to be there, believed the women were invading their school, had difficulty taking orders from women, and thought some women were only attending to prove a point. One VMI male cadet explained that some male cadets questioned why women wanted to attend VMI: "There are male cadets that are like 'why are you even here?' You know, 'what are you doing at this school?' and they have resentment that they are here" (VMI 1–2M). Another believed that the female cadets should have been more grateful to be attending *his* school.

I think a lot of them [female cadets] take for granted the fact that they're here and . . . I know this is wrong of me to think this but . . . they're in my school. They should be grateful that they're in my school because they weren't supposed to be and they don't act like that. (VMI 1–3M)

A third found it difficult taking orders from a woman because it conflicted with his machismo: "[D]uring the Ratline it was just when you heard a girl say, 'push' you were just like, 'what?' I mean, it's very hard especially just the macho attitude. It's hard to take orders from a higher ranking female cadet" (VMI 2–2M). A fourth believed that some women who attended VMI were doing so to prove a point as feminists:

For a guy to come here and get their butt kicked and yelled at, it might produce some sort of well being later on in life to take the lead and lead his family and/or make it through the hard times and for the girl to come here and then pursue no military career, it's almost as if she's crossing that line of being feminine to a feminist. (VMI 2–1M)

Other VMI male cadets were more conflicted. Although they too would have preferred to attend an all-male VMI, women were now tangible female cadets, and some females were their friends. This made rejecting coeducation outright more problematic. Asked how supportive male cadets were of female cadets, a VMI male cadet gave voice to this conflict between the tradition of being all-male and the reality of female cadets as individuals.

[L]ess supportive in an overall perspective just because of tradition that has been here and myself I would like to be here when there was no females but since they're here we have to accept it. You know we have all these alumni around here that's saying how the corps used to be and it kind of makes you feel well, this is a new corps—man, I wish I could experience the old corps. But I have female cadets who are friends of mine. . . . As a corps I believe that having women here is not really their wishes. They're against it I believe. (VMI 1–2M)

Others also had mixed feelings about coeducation but thought it was time to set aside their antagonism and accept coeducation. One VMI male cadet acknowledged that some male cadets regretted women being there but others had begun to accept it.

I think we still have many [male] cadets that are very unsupportive who, till they die, they're gonna regret that females came here, but on the other hand, you have quite a few males that are supportive and that realize that they're here and let's make the best of it so it's definitely mixed. (VMI 1–4M)

Many simply resigned themselves to the fact that VMI is now coed. Asked if there was anything males cadets could do to improve integration, a VMI male cadet replied, "They could just accept it, that they're here. Ain't nothing going to change that fact. Just move on and deal with it" (VMI

1–1M). For some, accepting coeducation meant developing a better attitude.

> I think, like a lot of people before they came, I was definitely dead set against it and I just think I've developed a better attitude about it. Now that they're here, we've got to make the best of it so, I mean, I've got quite a few friends who are female. (VMI 1–4M)

Others tried to reframe their experience in light of the skills they acquired from participating in the transition to coeducation.

> I feel like I've lived through history and I feel like it will serve me well later in life because I know I'll be faced with a situation like this whether it be male or female . . . and I know in the Army I will be given orders that I don't like but I'll have to execute but that's the way it is. And I feel like this will serve me well. (VMI 1–3M)

Before the women arrived, many male cadets had negative preconceptions about female cadets. At West Point, contact between men and women was found to help reduce male cadets' negative preconceptions about the first female cadets. Exposure to female cadets enabled West Point male cadets to perceive female cadets not simply as members of an unwelcome outgroup, but as individuals who were trying to achieve similar goals. Studies have repeatedly confirmed the contact hypothesis—that contact between male and female cadets reduced male bias (Adams, 1980, p. 49; Greene and Wilson, 1981).

At VMI, male cadets' preconceptions are also beginning to be challenged. Although many male cadets still did not like women as a group, some were starting to accept female cadets as individuals.

> My brother rats . . . when they got here they had their own preconceived notions . . . they didn't want any females with them. And then when you get to know that this female was doing push-ups three people down from you is another person and you get to know her and her personality, it's kind of hard to dislike somebody after you've gotten to know them as much as it is you just hate the fact of who they are. (VMI 2–1M).

Friendships between male and female cadets also helped ameliorate male cadet antipathy toward female cadets.

> I guess before they came here I didn't really look at them as people. I looked at them as someone coming here to ruin my school I wanted to be all-male and once I got to know them, they're real people too and some of them my good friends and I guess I was all wrong about them. Some of them are really here for good reasons, you know, the same reasons I'm here. (VMI 1–4M)

A few even began to see the advantages in coeducation, opening up the possibility for cross-sex friendships they hadn't known were possible.

> When I was a high school senior every single woman was a possible date, every single woman was hopefully something more than that. But coming here, after the

first week and a half, sweating then after that puking, slinking next to them, that left. And it opened the ground for a lot of other relationships to come up. One of my good friends is a female cadet and it's a different relationship that I know I couldn't have anywhere except out of here. That had we not gone through some of the experiences that we've gone through there'd be a lot of the so-called "hang-ups" that in general society we find. (VMI 1–6M)

Reflecting on the positive effects of coeducation, some male cadets granted that VMI had become more professional: "In the past you got away with a lot of profanity and mistreatment but now it's kind of cleaning up. It's starting to reflect more the military, [how] the military treats people" (VMI 1–1M), explained one VMI male cadet. Some VMI male cadets asserted that coeducation made them better prepared for the real world where they would be working alongside women as superiors, colleagues, and subordinates. Remarked a VMI cadet from the last all-male class, "In the real world you're going to be dealing with both males and females in day-to-day situations so with the women being here it is more like how it's going to be when we leave here" (VMI 1–4M).

Based on our evidence, however, it is clear that women have not been fully accepted at VMI. Many VMI male cadets still believe that women interfered with camaraderie and lowered corps morale, and several could think of no advantage to training with women. In fact, the majority of VMI male cadets maintained that the disadvantages of coeducation outweighed the advantages. In contrast, West Point male cadets maintained that the advantages of coeducation outweighed the disadvantages. Asserted a West Point male cadet, "It's a coed army. I'm gonna have female soldiers working for me. I'm gonna work for female officers and it doesn't matter what branch you go, they're in the Army so they might as well be here" (WP 4–6M). Remarked another:

When you're in the real world it's not going to be all male. You're not going to be sitting in the office with just all male . . . and when you get out into the real army it's not going to be all-male soldiers under you. It's not going to be all-male officers that are like superiors or inferiors." (WP 4–1M)

Female cadets at VMI agree with their male counterparts. They believe they are there to fit in as cadets, not stand out as women. One cadet stated:

I didn't come to this school to try to break a tradition, take away their all-male school. I had an opportunity. This is a good place to be. Everyone knows about it. . . . I think we should have as much opportunity and I think guys should understand that. (VMI 1–7F)

CONCLUSION

Changes in the experience of female cadets at West Point over a quarter century demonstrate that although integration is a gradual process, institutions, even highly masculine ones, can and do acclimate to women. The experience of female cadets at West Point has been improved by an organizational commitment to gender integration, an increase in the number of women attending, changes in the attitude of men, and mentoring by other women (Yoder, 1989). As gender integration at West Point demonstrates, women are able to succeed in masculine institutions, women can and do become valued members of these institutions, and women, men, and institutions are able to adapt to coeducation. In this sense, West Point's experience with coeducation rehearses the experience of gender integration in all formerly male-dominated professions, such as law and medicine, as well as the military for which cadets are training. (See, for example, Williams, 1989, 1995; on medicine, see American Medical Association, 2000; on the military, see United States Department of Defense, 1998; Women's Research and Education Institute, 2000).

VMI today is in the nascent stages of coeducation and will no doubt encounter growing pains as both the cadets and the institution acclimate to women within their ranks. Although VMI spent a great deal of time and energy preparing for women, gender integration is far from fully implemented. Our research suggests that it is not sufficient to establish coeducation at a formerly all-male institution and not expect antipathy on the part of at least some men who feel that their domain has been usurped. Dramatic changes—not only among the cadets but also among the superior officers and administrators who set the normative foundation for life in the school—will have to change as well. One thing is certain. Women will continue to enter formerly male domains in ever greater numbers. As more women enter these domains, men will need to learn how to work alongside women and institutions will need to develop strategies of inclusion and adaptation that build on the strength of all their members.

NOTES

1. West Point alumni and cadets were grouped into four cohorts: (1) the first coeducational cohort plus some alumni from the last all-male class, coded WP 1 (graduating classes: 1979 to 1984); (2) a cohort who attended West Point 8 to 12 years after women were first admitted to West Point coded WP 2 (graduating classes: 1988 to 1992); (3) a cohort who were attending West Point in 1997, twenty years after women were first admitted, coded WP 3 (graduating classes: 1997 to 2000); and (4) a cohort who were attending West Point in 2000, twenty-four years after coeducation began, coded WP 4 (graduating classes: 2000 to 2004). VMI cadets were grouped into two cohorts: (1) the first two coeducational classes plus cadets from the last all-male class, coded VMI 1 (graduating classes: 2000 to 2002); and (2) cadets in the third and fourth coeducational classes, coded VMI 2 (graduating classes 2003 to 2004). M or F at the end of the interview code indicates the subject's sex: male (M) or female (F).

2. The PT protest as it has come to be called is not limited to male cadets. Carol Cohn found that male military officers and enlisted men also interpret these different physical training standards as "'special treatment for women,' 'lowering standards for women,' and/or evidence that 'women can't cut it' in the military . . . [and link] *equal status* with *same fitness standards*'" (Cohn, 2000, p. 131).

3. The word dyke is "an early twentieth century corruption of the term 'decked out' to imply dressed up . . . [D]yke is the arrangement of crossed belts worn with a dress uniforms" (Norman, 1997, p. 66). In addition, dyke is the term used to denote the relationship between a Rat (freshman) and a first classman (senior) who serves as a mentor to the Rat.

4. Because many of VMI's first female cadets had athletic scholarships, they were dispropor-

tionately on sports teams. As a result, many female cadets did not participate in all of the Ratline activities. This led to resentment on the part of some male cadets.

REFERENCES

Acker, J. (1992). "From Sex Roles to Gendered Institutions." *Contemporary Sociology* 21:565–569.

Adams, J. (1979). *Report of the Admission of Women to the United States Military Academy at West Point: Project Athena III.* West Point, NY: United States Military Academy.

——. (1980). *Report of the Admission of Women to the United States Military Academy at West Point: Project Athena IV.* West Point, NY: United States Military Academy.

American Medical Association. Table: Physicians by Gender. (10 June 2001). *http://www.ama-assn.org/mem-data/wmmed/infoserv/data/table1.htm.*

Barkalow, C. (1990). *In the Men's House: An Inside Account in the Army by One of West Point's First Female Graduates.* New York: Poseidon.

Chandler, C. (1996). "Mentoring and Women in Academia: Reevaluating the Traditional Model." *NWSA Journal 8*(3):79–100.

Cohn, C. (2000). "'How Can She Claim Equal Rights When She Doesn't Have to Do as Many Push-Ups as I Do?': The Framing of Opposition to Women's Equality in the Military." *Men and Masculinity 3*(2):131–151.

Diamond, D., and Kimmel, M. (1999). "The Integration of Women at the United States Military Academy at West Point, 1976–1996." Paper presented at the 69th Annual Meeting of the Eastern Sociological Association. Boston.

Diamond, D., Kimmel, M., and Schroeder, K. (1997). "Determinants of Success for Women at Military Educational Institutions." Paper presented at the 92nd Annual Meeting of the American Sociological Association. Toronto.

Gilman, C. (1911). *The Man-Made World.* New York: Charlton and Company.

Goffman, E. (1961). *Asylums: Essays on the Social Situation of Mental Patients and Other Inmates.* Chicago: Aldine.

Greene, B. D. III, and Wilson, K. L. (1981). "Women Warriors: Exploring the New Integration of Women into the Military." *Journal of Political and Military Sociology 9*: 241–254.

Gumbiner, J. (1998). "Professors as Models and Mentors: Does Gender Matter?" *Psychological Reports 82*(1):94

Mellen, N. (1999). Personal website of VMI cadet Neil Mellen. 20 February 1999. http://www.mellennj.mellen.com/ed2.htm

Norman, G. (1997). *The Institute.* Wellington, FL: Edgeworth Editions.

Random House Dictionary of the English Language. (1967). New York: Random House.

United States Department of Defense. (September 1998). "Active Duty Military Strength Male/Female for September 1998." Statistical Information Analysis Division.

United States Military Academy at West Point Online Admissions Brochure. (1 April 2001). *http://www.usma.edu.admission/prosp-military.asp*

Virginia Military Institute Admissions Brochure. (1999). Lexington, VA: Virginia Military Institute Office of Admissions.

Virginia Military Institute Online Admissions Brochure. (10 April 2000). *http://www.vmi.edu*

VMI II, 44 F.3d 1229, 1234–35 (4th Cir.). *cert. granted,* 116 S. Ct. 281 (1995).

Williams, C. (1989). *Gender Differences at Work: Women and Men in Nontraditional Occupations.* Berkeley: University of California Press.

Williams, C. (1995). *Still a Man's World.* Berkeley, CA: University of California Press.

Wise, H. A. (1978). *Drawing Out the Man: The VMI Story.* Charlottesville: The University Press of Virginia.

Women's Research and Education Institute. (10 April 2000). "Active Duty Servicewomen by Branch of Service, Rank, Race, and Hispanic Origin, May 31, 1999." *http:www.wrei.org/military/fig7–1.pdf*

Yoder, J. (1989). "Women at West Point: Lessons for Token Women in Male-Dominated Occupations." In J. Freeman (Ed.), *Women: A Feminist Perspective,* 3rd ed. Palo Alto, CA: Mayfield.

CHAPTER 11

Studying Gender Consciousness in Single-Sex and Coeducational High Schools

Patricia Schmuck, Nancy G. Nagel, and Celeste Brody

After thirty-two years as an elite, all-male Catholic high school, Xavier Preparatory High School decided to enroll young women. We studied Xavier for two years with a multifaceted research design, making comparisons with two sister all-female high schools in the same diocese. One sister school chose to become coeducational, the other reaffirmed its commitment to remain all-female. We examined how society's collective consciousness about gender and its unspoken assumptions about male privilege influenced school learning environments. We also examined how the school's culture shaped experiences of students and faculty.

In this chapter we present brief background on research and policy about single-sex schools, describe our methods and summarize our findings to build a framework for understanding the gendered nature of school's environments, and present a continuum of gender consciousness and privilege to assess the equitability of school environments.

CONCEPTUAL FRAMEWORK

Although single-sex and coeducational schools are different from one another, our study did not judge which schools are better for females. What is good for females depends on the degree to which participants in a school are aware of societal assumptions about gender and how educational practices and policies in the school support learning. For instance, in some studies of all-female schools and classes, researchers (Shmurak, 1998; Streitmatter, 1998) found little gender awareness; the male point of view was continually presented in a curriculum that did not question gender assumptions, and counseling practices were stereotypical. Streitmatter (1998) also presented some excellent examples, however, of all-female schools, or all-female classes within coeducational schools, that addressed the unique and special needs of being female. She made the case, in part, for all-female learning environments. At the same time, putting females together without males does not necessarily provide a better education for females. Single-sex schools are different one from one another, and consequently we should not assume that all-female schools *promote gender consciousness* and *critique male privilege*.

THE CONCEPT OF GENDER CONSCIOUSNESS

Since the U.S. Congress passed Title IX in 1972, awareness or consciousness has grown about sex bias and discrimination among teachers and students in schools and society. Despite significant changes in policy and practice, LePore and Warren pointed out that "gender discrimination is a far more subtle and complex problem than is implied by past research. . . . Incidences of sexism occur in all school sectors regardless of gender composition" (1997, p. 506). Streitmatter's (1998) study of adolescent girls' in single-sex and coeducational environments found different types of sexist practices at different types of schools. Although females were less discriminated in all-female schools than in coeducational schools, some all-female schools were highly patriarchal using males as the model for performance and development of knowledge. They did little to affirm the experience of females and adopted the traditional, and often sexist, view of female behavior and knowledge. Today most educators verbally agree that schools should eliminate inequities based on sex; however, they differ in their levels of consciousness about how this could be accomplished.

Title IX presented a legal remedy to provide the *same* opportunities for females as for males; however, it does not represent a very advanced stage of gender consciousness. We believe to educate females and males equally is not necessarily to provide the *same* educational experiences. Same is not necessarily equal. The social context has defined separate spheres for females and males and same school experiences are not the "equalizer." Despite educator's good intentions, sex bias and sexist practices are often embedded in school policies, practices, and teacher behaviors. A more mature level of gender consciousness is to be aware of embedded sexism and inequality in our schools rather than simply focusing on sex bias or discrimination addressed in Title IX.

THE ROLE OF PRIVILEGE

Privilege is tied to concepts of status and wealth. Its traditional roots are in European nobility and the aristocracy and belies the American ideals of "equal rights for all, special privileges for none" (Jefferson as cited in George, 1906, p. 17). Defined in those terms, privilege is easy to identify, but not often claimed by any but the wealthy (Gosetti, 1995). Some researchers suggest, however, that privilege has other dimensions than its more narrow traditional meaning. Peggy McIntosh (1988) defined privilege as unearned and frequently taken-for-granted advantages accrued purely through one's birth into a certain group. She suggested that privilege exists, unseen, within our society. It gives people choices, opportunities, dominance, and permission to control members of less privileged groups, while making those power relationships seem natural. For example, social privileges of sex exist that grant cultural, professional, and personal status to men, allowing them "legitimate" ways to dominate and marginalize women (Sleeter, 1993).

As individuals become more conscious of gender, they view privilege as a person's special advantage that comes from being a member of a particular group. Our educational system, however, provides barriers to recognizing privilege by teaching members of the dominant cultural group that their lives are "morally neutral, normative, average, and also ideal" (McIntosh, 1988, p. 3). Many who enjoy the privileges of a social system that perpetuates their privileged status are not even aware that such a system exists. Indeed, privilege is more often recognized by those who do not have it as compared to those who do. In our study, we use these concepts of gender consciousness and privilege to understand the single-sex and coeducational schools we studied.

RESEARCH METHODS

In our study, the seven original authors (Brody et al., 2000) used typical social science qualitative and quantitative case study methods with a feminist stance. The feminist view challenged us to examine the schools critically from the standpoint of being female. We used women's experiences as a basis for our analysis (Harding, 1987) and put the social construction of gender at the center of our inquiry (Lather, 1991). We focused on embedded ideas of gender by identifying what Smith (1987) called "fault lines," those points of rupture that exist between traditional knowledge that tells women what they experience and what women actually experience in their everyday lives. Much of our research entailed listening to females talk about their experience and interpreting those data through a feminist lens.

Our study began when the Xavier principal asked Patricia Schmuck for consultative help in the transition from a single-sex to a coeducational school. An agreement was reached that a research team would help Xavier so long as we had an opportunity to study the transition. It was a serendipitous opportunity for research. Xavier's decision to become coeducational simultaneously affected two other Catholic high schools in the same diocese; Grove High School, a previously all-female school was also becoming coeducational, whereas St. Elizabeth's Academy reaffirmed its mission to remain all-female. Each school faced decisions about remaining single-sex or becoming coeducational and faculty; therefore, student and parent consciousness about gender was high.

The changes in three Catholic high schools brought about by Xavier's decision to become coeducational gave us the opportunity to examine gender consciousness and privilege because school members were questioning "the way it is." The dissonance created by transition opened the door for educators and students to uncover the gender and privilege assumptions in their cultures. In times of change, when "business as usual" is interrupted, participants may see more easily into their organizations' hidden dimensions.

Data came from six general research foci that included: (a) school policy and administration, (b) curriculum, (c) pedagogy, (d) student outcomes, (e) school culture, and (f) faculty action research. Data were derived from individual interviews of faculty, administrators, trustees, and students; classrooms observations of several teachers; recording and analyzing archival materials; and student focus groups and faculty focus groups. The steering committee guiding the consultation and research included members of the research team, administrators from the three schools, and several teachers. We worked most actively with Xavier from spring 1992, prior to becoming coeducational, to 1994, following the first year of coeducation. Grove and St. Elizabeth's were companion comparison schools.

THE SCHOOL SITES

Xavier Preparatory High School is inextricably linked to the tradition of Jesuits (Bryk, Lee, and Holland, 1993). The school opened in the 1950s and grew to about five hundred young men by the 1970s. After thirty years as a successful college preparatory school (close to 98 percent of the students attend a four-year college following graduation) with winning sports teams, Xavier's enrollment declined precipitously in the 1980s to its lowest point. Xavier's Board of Trustees and alumni were alarmed about enrollment decline and simultaneously parents began asking, "Why can't my daughter get the same Jesuit education as my son?" The Jesuit ideal of "leadership education for young men" began to be seen as important for young women as well. Coeducation became the solution; the coeducational school enrolled about one thousand students and was economically secure. Riordan (1990) suggested that conventional wisdom changes and coeducation is justified as "natural" after a precarious economic situation. In the case of Xavier, coeducation was to solve the economic problem and later developed into the rationale to implement the Ignation pedagogy into "leadership for men *and women.*"

The Congregation of Sisters founded St. Theresa of the Grove at the beginning of the twentieth century as a residential school including coeducational preschool, kindergarten, elementary, and junior high instruction. Traditionally the high school was an all-female school and during the late 1970s and 1980s, experienced a marked student decline in enrollment. Rumors abounded that the school might close. With Xavier's decision to become coeducational, the faculty and religious order members decided to become coeducational. They changed the school name from St. Theresa to the neutral designation of Grove Catholic High School, believing that young men would not attend a school with a female name. It maintained a steady enrollment at about four hundred students and was economically sound.

St. Elizabeth's Academy, one of the oldest high schools in the region was founded in the mid-1800s by the Congregation of Sisters. Located in the inner city, St. Elizabeth's has always been an all-female school. The Sisters believed in the power of education as exemplified by their founder, that "to educate a person is to educate a family, and regenerate a nation, and a world." With education, women could become leaders and change the world. Many families sent their sons to Xavier and their daughters to St. Elizabeth's; they were considered academically comparable schools. Unlike Xavier and Grove, St. Elizabeth's enrollment remained steady at about five hundred students. As Xavier altered its mission to coeducation, St. Elizabeth's reaffirmed its all-female mission but was concerned about a potential loss of students.

HOW GENDER CONSCIOUSNESS AND PRIVILEGE OPERATE

Our data indicated that gender consciousness operates in four domains: (a) social context; (b) school culture; (c) teacher and staff beliefs; and (d) student backgrounds, understandings, and perceptions. Our observations indicated that gender consciousness and privilege reside in intentions and behaviors whether or not individuals are aware of their influence. Peoples' intentions and behaviors interact and coalesce to form the cultural milieu—the symbols, actions, norms, and values that form the internal context of schools. Lisa Delpit wrote, "We all interpret behaviors, information and situations through our own cultural lenses; these lenses operate involuntarily, below the level of conscious awareness, making it seem that our own view is simply 'the way it is'" (1995, p. 151).

Peoples' intentions were an important part of the cultural lens we used in carrying out our data collection for understanding gender. Although a teacher may *intend* to act in sex-equitable or gender-aware ways, students may actually experience some of their practices as sex or gender biased, given their own cultural expectations and perceptions of what is fair and equitable. The reverse may also be true: The privileged practices associated with gendered expectations may be so ingrained within cultural norms that students or teachers may not even perceive those practices as sex or gender biased. How can one see the invisible? How can one make the familiar strange?

Privilege and gender are normative filters through which assumptions about reality are made and maintained, effectively excluding some people from opportunities and chances to be heard (Bohmer and Briggs, 1991).

Rusch and Marshall (1995), in their review of literature about school administrators wrote that, "deeply embedded gender filters function to maintain the privilege of dominant white-male culture by silencing ideas and people that on gender-consciousness continuum."

We saw the dialectic between privilege and gender within the schools we studied in two ways:

1. The unquestioned primacy of the male and the effects that patriarchy have in casting fundamental assumptions about what is and is not valued in a school
2. The privilege of elite schools, which fosters unquestioned assumptions about the reproduction of knowledge

THE PRIMACY OF THE MALE

Our research began with Xavier's plans to change from an all-male to a coeducational school with little concern for the effect of its decision on its sister schools.

THE SOCIAL CONTEXT

Xavier had power and privilege as a Jesuit school in the Catholic, male-dominated hierarchy and would have implemented coeducation earlier but earlier for the objections of the St. Elizabeth's principal. Xavier's power was curbed finally by the diocese and eventually came up with a delayed plan acceptable to St. Elizabeth's and Grove (Feeney, 1997).

The post-Title IX era proved a powerful social context. Educators believed the best policy for achieving sex equity was to be gender neutral. Gender neutrality was expressed differently, however, in the two schools becoming coeducational. Whereas Xavier tried to make its curriculum and instruction gender neutral by eliminating sex-biased language and behaviors as a way to make a favorable learning environment for young women, Grove sought to eradicate remnants of the all-female school that it believed would offend or turn away male students.

SCHOOL CULTURE

At each school, culture was communicated through the formal and informal norms and general expectations for behavior that provided clear evidence of gendered messages in disciplinary policies and dress codes, curriculum, grouping practices, athletics, extracurricular activities, informal student relationships, and even policies about sexual harassment. Xavier and Grove looked quite different in how they implemented coeducational schooling.

Xavier was known for its prestigious, well-developed, and cohesive culture. The major preparation for coeducation was to rewrite policies for dress and conduct with gender neutral language. In a culture where athletics was of primary importance they worked hard to create similar athletic opportunities for young women. The school hired new staff to coach women's athletics and installed a new women's locker room. An in-house joke was that a female teacher confronted the awareness of the male architectural team by pointing out they had not considered installing hair dryers in the locker room.

In contrast, Grove worked diligently on creating a different culture and environment from its all-female past. Grove enrolled boys gradually over four years, starting first with the freshman class. In the first year, when there were only a few freshman boys, a boys' basketball coach was hired, even though there were not enough boys for a team. Senior girls told us about the school brochure as a blatant example changing the school's image. One senior woman said:

> It just has guys in there. I mean tons of guys, and where are the girls? They have pictures of guys running track and guys' basketball, and then in the music group there should have been tons of girls but the focus was on the guys. The funny thing is when the brochure was made there were only about twenty guys in the whole school, so all the same boys you saw over and over again.

In addition, administrators acknowledged initially that they used lower admission requirements for boys than girls to increase the "male presence."

Both schools developed new policies about sexual harassment that had not been seen as necessary when they were single-sex (Stein, 1995). Xavier staff was aware that its school climate was heavily masculine and potentially deleterious to females. Some staff referred to the male culture as the "farting, burping, swearing culture," and others were concerned about "attitudes berating young women as less intellectual" and one teacher, concerned specifically about sexual harassment, referred to the young men as "heat-seeking missiles."

TEACHER AND STAFF BELIEFS

Our interviews revealed that most Xavier faculty saw little reason to change their pedagogy or goals; after all, when you believe you already have the best curriculum, why question it? They sought to create "fair" environments that were "sex-neutral," or "what is good for boys is good for girls." They focused on neutral language, to achieve the same disciplinary treatment of boys and girls, and to use "objective" academic assessment practices. Nevertheless, they did not always achieve equity. For instance, in discipline some teachers were perplexed because, what was good for boys was *not* necessarily good for girls, or more precisely, what boys would tolerate was not the same as what girls would tolerate. At Xavier gender consciousness was consistent with prevailing American standards about sex equity defined by Title IX; same is equal and gender consciousness is undeveloped. In contrast, we did find a few teachers who believed female and male life realities were different and they provided some differential instruction. For instance, Mr. Bronson, a math teacher at Grove High School, saw that female students often denigrated their mathematical ability with opening sentences such as "I'm not sure this is right. . . ." He discouraged such self-deprecating comments.

In each school, teachers were guided in part by local organizational norms of what was acceptable teaching practice about gender consciousness and privilege. One of the most progressive and feminist teachers at St. Elizabeth's, Mrs. North, probably could not have taught the same world history curriculum if she were teaching in an all-male or coeducational school. For instance, while studying *Henry V*, she portrayed one battle as "another example of 'Mine is bigger than yours.'"

STUDENTS

The students we studied were a critical force in shaping their high school culture. Because of their marginality within the adult-dominated culture, they were in a unique position to recognize and perhaps actively shape what it means to be "classed and gendered." Proweller referred to "work" in the border zone, where adolescent girls, in particular, seek "to exercise control over the conditions of their lives in spite of very real dynamics that have the potential to limit the possibilities" (1998, p. 16) of access to "membership" in activities reserved for white, male, and upper middle-class privilege.

We observed the new female students at Xavier exerted more gender consciousness than their teachers; for instance, a few young women, when they felt safe to voice their opinions, expressed dismay to their teacher that they were not reading female authors in English classes. Still, these same young women were just as likely not to see the deeply embedded male-normative standard. A powerful example of not seeing the embedded assumptions occurred with the writing of an editorial in the school newspaper. The male editor had written an editorial about how the standards were falling since young women had arrived; teachers were more lax and grading policies were easier. The article was approved by the female, senior assistant editor. It was printed and the principal called the two student editors into his office. He asked for data but they had none. They both defended the article's premise on their personal impressions. He asked, "Would you have written this article about African Americans in our school?" Both said they would not because it would be racist. He then asked, "How can you then write such an article about young women?"

At Grove young women became silent in the face of male dominance in class and the teacher's exclusionary practices; they noticed discriminatory practices even though they never directly challenged them. One young woman said:

Even though the boys were like half our size, they were still short in the eighth grade and they were asked to move stuff. It's the idea, "Boys are finally here; girls don't have to do anything." Almost all of us were brought up to be independent and to be able to do stuff like that, because obviously most of us are here for that reason, so that we could be independent women. It's just disgusting.

Senior women from the last all-female class voiced their concerns about being powerless to influence sex-biased practices under the guise of making the newly arriving young men feel welcome in their school.

PRIVILEGE AND ASSUMPTIONS ABOUT KNOWLEDGE REPRODUCTION

How teachers, administrators, and students thought about knowledge reproduction gave us a more poignant understanding of how privilege in elite schools fosters unquestioned gender-constructed assumptions and values. Topics for study, research, and debate, the actual primary and secondary sources of information encouraged for use and available through the library, and even the inquiry procedures within a particular discipline were subject to gendered constructions and privileged understandings.

At St. Elizabeth's, feminist views were in the informal curriculum, as evidenced in Mrs. North's social studies class. For example, Mrs. North, in teaching about footnoting for an academic paper, modified a Michigan State University handout for doing research to fit a "girl's point of view," changing the examples of author and topic. Her humor and knowledge of traditional footnoting procedures was evident when she put on the board an example of a proper form for citation: North, Nancy. *Woman and Superwoman.* Seattle, WA: Saint Elizabeth's Press, 1994. The young women saw it and laughed; they got the point.

At Xavier, on the other hand, Mrs. Wilson, a self-proclaimed feminist with a student-centered pedagogy, did not change her literature curriculum to include female authors or protagonists in her English class. Although she had wanted to make changes in the curriculum, she, the only female in the English Department, could not convince her colleagues that such changes were necessary, citing the mostly shared assumption that "what is good for boys is good for girls." No one questioned presumptions of male privilege inherent in the traditional Jesuit curriculum. Despite Mrs. Wilson's focus on her students and her attempt to include a more diverse curriculum, she was bound by the traditions and authority of the all-male school grounded in a patriarchal system.

THE GENDER CONSCIOUSNESS-PRIVILEGE CONTINUUM

The Gender Consciousness-Privilege Continuum emerged as we analyzed data from those three high schools. We wondered why most Xavier faculty, in particular, seemed to plateau at the level of sex neutrality—in intention as well as action—as their way of dealing with coeducation. In working with our data, we realized teachers needed and wanted a gauge to consider where they were developmentally. We found, too, our own limited "Title IX thinking" of sex equity. We learned that educators who attempt to create sex-same or sex-neutral learning typically ignored issues of male power and privilege. So how do we move forward?

The Gender Consciousness and Privilege Continuum shown in table 11.1, describes four positions of increasing awareness about unspoken assumptions undergirding valued status positions in the society, for example, sex, social class, race, age, and physical (dis)ability. We selected indicators drawn from our data to show where an individual or organization might be positioned. The four positions we describe are temporary markers or indicators along an infinite number of positions toward increased understanding of the meaning of gender and privilege and a more developed consciousness about the relationship between the two.

Our data point to the difference between teachers' intentions and their actual behaviors in relation to gender consciousness and privilege. Indeed, we found gender-focused intentions to be quite discrepant. A few Xavier teachers who articulated a well-developed commitment and even rhetorical passion on behalf of gender awareness, seldom took proactive actions to actualize those intentions. They did not have the pedagogical skill, nor were they willing to deviate from traditional Xavier norms and place themselves on the margin of the school culture. Individuals and organizations can be assessed on the continuum by using both intentions and behaviors. Indeed, looking at both intention and behavior may help surface contradictions that all people experience between what they think and how they act.

POSITION 0: UNEXAMINED THOUGHTS AND BEHAVIORS

Despite the positive changes brought about by Title IX, there are still many educators with unexamined assumptions about females and males in school and who unwittingly perpetuate sexism and sex biases. Position 0 is the place on the continuum where educators do not question, nor do they see, the social norms that result in bias or discrimination on the basis of sex, race, or social class. Neither their intentions nor their actions have changed.

POSITION 1: SEX EQUITY IN EDUCATION

The language of Title IX is deceptively simple, "No person shall, on the basis of sex, be excluded from participation in, be denied the benefits of, or be subjected to discrimination under any educational program or activity receiving federal funds." It emphasizes "sameness." If girls are equal to boys, then they should have the *same* opportunities as boys. It presumes what is good for boys is good for girls and eliminates differential treatment in materials,

TABLE 11.1
THE GENDER CONSCIOUSNESS-PRIVILEGE CONTINUUM

Position 0: Unexamined Thoughts and Behaviors	Position 1: Sex-Equity	Position 2: Gender Awareness Position	Position 3: Critical Transformation
Individuals unquestioningly accept social assumptions and stereotypes for females and males on the basis of sex. Individuals may deny bias and discrimination has occurred for them or for others. School implements different standards, policies, and behavioral consequences for females and males, or the unintended effects of unexamined practices is negative.	Individuals recognize females and males have been treated differently because of their sex; they make some corrective actions for same treatment. School changes standards and policies that differentiate on account of sex and provide deliberate compensatory opportunities to redress past inequities on account of sex.	Individuals recognize same is not alsways equal and cultural meanings of being female or male are deeply embedded in thinking and behavior; the concept of sex changes to the concept of gender, recognition of privilege as a factor in equity begins. School questions the assumptions guiding teaching and learning, curricular choices, extracurricular activities. The staff looks more deeply into how gender influences classroom teaching and organization functioning.	Individuals recognize the unspoken assumptions that privilege, which is determined by valued position in the society (sex, social class, and race), provides some individuals with access to social rewards. School helps students question issues of privilege and dominance in the society; the curricula move toward multiple perspectives of reality and encourage questioning how events of the world have been interpreted.
Indicators:	*Indicators:*	*Indicators:*	*Indicators:*
Different treatment and admission standards Student activities associated with specific group or another Demeaning sexist jokes and remarks More attention to the boys/to the girls The presence of the other lowers academic standards Boys carry/lift—girls clean/set up "What's good for boys is good for girls"	Standard dress code for males and females Equal-quality coaches, facilities, sport standards for males and females Nongender specific school profile of the student at graduation Uniform counseling and advising	Inclusion of greater variety of authors and diversity in English classes Increase in nonathletic extracurricular options for both sexes Changed teaching	Use of gender as a unit of analysis in curricular decision making Considers multiple points of view God as "He" or "She" Invites voices in the margin to name their position

Gender in Policy and Practice

interactions, participation, access to knowledge, and school structures. Educators at this level try to decrease differential treatment and increase "same" treatment by providing females the same opportunities as males. Xavier faculty and administrators worked diligently to do just that, as we explained.

POSITION 2: GENDER AWARENESS IN THE POST-TITLE IX ERA

We now realize, even with the positive consequences of Title IX, that "same is not equal. " *Same* opportunities are not necessarily *equal* opportunities. In Position 2, educators focus on the meaning of gender, and locate factors in the environment to explain performance differences between females and males. For instance, "How should *group* tendencies affect *individual* choices at one end of the spectrum and policies that support human growth and learning in schools at the other end?" When teachers question assumptions that guide teaching and learning, curricular choices, and extracurricular activities, they look more deeply into how gender influences classroom teaching and school organization functioning, and they realize how embedded gender is in thinking and behavior.

POSITION 3: CRITICAL TRANSFORMATION

We see critical transformation as a postmodern view; it is a change in how one views the world, a dramatic paradigm shift. The teacher who holds a critical transformative view understands that privilege is always present in society and thus concentrates on understanding the experiences of whomever is in the marginalized group. It eschews the romantic view that because we are all human, we are all the same. Moreover, things are not as they seem; thus, events, ideas, and viewpoints need to be "deconstructed" to explore multiple interpretations and focus on the power of context (Lather, 1991). Position 3 emphasizes consciousness about gender and privilege; educators are developing emancipatory curricula that focus on the spoken and unspoken assumptions of how social power is distributed and implemented. Critical transformation invites discussion about how best to develop education that is good for females and males, beginning by altering our thinking about the historical primacy and privilege of the white male. Although social class does not privilege all white young males, the white males we saw at Xavier and Grove carried a special sense of ownership of their school and school events.

We can only surmise what a critical transformative classroom would look like, because since we saw very few indications of it in the schools we studied. Fortunately, other feminist writers, such as Claire Hiller (1998), Jane Kenway and Sue Willis (1997), Patti Lather (1991), Catherine Marshall (1997), Patricia Murphy and Caroline Gipps (1997), Peggy Orenstein (1994) and Kathleen Weiler (1988) helped us struggle through the data to move beyond conventional thinking and think about what a critical transformative view would look like, and in table 11.1 we give examples of some possible indicators.

USE OF THE GENDER CONSCIOUSNESS-PRIVILEGE CONTINUUM

We suggest the Gender Consciousness-Privilege Continuum be used as a diagnostic tool for educators committed to analyzing their work with female and male students. Although our data come from Catholic schools, we surmise from other research and our public school experiences those data may not be so different from classroom practices in public coeducational institutions (Schmuck and Schmuck, 1992; Weis and Fine, 1993) and thus the continuum can be used in both public and private school sectors. Discussion about the descriptors and indicators at each of the positions can help educators to see their current beliefs and actions as well as the organizational structures that impede or help create new awareness. Increased consciousness does not simply "appear"; it is the result of new knowledge, reflection, action research, and proactive behavior. We describe how the continuum may be used by the individual teacher, and by the larger school or district organization.

An individual teacher might use the continuum to analyze and assess her or his curriculum, teaching, and personal beliefs about gender privilege in her or his classroom. Questions to be asked might include:

Position 1: Sex Equity. Are there different expectations for females and males? Are their different consequences for similar behavior?

Position 2: Gender Awareness. What are the assumptions present in curriculum? In a novel or a short story, what are the assumptions of the author? In history, are women and minorities represented or are they ignored? If they are present, how are they presented? Gerda Lerner (1979) tells us to read history with three questions in mind: (a) Where are the women (or other groups)? (b) What were they doing? and (c) Why were they doing that?

Position 3: Critical Transformation. Once students have critiqued the assumptions inherent in history (or science, literature, math), the teacher might ask the students to create alternative versions of what they have read.

At the organizational level, the continuum could be used to analyze educational policy and determine the school or district position on the continuum based on how those policies impact students. Most schools have policy written to adhere to the requirements for sex equity. Are these policies followed in the school and district or are they mere rhetoric? How do administrators work with teachers to develop concepts of equity, gender awareness, and critical transformation? Does the school help teachers question assumptions or accept the status quo? Honest discussions and reading of relevant literature will help school organizations create effective learning environments for their female and male students.

We hope educators will strive toward developing classrooms where students question the social meanings given to gender and privilege. We place the onus of responsibility on educators; how they organize their work and how they create environments for learning. Public and private schools can benefit from data drawn from other organizational settings to create classrooms and schools that are good for females and males.

REFERENCES

Bohmer, S., and Briggs, J. L. (1991). "Teaching Privileged Students about Gender, Race, and Class Oppression." *Teaching Sociology* 19: 154–163.

Brody, C., Fuller, K., Gosetti, P; Moscato, S; Nagel, N; Pace, G.; et al. (2000). *Gender Consciousness and Privilege.* New York: Falmer Press.

Bryk, A., Lee, V., and Holland, P. (1993). *Catholic Schools and the Common Good.* Cambridge, MA: Harvard University Press.

Delpit, L. (1995). *Other People's Children: Cultural Conflict in the Classroom.* New York: New Press.

Feeney, S. (1997). "Shifting the Prism: Case Explications of Institutional Analysis in Nonprofit Organizations." *Nonprofit and Voluntary Sector Quarterly* 26(4): 489–508.

George, H., Jr. (1906). *The Menace of Privilege: A Study of the Dangers to the Republic from the Existence of a Favored Class.* New York: Macmillan.

Gosetti, P. P. (1995). "Gender Privilege: A Case Study of an All-Male Catholic High School Transitioning to Coeducation." Unpublished doctoral dissertation. University of Oregon, Eugene.

Harding, S. (1987). "Introduction: Is There a Feminist Method?" In S. Harding (Ed.), *Feminism and Methodology.* Bloomington: Indiana University Press, 1–14.

Hiller, C. (1998). "Dis/Locating Gendered Readings: Moving Towards a Critical Pedagogy of Estrangement." Unpublished doctoral dissertation. University of Tasmania, Tasmania, Australia.

Kenway, J., and Willis, S. (1997). *Answering Back: Girls, Boys and Feminism in Schools.* New South Wales, Australia: Allen and Unwin.

Lather, P. (1991). *Getting Smart: Feminist Research and Pedagogy within the Postmodern.* New York: Routledge.

LePore, P. C., and Warren, J. R. (1997). "A Comparison of Single-Sex and Coeducational Catholic Secondary Schooling: Evidence from the National Educational Longitudinal Study of 1988." *American Educational Research Journal* 34(3): 485–511.

Lerner, G. (1979). *The Majority Finds Its Past: Placing Women in History.* NY: Oxford University Press.

Marshall, C. (1997). *Feminist Critical Policy Analysis.* Vol. 1. *The Primary and Secondary School Perspective.* London: Falmer Press.

McIntosh, P. M. (1988). *White Privilege and Male Privilege: A Personal Account of Coming to See Correspondences through Work in Women's Studies.* Working Paper No. 189, Wellesley College, Center for Research on Women, Wellesley, MA.

Murphy, P., and Gipps, C. (Eds.). (1997). *Finding Equity in the Classroom.* Melbourne, Australia: Falmer Press and UNESCO.

Orenstein, P. (1994). *Schoolgirls: Young Women, Self-Esteem, and the Confidence Gap.* New York: Anchor Books.

Proweller, A. (1998). *Constructing Female Identities.* Albany, NY: SUNY Press.

Riordan, C. (1990). *Girls and Boys in School: Together or Separate?* New York: Teacher's College Press.

Rusch, E. A., and Marshall, C. (1995, April). "Gender Filters at Work in the Administrative Culture." Paper presented at the annual meeting of the American Educational Research Association, San Francisco.

Schmuck, R., and Schmuck, P. (1992). *Small Districts: Big Problems.* Los Angeles: Corwin Press.

Shmurak, C. (1998). *Voices of Hope: Adolescent Girls at Single-Sex and Coeducational Schools*. New York: Peter Lang.

Sleeter, C. E. (1993). "Power and Privilege in White Middle-Class Feminist Discussions of Gender and Education." In S. K. Biklin and D. Pollard (Eds.), *Gender and Education: Ninety-Second Yearbook of the National Society for the Study of Education*. Chicago: University of Chicago Press, 221–240.

Smith, D. E. (1987). *The Everyday World as Problematic*. Boston: Northeastern University Press.

Stein, N.(1995). "Sexual Harrassment in School: The Public Performance of Gendered Violence." *Harvard Educational Review* 65(2): 142–162.

Streitmatter, J. (1998). *For Girls Only: Making a Case for Single-Sex Schooling*. Albany, NY: SUNY Press.

Weiler, K. (1988). *Women Teaching for Change: Gender, Class, and Power*. New York: Bergin and Garvey.

Weis, L., and Fine, M. (1993). *Beyond Silenced Voices*. Albany, NY: SUNY Press.

SINGLE-SEX SCHOOLING AND STUDENTS' ATTITUDES AND EXPERIENCES IN SCHOOL

CHAPTER 12

Perceptions of a Single-Sex Class Experience: Females and Males See It Differently

Janice Streitmatter

This study examines the perceptions of high school female and male students in single-sex math classes in a coeducational public high school. Interview and observation data were collected over a period of a school year. A qualitative research design and data analysis were used. Specifically, students were interviewed and asked how they felt about being in a class with students of their own sex and without students of the other sex. They also were asked to describe whether or not they felt the single-sex class construction had an effect on their math achievement. Results suggested that, with the exception of one male student, all students viewed their single-sex class as having been beneficial to them. However, the perceptions of why the class was important were differentiated by sex. The young women felt a sense of ownership and territoriality toward their single-sex math class, whereas the young men found the setting less distracting, but otherwise unexceptional.

Single-sex educational settings in the United States, those in the private as well as public sector have been studied, discussed, and debated by scholars, policy groups, and the courts in recent years. Policy groups such as the American Association of University Women (AAUW) and the federal courts have tended to focus on the legal issues regarding sex discrimination. The AAUW's report, *Separated by Sex: A Critical Look at Single-Sex Education for Girls* (1998), concluded that educational settings, organized as single-sex, were more detrimental than beneficial because of potential consequences of separating students by sex, and ultimately because this organization was based on principles of discrimination. The Supreme Court's decisions regarding admission policy to the Citadel and Virginia Military Institute rested on the assumption that denying women admission to these single-sex academies was sex discrimination and a violation of Title IX (1972). Despite policy and legal interpretations that clearly do not support single-sex educational organizations, scholars continue to examine the efficacy of these settings.

Increasing support at the local level as well as sustained practice in other countries of both single-sex schools and classes suggest that single-sex settings in the United States should not be rejected out of hand as an organizational option in schools.

The research on single-sex settings remains equivocal. (See Mael, 1998, for a partial summary of the literature.) Because the research designs and the settings for the research in this area are varied, it is difficult to summarize findings that apply to single-sex settings as a larger construct. In many cases findings are dependent on the variables studied and the research design used. Further, some research focuses on single-sex schools, some on single-sex classes, some is conducted in the private sector, and some in the public schools.

Some quantitatively analyzed data, comparing achievement of female and male students in Catholic single-sex and coeducational secondary schools, most notably that of Riordan (1985, 1990) suggest that some students in some cases benefit academically from single-sex educational settings, particularly those considered to be of at-risk populations. Other quantitatively constructed work (Lee, Marks, and Byrd, 1994; Marsh, 1991) has indicated that no significant benefits occur. These studies examined students in single-sex schools.

Less qualitatively designed research has been conducted, and that too has mixed results. Shmurak (1998) has studied females in private independent schools and found that no particular benefit with regard to achievement or career aspiration exists based solely on the single-sex setting. Streitmatter (1997, 1999) has studied the attitudinal, achievement, and psychosocial changes in female students in single-sex classes set in coeducational public schools. Data examining attitudes toward math and/or science suggest that female students in these classes sustain positive change in their attitudes toward these subject areas based on being in a single-sex class. Psychosocially, female students appear to exhibit more risk-taking behaviors, such as answering questions and initiating questions in single-sex classes than the same students do in their coeducational classes. The female students report these behaviors as being caused by the single-sex setting.

Despite the complex picture presented by the whole of the research on the effects of single-sex schooling, some current practice exists that suggests the development of single-sex classes has merit. Australian schools have supported the creation of single-sex classes in coeducational schools through teacher development policy for more than ten years. The work of Hildebrand (1996), and Parker and Rennie (1997) suggests that although the establishment of this class type is not without its problems (e.g., lack of appropriate and sufficient staff development) the work of creating, monitoring, and evaluating these classes continues with formal support from the government.

In England, where increasingly the government-funded schools recruit students and design schools in a way similar to the American charter school concept, some schools are turning to single-sex formats in order to draw larger numbers of students (interviews with head teachers and classroom observations, 1998). As examples, the secondary schools in Molsham and Chelmsford offer only single-sex classes to female and male secondary students. The schools' literature points out that girls and boys learn differently, need to be removed from the distractions provided by the other sex, and achieve better academically in single-sex classes. Although little if any systematic evaluation of the schools' claims appears to exist, parental response has been very positive, and both schools are operating at capacity. The United Kingdom has no public policy that limits the autonomy of the schools in separating female and male students.

Single-sex classes for girls in public middle schools have been developed in Edmonton, Alberta. This setting is perhaps more consistent culturally with the United States than are either Australia or England, although Canada also does not have any policy prohibition on separation of students by sex in public schools. Data from initial studies (Blair, in progress) suggest similar results to work done by Streitmatter (1999). The female students in the single-sex classes report a greater sense of empowerment and academic accomplishment in these classes than in their coeducational classes.

It is difficult to summarize the research to date on single-sex schooling benefits or disadvantages. The research venues are disparate, as are the research designs and questions. There are, however, several points upon which most of the scholars in the area of single-sex schooling agree. At-risk students, perhaps especially girls, in single-sex settings, whether Catholic schools, classes in public schools in Canada, or classes in public schools in the southwestern United States benefit attitudinally and academically because of being in single-sex settings (Schmuck, 1999). What is not clear is why specifically this is so. Is it simply that students of the other sex are not present; therefore, this distraction to learning is absent? Is it because students of the same sex create a particular climate in the single-sex class that facilitates greater learning?

THE STUDY

The purpose of this study was to examine girls' and boys' perceptions of being in a single-sex math class. Would female and male students view a single-sex class experience in the same ways? If not, how would these views differ? Although it might be expected that perceptions would differ by sex, the manner in which these differences would manifest themselves could hold important implications connected with implementation of single-sex classes. Given the increasing concern about boys' experiences in schools (Sommers, 2000), perhaps the most interesting question to be examined is whether the creation of single-sex classes is as efficacious for boys as for girls.

During the 1996 to 1997 academic year, as data were being collected and analyzed for a longitudinal study of girls-only classes in middle schools and high schools (Streitmatter, 1999), an unusual situation for study presented itself. A girls-only math class was formed in a high school. Because of the numbers of male and female students who needed that course, a boys-only class was inadvertently created as well. The same teacher taught both classes, back to back.

The high school in which these classes were created is an inner city school of approximately 2,100 students. Over 75 percent of the student body is minority and/or poor. The majority of the students are Latin-American, with European-American, African-American, Asian-American, and Native-American groups represented in that descending order.

The teacher, male and of European descent, first created a girls-only math class the year prior to when these data were drawn. The purpose of that class and the one the following year was to provide girls who had failed this course (Math Foundations) or pre-algebra, at least once, an opportunity to take the course in a single-sex setting. The teacher believed that having only girls in the class would lessen distractions and help the girls build their confidence and achievement as math students. The girls were either referred into the math class by their previous math teacher or counselor, or in the case of two girls, they requested the class themselves.

During the first week of school, the Math Foundations class following the girls-only section had only three girls enrolled. The teacher told the girls that they were free to change into a more mixed class. Two did so. The third girl chose to remain in the predominantly boys' section, but attended only a handful of classes before dropping out of school. This class was single-sex by the third week of school.

Seven other Math Foundations sections were offered during the 1996 to 1997 year. All were fairly evenly mixed by sex. Two were taught by the teacher of the single-sex sections, and the five others were taught by other math teachers at the school. All sections were developed for at-risk math students, and all followed the same curriculum.

METHODS

In order to observe student-student and teacher-student interactions, observations of both of the single-sex classes were conducted. A coeducational section, taught by this teacher, also was observed. Of particular interest in the observations were: whether the students would behave in ways that were connected to the arrangement of the class by sex; and whether the teacher would teach differently, dependent on the arrangement of the class. In previous work (Streitmatter, 1997; 1999), results of observations of girls-only classes have suggested that girls are likely to ask and answer questions more often in single-sex classes than when they are in their coeducational classes, and more often than other girls do in coeducational classes. In addition, the students in girls-only classes appear to cause the teacher to change her or his teaching style. Even in cases where the teacher expressed an intent to teach the single-sex class in exactly the same way as coeducational classes (usually a teacher-centered style), over time the teacher found that she or he taught in ways that allowed for greater collaboration among the girls than in the teacher's coeducational classes.

Each of the classes in the study was observed approximately every two weeks, usually on the same day. This allowed the observer to witness students in each of the classes being taught the same lesson. Of course, there were days when either the schedule was altered and the classes were shortened or not held, or when students in one of the classes were working on a lesson different from the other classes. This, however, was rare. The students in the three classes were generally on the same lesson on any given day. This pattern allowed for observations of student and teacher behavior by sex without the complication of considering student reaction to the content of the lesson.

Formal interviews were held with the teacher twice, once at the beginning and once at the end of the school year. The initial interview contained questions regarding the teacher's expectations of teaching two single-sex as well as one coeducational Math Foundations classes. He indicated that he wished to teach all of the classes in essentially the same way, although he expected the girls and boys in the single-sex classes would behave differently than the students in the coeducational section. He anticipated more discipline problems from the boys in the single-sex class and more interaction among the girls in the girls-only section than the coeducational students.

The interviewer at the end of the year reviewed his answers to the initial questions, and asked him to compare what his expectations had been with how he believed the classes actually had differed. After this interview was completed, the teacher had the opportunity to read the field notes.

Students in both of the single-sex classes were interviewed one time, between December and March. Twelve of the eighteen female and ten of the seventeen male students were interviewed. The female students were randomly chosen from among the class. The male students were selected based on attendance. Only ten of the boys regularly attended the class. The other seven had very sporadic attendance because of an array of difficulties ranging from suspensions to frequent household moves. It was decided that these boys were not at school enough to make them credible respondents about life in their math class, and that the ten boys included in the study would have a better sense of the class than the boys who were in attendance only occasionally.

The students were asked about their perceptions of being a student in a single-sex class as well as their attitudes toward math. All students were asked the same questions. Specifically, students were asked to comment on what it was like to be in a single-sex class, and how they felt about taking math with students of only their own sex and without students of the other sex. Other questions focused on if and how they thought their single-sex class differed from their other coeducational classes, and if and how this math class differed from their math classes in the past. The students also were asked how they felt the single-sex class arrangement did or did not affect their attitudes about math.

Observation data were analyzed according to the general categories that followed the purpose of the study. Interview data were transcribed and then analyzed according to the broad categories of student perceptions of single-sex classes and student attitudes toward math as it might be affected by a single-sex class arrangement.

RESULTS

The results from the interview data with the students in the girls-only class revealed almost identical findings to those collected since 1993 in other girls-only settings work of which this study was a part (Streitmatter, 1999). Every girl appreciated the opportunity of being in a single-sex class and each iterated similar reasons. The students believed they got more work done without the distraction of boys, they felt more comfortable in participating in class with only girls, and they felt more confident in their ability as math students as a result of being in the single-sex class. These excerpts from interviews with the girls are representative of their perceptions of the single-sex class experience.

> The guys distract. I think it's OK to have boys in other classes, but in here it's better with just us.

> Guys talk to you in class and want to give the answers. They take up a lot of attention. It's kind of like the whole class is spinning around that guy and not math.

> Guys yell out the answer. [In this class] you'd be more positive and in control. I think we work together better. The girls yell out and say, "Come on, you can do it, and all that."

> Guys take over a class. And like, for math, it's been good to have our own class.

The consensus from the girls about their experiences was particularly interesting in light of the fact that only three of the girls had deliberately chosen to enroll in the class. The majority had been placed with their consent by their counselor, and three had been placed in it without their knowledge at all. How the girls were placed in the class appeared to make no difference in their perception of the benefits of the class. Without exception, the girls indicated that this class was an important place for them. Here they could learn without distraction and not need to battle with male students for the teacher's time and attention. Perhaps most importantly, as the third quote in the preceding indicates, the girls felt they created a place where things were "positive and in control." In other words, they felt they had an important "girl place" that was theirs, and was without boys.

The boys were asked the same questions as the girls with regard to their experiences in a single-sex math class. The boys agreed with the girls that students of the other sex could be distracting, as illustrated through these representative quotes.

I guess I get more done in here. There aren't any chicks to look at.

It's pretty much the same environment, except we get more work done because there aren't any girls. Sometimes in other classes I look at the girls instead of paying attention to the teacher.

The idea that the single-sex class was better for getting work done was reiterated by all of the boys interviewed. Only one student, David, expressed concern about the organization of the class.

I get more done in here, and that's probably the same for the girls in their class. But I think it's wrong [separating students by sex] because it's segregation. You need to know how to get along with girls and women and stuff. So you should be in classes with them.

Other than David's concern about the philosophical consideration of separating students by sex, none of the boys voiced any particular interest in the single-sex organization of the class at all. They revealed neither irritation nor satisfaction about the construction of the class.

Although both girls and boys said that students of the other sex could interrupt their completion of their class work, a clear qualitative difference between the sexes is illustrated through their responses. The girls were much more specific about their issues regarding boys in class than were the boys. The girls talked about distractions but they also pointed to a concern about male dominance to the point where "the whole class is spinning around the guy." In contrast, the boys were much less specific about the issue of having only boys in their class. Three of them said that they really did not care one way or the other, aside from being able to get more work done. Being in class without girls was all right, and being with them was all right. The primary benefit of being in classes with girls was that you were able to "look at them."

Responses to the question of whether they would wish to have more single-sex classes further separated the respondents by sex. None of the boys wished for more classes, and two specifically said they did not want more. The other eight did not care whether they were in additional single-sex classes or not, although all boys stated that they did not want to be in an entirely single-sex environment.

The responses of the girls to this issue were quite different from that of the boys. All but one agreed that more single-sex classes would be a good thing. Some of their remarks follow:

They should be in math, English, science. Really anything where you don't want to be embarrassed.

You know, there's a life outside of class. No way would I want to be with just girls forever. But, like, it's easier to work in class with just us.

I think any class that's really hard should be just girls. That way you learn the stuff and don't worry about feeling stupid.

Maybe all of our classes should be just girls. That could be cool. But you wouldn't find me at an all girls school. I know some girls who went to St. Mark's. When they got to high school, they were totally party girls.

A particular incident occurred several months into the school year that reflected another issue of being in a single-sex class that was differentiated by student sex.

The class had been in session for about ten minutes. The girls were working on a word problem in small groups of two and three. The class-room door opened and a boy entered. The girls looked up and work was suspended. The boy told the teacher he had been enrolled in the class. Before the teacher could respond, one of the girls spoke up. "Hey sir, what's he doing in here? This is our class." A chorus of agreement followed from many of the other girls. The teacher explained to the boy that he had accidentally been placed in the wrong class and needed to return to the counselor's office to find another math class.

In looking back on the incident, several girls at the end of the year discussed their impressions. The context for the conversation was a group discussion during the final week of school.

We looked at him, and said, like what's a boy doing in here? This is our territory, our class. We didn't want to be mean about it, but we didn't want him there.

Yeah, he was odd in here. I know he was uncomfortable, but that's too bad. He didn't belong. This place is ours.

There have to be guys somewhere. Otherwise, what would be the purpose of coming to school? But not in our math class. It was like ours, you know? A girls' place.

As these data were analyzed, additional qualitative differences by sex emerged. For example, when asked about having boys in their classes, the female respondents focused on boys' behavior in a general sense, as well as the behavior of specific boys in their classes. The girls tended to see the boys as the center of attention, and as being assertive or aggressive. They also provided specific examples. "In my science class last year, Jose . . . ", "The guy next to me in English class . . . ", or "When I tried to answer the teacher's question in history, Jason . . . " The responses began as generalizations about "all boys" but soon became memories that were personal. Specific experiences involving individual male students were remembered. Further, the experiences were recalled as irritating, unpleasant, and negative.

The boys were pressed to discuss their perceptions of having girls in their classes. Qualitative differences in the boys' responses compared to the girls' were reflected. Although the boys considered girls as part of a general group (e.g., girls in general behave in a particular way) much in the same way the girls had done the boys, none of the boys remarked about any girls as individuals, even when invited to do so. The boys initially were asked, "What is it like having girls in your classes?" A follow-up question, "What specifically has occurred to you in school that might have shaped your opinion?" was then asked to try to elicit a more personalized response and to draw the boys away from generalized and stereotypic reflections. Only Martin identified real females, "my sisters." However, none of his observations had to do with classroom situations where he had personally been involved. Some examples of the boys' comments about "what girls are like in school" follow.

> Maybe girls just don't want to look smart. They think boys won't like them if they look smart. My sisters are like that. If the boys think the girls are smart, then the boys won't talk to them. At least that seems to be what they think.

> I don't think girls are as smart as boys in anything. Well, maybe in socializing and relationships and stuff like that. I guess girls are better at those things.

> Girls can kid around just like guys. But in classes, girls are usually better behaved and so teachers like them more. Girls are usually better students too, but I don't think they're smarter. It's about even in that.

> Men come from a more technical part of life. I'm not saying that men are smarter. But men think of technical things like they engineer things and build stuff. Women generally are more of a caring type. Girls are better in English and helping people and teaching.

Fennema and Sherman (1977) have suggested that the degree of girls' self-efficacy about math substantially decreases by the end of early adolescence and does not recover during the adolescent years of high school. Although grades or standardized test scores were not studied in this work in order to attempt to assess the possible affect of class organization on achievement, both female and male students were asked how they felt about themselves as math students as a result of being in a single-sex class. Following this question, they were asked if they thought the single-sex math class had made a difference in how well they performed in the class.

Student responses to this question were distinctly differentiated by sex. None of the girls said that they felt their math achievement or ability had declined during their single-sex class experience, one said she felt it made no difference, and eleven of the twelve girls interviewed said they believed their math ability had improved during the school year as a direct result of being in this math class. Of the ten boys interviewed, none reported a perceived decline in his math ability, three thought that they might have gotten more work done because they had concentrated more (although none of these three felt that there were any more lasting achievement or ability effects), and the remaining seven reported that they believed the class had made no difference in their sense of themselves as math students. Several representative statements from girls and then boys follow.

> Being in this class, I've been able to ask questions and get help from the teacher without being afraid of being made fun of. I'm not sure what it will be like in math next year, but at least I know I can do math and I'm not stupid in it (Cristina).

> I was going to take Consumer Math next year, cause I need one more year of math to graduate. But I think I'll do algebra instead. The teacher thinks I can do it, and so do I (Martina).

> I've always been bad at math. I still hate it, but like, I know that I can do it now. And I'm not afraid of it anymore (Kelly).

> It really helped to have all of us working together. When someone shouted out an answer, it was kind of like we were all doing it together (Sharla).

> Well, like I said before, it was easier to get work done without girls. But math has never bothered me, and it still doesn't. I feel the same about it (Ronaldo).

> This was like just a regular class, except there weren't any girls in it. I don't think anything else about it was different (Matt).

> Math has always been my worst subject. I guess I did about as well in here as I could in any class. I have one more year, and that's it for math forever (Juan).

In addition to assessment of student attitudes toward their own math ability, the teacher was asked to consider whether his anticipation of different dynamics in the classes had been realized. Field data from the observations support much of his assessment. The teacher felt that the girls had "more naturally" coalesced into groups, and had worked more collaboratively. He found them to be quite assertive and "labor-intensive."

> They asked millions of questions. It was never quiet in the class, even though it was a small group. They wouldn't just do their work, they wanted to talk about it together and with me. The groups worked pretty well. In fact, they preferred to have things set up that way. And they [the girls] were really clear that this was a class for only girls. Remember that time the boy was accidentally enrolled in the class? There was no way the girls were going to let him stay.

The teacher found the boys quieter, working more on their own, and in general the teacher was not surprised to find that the boys were not particularly concerned about the single-sex organization of the class. The primary difference in the teacher's interactions between the groups as he saw it, was that on occasion, he and the boys would engage in joking that often took the form of sexist jokes about girls.

> The jokes weren't really all that bad, but if there had been girls in the room they wouldn't have been said out loud. There was a short time when a female student was visiting from Minnesota, and came to the class a few times to tutor. She was a year or so older than most of the boys and very pretty. Needless to say, there would be jokes about who was doing the worst in the class and needed her help the most. But other than the few jokes and the boys' reaction to the tutor, there weren't any real discipline problems and this class pretty much ran like a regular Math Foundations class.

In that both observers were female, it is not surprising that the teacher's report of "sexist jokes" being an occasional part of the boys' math class milieu cannot be verified from observation data. We must take the teacher's word for it. The teacher clearly took the boys' behavior associated with the female tutor as "natural." The extent to which this and perhaps other sexist-related incidents further differentiated the dynamics of the girls' and boys' classes can only be supposed.

The teacher, in both single-sex classes, appeared to allow the dynamics of the groups to unfold, and then reinforced their construction. In the case of the girls' class, he placed the students into groups and then structured his teaching style around collaboration. Although there were always a few girls who chose to work alone on occasion, the general practice was for the teacher to give instruction to the entire group, and then have them work on problems in smaller groups of two or three. These groups often melded into one or two large groups where there was an exchange of information (usually, but not always about the math at hand). Whether the girls would have nudged the teacher into this structure without his first providing it, as has been observed in the past (Streitmatter, 1999), is not known. Certainly collaboration was the teacher's expectation, the girls worked well within it, and on final reflection, some of the students credited that construction with being responsible in part for their positive experience in the class.

The teacher's pedagogical style in the boys' class was much more traditional. He gave instruction, and then the boys worked on the examples, usually on their own. There was no restriction on collaboration, but neither was a collaborative format organized by the teacher. With regard to the sexist or sexual nature of some of the jokes in the boys' class, several questions can be constructed regarding their impact. Did the fact that the teacher engaged in the jokes influence some of the boys' statements about girls being objects to look at? The teacher seemed to believe that the situation with only one attractive girl in a boys' class would "needless to say" cause sexist or sexual comments from the boys. He perceived his role in these jokes as "going along" with the flow of events and not in any way directing them. Another interpretation is that his participation implicitly encouraged the boys to behave in this way. However, whether these male students would have made such comments in the same environment with a female teacher is unknown.

Would these jokes, as the teacher suggested, not have been uttered if the class had been coeducational? This seems likely. During the discussion with the teacher about the jokes, he added that he regretted they had occurred. He also mentioned that it was a "good thing none of the girls-only students heard the jokes." The teacher evidenced some sensitivity to this issue, and if for no other reason than to avoid angry female students, he probably would not have allowed this in a coeducational setting.

Would this dynamic have existed throughout the school year if the teacher had formally indicated that this would not be allowed? Given the well-documented fact that teachers have considerable influence over the climate established in their classrooms, this too seems unlikely.

Would the boys have felt more strongly about the math class being "their territory" if the class had been organized the same way as the girls? No data collected directly speak to this point. In the case of the girls' perceptions, a number of factors seem to have contributed to their strong sense of ownership of their class. The single factor of collaborative versus isolated groupings of students does not seem to sufficiently address this issue.

CONCLUSION

Much of the research that has examined females and males in single-sex educational settings has done so through comparing variables, such as achievement test scores and/or self-esteem measures (Lee and Marks, 1992; Marsh, 1989). The unique circumstance of this study allowed sustained observation and interview data with both girls and boys in single-sex classrooms, in the same course, taught by the same teacher, in a coeducational high school. The issue of what this setting meant to the students was the focus of this particular investigation.

There were three principal outcomes of this study. First, all students, regardless of sex, agreed that a single-sex class provided them with the opportunity to focus on work. Female and male students agreed that the single-sex class was beneficial with regard to getting their work done. All students of each group interviewed spoke of the other group providing distraction in the learning environment. This is a theme that is repeated in all of the ten single-sex classrooms that have been studied to date.

Second, there was a qualitative difference in how females and males explained their perceptions of how it was to have students of the other sex in their classes. The data from the male perspective suggest that male and female students in this investigation held qualitatively differing views about the essence of the distraction and the group responsible for it. The girls reported that boys generally, and some boys specifically, shouted out answers, took the teacher's attention, had a tendency to embarrass the girls, and dominated the classroom. When asked, the female students had a great deal to say about coeducational classroom dynamics by gender. Their examples of disruption or distraction were tied to individual male transgressors and the impact was described in ways that illustrated a personal effect: "Adrian made me feel stupid" or "Paul wouldn't let me talk. He kept interrupting." The girls reported scenarios that reflected feelings of hurt, embarrassment, or frustration. None suggested that boys were a positive force in their classrooms, or that they wished boys were part of the single-sex classroom. It should be noted that the group of girls in this class was not hostile to having boys in their lives. Most talked about dating and boyfriends, one was getting married immediately at the end of the school year, and one was pregnant. In the academic milieu, however, they held strong opinions about the role male students played in their classes.

Third, attitudes toward the single-sex class experience were differentiated by sex. The male students tended to speak about female students as belonging to a general group, "girls in classes," and other than Martin, cited no specific girls as examples of what they were discussing. The descriptions of "how girls are" were stereotypic and generalized. Young women were described as deficient in academics in comparison to boys, as pretending to be stupid for the sake of attracting boys, or skilled in nurturing roles. Only one boy suggested that female students were equally as skilled academically as male students. For nearly all of the male students, the girls represented sexual distractions, rather than "academic barriers" as the girls described the boys. The boys reported that they were kept from their work because they looked at the girls too often. The girls were a passive distraction, which was based on their sex, not because of any particular behavior on their parts.

The third finding suggests that female and male students perceived the experience of participating in a single-sex class differently in yet one other way. An incident described earlier underscores the girls' sense of ownership of their single-sex class. The boy who was inadvertently admitted to their math class found himself in hostile territory. The girls were clear in their message to the boy as well as to their teacher; boys were not allowed in their space. The class was girls-only, and they would not tolerate a male student in their class.

By way of comparison, a situation occurred in the boys' class that illustrated a very different attitude on the part of the students in the boys-only class toward the issue of turf or ownership based on student sex. As was described, one girl remained enrolled in the boys' class for a time. Although it is true that this student was absent much more often than she was present, and eventually dropped out after several months, her intermittent presence was ignored by the boys. When interviewing began, the boys identified, or at least agreed with the interviewer's identification of the class being single-sex. During the interview of the fourth male student, the female student was present that day in class. This was the first time the interviewer had been aware that a girl still was part of the boys-only class. The boy being interviewed was perfectly comfortable with the idea that his math class was single-sex. When asked directly about girls in the class, he looked around the room, spotted the girl, and replied, "Oh, I guess there's a girl in this class." He was asked what having a girl in the boys-only class meant to him, and he said it was "No big deal." The other boys interviewed were equally disinterested.

The boys did not view their classroom as a place that belonged only to them. The strong sense of turf that was present for the girls in having their own class was absent from the perceptions of the boys. Finally, with the exception of presenting girls as sexually related distractions, no boys attributed the absence of girls as being connected with better achievement in math. They also mentioned nothing about a greater sense of empowerment that was implicit in many of the girls' explanations of why they liked their math class.

It is not possible to assess any long-range effects of the single-sex experience on either the girls or the boys in this investigation. Similarly, these results cannot be generalized. However, the results of this study are consistent with work done previously regarding girls' perceptions of single-sex class experiences (Riordan, 1998; Streitmatter, 1997) and provide some substantiation of their veracity. The dimension added here is the comparison of views held by boys compared to those of girls in the same subject single-sex classes, taught by the same teacher. The girls placed a much higher value on their single-sex class than did the boys. The girls felt that the class was their place, whereas the boys felt their class was just a class, incidentally without girls to distract them. It is apparent, especially through their discussion about wishing more or perhaps all classes were single-sex, that the girls found benefit in being in this class. As in other studies where there has been evidence suggesting that the girls have created their own community (Streitmatter, 1997, 1999) these girls indicated the same, as they rejected the addition of a boy to their group. Further, the girls identified a need being met that was not referred to by the boys. The girls relished having a setting where there were no negative intrusions; no boys making fun of their questions or answers, and no boys overshadowing their presence in the classroom. The girls' emphasis on having "a girls' place" suggests a reaction to the broader environment as not being a girls' place, but perhaps a boys' place. In their single-sex math class, the girls could own the space, even if they perceived they did not own the remaining space in the school. The passion with which these girls spoke about their class seemed to suggest that a very important need was being addressed; creating a space for girls that is not male dominated. The female students in this study have clearly iterated their need to control and dominate part of their learning environment. The implication seems clear. Single-sex classes for girls in secondary coeducational settings is important. Further, this option appears, at least from these limited data, not to be as critical for male as female students. Certainly boys as a group appear to have important educational issues that must be addressed (Sommers, 2000). Providing them with a single-sex classroom environment may produce some positive effects for male students, but filling a need for classroom presence or domination is not one of them.

REFERENCES

American Association of University Women (AAUW). (1998). *Separated by Sex: A Critical Look at Single-Sex Education for Girls.* Washington, D.C.: American Association of University Women Educational Foundation.

Fennema, E., and Sherman, J. (1977). "Sex-Related Differences in Mathematics Achievement, Spatial Visualization, and Affective Factors." *American Educational Research Journal 14*: 51–71.

Hildebrand, G. (1996). "Single-Sex Classes in Co-educational Schools: Highlighting Issues of Gender." Paper presented at the American Educational Research Association, New York.

Lee, V.E., and Marks, H. (1992). "Sustained Efforts of the Single-Sex Secondary School Experience on Attitudes, Behaviors, and Values in College." *Journal of Education Psychology* 82 (3): 578–592.

Lee, V. E., Marks, H., and Byrd, T. "Sexism in Single-Sex and Coeducational Independent Schools." *Sociology of Education* 67: 92–120.

Parker, L. H., and Rennie, L. J. (1997) "Teachers' Perceptions of the Implementation of Single-Sex Classes in Coeducational Schools." *Australian Journal of Education 41* (2): 119–133.

Mael, F. A. (1998). Single-Sex and Coeducational Schooling: Relationships to Socioemotional and Academic Development. *Review of Educational Research 68*: 2 101–129.

Marsh, H. W., (1989). "Effects of Attending Single-Sex and Coeducational High Schools on Achievment, Attitudes, Behaviors, and Sex Differences." *Journal of Education Psychoology 81* (1); 70–85.

———. (1991). "Public, Catholic Single-Sex and Catholic Coeducational High Schools: Their Effect on Achievement, Affect, and Behaviors." *American Psychologist 45*: 513–520.

Riordan, C. (1990). *Girls and Boys in School: Together or Separate?* New York: Teachers College Press.

———. (1985). "Public and Catholic Schooling: The Effects of Gender Context Policy." *American Journal of Education* (August): 518–540.

Schmuck, P. (1999). Discussion Notes from Pre-Conference Session American Education Research Association Seg: Women in Research, Hempstead, Long Island, N.Y. October.

Shmurak, C. (1998). *Voices of Hope: Adolescent Girls at Single-Sex and Coeducational Schools.* New York: Peter Lang.

Sommers, C. H. (2000). *The War against Boys.* New York: Simon and Schuster.

Streitmatter, J. (1997). "An Exploratory Study of Risk-Taking in a Girls-Only Middle School Math Class. *Elementary School Journal 98* (1): 15–26.

Streitmatter, J. (1999). *For Girls Only: Making a Case for Single-Sex Schooling.* Albany, NY: SUNY Press.

CHAPTER 13

Single-Gender or Coeducation for Middle-School Girls: Does It Make a Difference in Math?

Judith Gilson

INTRODUCTION

Competency in mathematics has been identified as a crucial skill that is related directly to educational and occupational choices. A strong background in mathematics is key for many career and job opportunities in an increasingly technological society. Math skills, however, have often appeared elusive for many girls. Fennema (1990) described mathematics as the "critical filter" that successfully inhibits the participation of women in many careers and occupations. Fennema and Hart (1994) reported that, although gender differences in mathematics achievement are declining, there are indications that differences still exist in areas involving the most complex mathematical tasks, especially as girls progress from middle school to high school.

Previous research has investigated different learning environments that may affect female students' performance in mathematics and their attitudes toward mathematics. Many of these studies have been focused on students at the high-school and college levels and have been confined largely to Roman Catholic schools or to schools outside the United States. The purpose of the study described in this chapter is to identify differences in mathematics achievement and attitudes toward mathematics of American female students in independent single-gender and coeducational eighth-grade classes. A secondary purpose is to identify successful pedagogies or school organizations that could be transferred to public schools. The study is confined to independent schools because single-gender public schools are quite rare in the United States.

REVIEW OF THE LITERATURE

Academic self-concept, the component of self-concept related to students' feelings about themselves as learners, interacts strongly with school performance. Students who are confident in their ability to perform an educational task are more likely to be successful at that task than students who lack confidence in their ability (Sarah, Scott, and Spender, 1980). Students who have positive self-concepts of their mathematical ability, tend to perform better in mathematics than students who do not interpret their mathematical ability as strongly (Meece, Wigfield, and Eccles, 1990; Tobias, 1987).

Meyer and Koehler (1990) and Posnick-Goodwin (1997) reported that at both the middle school and high school levels, females expressed less confidence in their ability to learn mathematics than did males. Fennema and Sherman (1977, 1978) found that students' perceived ability, or confidence, in learning mathematics was correlated more strongly with achievement ($r =$ .40) than with any other affective variable they measured.

Classroom environments can affect student attitudes and student achievement-related behaviors; subsequently, they can affect student academic achievement (Reyes and Stanic, 1988). Females have been found to be more socially oriented than males, and females pick up cues from their environment more readily than males do. As a result, classroom experiences of males and females may differ (Linn and Petersen, 1985), and females have been found to exhibit a greater susceptibility to both the positive and negative effects of the classroom environment than do males (Mitchell and Gilson, 1997).

Although intuitively one might predict that all-female schools have a beneficial effect on girls' self-esteem, some research has shown otherwise (Foon, 1988; Monaco and Gaier, 1992). Foon (1988) reported that school type did not produce consistent differences in patterns of self-esteem for females. According to Lee, however, by itself self-esteem is not an appropriate educational outcome. Self-esteem must be seen as a means, not merely an end. "Our efforts are better directed to raising [girls'] performance. Children's self-esteem goes up when they are successful in school" (1997, p. 143).

Confidence was found to be the most consistent variable in predicting achievement in mathematics for females (Tartre and Fennema, 1995). In a study of twelfth-grade female high-school students, Armstrong and Price (1982) found that, for females, participation in mathematics classes was weakly correlated with a nonstereotypic perception of mathematics (i.e., the perception that either males or females can succeed in math) ($r = .20$), but more highly correlated than it was for males ($r = .10$). In an attempt to further understand the impact of gender stereotyping, Colley, Comber, and Hargreaves (1994) studied the school-subject preferences of 327 female eleven- and twelve-year-old students and 240 female fifteen- and sixteen-year-old students in three single-gender and four coeducational schools in England. Participants were asked to rank order thirteen school subjects, including mathematics, in order of preference, excluding subjects that they had not personally studied. For the eleven- and twelve-year-old female middle-school students from the single-gender schools, mathematics ranked the highest, whereas for their female counterparts from the coeducational schools, mathematics was one of the lowest ranked subjects. At the high-school level, female students in both school sectors ranked mathematics similarly.

Steinback and Gwizdala (1995) investigated differences in mathematics attitudes of female high-school students in the United States before and after their single-gender Roman Catholic high school merged with a similar all-male high school. The same questionnaire, which was designed to determine students' like or dislike of mathematics, their self-esteem in mathematics, and their view of the importance and usefulness of mathematics, was administered to participants in both years of the study, and a comparison of responses was made for those female students who took mathematics classes both years of the study. Despite an observed decline in the female students' positive feelings, particularly in self-confidence in mathematics, after the school became coeducational, the researchers concluded that the female student's attitudes toward mathematics and their own performance in mathematics remained generally positive.

Some research on the effectiveness of single-gender education for girls mathematics achievement has produced results unfavorable to single-gender schools (AAUW, 1998; Belash, 1992; Daly, 1996; Lee, 1997; LePore and Warren, 1997; Shmurak, 1998; Signorella, Frieze, and Hershey, 1996). The Association of University Women (AAUW) concluded, "There is no evidence that single-sex education in general 'works' or is 'better' than coeducation" (1998, p. 2). Specific practices and characteristics of single-gender environments have contributed to the success of single-gender education, and many of these practices may be translatable to coeducational environments. In her longitudinal study of fifty-six female students from two single-gender schools and two coeducational schools, Shmurak (1998) concluded that most of the data showed no differences between the two types of schools. Shmurak followed the students from the ninth grade through their freshman year in college. She concluded that there were no statistical differences in SAT scores (average SAT math scores for single-gender students = 566.5; average SAT math scores for coeducational students = 594.7) and no statistically significant differences in grades in mathematics courses between students at the different types of schools.

Riordan (1990), however, found that female students in single-gender schools have an advantage over their peers in coeducational schools. Riordan concluded that girls in single-gender schools did more homework than the girls in coeducational schools did. Because success in mathematics may depend on repeated application and practice of new concepts, Riordan attributed higher achievement in mathematics for the girls in the single-gender schools to the greater amount of mathematics homework they did compared to girls in the coeducational schools.

Young (1994) reported that the socio-economic and educational levels of students' families contributed more to student academic achievement in math than did the gender composition of Australian schools. Higher SES corresponded with higher student achievement. Ware and Lee (1988) concluded that personal and family background affect students' achievement and educational aspirations, and for women, these aspirations are stronger predictors of mathematics enrollment in college than for men.

Marsh (1991) and Bell (1989) similarly concluded that variances in achievement in different areas of the curriculum between coeducational and single-gender schools could be explained more by the characteristics of the students who attended the schools than by school-type effects. Bell reported that there was no evidence to ascribe differences in academic achievement directly to the separation of students in schools based on gender. Similarly, Stoecker and Pascarella (1991) concluded the career attainments that had previously been ascribed to attending a women's college were more likely to be artifacts of differential student recruitment at those schools than of socialization occurring in the single-gender environment. In their 1998 report, *Separated by Sex*, the AAUW proposed that it is unwise to view a school's gender composition as "the key variable" in assessing the effectiveness of a school.

Interest in single-gender education in the United States is increasing. Yet there is little clear evidence supporting the idea that single-gender education promotes higher achievement levels in or more positive attitudes toward mathematics for girls than coeducation does. Few studies have addressed the practices of different school environments that promote better educational outcomes specifically for females at the middle-school level. One approach is to compare single-gender schools with coeducational middle schools that provide similar mathematics curriculums in order to assess whether one environment is more advantageous for female students than the other.

PURPOSE OF THE STUDY

The study described in this chapter continued the investigation of the relationship between achievement and self-concept, specifically in mathematics, and looked for factors inherent in two different school sectors (independent all-girls middle schools and independent coeducational middle schools) that may affect female students' attitudes toward mathematics. The expectation was that if differences in either attitude toward mathematics or mathematics achievement between the two school types were discovered, it would be possible to identify factors that were contributing to the student's attitudes toward mathematics and their achievement in mathematics. These elements could be translatable to the public sector.

The study focused on 467 eighth-grade girls from ten independent all-girls middle schools and 208 eighth-grade girls from ten independent coeducational middle schools. Independent schools refer to nonsectarian, private schools that charge tuition. The participating schools were all members of the National Association of Independent Schools (NAIS) and included schools from across the United States. The schools were all in large metropolitan areas across the United States. This study intended to extend the existing research on mathematics education and gender to include students at the middle-school level because prior research has not looked at the middle-school level.

METHODS

The schools participating in this study were selected from a random sample of independent schools across the United States that were members of NAIS. By nature, NAIS schools are selective, and students attending NAIS-member schools are largely of the same middle- to upper-middle socioeconomic classes and of comparable achievement levels (National Association of Independent Schools, 1997). Because the study compared schools that served similar student populations, it was anticipated that any differences in student achievement or outcome could be attributed to differences in the school sectors.

A letter was sent to sixty single-gender schools and to sixty coeducational schools inviting their participation in the study. The 120 schools originally invited to participate in the study were chosen at random from the NAIS 1998 roster. The only criteria for inclusion were that the schools have a middle-school program and be located in major metropolitan areas. Twenty schools agreed to furnish test results and allow their students to complete a mathematics-attitude questionnaire. School personnel at nineteen of the twenty schools completed a separate questionnaire that was used to gather specific information about the participating middle schools (one coeducational school did not return the questionnaire). Information was collected identifying the gender of the administrative personnel and of the eighth-grade mathematics teachers, the size and class length of the eighth-grade mathematics classes, the size of the eighth-grade classes, and what efforts the schools had made to address issues of gender equity. Phone conversations were conducted with mathematics teachers, school administrators or both at four of the schools (two single-gender, two coeducational) who volunteered to be interviewed.

An attitude questionnaire constructed and previously piloted by the researcher was used to assess students' attitudes toward mathematics (see Appendix). On the response sheets, students identified whether they attended single-gender or coeducational middle schools, the number and level of mathematics courses they had taken, and the mathematics courses in which they were enrolled. Collected test score data were students' most recent quantitative achievement and ability scores from the Comprehensive Testing Program III (CTP III) published by the Educational Records Bureau (ERB), which is a requirement for membership in NAIS. Depending on the school, these test data either were from spring of the seventh grade or fall or spring of the eighth grade.

RESULTS

MATHEMATICS ACHIEVEMENT AND QUANTITATIVE ABILITY SCORES

Scores on the CTP III can be compared across grade and test levels (D. Hall, personal communication, May 28, 1998; Educational Testing Service, 1997). A t test for independent samples was computed on the mean mathematics achievement and quantitative ability scores from each school sector. In a t test, the more the means of the samples differ, the greater the value of the t statistic will be. No statistically significant differences at the .01 level were found between the two groups for mathematics achievement ($t = -.64$, $df = 576$) or for quantitative ability ($t = -.80$, $df = 672$).

The strength of the relationship of school sector to student's mathematics achievement was measured using an effect size. Effect sizes are estimates of the degree to which a phenomenon may exist in a given population. Cohen's d was calculated by subtracting the mean scores for the two school sectors and dividing the difference by the standard deviation of the appropriate test from the Independent School Norms® (Educational Testing Service, 1997). No meaningful effects were found for quantitative ability scores ($d = .06$) or for mathematics achievement scores ($d = .05$) and school sector. The means and standard deviations for each group are reported in table 13.1.

Regression analyses were conducted to determine the effect of school sector (single-gender or coeducational) on mathematics achievement and quantitative ability defined by student scores on the CTP III and on students' attitude toward mathematics defined by student responses on the attitude questionnaire (table 13.2). Three series of regression analyses were conducted. The first set of analyses regressed the variable of school sector on the total group of 578 individual CTP III mathematics achievement scores. The second set of analyses regressed school sector on the total group of 674 individual CTP III quantitative ability scores. The third analysis regressed school sector on attitude toward mathematics. Attitude toward mathematics was then regressed on mathematics achievement and quantitative ability scores aggregated by school. Only the three scales with acceptable reliability levels were used in the regression analyses. The reliability coefficient for interest in mathematics was .68; for perception of ability in mathematics .76; and for perception of effort in mathematics .72. Inspection of the regression analyses indicates that variations in mathematics achievement and quantitative ability scores are not attributable to differences in school sector.

ATTITUDE TOWARD MATHEMATICS

Overall, positive attitudes toward students' sense of their ability and academic identity in mathematics were found in both school sectors. Raw scores on the attitude instrument were transformed based on Rasch estimates (Cohen, 1988) (table 13.3). The new scale is a linear transformation of the Rasch logits with a mean of 50.

TABLE 13.1

MEANS AND STANDARD DEVIATIONS FOR CTP III SCORES[a]

School Sector	Mathematics Achievement				Quantitative Ability	
	n	Mean	SD	n	Mean	SD
Single-gender	392	369.36	28.30	467	366.33	19.56
Coeducational	186	367.83	23.64	207	365.08	17.01
Total	578	365.74	25.38	674	365.02	18.16

[a]. Not all schools submitted both test scores for all students.

TABLE 13.2

REGRESSION RESULTS OF SCHOOL SECTOR EFFECTS ON
MATHEMATICS ACHIEVEMENT AND QUANTITATIVE ABILITY

Source	df	Sum of Squares	Mean Square	F	R Square	Adjusted R Square
Total Mathematics Achievement						
Regression	1	293.89	293.89	0.41	0.001	−0.001
Error	576	416450.12	723.00			
Total	577	416744.01				
Total Quantitative Ability						
Regression	1	224.22	224.22	0.63	0.001	−0.001
Error	672	237817.64	353.90			
Total	673	238041.86				
Attitude toward Mathematics						
Regression	1	1.01	1.01	1.44	0.002	0.002
Error	674	521.65	0.70			
Total	675	522.66				
Attitude toward Mathematics Regressed on Mathematics Achievement						
Regression	6	0.49	0.08	0.62	0.19	−0.12
Error	16	2.19	0.14			
Total	22	2.61				
Attitude toward Mathematics Regressed on Quantitative Ability						
Regression	6	133.98	22.33	0.26	0.12	−0.30
Error	13	1102.71	84.82			
Total	19	1236.69				

A *t* test for independent samples was computed on the attitudinal mean responses of the participants from each school sector. No statistically significant differences at the .01 level were found between the two groups for perception of ability in mathematics ($t = -0.99$, $df = 615$), for perception of effort in mathematics ($t = 1.09$, $df = 605$), for academic identity in mathematics ($t = 1.78$, $df = 555$), for interest in mathematics ($t = -2.06$, $df = 630$), for the relationship of effort to achievement ($t = -0.83$, $df = 634$), or for the relationship of ability to achievement ($t = -2.25$, $df = 625$).

From the regression analyses (table 13.2), it was concluded that students' attitude toward mathematics scores were not related to mathematics achievement scores or to quantitative ability scores. Any differences in students' attitudes toward mathematics could not be attributed to school sector.

Higher means on the attitude instrument (see Appendix) indicate attitudes that are more positive. In comparison to the other constructs, means for interest in mathematics and for the perception of the relationship of ability to achievement are lower for both groups. The standard deviations are similar for both groups, but there is more variability in both school sectors on responses to items related to perceptions of ability and effort than on items related to the relationship of ability to achievement and the relationship of effort to achievement.

On the average, students in coeducational schools reported a slightly stronger sense of their ability in mathematics, the relationship of effort to achievement, the relationship of ability to achievement, and interest in mathematics than students from single-gender schools. On the average, students in single-gender schools reported a slightly stronger sense of their academic identity in mathematics and the effort they apply to their mathematics classes than students from coeducational schools. However, none of these results were statistically significant.

Overall, positive attitudes toward participants' sense of their ability and academic identity in mathematics were found in both school sectors. Students in both school sectors reported less interest in mathematics and less agreement that being intelligent is the only way to do well in mathematics. Despite their demonstrated academic achievement in mathematics, only 39.8 percent of the coeducational students and 34.4 percent of the single-gender students responded that mathematics was one of their favorite subjects. Overall, 57 percent of the students responded that doing well in mathematics depends on how hard you work, yet only 34.6 percent of the coeducational students and 38.7 percent of the single-gender students claimed that they try very hard in mathematics compared with other school subjects.

Chi-square tests were conducted on data reported by the students on the attitude questionnaire (table 13.4). A chi-square test was utilized to identify whether the differences in the number of eighth-grade students from single-gender middle schools and coeducational-middle schools taking dif-

TABLE 13.3

MEANS AND STANDARD DEVIATIONS FOR SUBSCALES OF
ATTITUDE INSTRUMENT TRANSFORMED TO RASCH ESTIMATES

Subscale	Single-Gender Schools			Coeducational Schools		
	n	Mean	SD	*n*	Mean	SD
Ability	467	61.82	17.07	208	62.68	17.76
Effort	467	61.18	15.48	208	59.62	17.10
Academic ID	467	68.30	12.32	208	66.79	12.48
Effort/Ach	467	55.74	8.81	208	56.39	8.72
Ability/Ach	467	52.50	8.72	208	53.68	8.49
Interest	467	53.73	10.87	208	55.80	12.60

ferent levels of mathematics courses at the eighth-grade level were large. Traditionally, students at the eighth-grade level take pre-algebra or general mathematics. "More advanced" or "more capable" students only are encouraged to take algebra at that grade level. Of the students who participated in this study, 78.4 percent of the students from the single-gender schools, and 74 percent of the students from the coeducational schools reported they were taking algebra in the eighth grade (table 13.4). No statistically significant differences were found between the groups (χ^2 [2, N = 675] = .94, p < .05) in taking different levels of mathematics courses.

DESCRIPTIVE RESULTS

In addition to test scores and completed attitude questionnaires, other data were collected from each of the participating schools. These data included specific information about each school's mathematics program, as well as general information about the school. An administrator or mathematics teacher from each of the independent coeducational and single-gender middle schools in this study reported details about the school and its mathematics program. All reported small mathematics class sizes (fewer than twenty students); the presence of adult female role models, including heads of school, department heads, and teachers; high expectations for all students in mathematics; and accessible and concerned mathematics teachers (table 13.5). These reports indicate that these independent schools are attentive to issues concerning gender equity in education, and they are becoming sensitive to the needs of female learners. Seventy-eight percent of the participating coeducational schools (*n* = 7) and 100 percent of the single-gender schools (*n* = 10) reported that their schools had made specific efforts to address issues of gender equity. These efforts included workshops for faculty, parents, and students, as well as con-

TABLE 13.4

STUDENTS' SELF-REPORTED DESCRIPTIONS OF GRADE, SCHOOL
TYPE, AND MATHEMATICS-COURSE TAKING

	Single-Gender Middle Schools		Coeducational Middle Schools		Total	
	n	%	n	%	n	%
8th-grade students	467	100.0	208	100.0	675	—
General math	63	13.5	37	17.8	100	14.8
Algebra or geometry	366	78.4	154	74.0	520	77.0
No math course	1	2.1	0	0.0	1	0.15

sultations with well-respected experts on issues of gender equity and attention to methods advocated for helping females succeed in school. These methods include the use of challenging academic curriculums, fostering positive professional relations among school members, teachers who are responsive and attentive to the needs of their students, small class sizes; and an abundance of adult female role models. In both the single-gender and coeducational schools in this study, 85 percent of the eighth-grade mathematics teachers were female. Female mathematics teachers have the potential for being powerful role models for female students. Slightly smaller mean eighth-grade math-class sizes (m = 14.35, SD = 2.19) were reported in the single-gender schools than in the coeducational schools (m = 15.83, SD = 2.87).

DISCUSSION

The results of this study contribute to earlier studies that conclude that single-gender schools are not automatically better learning environments for females (AAUW 1998; Belash, 1992; Daly, 1996; Lee, 1997; LePore and Warren, 1997; Shmurak, 1998; Signorella, Frieze, and Hershey, 1996). Indeed, it appears that similar educational practices and pedagogies employed by the two school sectors have a more important impact on student achievement than does the school type.

These findings provide evidence that there is no clear advantage to single-gender education for girls in the area of mathematics education at the middle-school level. Contrary to assumptions and some previous research about single-gender schools, the all-girls schools in this study do not appear to have a more meaningful positive effect on their students' attitudes toward mathematics than coeducational schools do. Differences in students' attitudes toward mathematics between the two school sectors are not statistically significant.

Gender in Policy and Practice

TABLE 13.5

CHARACTERISTICS OF PARTICIPATING MIDDLE SCHOOLS

Characteristic	All Girls Middle School n = 10				Coeducational Middle Schools n = 10					
	Female		Male		Female		Male		None	
	f	%	f	%	f	%	f	%	f	%
Head of school (all grades)	10	100	0	0	2	22	7	78	0	0
Head of middle school (5–8)	9	90	1	10	3	33	5	56	1	11
Eighth-grade math teachers	17	85	3	15	11	85	2	15	0	0

	Mean	SD	Range	Mean	SD	Range
Number of eighth-grade students	52.00	15.31	34–81	41.9	22.10	8–77
Number of female eighth-grade students	52.90	14.71	34–81	21.89	11.06	5–40
Eighth-grade math class size	14.35	2.19	12–18	15.83	2.87	12–21
Eighth-grade math classtime/ minutes/week	222.25	33.67	180–285	231.11	28.15	200–270

	Yes		No		Yes		No	
	f	%	f	%	f	%	f	%
School effort to deal with issues of gender equity	10	100	0	0	7	78	2	22

Girls in both school sectors are performing well in mathematics as indicated by the test scores. There is no statistical significance in the different levels of achievement in mathematics. The schools involved in this study are clearly providing outstanding educational opportunities for their students.

Students in this study profess positive attitudes about their ability in mathematics that in turn may affect their performance in mathematics. Despite their high achievement scores in mathematics, the students in this study assert little interest in mathematics and see little need for mathematics in their lives. Regardless of their accomplishment in mathematics, these attitudes have the potential to dissuade the students from pursuing mathematics later in school and subsequently from choosing careers that involve mathematics.

Because there are no statistically significant differences in student achievement between the two school sectors, it is considered that the schools' reported attention to issues of gender equity in mathematics education is contributing to the girls' achievement in mathematics. All the schools in this study have made conscious efforts to provide optimal learning environments for female students in mathematics. The adaptations and considerations made by these schools can apply to schools in both the public and private sectors. These include workshops for parents, faculty, staff, and students on issues of gender equity, training for faculty on pedagogy dealing specifically with girls, small class sizes especially in math and science, and an effort to recruit female teachers for math and science.

In both the single-gender and coeducational schools in this study, most of the eighth-grade mathematics teachers are female. The effect of female mathematics teachers as powerful role models for female students has been documented in studies of single-gender high schools and colleges (Monaco and Gaier, 1992; Riordan, 1990). Other studies have shown that female teachers can influence girls' attitudes toward mathematics and subsequently their achievement in mathematics (Carpenter, 1985; Oakes, 1990). Several other studies (Belash, 1992; Finn, 1980; Riordan, 1994) have attributed the academic achievement of students in single-gender schools partially to the presence of mostly female teachers in those schools. NAIS reported that, in 1997, female teachers outnumbered male teachers in coeducational day schools two to one. In all-girls schools, however, the ratio of female teachers to male teachers was almost five to one (National Association of Independent Schools, 1997). Results from this study confirm that female teachers may be powerful influences on female students in areas such as mathematics, which typically have been identified as male regardless of the configuration of the school. Proponents of single-gender education for females argue that when girls see women heading mathematics departments, they conclude that women can excel at mathematics.

Despite the fact that personnel in the single-gender schools in this study report on the average slightly smaller mean eighth-grade math class sizes than in the coeducational schools, the class sizes in both sectors was smaller than in the average class size in public schools. Small class size has been cited as a factor that works to the advantage of girls in mathematics (AAUW, 1992). Small class sizes are more typical of the independent school sector and may be a characteristic transferable to public schools.

Stipek (1993) claimed that age-related perceptions of ability are affected by the classroom environment and by performance feedback. Participants from both school sectors rated themselves particularly high on items related to their ability in mathematics ("I think I'm a good student in math") and on items related to their academic identity in mathematics ("When I do well in math I feel really good about myself"). Students who ascribe their success in mathematics to their mathematical ability are more likely to experience future success in mathematics and experience positive self-concept than students who attribute their success to luck or to the assistance of others (Weiner, 1984). Self-perception of mathematics abilities, not objective ability-achievement measures, is described as an important component for the formation of academic self-concept (Marsh, 1987).

Although students in both the single-gender and coeducational independent schools in this study are achieving high levels in mathematics, they are not coming away imbued with a consciousness about the utility and importance of mathematics in the real world. C. Shmurak (personal communication, October 23, 1999) claimed that the independent school culture subtly may be discouraging girls from aspiring to fields in engineering and computer science. These female students might be achieving equity with their male counterparts in mathematical understanding, but they may continue to lag behind in educational and career choices that require mathematics.

In spite of the fact that 77 percent of the student respondents felt it was important to do well in mathematics, only 58 percent of them recognized connections between what they did in mathematics class and real-world applications, and only 50 percent claimed that mathematics would be useful to them in the future. These students appear to place a higher value on school performance in mathematics classes than on the practical uses of mathematics. This may be a socioeconomic phenomenon related to the students' perceptions that good grades in mathematics will get them into good colleges, and after that they do not need mathematics. Even the female mathematics teachers at these schools seem unable to dispel that thinking.

Given the relatively large number of schools and students that were sampled from across the United States, the results of this study should be generalizable to other similar independent middle schools. From this study, one may conclude that at the middle-school level in independent schools, segregating girls in single-gender schools has no obvious advantages for their achievement in mathematics or influencing their attitudes toward mathematics.

Despite the reported attention to issues of gender equity and instructional methods that may be contributing to the mathematics achievement of their female students, the independent schools in this study are producing female students who profess little interest in mathematics and who identify little future need for mathematics in their own lives. Although educational pedagogies that enhance female learning of mathematics have been identified and employed, it is clear from this study that even in the elite independent schools in the United States, more attention needs to be given to strategies that will improve female's attitudes toward mathematics and thereby enhance their occupational opportunities.

REFERENCES

American Association of University Women (AAUW). (1992). *How Schools Shortchange Girls.* Washington, D.C.: Author.

American Association of University Women Educational Foundation. (1998). *Separated by Sex: A Critical Look at Single-Sex Education for Girls.* Washington, D.C.: Author.

Armstrong, J., and Price, R. (1982). "Correlates and Predictors of Women's Mathematics Participation." *Journal for Research in Mathematics Education* 13(2): 99–109.

Belash, R. (1992). "Girls' Schools: Separate Means Equal." In P. Kane (Ed.), *Independent Schools, Independent Thinkers.* San Francisco: Jossey-Bass, 73–90.

Bell, J. (1989). "A Comparison of Science Performance and Uptake by Fifteen-Year-Old Boys and Girls in Co-educational and Single-Sex Schools: APU Survey Findings." *Educational Studies* 15: 193–203.

Carpenter, P. (1985). "Single-Sex Schooling and Girls' Academic Achievements." *The Australian and New Zealand Journal of Sociology* 21: 456–472.

Cohen, J. (1988). *Statistical Power Analysis for the Behavioral Sciences,* 2nd ed. Hillsdale, NJ: Lawrence Erlbaum Associates.

Colley, A., Comber, C., and Hargreaves, D. (1994). "School Subject Preferences of Pupils in Single Sex and Co-educational Secondary Schools." *Educational Studies* 20: 379–385.

Daly, P. (1996). "The Effects of Single-Sex and Coeducational Schooling on Girls' Achievement." *Research Papers in Education,* 11, 289–306.

Educational Testing Service. (1997). *Comprehensive Testing Program III Fall Norms Booklet: National Norms, Suburban School Norms®, Independent School Norms®.*Princeton, NJ: Author.

Fennema, E. (1990). "Justice, Equity, and Mathematics Education." In E. Fennema and G. Leder (Eds.), *Mathematics and Gender.* New York: Teachers College Press, 1–9.

Fennema, E., and Hart, L. (1994). "Gender and the JRME." *Journal for Research in Mathematics Education* 25: 648–659.

Fennema, E., and Sherman, J. (1977). "Sex-Related Differences in Mathematics Achievement, Spatial Visualization and Affective Factors." *American Education Research Journal* 14: 51–71.

Fennema, E., and Sherman, J. (1978). "Sex-Related Differences in Mathematics Achievement and Related Factors: A Further Study." *Journal for Research in Mathematics Education* 9: 189–203.

Finn, J. (1980). "Sex Differences in Education Outcomes: A Cross-National Study." *Sex Roles,* 6, 9–26.

Foon, A. (1988). "The Relationship between School Type an Adolescent Self-Esteem, Attribution Styles and Affiliation Needs: Implications for Educational Outcome." *British Journal of Educational Psychology* 58: 44–54.

Lee, V. (1997). "Gender Equity and the Organization of Schools." In B. Bank and P. Hall (Eds.), *Gender, Equity, and Schooling: Policy and Practice.* New York: Garland Publishing, 135–158.

LePore, P., and Warren, J. (1997). "A Comparison of Single-Sex and Coeducational Catholic Secondary Schooling: Evidence from the National Educational Longitudinal Study of 1988." *American Educational Research Journal* 34: 485–511.

Linn, M., and Petersen, A. (1985). "Facts and Assumptions about the Nature of Sex Differences." In S. Klein (Ed.), *Handbook for Achieving Sex Equity through Education*. Baltimore: The Johns Hopkins University Press, 53–77.

Marsh, H. (1987). "The Big-Fish-Little Pond Effect on Academic Self-Concept." *Journal of Educational Psychology* 79: 280–295.

——. (1991). "Public, Catholic, Single-Sex, and Catholic Coeducational High Schools: Their Effects on Achievement, Affect, and Behaviors." *American Journal of Education* 41: 320–356.

Meece, J., Wigfield, A., and Eccles, J. (1990). "Predictors of Math Anxiety and Its Influence on Young Adolescents' Course Enrollment Intentions and Performance in Mathematics." *Journal of Educational Psychology* 82: 60–70.

Meyer, M., and Koehler, M. (1990). "Internal Influences on Gender Differences in Mathematics." In E. Fennema, and G. Leder (Eds.), *Mathematics and Gender: Influences on Teachers and Students* (pp. 60–95) Stanford, CA: Stanford University Press.

Mitchell, M., and Gilson, J. (1997, March). "Interest and Anxiety in Mathematics." Poster session presented at the annual meeting of the American Educational Research Association, Chicago.

Monaco, N., and Gaier, E. (1992). "Single-Sex Versus Coeducational Environment and Achievement in Adolescent Females." *Adolescence* 27: 579–594.

National Association of Independent Schools. (1997). *NAIS Statistics 1997, Vol. I*. Washington, D.C.: Author.

Oakes, J. (1990). "Women and Minorities in Science and Math." In C. Cazden (Ed.), *Review of Research in Education*, Vol. 16. Washington, D.C.: American Educational Research Association, 153–222.

Posnick-Goodwin, S. (1997). "Girls in the Middle." *California Educator* 2 (4): 7–9.

Reyes, L., and Stanic, G. (1988). "Race, Sex, Socioeconomic Status, and Mathematics." *Journal for Research in Mathematics Education* 19: 26–43.

Riordan, C. (1990). *Girls and Boys in School: Together or Separate?* New York: Teachers College Press.

——. (1994). "The Value of Attending a Women's College: Education, Occupation, and Income Benefits." *Journal of Higher Education* 65: 486–510.

Sarah, E., Scott, M., and Spender, D. (1980). "The Education of Feminists: The Case for Single-Sex Schools." In D. Spender and E. Sarah (Eds.), *Learning to Lose: Sexism and Education*. London: The Women's Press, 55–66.

Shmurak, C. (1998). *Voices of Hope: Adolescent Girls at Single-Sex and Coeducational Schools*. New York: Peter Lang.

Signorella, M., Frieze, I., and Hershey, S. (1996). "Single-Sex Versus Mixed-Sex Classes and Gender Schemata in Children and Adolescents." *Psychology of Women Quarterly* 20: 599–607.

Steinback, M., and Gwizdala, J. (1995). "Gender Differences in Mathematics Attitudes of Secondary Students." *School Science and Mathematics* 95: 36–41.

Stipek, D. (1993). *Motivation to Learn: From Theory to Practice*. Boston: Allyn and Bacon.

Stoecker, J., and Pascarella, E. (1991). "Women's Colleges and Women's Career Attainments Revisited." *Journal of Higher Education* 62: 394–406.

Tartre, L., and Fennema, E. (1995). "Mathematics Achievement and Gender: A Longitudinal Study of Selected Cognitive and Affective Variables [Grades 6–12]." *Educational Studies in Mathematics* 28: 199–217.

Tobias, S. (1987). *Succeed with Math*. New York: The College Entrance Examination Board.

Ware, N., and Lee, V. (1988). "Sex Differences in Choice of College Science Majors." *American Educational Research Journal* 25: 593–614.

Weiner, B. (1984). "Principles for a Theory of Student Motivation and Their Application within an Attributional Framework." In R. Ames and C. Ames (Eds.), *Research on Motivation in Education: Student Motivation*. Vol. 1. Orlando: Academic Press, 15–38.

Young, D. (1994). "Single-Sex Schools and Physics Achievement: Are Girls Really Advantaged?" *International Journal of Science Education* 16: 315–325.

APPENDIX: ATTITUDE QUESTIONNAIRE ITEMS

PERCEPTION OF ABILITY IN MATHEMATICS
I think I'm a good student in math.
I'm not very good at math.
Compared with other subjects I am studying, I know a lot about math.
I don't know much about math.

PERCEPTION OF EFFORT IN MATHEMATICS
Compared with other school subjects, I try my hardest in math.
I don't try very hard in math compared with other school subjects.
In math I usually try very hard compared with other school subjects.
I don't put much effort into my math work.

ACADEMIC IDENTITY IN MATHEMATICS
Being a good math student is not important to me.
When I do well in math, I feel really good about myself.
I don't care if I get grades in math.
It is important to do well in math.

INTEREST IN MATHEMATICS
Much of what I learn in math classes will be useful to me in the future.
Math is one of my favorite subjects.
Math classes are boring.
What we do in math classes has nothing to do with the real world.

RELATIONSHIP OF ABILITY TO ACHIEVEMENT
You have to be smart to do well in math.
Doing well in math does not depend on how smart you are.
How much math you can learn depends on how smart you are.
Even if you're not smart, you can still do well in math.

RELATIONSHIP OF EFFORT TO ACHIEVEMENT
Some people will never be good at math no matter how hard they try.
If I try, I can do well in math.
You can work really hard and still not get good grades in math.
Doing well in math depends on how hard you work.

CHAPTER 14

Participation in Science Courses in the Final Year of High School in Australia: The Influences of Single-Sex and Coeducational Schools

John Ainley and Peter Daly

The subjects studied in the senior secondary years have a major influence upon subsequent educational and career options, and the choice of subjects has been seen as involving issues about equity between various social groups (Oakes, 1990). Concern over equity in subject choice is expressed in relation to science because it is regarded as the basis for entry to many programs of professional education. It is argued that the much lower levels of participation by young women in physical science courses at school means that a range of vocational choices is subsequently denied to them. In a number of Western countries single-sex secondary schools or single-sex classrooms in coeducational schools are proposed as a means of improving the participation of young women in science courses. This chapter explores the influence of single-sex secondary schools, as well as other factors, on participation by young Australians in science in the final years of high school.

In Australia in 1998 some 24 percent of students in their final year attend a single-sex school. Attendance at a single-sex school is more common for girls than boys; 29 percent of girls are in single-sex schools compared to 19 percent of boys. This difference appears to reflect a view of parents that single-sex school settings are more important for their daughters than for their sons. Baker, Riordan and Schaub (1995) argue that the effects of single-sex grouping on achievement outcomes is greater in national contexts where single-sex settings are rare rather than a regular feature of the national context. On that basis, Australia occupies an intermediate position. A minority of the student population attends single-sex schools but they are not rare; and certainly not rare for girls. They provide the settings for nearly one quarter (24 percent) of all students in the final year of secondary school.

Single-sex schools are found predominantly in the nongovernment school sectors. In Australia 60 percent of final year secondary school students attend government schools, 24 percent attend Catholic schools and 15 percent attend private schools (Australian Bureau of Statistics, 2000). However, only 8 percent of final year students in government schools are in a single-sex environment compared with 55 percent of their peers in Catholic schools and 45 percent of those in private schools. Single-sex schools also tend to enroll more students of higher socioeconomic status than coeducational schools (the difference is .4 standard deviation units) and are more frequently located in metropolitan than nonmetropolitan locations.

Australia provides a fertile context in which to examine the uptake of different subjects for two reasons. First, the common structure is for high schools to provide five or six years of secondary education in one institution with increased student choice of areas of specialization as the years progress. Second, although there is a wide choice of subjects available in the final years of high school that choice is more constrained in range and structure than in the United States. This means that students more often make clear choices about their combinations of subjects in the final years of high school with those choices being focused on an area. In Australia the first one or two years of high school typically consist of a general program followed by all students and the next two years involve a basic core of subjects supplemented with optional subjects. In the final two years of high schools students have more scope to specialize, and a range of elective studies is provided from which students choose five or six.

Typically the subjects chosen in the final year of high school are a continuation of those chosen in the second last year (usually with one fewer subject studied in that final year). Almost all final year students study English and 85 percent study a mathematics subject. Nearly three-quarters (72 percent) of each cohort complete the final year of school. Since 1976 the school completion rate has been higher for girls than boys. In 1998, 78 percent of girls, compared to 66 percent of boys, remained to the final year of school.

The central research questions for the Australian context investigated in this chapter are the following:

- Are differences in science course participation rates between Australian senior school students associated with differences in educational and social background?
- Are these differences in science course participation linked to the single-sex or coeducational nature of the schools?

Before we describe the results of our study, the following review of the literature draws attention to developments with regard to single-sex schools in England and Ireland where a tradition of single-sex schools is being redirected to coeducational schools.

PERSPECTIVES FROM RESEARCH ON SUBJECT PARTICIPATION IN SINGLE-SEX AND COEDUCATIONAL SCHOOLS

There is an important body of research on student participation in science in single-sex and coeducational schools from Australia, England, and Ireland. In this review we draw attention to some general considerations concerned with the progressive focusing view of student participation in science studies at school and its implications for the roles of single-sex and coeducational schools. We then review a series of studies from England that compare science participation in single-sex and coeducational schools and offer interpretations of potential school influences on subject choice. Finally, we review a similar body of ongoing research from Ireland that provides broadly similar findings to those from England.

SUBJECT PARTICIPATION AS PROGRESSIVE FOCUSING

Participation in science courses in senior years of high school can be regarded as a function of abilities, interests, background, and opportunities. As students move through school they develop a sense of competence in mathematics and science and interests in investigative activities in response to social influences and experiences both in and outside of school. An understanding of the differences in the uptake of science between young women and men needs to take account of the interests and competencies developed in earlier years of schooling as well as the situational constraints (such as the availability of subjects), which operate at the time choices are made. One view of these influences is to envisage subject preferences as being formed over a longer time frame and subject uptake as the manifestation of those preferences within a context of more immediate constraints (e.g., the availability of subjects), and opportunities (Elsworth, Harvey-Beavis, Ainley, and Fabris, 1999). Patterns of science uptake among high school students should not be seen as simply arising from decisions taken in the final year of high school.

The extensive body of international literature concerned with gender differences in participation in individual science subjects has consistently shown substantial differences in favour of males in the physical sciences. Although the size of these differences may have reduced a little in recent times the gap remains wide (Fullarton and Ainley, 2000).

Explanations for gender differences have often invoked ideas related to general vocational interests (Elsworth et al., 1999), social influences in school and outside (Gamoran, 1987), curriculum tracking that limits opportunities to study foundations for science in the earlier years of school (Dauber, Alexander, and Entwistle, 1996; Spade, Columba, and Vanfossen, 1997), the nature of science curricula in schools (Willis, 1989) and subject stereotyping (Kelly, 1988). Sophisticated analyses from the Netherlands not only highlight the similarity of the effects of gender, social class, and ethnicity on participation in the sciences in another national context, but also identify a range of complex interactions among gender, social class, and ethnicity (Dekkers, Bosker, and Driessen, 1999).

Subject participation arguments in favor of single-sex schools (and classrooms) tend to focus on the participation by girls in the physical sciences. It is argued that in a single-sex environment the social pressures of coeducational peers that limit girls' choices of nontraditional subjects will not be so pervasive (Stables, 1990). This argument sees girls establishing greater confidence in their abilities in mathematics and science in single-sex settings and this having an impact on both achievement and patterns of subject choice (Rowe, 1988, 2000). The assumption appears to be that if boys are physically absent from girl's educational environments during adolescence so also will be their influence. On the other hand, opportunities to study the physical sciences may be more limited in single-sex environments, especially in small schools with limited resources where there may not be sufficient numbers of students to ensure that a physics class is viable (Bone, 1983). Parker and Rennie (1997) point to the complex issues of management organization and teaching that are involved when single-sex classes are introduced into a coeducational school. Furthermore, an argument is advanced that in some single-sex schools a culture that asserts a feminist view of the world may operate to influence girls not to choose subjects that boys have traditionally chosen. It is important to recognize that even if single-sex settings reduce overt pressures on girls to conform to established gender patterns of subject uptake, there are other factors that may constrain their choices.

COMPARATIVE STUDIES FROM ENGLAND

Research on the effects of single-sex and coeducational high schools on subject choice has been inconclusive. Elwood and Gipps (1999) concluded that subjects such as mathematics and science at single-sex schools tended to be more popular among girls and that music and languages tended to be more popular among boys in single-sex schools. However, the evidence was not strong, was not evident among older students, and often did not take account of other differences between single-sex and coeducational schools. They also observe that girls from girls' schools were more likely to study mathematics or physical sciences in the final years of school than girls from coeducational schools, and that boys from boys' schools were more likely to study modern languages than boys from coeducational schools.

The work of Dale (1969, 1971, 1974) on English and Welsh secondary schools is among the best-known early studies in this field. His overall conclusion expressed cautiously was that coeducational schooling did not harm girls' progress. This general conclusion in regard to girls' achievement was supported by findings from a more representative and longitudinal study carried out by Steedman (1984, 1985). Steedman's study, which included controls for prior pupil performance and family background, found little support for the advantageous impact of single-sex schooling. Steedman concluded:

> These complex findings add up to suggest that very little in their examination results is explained by whether schools are mixed or single-sex once allowance has been made for differences in intake. (1985, p. 98)

In England there has been a dramatic decline in the public provision of single-sex schools since the 1960s (Robinson and Smithers, 1999). There has also been a shift in the focus of public concern about gender differences in achievement, over this period. An earlier concern about the overall poorer performance of girls relative to boys has given way to a growing concern in the 1990s and onward about the gap in achievement terms between girls and boys, reflecting international trends in favor of girls (Arnot et al., 1998; EOC/OFSTED, 1996; Riordan, 2000a). As far as England is concerned, the pattern of findings in regard to the uptake of science-related courses is a complex one (Arnot et al., 1998; Bone, 1983; Elwood and Gipps, 1999). Available data and sampling restrictions make it difficult to get beyond very tentative conclusions about the influence of single-sex or coeducational schooling.

A study by Cheng, Payne, and Witherspoon (1995) carried out on behalf of the Department for Education and Employment concentrated on students over the age of sixteen years continuing in full-time education at a range of educational institutions, with particular reference to enrollment on advanced science and mathematics courses. These students were aged sixteen to eighteen years in the senior cycle of high school education. The students were mainly preparing for university entrance or for entry to the nonmanual labor market. Cheng, Payne, and Witherspoon (1995) reported pattern differences in uptake related to whether or not these senior cycle (advanced level) students had previously attended single-sex or mixed high schools at age sixteen. Girls who had attended all-girls schools were more likely than girls from mixed schools to have taken physical sciences in the senior cycle (25 percent compared with 19 percent). This school difference, however, was not found in the case of girls who took life science subjects. The pattern for boys was something of a mirror image of this. Boys who had been attending a single-sex school at age sixteen were less likely to have taken the advanced physical route science at the senior cycle stage than those who had been attending a mixed school and furthermore, were more likely to have taken the life science route than boys who had attended a mixed school earlier.

A subsequent multilevel regression analysis of the data controlling for background differences (Cheng, Payne, Witherspoon, 1995) indicated that girls at girls' schools were significantly less likely than girls or boys from any other school type to take up advanced physical sciences at the senior cycle stage (sixteen- to eighteen-year-olds). Cheng, Payner, and Witherspoon (1995) noted that their evidence "contradicts the idea that single-sex schools help to free girls from pressure to conform to gender stereotypes." The researchers concluded their investigation by stressing the overriding importance of student levels of achievement at age sixteen, irrespective of the type of school attended up to that point, for continued enrollment on advanced courses during the senior cycle stage.

STUDIES FROM IRELAND

As in other parts of the United Kingdom, public provision of single-sex schools declined in Northern Ireland as the new century approached. This decline reflects, in part, economic concerns in line with increasing government demands for educational reform as school curricula become more clearly aligned to economic development. Accountability in efficiency and effectiveness terms has been a concern of publicly assisted schools, such as church schools with continuing contentious mergers of single-sex "voluntary" schools, forming coeducational institutions.

Aspects of single-sex schooling have long been of interest to educational researchers in Ireland. In Northern Ireland the education system has many similarities to the English one. However, it is characterized by a higher proportion of single-sex, state-supported high schools reflecting, in part, the stronger influence of the Christian churches in public education service provision. Prior to the introduction of a statutory curriculum in 1988, Northern Ireland also had a lower record of science course participation on the part of fifteen-year-old students than was the case in England.

Daly (1995) reported findings from a reanalysis of two high school surveys carried out originally in the 1980s that considered, among a range of issues, science course participation in single-sex and coeducational schools on the part of sixteen-year-old students in Northern Ireland. The first survey featured data on a representative sample of thirty schools and the second survey contained data on a representative sample of primary school students whose subsequent progress was tracked across more than two hundred high schools. Use was made of multilevel modeling software not available for the original analysis. After controlling for background differences there was evidence from the first survey that girls were less likely than boys to take up science courses leading to public examinations at age sixteen. The later survey, however, indicated a narrowing of this gender gap that by then had ceased to be statistically significant. As far as single-sex and coeducational school differences were concerned, girls were more likely to take science courses at coeducational schools, perhaps reflecting the better provision of additional laboratory resources for such publicly examined courses in coeducational schools. The second survey found no significant difference between these school types in science course enrollment terms.

A study carried out by Gallagher, McEwen, and Knipe (1996) for the Equal Opportunities Commission for Northern Ireland reported that students were more likely to take advanced science/mathematics courses at coeducational schools rather than at single-sex schools and that the boys were more likely to have higher achievement at coeducational schools. These pupils attended grammar (selective) schools only. Because of the selective, academic status of these schools, variation in school resources available to the students was very much reduced. Historically grammar schools were much better resourced than nongrammar (nonselective) schools. Pupils from upper socioeconomic backgrounds continue to be overrepresented in grammar schools.

Shuttleworth and Daly (1997), using data from the 1991 School Leaver's Survey in Northern Ireland, looked at inequalities in the uptake of science courses preparing students for the public examinations taken typically by sixteen year olds. A distinction was made between "hard" sciences, mainly physics, chemistry, and technology on the one hand, and "soft" sciences, mainly "general" science and biology, on the other. As far as enrollment on "hard" science courses was concerned, boys were significantly more likely to take this route than girls. However, for the boys and girls who actually took this "hard" science route, no significant differences were found between single-sex and coeducational schools in a multilevel regression analysis that allowed for background differences.

Following a small-scale study by Hanafin and Ni Chartaigh (1993), which had concluded that girls in girls' schools performed better in public school-leaving examinations than girls in coeducational schools, the government of the Republic of Ireland funded a national study of coeducation (Hannan et al., 1996). This investigation showed the considerable decline in enrollments in single-sex schools over a fifteen-year period, whereas the enrollment figures for second-level schooling had risen over that period. The number of boys schools had dropped by one-third and the number of girls schools had dropped by one-quarter, whereas the number of mixed schools had increased by one-fifth.

Continuing earlier work involving an investigation into coeducation and gender equality in the Irish Republic, Smyth and Hannan (2000) embarked on a major survey of science course participation by high school students making use of the data from the earlier study. The authors examined the school characteristics associated with the take-up of science subjects for public examination in the senior cycle. In a preliminary report, they have rejected the more traditional "hard/soft" science distinction on the grounds that this categorization was not sensitive enough to take account of recent pattern changes they have found. For example, in the case of chemistry, they noted the much more equitable take-up in gender terms in recent years. The case of physics, however, is quite different with girls being five times less likely than boys to continue studying physics at advanced (honors) level during the senior cycle. Nevertheless, in regard to enrollment for both physics and chemistry courses, single-sex and coeducational school differences were not found after allowing for pupil intake and other school type differences in a multilevel regression analysis.

SUMMARY

The studies from England and Ireland cast doubt on the proposition that single-sex schools provide an impetus for girls to participate in science subjects in the senior years of school. They suggest that differences in science participation between schools of different gender contexts could be the result of the confounding effects of other factors. The Australian analysis that follows provides the opportunity to analyze science participation in a nationally representative sample of final-year students using data that include a comprehensive range of student-level and school-level background characteristics.

AN ANALYSIS OF AUSTRALIAN DATA

The combination of subjects studied by students in the senior secondary years says more about a student's educational orientation than does enrollment in any given subject. Previous analyses of large national surveys of subject participation have identified two science-oriented course types in the final year of secondary school in Australia (Ainley et al., 1990; 1994). The first is a "physical science" course type that includes both physics and chemistry (and usually substantial mathematics study as well). The second is a "biological and other science" course type that includes two science subjects other than the combination of physics and chemistry (although it may include one of physics or chemistry in combination with another science). Previous analyses have indicated that the educational and social backgrounds of those participating in a physical science course are somewhat different from those in a biological science course.

DATA

The analyses reported in this chapter are based on a longitudinal survey of a nationally representative sample of young people in Australia.[1] The sample of more than ten thousand students in grade nine at school was established in 1995. In that year students completed achievement tests in reading and numeracy and answered a questionnaire about their background, attitudes, and educational plans. In 1996 a questionnaire was sent to students' home addresses; through that questionnaire they provided more detail about their plans. These students were contacted again in 1997 and 1998; through a

Gender in Policy and Practice

telephone interview, they provided considerable detail about their activities over the year, including the school subjects they studied (for those who were still at school). They have been contacted by telephone each year since then. The present chapter is based on analyses for just fewer than 7,500 students who completed their final year of high school in 1998 and with whom contact had been maintained over that time. These students came from 297 schools so that there were approximately twenty-five students per school.

METHODS OF ANALYSIS

In the investigation of influences on science course participation two approaches are used. In the first approach we use simple analyses that compare participation rates for the groups of interest. Using these methods it is possible to estimate the differences in science course participation, for example, between males and females, students of different earlier achievement levels, and (for girls and boys) differences between single-sex and coeducational settings.

In the second approach we use statistical techniques that make allowance for the associations among the predictor variables of interest. In the Australian context this is important because single-sex schools are more frequently found among private schools where there are higher levels of socioeconomic background and higher levels of earlier school achievement. Through the application of multilevel modeling it was possible to identify factors at an individual and school level that are associated with participation in each science course type. Although it was not possible to control directly for "constrained curriculum" effects (Lee, Croninger, and Smith, 1997) such as the availability of subject data on pupils' prior achievements at age fourteen, school location (metropolitan, nonmetropolitan), and school governance (government, independent, and Catholic) provided an indirect means of addressing these concerns. Through these analyses it was possible to estimate the effect of school gender context on science participation controlling for other variables. A multilevel modeling approach to such data analysis was required to allow for the clustering of students within schools.[2] Two-level (student and school) logit models were specified to deal with binary data concerning students' science course uptake using the MLwIN program (Goldstein, 1995).[3]

RESULTS

Patterns in Science Course Participation Rates

Before considering differences in science course participation, it is worth noting that through the 1990s there was a significant decline in the percentage of Year 12 students in Australia taking a physical science course (i.e., taking both physics and chemistry). Whereas in 1992 approximately 15 percent of students took these courses (Daly, Ainley, and Robinson, 1996) in the present data that refer to 1998 the figure had dropped to 9.3 percent. Moreover, the decline in participation in this course was more marked among boys (a drop of nearly ten percentage points from 23 to 13 percent) than girls (a drop of four percentage points from 10 to 6 percent).

Table 14.1 records the unadjusted participation rates in the two types of course. In these unadjusted participation rates some striking pattern differences are evident. The higher the student's achievement at age fourteen the more likely they were to take physics and chemistry in Year 12.[4] Students from the top achievement quartile were more than ten times more likely to choose a physical science course than students from the bottom quartile. Higher levels of socioeconomic background were associated with a greater likelihood that their children would take physical science courses. Students from the top of four socioeconomic categories based on parental occupations were twice as likely to choose a physical science course than students from the lowest socioeconomic category. Students from non-English speaking backgrounds were more likely to take physical science than other students. There was an effect of the type of school governance, with independent schools having far stronger representation in the physical sciences than either government or Catholic schools. School location differences were very small.

Differences between girls and boys in physical science participation were pronounced. Boys were more than twice as likely as girls to take physical science. There were also differences in terms of the gender mix of schools. Participation in physical science courses in boys' schools was almost twice that for girls' schools, which in turn were similar to those for coeducational schools. However, it is not clear from these analyses whether this effect arises from the single-sex characteristic of the schools or is simply what would be expected for boys as a group. For a range of reasons, including vocational interests (Elsworth et al., 1999) and traditional community expectations, boys have had stronger participation in chemistry and physics than girls.

Table 14.1 also contains information about participation in "other" science courses. For this type of course the effect of earlier school achievement is less pronounced than observed for the physical science course. It is also nonlinear in that participation is the same in the third and top quartile, suggesting that this course type attracts moderately capable students but not proportionately more from the top quarter of the achievement distribution. Students from the highest socioeconomic background category participated to a smaller extent than other students in this course and the effect of language background was small and in the reverse direction from that for physical science. For the other science courses, participation was stronger in nonmetropolitan than metropolitan schools. Participation in biological science course types was higher for girls than boys but the differences were less than had been observed for the physical sciences. Boys' schools had the low-

TABLE 14.1

PARTICIPATION RATES FOR TWO SCIENCE COURSES BY PUPIL
AND SCHOOL CATEGORIES (1998)

		Percentage Participation	
Variable	Category	Physical Science	Other Science
Sex	Male	13.3	8.4
	Female	5.9	11.9
Achievement	Lowest	1.8	5.3
	Lower-middle	3.7	9.3
	Upper-middle	8.0	12.4
	Upper	19.9	12.4
Socioeconomic status	Lowest	7.8	8.3
	Lower-middle	6.8	11.4
	Upper-middle	10.4	11.2
	Upper	16.4	11.4
Language background	English	8.8	10.6
	Other than English	12.6	8.7
Location	City	9.8	9.4
	Rural	8.5	11.6
Governance	Government	8.0	9.7
	Catholic	9.1	11.1
	Independent	15.0	11.6
School gender context	Boys	15.7	7.1
	Coeducational	8.7	10.2
	Girls	8.3	12.8

est participation rates for biological science with girls' schools ahead of coeducational schools.

Differences in Science Participation between Single-Sex and Coeducational Schools
Data such as those in Table 14.1 reveal little about the influence of the gender composition of the school on science course enrollments. Participation in physical science courses is highest in "boys-only" schools and lowest in "girls-only" schools but this could be a result of the difference in course taking patterns of boys and girls rather than any influence of the gender composition of the setting. A similar explanation could apply for the observed differences in participation in biological and other science courses where the highest rate occurs for "girls-only" schools and the lowest for "boys-only" schools.

Table 14.2 provides greater detail regarding the differences between school settings of different gender composition. From Table 14.2 it is evident that girls in single-sex schools participate in physical science courses to a greater extent than girls in coeducational schools. Similarly, it is also evident that boys in single-sex schools participate in physical science courses to a greater extent than boys in coeducational schools. These data appear to support the argument that there is a benefit for girls' physical science participation that arises from being in a single-sex school. These unadjusted data are in accord with much of the conventional wisdom on the topic.

The difficulty with the data in Table 14.2 is that they do not take account of other characteristics of the students and their schools. Single-sex schools are more frequently nongovernment schools, enroll students from wealthier socioeconomic backgrounds, and attract students with higher levels of earlier school achievement. Each of these factors would be expected to favor participation in a physical science course. It is not evident whether the difference between single-sex and coeducational schools is a result of the gender composition of those schools or is associated with differences in school governance and the educational and social background of individual students. A multivariate (multilevel) analysis is required to estimate the relative impact of these student and school differences on science course uptake.

Results of Multilevel Analyses

It was noted previously in this chapter that participation in single-sex schooling in grade twelve in Australia was associated with other factors. Single-sex schools were more frequently found in Catholic and private schools and were more likely to enroll students of relatively higher socioeconomic background as well as having students with higher earlier levels of achievement. To allow for the confounding effects of these other correlated influences at student and school level multilevel modeling was used to investigate participation in each type of science course. Through these analyses it was possible to estimate the effect of school gender context on science participation controlling for other variables. The multilevel modeling approach to the data analysis also allowed for the clustering of students within schools when estimating the statistical significance.[5] Results of these analyses are recorded in Table 14.3.

Physical Science

It is clear from Table 14.3 that there are significant gender differences in terms of the likelihood of participating in physical science favoring boys. There was also evidence of background differences related to home language and socioeconomic status as well as students' prior achievement influenced participation in physical science courses. The effect of socioeconomic status

TABLE 14.2

SCIENCE COURSE PARTICIPATION RATES BY GENDER AND TYPE OF SCHOOL: AUSTRALIA, 1998

	Single-sex		Coeducational		All Schools		
	Boys	Girls	Boys	Girls	Boy	Girls	All
Physical science	15.9	8.3	12.7	5.1	13.3	5.9	9.3
Other science	7.2	13.0	8.7	11.5	8.4	11.9	10.3

TABLE 14.3

TWO-LEVEL LOGIT MODELS: ESTIMATES FOR LOG ODDS OF SCIENCE COURSE PARTICIPATION: AUSTRALIA, 1998

Explanatory Variables	Physical Science	Other Science
Fixed Part		
Intercept	-3.45 (.36)	-3.02 (.29)
Gender (ref. boys)		
Girls	-.95 (.10)	.18 (.09)
Language background (ref. English)		
Other than English	.98 (.14)	.11 (.15)
Socioeconomic background (ref. highest)		
Upper-middle	-.32 (.12)	.03 (.12)
Lower-middle	-.56 (.12)	-.04 (.12)
Lowest	-.39 (.13)	-.26 (.14)
Earlier school achievement (ref. lowest quartile)		
Lower middle	.81 (.29)	.47 (.17)
Higher middle	1.66 (.27)	.81 (.16)
Highest	2.69 (.27)	.92 (.16)
Residential location (ref. metropolitan)		
Nonmetropolitan	-.15 (.11)	.24 (.11)
School governance (ref. government)		
Independent	.46 (.16)	.00 (.16)
Catholic	.19 (.16)	.03 (.16)
School gender context (ref. coeducational)		
Single-sex boys	-.35 (.21)	-.36 (.24)
Single-sex girls	.17 (.19)	.20 (.18)
Random Part		
School level variance Intercept	.31 (.07)	.34 (.07)
Pupil level variance Intercept	1.00 (.00)	1.00 (.00)

Note: Standard errors are shown in parentheses. Coefficients significant at the 5 percent level are shown in bold.

and earlier achievement is probably understated because fewer students from lower socioeconomic backgrounds, and lower achievement, stay at school to the final year. At school level there was evidence of the significant impact of independent schools (relative to government schools) but not of Catholic schools on participation in science. On average, girls' schools appeared to confer some advantage in terms of the likelihood of participation in physical science courses but not to a significant extent. In addition there was evidence of significant residual variation across schools. Schools made a difference to participation in physical science, although this difference was not related to gender composition.

Other Science

Results from regression analysis of other science course participation were strikingly different. As expected, girls were significantly more likely than boys to take these courses. In contrast to the physical science results, there was no evidence of a difference between students of a language background other than English and other students in the uptake of other science. Estimates of the influences of prior achievement revealed an influence that was not as strong as that observed for the physical sciences. Students from nonmetropolitan areas were a little more likely to enroll in these courses than students from metropolitan schools. Single-sex girls' schools tended to have higher participation in biological science courses than single-sex boys' schools. However, in neither case was the effect statistically significantly different from that for coeducational schools. There was evidence of significant variation remaining across schools.

Summary

A number of student characteristics, including gender (boys participate at a higher rate than girls), earlier achievement, socioeconomic background, and language background are associated with students taking a physical science course in the final year of school. In addition the uptake of such a course was higher in independent schools than other schools. It also appeared that the uptake of physical science courses by girls was higher in single-sex than coeducational settings. However, a multivariate analysis showed that this apparently greater participation in physical science by girls in single-sex schools was not statistically significant after allowance was made for other influences that were associated with school gender context. There is a tendency for female participation to be higher in single-sex schools but the difference from coeducational schools is not statistically significant.

For "other science" courses participation by girls was greater than boys. Other related research suggests that this is partly a result of more socially oriented vocational interests of girls: an observation that offers the possibility that curriculum change might reduce the disparity in physical science participation (Ainley and Elsworth, 1997). Higher levels of earlier school achievement were associated with higher participation rates (although the effect was not as strong as for physical science). Living in a nonmetropolitan area was also associated with higher levels of participation in other science courses, but neither school governance nor school gender context influenced participation in this type of course.

DISCUSSION AND IMPLICATIONS

The results of the analyses of data concerned with participation in physical science and other science courses during the final year of high school in Australia during 1998 are similar to those found for the early 1990s when participation in physical science courses was higher (Daly et al., 1997). The findings are also consistent with the international evidence based on longitudinal studies reported for England (Cheng, Payne, and Witherspoon, 1995) and Ireland (Daly, 1995; Smyth and Hannan, 2000). The studies all find that apparent differences between single-sex and coeducational schools in the uptake of science courses are reduced to the point of not being significant after allowance is made for the concomitant influence of other factors. Studies from Europe do not typically identify gender composition of schools as a potential influence on the uptake of science courses, although the results of those studies with regard to the influence of other are similar to the results reported for Australia (Bosker and Dekkers, 1994; Dekkers, 1996; Dekkers, Bosker, and Driessen, 1999).

With regard to students in the final year of high school, at any rate, there does appear to be consistency across these studies, suggesting that popular beliefs about the supposed benefits of moving beyond coeducation be treated with caution, especially where subject-uptake is a focal concern and public sector funding is involved. Any effects of whether a school is single-sex or coeducational appear to be small and not statistically significant, although the tendency is generally in the direction of higher physical science participation for girls if they are in single-sex schools.

There are some similarities between these findings and those concerned with differences in achievement outcomes between single-sex and coeducational schools. The apparent superiority of single-sex girls' schools in raw achievement data is not always evident, or is greatly reduced when statistical allowance is made for the influence of differences in the educational and social backgrounds of students (Daly, 1996). In many contexts single-sex schools are frequently private schools that enroll a larger percentage of students from upper socioeconomic backgrounds or who have relatively high levels of ability. Researchers have to be mindful of the dangers of identifying higher-level group effects when these so-called "effects" are merely artefacts arising from underspecified models of individual level influences. Smithers and Robinson concluded an analysis of 1995 senior school examination results in England with the observation that "the pattern of differences similarities strongly suggests that the performance of a school in terms of examination results has much less to do with whether it is single-sex or not than with other factors" (1997, p. 5). They noted the importance of student intake in terms of ability and socioeconomic background as well as the school's historical standing in its local context.

The analyses of the Australian data in this chapter only refer to the 72 percent of each cohort that reaches the final year of high school. It is known that educational and social background is strongly related to staying at school to the final year. For example, in Australia, only 30 percent of indigenous students stay to the final year of high school (Long, Frigo, and Batten, 1999). Underrepresentation of minority pupils can go unnoticed in studies of senior years of school when the outcome variables refer to advanced course participation. Some minority group students will have dropped out by this later stage. Riordan's (2000b) discussion of American studies of private single-gender schooling, suggests that minority groups rather than mainstream pupils gain, nowadays, from single-gender school experience (Salamone, 1999). Dekkers and colleagues (1999) argue that interactions between gender and ethnicity are important factors in the choice of science studies. Studies of interventions in the detailed curriculum (e.g., socially oriented physics and chemistry curricula) and organization (e.g., single-sex classrooms) may inform our understanding the role of the sex composition of educational settings on student subject choice, achievement, and motivation. In England there are studies that monitor the effects of single-sex classes in mixed schools on outcomes for girls and boys (Sukhnandan, Lee, and Kelleher, 1999). Critical policy evaluation of American public sector single-gender school pilot projects is another important development (Datnow, Hubbard, and Conchas, 2001).

In the Australian context there are competing influences in single-sex schools that may influence participation in the physical sciences. Although it may be argued that girls feel fewer psychological constraints when choosing a physical science course in an all-girls school than in a coeducational school, there are other constraints that may operate. In a small all-girls school there may be resource constraints if the overall demand for physical science is low. This may restrict choice either because of the lack of availability of subjects or because a particular subject is only able to offered in limited locations in the timetable. Moreover, in an all-girls school there may be an orientation to emphasize the importance of subject more traditionally taken by girls to the exclusion of the physical sciences. The special ethos of an all-girls school may not necessarily be favorable to study in the physical sciences. Given these competing influences, it is not surprising that the influence of the gender composition of a school is small and often not statistically significant.

Many challenges still face researchers in the area of subject take-up. We have moved away from simple notions of subject "choice." Studies such as those by Lee, Croninger, and Smith (1997) and Smyth and Hannan (2000) identify the complexities surrounding the systematic estimation of classroom, school, and higher-level constraints on student decisions. We are becoming more aware of the need for better coordination of qualitative and quantitative research studies. The question of single-sex class teaching for selected subjects in public schools remains a troubling, complex, controversial policy issue. Although it may seem rather optimistic to accept an aspiration that Susan McGee Bailey articulated, it remains appealing:

> Rather than assuming that we must isolate girls in order to protect them from boys' boisterous behavior or that boys will be unduly feminised in settings where girls are valued and comfortable we must look carefully at why some students and teachers prefer single-sex settings for girls. We must understand the positive aspects of these classrooms in order to begin the difficult task of bringing these positive factors into mixed sex classes. (1996, p. 76)

Gill (1993) urges a rephrasing of the question of single-sex schooling to focus more on the question of educational reforms that promote more equal and better educational outcomes. She observes that in much of the debate about single-sex schools the word *return* occurs frequently, both from opponents of single–sex schooling and from its proponents. Proponents of single-sex schools speak of returning to an imagined age when young women enjoyed rewarding educational experiences, whereas opponents see the return as regressive. Gill subsequently argues for rephrasing the debates to take account of the differences in the issues facing educators in the current era and to seek a way forward in educational reform (Gill, 1998). In terms of the differences in science participation between boys and girls, the way forward may focus on questions of curriculum and pedagogy rather than the structure of schools. Those changes might well focus on stimulating interest in science among both boys and girls.

NOTES

1. The sample was stratified so that students from smaller states were oversampled and, correspondingly, students from larger states were undersampled. Selection of students within States was proportional by sector (government, Catholic nongovernment, non-Catholic schools). Within strata, schools were selected with a probability proportional to their size, with an implicit stratification by geography because of the postcode-order of the sampling frame. Weights based on actual numbers of respondents in comparison with official enrollment figures were used to calculate results representing the populations from which the samples were drawn.

2. Ignoring the correlations induced by clustering biases estimates of standard errors.

3. Categorical (dummy) variables are used throughout the analysis.

4. Quartiles were used to place pupils in four achievement groups based on performance in English and mathematics.

5. Ignoring the correlations induced by clustering biases estimates of standard errors.

REFERENCES

Ainley, J., and Elsworth, G. (1997). "Measured Interests, Gender, Socioeconomic Status and Participation in Science and Technology." Paper presented to the Seventh Conference of the European Association for Research on Learning and Instruction, Athens, Greece, August.

Ainley, J., Jones, W., and Navaratnam, K. K. (1990). *Subject Choice in Senior Secondary School.* Canberra: Australian Government Publishing Service.

Ainley, J., Robinson, L., Harvey-Beavis, A., Elsworth, G., and Fleming, M. (1994). *Subject Choice in Years 11 and 12.* Melbourne: Australian Council for Educational Research.

Arnot, M., Gray, J., James, M., Ruddock, J., and Duveen, G. (1998). *Review of Recent Research on Gender and Educational Performance.* London: HMSO.

Australian Bureau of Statistics. (2000). *Schools Australia: 1999.* Catalogue No. 4221.0, Canberra: Australian Bureau of Statistics.

Baker, D., Riordan, C., and Schaub, D. (1995). "The Effects of Sex-Grouped Schooling on Achievement: The Role of National Context." *Comparative Education Review 39:* 468–482.

Bone, A. (1983). *Girls and Girls-Only Schools.* Manchester, UK: Equal Opportunities Commission.

Bosker, R., and Dekkers, H. (1994). "School Differences in Producing Gender-Related Subject Choices." *School Effectiveness and School Improvement 5:* 178–195.

Cheng, J., Payne, J., and Witherspoon, S. (1995). *Science and Mathematics in Full-Time Education after 16.* (Youth Cohort Report No. 36). London: Policy Studies Institute, Department for Education and Employment.

Dale, R. (1969, 1971, 1974). *Mixed or Single-Sex Schools;* Vols. 1–3. London: Routledge and Kegan Paul.

Daly, P. (1995). "Science Course Participation and Science Achievement in Single-Sex and Coeducational Schools." *Evaluation and Research in Education 9:* 91–98.

Daly, P. (1996). "The Effects of Single-Sex and Coeducational Secondary Schooling on Girls' Achievements." *Research Papers in Education 11:* 289–306.

Daly, P., Ainley, J. and Robinson, L. (1996). "The Influence of Single-Sex Secondary Schooling on Choices of Science Courses." Paper presented to the American Educational Research Association, New York, April.

Datnow, A., Hubbard, L., and Conchas, G. Q. (2001). *"How Context Mediates Policy: The Implication of Single-Gender Public Schooling in California." Teachers College Record, 103:* 184–206.

Dauber, S., Alexander, K., and Entwistle, D. (1996). "Tracking and Transitions Through the Middle Grades: Channelling Educational Trajectories." *Sociology of Education 69:* 290–307.

Dekkers, H. (1996). "Determinants of Gender-Related Subject Choice: A Longitudinal Study in Secondary Education." *Educational Research and Evaluation 2:* 185–209.

Dekkers, H., Bosker, R., and Driessen, G. (1999). "Complex Inequalities of Educational Opportunities: A Large-Scale Longitudinal Study on the Relation between Gender, Class, Ethnicity and School Success." *Educational Research and Evaluation 6:* 59–82.

Elsworth, G., Harvey-Beavis, A., Ainley, J., Fabris, S. (1999). "Generic Interests and School Subject Choice." *Educational Research and Evaluation 5:* 290 - 318.

Elwood, J., and Gipps, C. (1999). *Review of Research on the Achievement of Girls in Single-Sex Schools.* London: Institute of Education, University of London.

Equal Opportunities Commission/Office for Standards in Education. (1996). *The Gender Divide.* London: HMSO.

Fullarton, S., and Ainley, J. (2000). *Subject Choice in Years 11 and 12.* (LSAY Research Report No. 15). Melbourne: ACER Press.

Gallagher, A. M., McEwen, A., and Knipe, D. (1996). *Girls and a Level Science, 1985–1995.* Belfast: Equal Opportunities Commission for Northern Ireland.

Gamoran, A. (1987). "The Stratification of Learning Opportunities." *Sociology of Education 60:* 135–55.

Gill, J. (1993). "Rephrasing the Question about Single-Sex Schooling." In A. Reid and B. Johnson (Eds.), *Critical Issues in Australian Education in the 1990s.* Adelaide: Painters Prints, 85–106.

Gender in Policy and Practice

Gill, J. (1998). "Knowing What Counts: Lessons for Effective Teaching." Paper presented to the annual conference of the British Educational Research Association, Belfast, Northern Ireland, August.

Goldstein, H. (1995). *Multilevel Statistical Models*, 2nd ed. London: Edward Arnold; New York: Halstead Press.

Hannafin, J., and Ni Chartaigh, D. (1993). *Co-education and Attainment*. Limerick, Ireland: University of Limerick.

Hannan, D.F., Smyth, E., McCullagh, J., O'Leary, R., and McMahon, D. (1996). *Coeducation and Gender Equality*. Dublin: Economic and Social Research Institute.

Kelly, A. (1988). "Option Choice for Girls and Boys." *Research in Science and Technological Education* 6: 5–24.

Lee, V., Croninger, R., and Smith, J. (1997). "Course-Taking Equity and Mathematics Learning: Testing the Constrained Curricular Hypothesis in US Secondary Schools." *Educational Evaluation and Policy Analysis* 19: 99–121.

Long, M., Frigo, T., and Batten, M. (1999). *The School to Work Transition of Indigenous Australians: A Review of the Literature and Statistical Analysis*. Canberra: Department of Education, Training and Youth Affairs.

McGee Bailey, S. (1996). "Shortchanging Girls and Boys." *Educational Leadership* May, 75–79.

Oakes, J. (1990). Opportunities, Achievement and Choice: Women and Minority Students in Science and Mathematics." in C. B. Cazden (Ed.), *Review of Research in Education*, vol. 16. Washington, D.C.: American Educational Research Association, 153–222.

Parker, L., and Rennie, L. (1997). "Teachers' Perceptions of the Implementation of Single-Sex Classes in Coeducational Schools." *Australian Journal of Education* 41(2): 119–133.

Riordan, C. (2000a). "What Do We Know about the Effects of Single-Sex Schools in the Private Sector: What Are the Implications for Public Schools." Paper presented at the annual meeting of the American Educational Research Association, Seattle.

——. (2000b). *Student Experiences in Home and School: Gender Gap Comparisons among 1990 Sophomores in the National Educational Longitudinal Study*. Paper projected at the annual meeting of the American Sociological Association, Washington, D.C.

Robinson, P., and Smithers, A. (1999). "Should the Sexes be Separated for Secondary Education? Comparisons of Single-Sex and Coeducational Schools." *Research Papers in Education* 14: 23–49.

Rowe, K. J. (1988). "Single-Sex and Mixed-Sex Classes: The Effects of Class Type on Student Achievement, Confidence and Participation in Mathematics." *Australian Journal of Education* 32: 180–202.

Rowe, K. J. (2000). "Schooling Performance and Experiences of Males and Females: Exploring Real Effects from Evidence-Based Research in Teacher and School Effectiveness." Paper presented at Australian Institute of Political Science and Department of Education, Training and Youth Affairs Education Symposium, Melbourne, Australia.

Salamone, R. (1999). "Single-Sex Schooling: Law, Policy and Research." In D. Ravitch (Ed.), *Brookings Papers on Education Policy*. Washington, D.C.: Brookings Institution Press.

Shuttleworth, I., and Daly, P. (1997). "Inequalities in the Uptake of Science at GCSE: Evidence from Northern Ireland." *Research Papers in Education* 12: 143–155.

Smithers, A., and Robinson, P. (1995). *Coeducation and Single-Sex Schooling Revisited*. Uxbridge: Brunel University.

Smyth, E., and Hannan, C. (2000). *Who Chooses Science? School Factors and Subject Take-up*. Dublin: The Economic and Social Research Institute.

Spade, J. Z., Columba, L., and Vanfossen, B. E. (1997). Tracking in mathematics and science: courses and course-selection procedures. *Sociology of Education* 70: 108–127.

Stables, A. (1990). "Differences between Pupils from Mixed and Single-Sex Schools in their Enjoyment of School Subjects and in their Attitudes to Science and School." *Educational Review* 42: 221–230.

Steedman, J. (1984). *Examination Results in Mixed and Single-Sex Schools: Findings from the National Child Development Study*. Manchester, UK: Equal Opportunities Commission.

———. (1985). "Examination Results in Mixed and Single-Sex Schools." In D. Reynolds (Ed.), *Studying School Effectiveness*. London: Falmer Press.

Sukhnandan, L., Lee, B., and Kelleher, S. (2000). *An Investigation into Gender Differences in Achievement. Part 2. School and Classroom Practices*. Slough, UK: National Foundation for Educational Research.

Willis, S. (1989). *Real Girls Don't Do Maths: Gender and the Construction of Privilege*. Geelong: Deakin University Press.

Section Five

CONSTRUCTIONS OF GENDER IN SINGLE-SEX SCHOOLING

CHAPTER 15

Girls in the Company of Girls: Social Relations and Gender Construction in Single-Sex Drama Education

Kathleen Gallagher

I AM A FEMINIST and i'm not scared to say it. i'm not scared of what the word means. I'M NOT SCARED OF HOW YOU'LL TAKE IT. and if you're intimidated, then please Don't blame your FEAR on me. Don't let it close you off from reality, Cuz in realty . . . shit happens. . . . I AM A FEMINIST, and it doesn't mean i hate all men. . . . Although i may be concerned about a few of them . . . it doesn't mean i think the whole world should be governed only by women. though on a second thought, maybe that wouldn't be such a bad option. . . . TWIST my words 'til NOTHING'S WHAT I REALLY SAID, You can make it sound absurd, make it all LOSE SENSE. it still doesn't mean a thing, since in the end I KNOW WHERE I STAND, sometimes i wonder if you have a clue of where you do . . . i listen to people saying that the feminist mOveMeNt is over, so baby, baby, baby, why don't you take that chip off your shoulder, i guess MY STANDING HERE is proof that it's not, there's thousands others who would agree, thing is, they do it SILENTLY . . . and Statistics will say a certain number of women are raped by men, I WANT TO KNOW about the ones who didn't announce it to the government, CALLME CRAZYCRAZYCRAzY, call me anything you like, Cuz i'm screaming TRUTHS out in the streets, and i didn't think you'd like it. i knew you wouldn't like it. I AM A FEMINIST, and i claim the word proudly, it doesn't necessarily mean I'm a lesbian, but then again, maybe i am. and maybe my sexual preference is really NONE OF YOUR BUSINESS I said it's none of your business, but YOU STILL DON'T GET IT. maybe I'm living in a world full of ISMS, but I'm not singing to you, cuz i've got nothing better to do. and maybe if you still don't understand the word then for god's sake open up a book and LOOK IT UP. it's all about respect, such a simple thing really. too bad that in 1997, so many of us still don't get it. it doesn't mean that i'm ugly, or that i'll die lonely, or that I have to be ANGRY all the time. in fact, it doesn't mean much of what you think. I AM A FEMINIST, and I claim the world proudly, it doesn't mean i hate all men, it doesn't mean i want them dead. it doesn't mean I have to have hairy armpits or hairy legs, or that I have to shave my head, it doesn't mean that I'm bitter cuz I can't get laid, cuz honey I can (sorry mom!) I AM A FEMINIST, and i'm not scared to say it, i'm not scared of what the word means, i'm not scared of how you'll take it, and if you're intimidated, then please don't blame your FEAR on me. i have no use for it. I simply won't have it.

Andrea Florian
Independent Artist/Bathsheba Records 1998
Lyrics from FeMiNiSt
somehurrygood CD

INTRODUCTION

Musician Andrea Florian's lyrics celebrate the agency of young women who claim their identity proudly. In the latter years of the 1990, I conducted research in a single-sex, Catholic, publicly funded, urban school in Toronto, Canada. This research examined the ways in which girls often make sense—and take charge—of their learning. My current research project represents a collaboration with such a group of young women in their early to mid-twenties, who are interrogating their earlier Catholic single-sex school education and bringing this experience into active relationship with their current identities as artists. This research has evolved from the original line of inquiry, which transported me into the worlds of the vastly diverse and complex group referred to as "adolescent girls." My recent book, *Drama Education in the Lives of Girls: Imagining Possibilities* (Gallagher, 2000), is the result of this earlier ethnographic research. The grade ten girls of that study challenged me to know more fully the unique and imaginative aspects of identity and agency in their school lives and opened up for discussion the complex and contradictory nature of their adolescent selves. Before outlining the goals and particular considerations of my current project it will be useful to provide a brief synopsis of the original single-sex research and a summary of significant findings.

My research, which began as a study of drama education in a particular context, led me to some very provocative questions concerning gender, class, multiracial/culturalism and girls' gender constructions in schools. That context was a single-sex school for girls in the Metropolitan Separate School Board (now called the Toronto Catholic District School Board). This single-sex girls' school was founded by an order of nuns originally from Le Puy, France. They opened their first girls' secondary school in Toronto in 1857. But, in 1984 when Catholic schools in Ontario won the legal right to full funding (previously government funding for Catholic schools extended only to grade eight), they became public institutions despite their special denominational status. What has resulted in a cosmopolitan urban center like Toronto is a rather odd combination of the former private secondary system (middle and upper-middle class signs and symbols like uniforms, liturgical celebrations, single-sex schools) with a truly inner city, urban population largely of lower socioeconomic status, mainly not of Anglo-Saxon heritage, and many being first generation Canadian or refugee students.

For ten years I taught drama in the single-sex school where I conducted ethnographic research and was witness to the many ways in which girls' work in educational drama created opportunities for them to interrupt the limited and limiting discourses and possibilities assigned to them in schools. Instead, they were invited to—in the words of bell hooks (1994)—exercise their transgression. Drama asks them to mediate reality by working with metaphor, analogy, symbolism, and most significantly, it asks girls to speak their own understandings of the world. The fictions students engaged in were often so deeply connected to their own reality that they were at once moving from distraction, fun, and entertainment, into meaning-making, risk, contention, and self-disclosure. What I found in my research is that in trying on these different "selves," girls were not slipping deeper inside a role, but rather were surfacing as themselves—full of contradictions and ambiguity—more and more strongly as they gazed, in safety, through a "character" self.

I wanted the study to make an original contribution to the familiar and much-studied questions concerning gender and equity in schooling, from its unique perspective of a publicly funded, heterogeneous, single-sex environment. I also hoped to provide strong classroom-based qualitative evidence of the aesthetic, social, and academic advantages of drama education practices in secondary schooling. A recent, comprehensive, quantitative study was conducted by Winner and Hetland (2000) of the Reviewing Education and the Arts Project at Harvard Graduate School of Education. Based on eighty reports (107 positive effect sizes), they found that there was a significant causal link between classroom drama and a variety of verbal areas. Drama, they have established, helps to build verbal skills that transfer to new materials. When one considers that drama helps to build verbal skills that are highly prized in schools and in life, the natural corollary to this begs the question: Does greater verbal proficiency and confidence in school influence later life choices and successes? In Walter Pitman's (1998) recent work on the arts in Canada and in Canadian schools, he describes the capacity of the arts to give meaning to the rest of the school curriculum. Despite this unifying and integrating function of the arts in schools, there still remains a hierarchy of knowledge that places the measurable and objective subjects at the top, leaving the experiential and subjective at the bottom. Over his many years of observation of Canadian schools, he concludes that there continues to be a perception of the arts as "play," entertainment, a kind of relaxation at the end of the day:

> Yet arts education programs in some schools are rigorous. They stretch the mind
> and the emotional capacity of the student. In good arts education classes there is a
> seriousness, an intensity that is a wonder to behold. This quality can sometimes be
> experienced by attending a play, a musical or a concert in the local school gymna-

sium. Even during those mythical years of the '70s and '80s, when it was assumed that excellence had disappeared from the classrooms of North America entirely, the quality of music or drama at such events left the adult audience in awe. Yet arts classes are still viewed as unimportant. (p. 51)

This was a view I hoped my research would seriously challenge.

Not wanting to divorce the "subjects" from the drama work they were involved in, I videotaped—as the primary means of data collection—five grade ten drama classes over two school years. I also included students' writing-in-role and their reflective writing. A group of nineteen girls, a self-selected cross-section of the 139 girls in the five grade ten drama classes in the study, volunteered to be interviewed individually in order to include their own analyses of what they do in role and how they think about their own thinking. Finally, I sought other expert eyes—the "insider-outside eyes"—of the videographers (senior-level drama students), to achieve a kind of second level of participant observation. The research became a multicase ethnographic study in a reflective practice design.

I learned many things by analyzing key classroom episodes and by listening to the girls talk about their experiences. These findings certainly have curricular implications for arts education, but I would argue that they also render important pedagogical and policy implications for decisions regarding the education of girls generally. Observations of the process of working in drama suggest that drama education is not a reactive stance, but a creative one. It is not a correction of previous understandings but a reorientation in thinking. I found that dramatic role play can poignantly challenge previous understandings. Through a collaborative, but rarely consensual process, the girls were concerned with the framing, interpreting, and communicating of meanings rather than with intentional outcomes or finalities. As Grumet has described it, this kind of drama education can create "exercises and improvisations that ask students to tumble off the linear curriculum so that they can explore all the ramifications of the problem they are studying" (2000, p. x). Drama also offers girls a multitude of subject positions; discussions in and out of role highlight different voices in the collectively created, imagined world. Drama education practices can engage the polyphony of voices in a diverse classroom, inviting participation from within many different frameworks, and bringing students into relation with each other. In the process of adopting new positions and entering into new relations, the girls described shifts in thinking and feeling; in fact, in knowing.

WORKS IN PROGRESS: AN ORIENTATION TO THE FOLLOW-UP STUDY AND STUDY PARTICIPANTS

Because the high school participants of my study had such strong opinions about experiences of gender inequities in mixed-sex classrooms and reported a stronger sense of self and greater access to personal and academic successes in single-sex environments, I became interested in fixing the lens of retrospection on the experiences of my new study participants as they considered the implications of earlier adolescent experiences for current life choices and actions. Psychological-cognitive (AAUW, 1992, 1998; Gilligan, 1993), physiological-hormonal (Kimura, 1992, 1987; Sylwester, 1995) and education gender research (American Institutes for Research, 1999; Blair and Sanford, 1999; Brown and Gilligan, 1992; Canadian Teachers' Federation, 1990; Gaskell and Willinksy, 1995; Hollinger and Adamson, 1992; Riordan, 1990; Sadker and Sadker, 1994; Sedgwick, 1997; U.S. Department of Education, 1996) expose forcefully the diminishing sense of self experienced by too many adolescent girls. A qualitative study of young women at another crucial point in their lives—as their adult identities emerge—has much to bring to the single-sex schooling debate. As well as having been educated in Catholic, urban, publicly funded, single-sex settings, these four young women I have begun to work with share another significant characteristic: They are currently studying and/or working in some area of the arts and claim the identity of "artist."

Francine is twenty-five years old and describes herself as a black, Canadian Jamaican who speaks English and is a Baptist. In high school, she studied drama and music and went on to study drama in university. Following this, she toured with an African modern dance company for a few years before beginning the journalism program in which she is currently enrolled. She remembers her peers in a single-sex school as "more open-minded and forced to be more creative." For a drama festival one year, Francine remembers playing a male role in a French farce that she would have had no chance of playing in a coeducational school. Now on reflection, she considers her ability to concentrate on her studies without the added pressure of seeing boys every day as the greatest positive effect of her single-sex education and further that this milieu allowed her to "see girls for who they really were: evil, shy, loud, smart, dumb."

Danielle is twenty-five years old and describes herself as a white, Italian, English-speaking, "hetro" [sic] who was raised Catholic. Having just finished a university degree in drama education, she is directing some small theater works in Montreal and is the arts administrator for Montreal's Black Theater Workshop. In high school, she studied drama and also music privately. She remembers studying drama in her first year of high school only because it was a school requirement but believes that had she been in a coed school, she would have been too shy to continue with drama: "Being surrounded by males would have made me doubt my abilities." Like Francine, Danielle, too, thinks that "playing male roles in high school made the experience more complete." Considering the competitive nature of many schools, she remembers of her single-sex classroom "praising and being praised for a scene well done. It is as though many share in your accomplishments." Most importantly, Danielle thinks now that single-sex education gave her the "courage and strength to continue my education in theater and to now work in the field without feeling as though I couldn't compete with men. This is not to say that I haven't been discriminated against while studying at the university level within the field, but I am able to carry myself independently despite that."

Alex describes herself as a twenty-one-year old, white, Canadian-Hungarian who speaks English and Hungarian, has no religious affiliation, and considers herself a person of low socio-economic status. Currently she is in her third year of a university theater degree and is involved in community theater projects outside the university. In high school, she studied music, drama, and visual arts. Of her single-sex arts experiences, she recalls that:

> with the elimination of awkward sexual tensions I feel adolescents have more incentive to express themselves creatively. My experience in a single-sex environment tells me that I had more confidence in what I produced or attempted, and more time to spend focusing on the project at hand. In a course like drama often people have trouble standing up in front of the class or presenting a scene. In a single-sex environment the need or want to sexually impress is eliminated and the work is given more importance.

Alex states unequivocally that her single-sex schooling was directly responsible for her current actions and achievements. She further explains:

> In my situation, single-sex schooling has had a very positive influence on my education. Being in a school with all girls allowed me to thrive as a student. I never felt insecure physically or intellectually. I did not have to deal with sexual tensions that you experience in co-ed schools. No sexual pressures helped me develop self-confidence. This confidence gave me incentive to participate in extra-curricular activities, maintain excellent marks, be socially involved outside of school, and hold part-time jobs. The list is long but revealing. I never was pressured by my parents to achieve good grades, or attend a post-secondary education institute. Now I fully support myself and attend university full-time. If it was not for my training in a single-sex environment I think my perspective would be different. I notice amongst my peers at university different systems of prioritizing. What stays my priority is school.

Andrea describes herself as a twenty-five-year-old, white, Maltese-Canadian who speaks both Maltese and English and is a nonpracticing Catholic. Currently she is a recording artist who has produced three CDs with the assistance of the Ontario Arts Council and she continues to tour in Canada and abroad. She completed a university music degree and earns her living as a professional musician. Andrea studied music and drama in high school and explains that she never had an image problem because she was extremely focused on her dreams and goals: "I was allowed to be silly not because of male presence. I was more secure because I never had to endure heartbreaking crushes in 'public.'"

Taking my lead from these early conversations, I am persuaded that pursuing this perception of "judgment" is a fruitful longitudinal avenue to take. A study, therefore, that centers on young women who have explored other possibilities for themselves through the arts will help to direct the imagination into new realms, a creative shift that gender research might well use. Fiona Shaw, who played the role of Richard II in 1995 in a daring production at the National Theatre in England said of this performance that "the experiments in gender, both socially and artistically, can remind us all of the constant bravery necessary to force the universe of the imagination outwards." (Goodman and de Gay, 1998, p. xxiv)

SOME SPECIFIC CONSEQUENCES OF SINGLE-SEX DRAMA EDUCATION

Conflicts in drama become sites of struggle for divergent perspectives. When gender is relaxed, other categories or components of identity emerge more strongly. By "gender-relaxed," I am referring to the hierarchy of identity markers for adolescent girls that typically place "femaleness" and constructs of femininity at the top. In my experience, in a diverse, single-sex context, markers other than sex and gender, such as racial, ethnic, and linguistic identities, class-based experiences, and sexual orientation that delineate "differences" among girls become more pronounced. Cultural knowledge and experiential knowing, for instance, figure prominently in classroom drama work when gendered knowledge is not foregrounded. In an interview discussing her development of fictional characters, Fenny explained:

> Yeah, 'cause you take all of *your* surroundings and you use that to make the character. Yeah, I think the character you play is always a part of you, like even though you could be playing something totally opposite. (Student interview session)

Students' understandings, then, of a dramatic world that is based on their experience of an actual world and their personal criteria for making judgments can be poignantly challenged by dramatic role-play:

> *Alex:* When I roleplayed as Kelly's teacher, it changed the way I was looking at the situation because now I was looking through someone elses [*sic*] eyes. Since we started this "Kelly Turner" story, we were always asking the question "How would Kelly feel?" When I role played as her teacher I asked the question "How do *I* feel about this situation?" Looking from someone elses [*sic*] point of view changed your whole outlook on the situation changed because you begin to realize everything and everyone was a factor in Kelly's decision. (Student postdrama reflective writing)

The process-oriented way of working in a single-sex drama classroom for girls can ask afresh what counts as knowledge. When girls become the substance or the essential content of their fictional worlds they can construct fresh understandings and reconstruct themselves. The arts' ability to "humanize" is in enlarging the concept of "human" through critical inquiry by discussion. When asked whether they see themselves differently in drama class as compared to other classes, two students explained it this way:

Nicole: Yeah. I'm more outspoken. I don't know . . . this class doesn't really feel like a class. It just feels like . . . like you're teaching me new things and I'm just exploring it. It doesn't feel . . . I don't feel, like, you know . . . straight. Usually like in math and science there's a way you have to act, like . . . you can't express yourself . . . freely . . . like . . .

KG: What do you mean when you say that?

Nicole: I mean like . . . like . . . sometimes you show really high feelings or what you think about and sometimes you just, like, see things in your environment. I don't know, drama just brings out that. (Student interview session)

Danielle: Well yeah in a way 'cause you just feel you can be more yourself. It's not like, "O.K. do this, do that, do this, do that." It's more like everybody works together. In other classes it's more independent, but in drama it's like everybody works together. (Student interview session)

From the nineteen interviews, I learned that 95 percent of these students believed that they personally identify with some aspect of the created story in order to build the characters and the world they inhabit. Students of color and new Canadians (those living in Canada for fewer than five years) felt particularly strongly about including aspects of their own lives and "attitudes" in their process of character development, whereas this seemed somewhat less significant to white students. One might reflect upon Sherene Razack's analysis of gender, race, and culture in classrooms here:

What makes the cultural differences approach so inadequate in various pedagogical moments is not so much that it is wrong, for people in reality are diverse and do have culturally specific practices that must be taken into account, but that its emphasis on cultural diversity too often descends, in a multicultural spiral, to a superficial reading of differences that makes power relations invisible and keeps dominant cultural norms in place. The strategy becomes inclusion and all too often what Chandra Mohanty has described as "a harmonious, empty pluralism." (1998, pp. 9–10)

In other words, if there were common practices in schools that engaged "difference" beyond the "harmonious, empty pluralism" often encountered by students, they may not have felt so vehement that their "different attitudes" be central. However, they know, too well, how inadequate "inclusion" can feel.

Almost all students made some reference to their feelings, or values, or understanding of "important issues" as guiding their work. When asked whether they included aspects of themselves and their experiences in their drama work, three students explained:

Lily: Probably because I've been in a similar situation `cause of where I live. `Cause I live in an Irish area and I went to a party with a bunch of Irish friends and these guys are like "Is she latin? Is she dirty?" And I was like "No, I'm Portuguese" and they're like "O.K. you can stay then." Yeah really, like, big time racist there.

KG: So you related in some way to our Kelly Turner drama?

Lily: I seen them beat up on so many people and you keep your mouth shut `cause you know you would be the next one. (Student interview session)

Christina: Yeah, Earthwoman, she went up to the sky and she didn't know anything about it. She had to, in a way, adjust to the whole environment and that's what happened to me when I got to Canada . . . uhm . . . I didn't know how to talk. I didn't know anybody `cause everybody's customs are different.

KG: And has that changed at all for you now?

Christina: Well by going to school you become aware of everything around you. You get in with it.

KG: You understand the culture more?

Christina: Yeah.

KG: Do you think you've lost any aspects of your own culture?

Christina: Not at all. At home we talk our language and we're really involved in the community. I mean, I am who I am and I'm not gonna change that. I'm Portuguese. (Student interview session)

Marcella: Oh, like Mary Morgan. I thought that was such a good story `cause it's like my family. "You can't have a boyfriend, you can't do this, you can't do that" and all this stuff. And I think, well what if something accidentally happens? What if I accidentally get pregnant. There were so many different, interesting characters . . . like how everyone acted and it was just so good and so . . . dramatic. (Student interview session)

In improvised drama, we can have a depiction of character that is insufficient and open, that can be explored using drama conventions. Using a process of alienation (*Verfremdungseffekt*) in the tradition of Brecht (1964), that is, setting life up as a site for struggle and change is one means of dismantling seductive, stereotypical images, and resisting the limited and limiting discursive and aesthetic representations of self/other. As one student, Bianca, explained in her reflective writing, "When I was role playing as Kelly's teacher, it changed the way that I was looking at the situation quite a bit, because when I was actually *in the teacher's shoes*, I tended to think differently than I would have if I just *thought* of what the teacher would have done." These shifts in thinking reveal an embodied knowledge, a felt knowledge that often measures what is spontaneously experienced against what was preconceived. Fostering multiperspectival views of life is the hallmark of drama education.

Much has been written in the field of drama education about its ability to teach "empathy." In my view, however, drama often fails to move beyond what Megan Boler (1997) has described as a "consuming" of the other, what she calls "passive empathy." Boler persuasively argues that passive empathy promoted as a bridge between differences is not a sufficient educational practice. In particular, she argues, the ability to empathize with a very distant "other," without recognizing oneself as implicated in the social forces that created the climate of obstacles that others must confront is a very dangerous practice indeed. In my experience, teenagers working in drama often begin by knowing who they *are not*. It is frequently the pedagogical/political commitments of the facilitator that push students to explore who *they are*, as well as where they stand in relation to others. The key here is not to consume the "other's story," but to position oneself and better understand oneself in relation to it. To support her argument, Boler[1] points to Aristotle's discussion of pity; a practice more about the projection of self than the understanding of another. When working with stories of oppression and injustice, then, it is neither guilt nor pity that motivates new understanding, but a critically "distanced" reading that moves increasingly closer to "self" as a positioned self and one that resides within systems that shape human agency. The problem with a good deal of classroom drama is that we consume "good stories" without taking on the required work of positioning ourselves and finding responses other than guilt and pity to rethink stories so familiar they have often lost meaning and commonly elicit a set of stock responses. In this regard, I agree strongly with Boler's analysis of the "risks" of empathy. If we remain at the level of superficial points of nonidentification, even pity, the work might well engage activity but will not challenge a priori assumptions. Reflective writing in drama can, nonetheless, call on the participant to "cast her gaze at her own reflection" (p. 259) in significant ways. For example, Rosa explains:

> I learned that in every situation everyone views their own story as the truth, builds up their own truth. And through acting out different points of view we understood why everyone wanted their story to be the truth. (Student post-drama reflective writing)

This observation, from her reflective writing after the improvisational drama, marks merely a beginning of an understanding that "we choose our ignorances, just as we choose our challenges" (Boler, 1997, p. 269). This is a not "passive empathy" and is different from it in notable ways. Rosa's comments represent her understanding that realities are constructed, contingent, and changeable.

ARE SINGLE-SEX CLASSROOMS DIFFERENT FROM COEDUCATIONAL ONES?

These students functioned in a single-sex environment every day. It is the context they knew best. I had imagined they would no longer necessarily think consciously about it because it was the context they could take for granted. But when I posed the question in the interview that asked them to think deliberately about themselves in this environment, they responded with strongly held views about single-sex and mixed-sex learning environments, evaluating their own sense of self in these milieux:

"The way I think of it is like girls will be more hush around guys and guys like to show off around girls and they'll be more to impress girls and girls will be more down. With no guys here we're able to project a lot more. I think it's better."

"I wouldn't talk as much. I'd be scared they'd [boys] laugh at me."

"Yeah with girls it's ok if you screw up. In elementary school I used to be so quiet, now it's like I just say it. "

"In class, it's not like, can't say that a guy's here."

"With guys watching? I don't know. I don't think I'd express myself deeply. And plus when you express yourself in drama people learn a lot about you. I'm sure you know a lot of things about me and I wouldn't want guys knowing, you know, things that hurt me and things that make me laugh."

"With boys I'd feel more self-conscious. In elementary school with guys there, they always have an opinion about what you do. Girls, like I find, are more accepting."

"In a coed class, girls don't really have a lot to say and girls don't get as much attention as they should. Not me, but some girls would be afraid to talk, like express themselves in front of guys."

"If guys were in this school I think you'd be more afraid to show that you're smarter. You'd want to hide that cause they might criticize you."

However I looked at the responses from the nineteen interviews conducted with the self-selected cross-section of the 139 girls in the study, it was impossible not to see their feelings of intimidation and sense of judgment, whether actually experienced in previous coeducational contexts or merely perceived. It is this sense of judgment, or more accurately, their belief that they were freer to have impact on their learning environments in single-sex settings, which compelled me to begin conversations with a group of young women graduates of Catholic urban single-sex schools. Together, we are considering what role this setting may ultimately have had on their self-concepts, their productive and artistic lives, and later gender relations.

WHAT LIES AHEAD?

The very future of single-sex schools is uncertain, however, in a political climate of economic viability and "equal" opportunity. In the Toronto Catholic District School Board, the threat of school mergers looms large. When enrolment drops in public, single-sex schools, the first response is often to "go coed." In the United States, a qualitative study looking at a single-sex physics classroom within the Illinois Mathematics and Science Academy (IMSA) (1995), a public, state-funded residential high school for high-achieving mathematics and science students developed a girls-only section of physics as an experimental program. The purpose of the study was to see whether girls in the single-sex classroom would participate more, exhibit greater confidence, and demonstrate higher achievement in later science classes than girls in mixed-sex physics classes in the same school. The authors of this study report data that support significant growth and achievement in all areas for the single-sex groupings over the mixed-sex ones. Despite what the authors describe as overwhelming evidence to support single-sex classes for girls, the school discontinued the classes after only one semester because they were not "the most appropriate long-term solution."

In Ontario, it is uncertain whether the province will continue to support its historic commitment to two publicly funded systems of education and those who most vehemently oppose what they see as outright discriminatory practice on the basis of religion are raising some important questions. In the meantime, Ontario's Catholic single-sex schools (unlike their more homogeneous private school counterparts) have a unique opportunity, at this juncture in history, to examine complex questions of gender within ever widening frames of diversity. Although the history of single-sex schooling may tell a story of exclusion and elitism, the publicly funded, Ontario Catholic single-sex schools of the late twentieth and early twenty-first century tell a very different story indeed. Granting girls the time and space in adolescence to continue relationships with themselves as subjects rather than objects, and to foster collaborative relationships across difference, may prolong the strong sense of solidarity and community that younger girls feel[2] and adolescent girls lose. Allowing differences to emerge, rather than assuming a group identity, is a strengthening force in girls' development. And graduates of these anomalous environments, who are getting on with their adult lives, have perhaps, even more to teach us. I would hope that my follow-up study would illuminate new questions about why these environments—decreasing in number as school mergers loom—deserve a closer look.

In my experience, there are few places in schools where "differences" can be negotiated between people and analyses of structural and institutional inequities are exposed. Razack advocates:

> Instead, we need to direct our efforts to the conditions of communication and knowledge production that prevail, calculating not only who can speak and how they are likely to be heard but also how we know what we know and the interest we protect through our knowing. (1998, p. 10)

How drama, within the imperatives of feminist, antiracist education, might contribute particularly to ongoing struggles of social justice in single-sex and mixed-sex schools is by offering other modes of critical analysis and equity-focused creative projects that recognize and communicate differences in active and productive ways. With its focus on perspectives and processes, drama can demand a way of thinking and relating not expected by other disciplines. Significantly, it can straddle the entirely-too-often mutually independent worlds of critical analysis and creativity, or deconstruction and production.

Freire, in *Pedagogy of Freedom,* offers some hope for these projects that aim to redress systemic inequities in schools and societies by foregrounding the place of agency and creativity in our educational projects. He says:

> I like being human because I know that my passing through the world is not predetermined, preestablished. That my destiny is not a given but something that needs to be constructed and for which I must assume responsibility. I like being human because I am involved with others in making history out of possibility, not simply resigned to fatalistic stagnation. Consequently, the future is something to be constructed through trial and error rather than an inexorable vice that determines all our actions.
>
> I like being human because in my unfinishedness I know that I am conditioned. Yet conscious of such conditioning, I know that I can go beyond it, which is the essential difference between conditioned and determined existence. (1998, p. 54)

Scottish writer, director, and producer John McGrath (1981) claims that theater is the most clearly political of the art forms:

> Theater is the place where the life of a society is shown in public to that society, where that society's assumptions are exhibited and tested, its values are scrutinized, its myths are validated and its traumas become emblems of its reality. Theater is not about the reaction of one sensibility to events external to itself, as poetry tends to be; or the private consumption of fantasy or a mediated slice of social reality, as most novels tend to be. It is a public event, and it is about matter of public concern. (1981, p. 83)

Drama is, conceivably, the best able of all the arts in schools to intervene in ways that move us (in our minds, our hearts, with our senses, in our bodies) to see others and ourselves differently and to think and act with these new understandings.

Policymakers and educators need to better appreciate what is possible in arts-rich, single-sex learning environments. Performance in math and the sciences has long been an area of interest and attention for researchers of gender equity in schooling. Casting light on those areas often deemed "less academic" in secondary schools may reveal different prospects for girls in single-sex environments and force a needed reevaluation of what "achievement" and "success" mean. Asking young women to critically reflect on their education in such environments will indicate important future directions for equity-centered teaching and research.

I close with another excerpt of Andrea's song writing. In it, she insinuates the focus on "processes" that is a defining feature of arts education in schools, often demanding a way of thinking not expected by other disciplines. In her music, Andrea celebrates her own freedom from what she and others have too often described as an immobilizing sense of judgment in those years when it most matters, as girls carve out directions for future life and construct their very selves in view of the world around them.

> i am a work in progress, this is a work in progress,
> we are all someplace in between,
> it may not be so beautiful, but as long as it is honest,
> then i guess it doesn't really have to be.
>
> i'm trying to remember it's not all a pretty picture
> and sometimes half of what we say,
> is not really what we mean.
>
> and i'm trying to hold onto
> the things that really matter
> i'm trying to remember the precious things.
>
> i am a work in progress.
>
> when there are no more words
> and there's no peace in silence.
> i'm trying to remember all these things.
>
> holding on sometimes means letting go
> and i've got a firm grip on all of this pain.
> i am a work in progress.
>
> i'm trying to remember, it's not all what it appears.
> this is not real, but this is not a dream.
> and i'll find my peace in silence, and all the noise around us.

and i'm holding on to all these precious things.

i am a work in progress.

Andrea Florian
Independent Artist/Bathsheba Records 1998
Lyrics from: i am a work in progress
Only Human CD 1997

NOTES

1. Boler also documents from her own teaching the often cathartic, innocent and sometimes voyeuristic sense of closure that is associated with "empathic" readings of the stories of the "other". This is an especially important concern for drama practitioners. It is, however, a subject for another article and will not be addressed here.

2. See Brown and Gilligan's (1992) *Meeting at the Crossroads: Women's Psychology and Girls' Development,* in which they describe the seven- and eight-year-old girls they interviewed as the "whistle blowers" in the relational world, who easily disagree with others, sometimes refuse to take no for an answer, and often resort to disruptive ways to be heard if they think someone is not listening. These young girls have powerful friendships and determined voices.

REFERENCES

American Institutes for Research. (1999). *Gender Gaps: Where Schools Still Fail Our Children*. New York: Marlow and Company.

American Association of University Women Education Foundation. (1992). *How Schools Shortchange Girls*. Washington, D.C.: AAUW.

———. (1998). *Single-Sex Education for Girls*. Washington, D.C.: American Association of University Women Educational Foundation.

Blair, H., and Sanford, K. (1999). "Single-Sex Classrooms: A Place for Transformation of Policy and Practice." Paper presented at the American Education Research Association. Montreal, Quebec.

Boler, M. (1997). "The Risks of Empathy: Interrogating Multiculturalism's Gaze." *Cultural Studies* 11(2):253–273.

Brecht, B. (1964). *Brecht on Theatre*. J. Willett (Trans.). London: Methuen.

Brown, L., and Gilligan, C. (1992). *Meeting at the Crossroads: Women's Psychology and Girls' Development*. Cambridge: Harvard University Press.

Canadian Teachers' Federation. (1990). *The A Capella Papers of the Canadian Teachers' Federation*. Ottawa: Canadian Teachers' Federation.

Freire, P. (1998). *Pedagogy of Freedom: Ethics, Democracy, and Civic Courage*. Lanham, Boulder, New York: Rowman and Littlefield Publishers.

Gallagher, K. (2000). *Drama Education in the Lives of Girls: Imagining Possibilities*. Toronto, Buffalo, London: University of Toronto Press.

Gaskell, J., and Willinsky, J. (Eds.) (1995). *Gender In/forms Curriculum: From Enrichment to Transformation*. New York: Teachers College Press.

Gilligan, C. (1993). *In a Different Voice: Psychological Theory and Women's Development*. Cambridge: Harvard University Press. Originally published in 1982.

Goodman, L., and de Gay, J. (1998). *The Routledge Reader in Gender and Performance*. New York: Routledge

Grumet, M. (2000). Foreword in *Drama Education in the Lives of Girls: Imagining Possibilities*. Toronto, Buffalo, London: University of Toronto Press.

Hollinger, D., and Adamson, R. (1992). "Single-Sex Schooling: Proponents Speak," Vol. 2. *A Special Report from the Office of Educational Research and Improvement*. U.S. Department of Education.

Hooks, B. (1994). *Teaching to Transgress: Education as the Practice of Freedom*. New York: Routledge.

IMSA. (1995). *Statement: 1993–1994 Calculus Based Physics/Mechanics Study.* Illinois Mathematics and Science Academy, 1500 W. Sullivan Road, Aurora, IL 60506-10000.

Kimura, D. (1992). "Cognitive Function: Sex Differences and Hormonal Influences." *Neuroscience Year: Supplement 2 to the Encyclopedia of Neuroscience,* Boston: Birkhauser.

Kimura, D. (1987). "Are Men's and Women's Brains Really Different?" *Canadian Psychology* 28:2.

McGrath, J. (1981). *A Good Night Out: Popular Theatre, Audience, Class and Form.* London: Nick Hern Books.

Pitman, W. (1998). *Learning Through the Arts in an Age of Uncertainty.* Toronto: Aylmer Express Limited.

Razack, S. (1998). *Looking White People in the Eye: Gender, Race, and Culture in Courtrooms and Classrooms.* Toronto: University of Toronto Press.

Riordan, C. (1990). *Girls and Boys in School: Together or Separate?* New York: Teachers College Press.

Sadker, M., and Sadker, D. (1994). *Failing at Fairness: How America's Schools Cheat Girls.* Toronto: Maxwell MacMillan International.

Sedgwick, J. (1997). "What Difference Does Single-Sex School Make to a Girl in Later Life?" *Self Magazine* (March).

Sylwester, R. (1995). *A Celebration of Neurons: An Educator's Guide to the Brain.* Alexandria, VA: Association for Supervision and Curriculum Development.

U.S. Department of Education. (1996). Office of Educational Research and Improvement, Washington, D.C.

Winner, E., and Hetland, L. (2000). "The Arts and Academic Achievement: What the Evidence Shows." *Journal of Aesthetic Education.* 34 (3/4): Fall/Winter, 2000.

CHAPTER 16

Constructions of Masculinity in California's Single-Gender Academies

Elisabeth L. Woody

INTRODUCTION

At this point, we have little understanding of social and cultural influences on students', and in particular boys' experiences of single-sex schooling. Based on research in California's public single-gender Academies, this chapter provides a much-needed analysis of constructions of masculinity in single-sex schools. In a recent review of research on single-sex education, Mael finds a noticeable gap in the literature, namely, in the lack of attention to the experiences of boys, as "the overwhelming preponderance of research has focused on females and female concerns" (1998, p. 117).

In an effort to contribute to the scholarship on boys, this chapter examines how students construct, enact, and challenge notions of masculinity, through personal ideologies, relationships with peers and teachers, and institutional practices and assumptions. Within the context of sex-segregated academies, boys were defined in opposition to girls, and, more often than not, as "bad" and in need of discipline. Despite an acknowledgment of complexities among boys in the single-gender Academies, both boys and girls upheld hegemonic notions of masculinity through limited expectations of how boys should act. Ultimately, any efforts to challenge definitions of masculinity were tempered by a recognition of the inevitable privileges of being a boy.

This research also expands our understanding of gender as a salient factor in students' lives. Any school reform, which highlights gender as a significant marker of identity, must consider the implications of such policy on students' lives. Girls and boys attending California's single-gender Academies were no longer merely "students," but were systematically defined by gender. How students respond to, interpret, and act on those definitions is of central relevance to educators. Beyond simply a study of single-sex education, this research brings considerations of gender into discussions of school reform and has implications for raising awareness of students' gendered experiences across school contexts.

PROJECT OVERVIEW

In 1997, California's former Governor Pete Wilson introduced single-sex education into the public secondary school system through the funding of "single-gender academies," in an effort to expand choice in the public sector and address the perceived "different" needs of boys and girls. (For a comprehensive analysis of the California single-gender "experiment," as it was called, see Datnow, Hubbard, and Woody, 2001.) Districts were invited to submit proposals for the creation of one girls' and one boys' academy within the same school site. Each district would receive $500,000—a significant amount of money for a state-funded reform effort—for the start-up and continuation of the academies for two years, with the expectation that the academies would become self-sufficient after that time. The twelve resulting academies (six girls' and six boys' academies in six participating districts) represent a renewed interest in single-sex education within the context of public school reform.

California's single-gender academies are one of the most comprehensive efforts to establish single-sex schooling within the public sector since the passing of Title IX in 1972.[1] Most recent efforts, whether in the form of separate classes or entire schools, have been criticized and eventually shut down. California was quick to realize that any attempts to provide separate schooling would have to be offered equally to boys and girls. Therefore, the legislation explicitly called for "equal access to the schools," and required that for "all aspects of the curricula, the educational opportunity must be equal for boys and girls" (CA Education Code 58522).

The school sites include a rural, predominantly white, lower-class community, a suburban middle-class community, and several urban Latin-American and African-American communities. There was a significant amount of racial and socioeconomic diversity among students at each of the academies. This is a key difference between this study and other studies of single-sex education, which have primarily been conducted in private or Catholic institutions.

Four of the sites served middle school students, and two sites served high school students. Only two sets of academies operated as self-contained schools, with the remaining four sets established as schools within a school. Thus, the extent to which each site was sex-segregated varied; students attending academies within a larger school had more opportunities for coed interactions during lunch and break periods than their peers at self-contained academies.

Five of the six districts decided to close the academies, not coincidentally at the end of the two-year funding period. In most cases, administrators initiated the closures in the face of strong student, faculty, and parent support for the academies. The demise of the Single-Gender Academies resulted from a lack of district-level support, an absence of a strong theory as to why schools were implementing single-sex education, and high turnover rates among faculty and staff (See chapter 7 of this volume).

METHODOLOGY

The recent interest in public single-sex education is notable, given the absence of consistent research findings. Indeed, the research conducted thus far reveals far more contradictions than patterns of commonalty (AAUW, 1998). Existing research on single-sex schooling tends to employ quantitative approaches, using student outcome measurements (standardized test scores, grades, career aspirations) to assess its effectiveness as compared to coeducational environments (Lee and Bryk, 1986; LePore and Warren, 1997). Although these measurements are important to consider, they provide little attention to the complexities of students' experiences.

Significantly, this chapter draws on the first comprehensive qualitative study of public single-gender schools (Datnow, Hubbard, and Woody, 2001), with a specific focus on student experiences (Woody, 2001). Qualitative data from over three hundred interviews with students, teachers, administrators, and parents conducted during three years of site visits, provides insight into adolescent articulations of gender within the context of single-sex public schooling. This research adds the necessary layers of complexity to existing quantitative data, offering insight into current assumptions of single-sex education.

In California, the establishment of "equal" academies for boys and girls at one school site provided a unique dimension for research. Most single-sex institutions serve only males or only females, thus limiting researchers' ability to consider the experiences of both girls and boys within the same school. The students in these six schools share physical spaces, curriculum and resources, and in many cases, the same teachers. Thus, this chapter draws on interviews with both boys and girls to provide a more complete understanding of student articulations of masculinity.

Teams of two or three researchers visited each site for a period of two to three days during each school year from 1997 to 2000, conducting interviews and classroom observations. Despite the closures, site visits continued through a third year, in an effort to explore students' transitions back into a coed environment. Following a semistructured interview protocol, the majority of students enrolled in the academies were interviewed individually or in same-sex focus groups of two to four students. Students were asked their reasons for enrollment in the academies, and their impressions of the impact of the academies on their social and academic experiences, as compared to coed experiences.

To a certain extent, the event of single-sex education allowed for further consideration of issues of gender, which might otherwise be a challenge in interviews with adolescents (Martin, 1996). Growing out of discussions of the single-sex environment, students offered insight into issues of gender and sexuality. Students articulated an awareness of societal expectations for boys' and girls' behavior, as well as an awareness of the complexities of gender as exhibited in their own lives. Both boys and girls were willing to reflect on issues of gender within the context of discussing their experiences in a single-sex environment.

All interviews were taped and transcribed, along with field notes from school and classroom observations. Using qualitative data analysis software (HyperResearch), transcripts were coded according to predetermined as well as emergent themes. Case reports were written for each site, in an effort to illuminate cross-site similarities and complexities. The themes discussed in this chapter are all the more significant given their salience across sites, representing a diversity of voices and contexts.

CURRENT DISCOURSES OF BOYHOOD AND MASCULINITY

California's single-gender academy experiment is situated within the context of shifting discourses on gender issues in education. In particular, there is growing interest in issues of boyhood and masculinity in both popular and academic arenas (Kimmel and Messner, 2000; Pollack, 2000). However, surprisingly little has been written about all-male secondary institutions; the literature that does exist focuses either on elite, private schools (Hawley, 1991; Ruhlman, 1996), or public academies geared toward African-American boys (Leake and Leake, 1992; Watson and Smitherman, 1996). This chapter draws from and contributes to research on single-sex education and gender issues in education, in an effort to illuminate the experiences of adolescent boys and constructions of masculinities in schools.

Within the scholarship on gender and education, a rich theoretical discussion of masculinities has emerged. Although recognizing the prevalence of a hegemonic masculinity in schools, theorists point to contradictions and complexities, reminding us that this is not the only form of masculinity, nor even the most common (Connell, 1995). Furthermore, masculinity is understood not as a fixed or innate concept, but as shaped through formal and informal school practices:

> Masculinities do not exist prior to social behavior, either as bodily states or as fixed personalities. Rather, masculinities come into existence as people act. They are accomplished in everyday conduct or organizational life, as configurations of social practice. (Connell, 1996, p. 208)

Haywood and Mac an Ghaill (1996), for example, describe the construction of "multiple masculinities" in schools, across relationships and institutional contexts. They locate "sites of masculinities" within school practices, including discipline, curriculum, and language among male peers.

The physical layout of elementary school classrooms, with segregated spaces like the doll corner, contributes to a construction of masculinity in opposition to femininity (Dyson, 1994; Paley, 1984). Play and sporting events provide opportunities for students to define and enact gender (Messner, 1990; Thorne, 1993). Curriculum and teaching styles are also sites of masculinity construction, including the privileging of math and science courses and a reliance on a competitive, hierarchical system of grading (Gilbert and Gilbert, 1998). The same gendered assumptions, which steer girls away from math and science courses, are influencing boys' participation in language arts courses (AAUW, 1998).[2] Just as they learned on the playground, students understand that certain academic pursuits are more appropriate for boys or girls.

Alongside academic studies of masculinity, several popular works have emerged, fueling discussions of a "crisis of boyhood" in the public discourse. Using similar voice-centered approaches to research on girls, psychologist Pollack relies on boys' voices to explore what he calls the "boy code," or "gender straightjacketing" in which "there is often only a very narrow band of acceptable male or masculine behavior" (2000, p. 19). Pollack's work is just one example of a body of literature, which has achieved significant popularity in the last few years (Biddulph, 1998; Gurian, 1997; Kindlon and Thompson, 1999). These books combine a psychological analysis of the adolescent male experience with advice for parents and educators.

Just as popular psychology books fueled the girls' movement of the last decade (Orenstein, 1994; Pipher, 1994), we are now seeing a focus on boys in newspapers, talk shows, and bestseller lists across the country. Yet, although this work has been effective in bringing boys' voices into the educational and popular arenas, the focus on individual and psychological perspectives often does not allow for a complex understanding of masculinity (Kimmel, 1999). In the end, we are left with incomplete caricatures of quiet girls and violent boys, essentialized notions of gender, which fail to acknowledge the diversity of experiences among boys or girls.

The result of this public awareness is something of a "moral panic," which Titus (2000) explains is in response to "a perceived threat to values or interests held sacred by society." In this case, a traditional, and many would argue, male-centered, approach to education has been threatened by recent efforts to improve the status of girls and women in schools (Kenway and Willis, 1998). In response to what Yates (1993) calls "girl-friendly schooling," including efforts to incorporate women's lives into the curriculum or to employ more inclusive pedagogies, some educators are now asking, "What about the boys?"

Embedded in such a question is the assumption that previously documented gender bias against girls has been eliminated and that boys are now actually being shortchanged. There is concern that the last decades' efforts to achieve gender equity have actually tipped the scales in favor of girls, and it is now boys who require special attention. Supporters of this argument point to decreasing college enrollments among young men, boys' lower test scores in reading and languages, and the predominance of boys in special education programs (Kleinfeld, 1998). The recent attention to boys has served to distort the issues of gender equity in schools by implying that either girls or boys are at risk, but not both.

One result of this backlash has been a renewed interest in all-male institutions as a means to restore boys' sense of self. The belief is that a cure for current social problems (e.g., violence, drugs, gang involvement, and truancy), which many boys (including those enrolled in the single-gender Academies) face, lies in a moral and culturally specific education (Grant-Thomas, 1996). Furthermore, single-sex education for boys is often conceived as an opportunity to restore traditional sex roles. African-American male academies in particular advocate "gender training," by men for men, to combat the prevalence of female-headed households. As the principal of a Detroit boys' academy explained, "Only a man can raise a man. A woman can raise a boy, but not a man" (quoted in Grant-Thomas, 1996, p. 13). Similarly, the creators of Milwaukee's African American Immersion schools proposed "gender socialization courses," which would "help students examine and establish personally and culturally appropriate notions of femininity and masculinity" (Leake and Leake, 1992).

Although the relative newness of most all-male African-American academies precludes the availability of conclusive, long-term research, early studies show positive benefits for students. Hudley's (1997) study of a middle school program for African-American boys found an increase in students' sense of academic competence as well as attendance. Positive outcomes may be attributed to rigorous curriculum, a safe classroom environment, and supportive teachers. Understandably, Governor Wilson hoped to achieve similar results with his Single-Gender Pilot Program. The danger, of course, is that such programs place an emphasis on individual change and do little to address the larger social structures in which those problems occur, namely, poverty and a lack of community support services (Noguera, 1997).

Embedded within efforts to "restore" boys' sense of self through single-sex education are assumptions about an innate masculinity. The belief in biological determinism, that the physical differences between boys and girls result in distinctly different behaviors, is heard most often in the remark, "boys will be boys."[3] Much of the current popular literature on boys echoes these essentialized notions of gender, setting up "male" as a static category. Authors write about "boy energy" (Kindlon and Thompson, 1999) or "boy biology and culture" (Gurian, 1997), which at once assumes an innateness and universality of boys' experiences. Single-sex schooling, in a sense, is grounded in a belief in boys' and girls' inherent (and different) qualities. Yet, as the following sections suggest, limited conceptions of masculinity do not provide a full representation of boys' experiences in schools.

CONSTRUCTING BOYS AS BAD: INSTITUTIONAL ASSUMPTIONS AND PRACTICES

The structure of the Single-Gender Academies, with separate spaces for boys and girls on the same campus, served to promote a way of thinking about gender that highlighted boys' and girls' differences. Differences between boys and girls were made paramount to any commonalties. The danger, of course, in a presumption of difference is twofold; first, it may imply inequality, as one group is compared against another; and second, it suggests a universality of experience within each group, ignoring intragroup complexities. Furthermore, as Levit (1999) warns, "The separation inevitably comes with a stigma. . . . Constructing separate schools and even creating separate classes not only implies, it explicitly states and physically embodies that the problem is the presence of the opposite sex" (1999, p. 517). In the case of the California Single-Gender academies, boys as a group were most often identified as the "problem" within a dichotomous framework of gender.

Among academy administrators, there was a general consensus that boys needed a strict disciplinary environment, a "boot camp" approach to education. Boys were seen as a disruption (distraction), a threat to girls' safety (sexual harassment), and generally in need of stricter discipline and stronger male role models. Indeed, Governor Wilson's original intent for the academies was to provide discipline for at-risk boys.[4] It was no coincidence that the "at-risk" boys targeted for the academies were primarily lower-class, African-American and Latin-American students. As Ferguson argues, "The modal category for African American boys is "at-risk." . . . The concept of "at-riskness" is central to a discourse about the contemporary crisis in urban schools in America that explains children's failure as largely the consequence of their attitudes and behaviors" (2000, p. 91). Within the Single-Gender Academies, boys' at-risk status was explained largely as a consequence of their "bad" behavior, rather than asking how issues of race and class in California's public schools contributed to these students' risk.

Assumptions about boys' bad behavior were enacted through disciplinary practices in the single-gender academies. Administrators at one school installed a metal detector at the boys' entrance to the academies, but did not require girls to pass through any security system at their entrance. Another campus included a "lock down" room where the overwhelming majority of "visitors" were boys. Indeed, both boys and girls agreed that boys were more likely to be punished, even in situations where a girl and a boy were equally involved. In her study of disciplinary practices in public schools, Ferguson

(2000) found a similar pattern of males, and African-American males in particular, being punished disproportionately. Given the racial and socioeconomic diversity throughout the academies, it is impossible to ignore the influence of race and class on gendered disciplinary practices. The principal of one set of academies advocated an "academic boot camp" for the boys, whom he described as "at-risk" in part because of their upbringing in lower income, single-parent homes with few male role models.

> I don't want to sound mean, but they need to be brought to the point where they're kind of reduced down to the lowest level. And it maybe sounds like boot camp or something like that. . . . And then just brought down to that and then rebuilt back up by means of accomplishments. As simple as they may be. You know okay now you've got to run the mile today. Now you're going to do this. And then now you're going to do this.

A strong classroom management style, enforced through physical discipline if necessary and adult male role models, was seen as most effective for the lower income, racially diverse population of boys at this academy. Masculinity as constructed within the single-gender academies was influenced not only by adults' assumptions of gender, but of race and class as well.

Boys' apparent need for discipline was also reflected in differential teaching styles for girls and boys in the academies. Many teachers felt their role in the boys' academy included discipline:

> *ST*: Yeah, Mr. Sanders said to my mom, we need to show those academy boys how things work here, he said that to my mom on the phone.
>
> *I*: Really, what does he mean, show them how it works?
>
> *ST*: By picking on them and giving them detentions for like un-legitimate reasons.

Although boys certainly complained about the increased authoritarianism of the academies, they also embraced it as a necessary step to becoming a man:

> *ST*: Because he's harder on us. As a guy he said if we're going to be men we've got to be treated like men.
>
> *I*: What does that mean? Can you explain that to me?
>
> *ST*: He says like when he treats us bad he's like you know I treat you guys like you guys are my age. And then he says . . .
>
> *ST*: He says, "I hate doing this but if whatever it takes to get you guys in line. Then that's just what it's going to be."

Stricter classroom practices were seen as an unpleasant, but necessary step in their development of a masculine identity. Haywood and Mac an Ghaill note the predominance of discipline as a teaching method for boys. In reviewing studies of boys' schools in Australia, they find that "coercive methods used in the classroom represent 'good' teaching. Physical coercion through shaking, cuffing and pushing were seen as acceptable everyday forms of discipline. This discipline complemented the ethos of a 'school for boys and men'" (1996, p. 54). Similarly, in the single-gender academies, disciplinary practices included physical punishment:

ST: Because if you mess up they're really rough on you.

I: They're really rough? What do they do? What kind of things?

ST: They make you run laps. They make you do a lot of pushups and all other kinds of hard exercises.

It is through a disciplinary, and at times physical approach to teaching, Haywood and Mac an Ghaill argue, that hegemonic masculinity is reinforced. The presumption is that boys can, and indeed should be able to tolerate a stricter, more direct approach.

Discipline was embedded within the predominant theory of teaching boys in the single-gender Academies, which in turn, led to a process of "masculinity formation" (Connell, 1996). Academy educators often espoused a belief that the male students needed more discipline in "becoming a man." Such beliefs are in line with recent concerns about the "feminization" of teaching (and subsequent rationales for all-male academies), including the lack of male role models to instill a masculinity ideology in boys (Grant-Thomas, 1996). One academy in particular advocated a code of conduct for gendered relations based on discipline. When a "lady" entered the classroom, such as one of the researchers on this project, the teacher insisted that his students stand and formally greet her. Within such efforts to instill respect were assumptions about gender; women were presented as deserving of a traditional, "genteel" respect, through such actions as opening the door or using a formal address.

Although the boys were capable of enacting this gendered discipline, it did little to influence their daily behaviors and attitudes toward girls and women. Girls at this academy were most likely to express fears and frustration about persistent sexual harassment from their male peers. Likewise, as researchers, we experienced discomfort and disrespect, including foul language and sexual innuendos, in interviews with boys at this school that were never experienced anywhere else throughout the project. If anything, the strict discipline at this school instilled a strong sense of male privilege and authority. Men were either positioned as the protector and provider or as the predator, and women were either in need of assistance or in a position of sexual objectification.

Teachers in the girls' academies were equally involved in the construction of boys as "bad," and as sexual predators. Girls consistently heard negative messages about boys, often presented as a warning: "Miss Hillman really thinks just stay away from boys, they're bad. She used to say that like every week. Stay away from boys." Embedded in such warnings are assumptions about boys' (and girls') sexuality. Boys were presented as aggressive, as physical and psychological predators; girls, in turn, were seen as victims in need of protection. Certainly, the reality of sexual harassment in many girls' lives justified concerns about boys. Yet stereotypes of bad boys and vulnerable girls did not allow for variability among boys or among girls. Furthermore, such stereotypes imply that boys' bad behavior is an inherent aspect of masculinity, grounded in an essentialized theory of gender. Interestingly, teachers interpreted their negative messages about boys not as harmful to boys, but as empowering for girls. As this teacher explained:

I said, "How many of the relationships that you've seen—the woman is on welfare and the boyfriends trying to do something, he gives her two or three babies and he takes off?" I said, "is that what you want to be?" So we talked about being the dog-catcher. Don't let them run you. You run them. And so that's a skill that I've given them.

Unfortunately, messages of empowerment for girls came at the expense of boys. Essentialized notions of gender allowed for a limited construction of masculinity, where boys were portrayed as sexually single-minded and adversaries in relationships.

STUDENTS REINFORCING PERCEPTIONS OF BOYS AS BAD

Clearly, the institutional policies and teaching practices of the single-gender Academies grew out of a definition of boys as "bad," or problem students. It is important to consider, then, how boys and girls internalized or challenged such a definition of boys and masculinity. Overwhelmingly, students throughout all academies reiterated institutional assumptions about boys' "bad" behavior and need for discipline. Both boys and girls recognized that the single-gender Academies were created with the hope that segregated education would reduce incidents of disruption in the classroom. More importantly, they were acutely aware that boys were seen as the primary cause of those disruptions. Indeed, the pervading sense that boys were "trouble" served as a primary marker for defining masculinity in the academies. The physical design of a boys' and girls' academy on the same campus provided teachers with the opportunity to compare boys and girls. More often than not, the resulting comparisons presented boys in a negative light. The general consensus among students was that teachers were "kind of like annoyed by the boys, I think."

For boys, the expectation of bad behavior became an attribute to claim as part of a masculine identity. Students noted how boys responded to getting in trouble in the classroom with such comments as, "Ooh. I'm the man." In describing his all-male classroom, this boy noted, "Like being in a classroom full of guys it's just like—I don't know it's like—it would be like a teacher's nightmare, you can ask the teachers." With a tinge of pride in his voice, he recognized that a group of boys pose a menace to teachers. As Connell argues, boys' involvement in violence and disciplinary problems can be explained "not because they are driven to it by raging hormones, but in order to acquire or defend prestige, to mark difference, and to gain pleasure" (1996, p. 220). Institutional assumptions about boys' need for discipline perpetuated a definition of masculinity as "bad." Many boys, in turn, embraced the reputation of "problem student" as a sign of their masculinity.

Girls, for the most part, reiterated adults' opinions of boys as troublesome. When asked to tell us about boys, girls consistently made comments such as, "boys are bad," or "boys are just [yuck]." Boys were described as immature, irresponsible, "savage." Girls' opinions of boys were influenced by the messages and warnings heard from teachers, as well as their own experiences of boys in coed settings. For example, girls in the academies remembered how boys would behave in coed classrooms:

ST: The boys are louder. They're more rowdier.

ST: They were just immature.

Girls complained about how boys presented a constant interruption in coed classrooms, often capturing the teacher's attention with disruptive behavior. In terms of academic participation, girls enjoyed fewer distractions from boys in the all-girl classrooms (Datnow, Hubbard, and Woody, 2001). Interestingly, the single-sex classroom also provided a unique opportunity for girls to form opinions about boys based on their female peers' experiences. The increased instances of "girl talk" allowed girls to confirm assumptions that boys were bad:

I: Well, what do you think of the guys here?

ST: Immature.

ST: They're all dogs.

ST: Sloppy.

ST: Dumb, stupid.

I: Have you always thought that about guys? No, so ok, and when have you learned, how have you learned more about guys?

ST: Talking about the experiences we have with boys.

Discussions among girls mirrored the messages from teachers; these girls learned that boys are "dogs" from their teachers as well as by sharing mutual experiences. Girl talk in the single-sex classrooms included stories of sisters and cousins who had been mistreated by boyfriends. They were all too familiar, for example, with boys who shirked responsibility when a girl was pregnant:

I: What happens to the boys? I mean, after the girls get pregnant where are the boys?

ST: They get lost.

I: Why?

ST: . . . 'cause they don't want responsibility.

ST: The only thing they want to do is have sex and [inaudible] that's all they want.

The negative assumptions of boys put forth by teachers and administrators were confirmed in girls' own lived experiences. Again, the structure of single-sex classrooms had direct implications for students' articulations of a dichotomous theory of gender. Within the context of segregated academies, it became easy for girls to define boys as a uniform "other." Armed with warnings from teachers and shared negative experiences with boys, girls bonded as a group in opposition to boys. With fewer daily interactions, boys' individual differences were lost under the category of gender as a singular marker of identity.

COMPLICATING MASCULINITIES WITHIN THE SINGLE-GENDER ACADEMIES

Separating girls and boys heightened students' sense of boys as a unified group in opposition to girls, which in turn allowed for generalizations about boys. Yet at the same time, students raised complexity and contradictions in their definitions of masculinity. It is important to note, for example, that girls' perceptions of boys were not all negative. Despite their complaints about boys, girls also recognized positive attributes in their male peers. Going to school in sex-segregated environments made them realize how much they appreciated boys' unique ability to "make you laugh." Although they may have enjoyed fewer interruptions in the single-sex classrooms, girls missed boys' tendencies to liven up a situation, "I think guys—they're a lot more—like if they were to say something it would turn into a joke. They'd laugh about it." Similarly, girls recognized that not all boys were "bad." Many girls rejected assumptions about boys being trouble, citing examples of friendships with boys outside of school or supportive relationships with brothers. Although girls were quick to agree to a collective definition of boys as bad, they raised complexities and contradictions when discussing individual boys.

Boys, too, articulated similar complexities in their discussions of masculinity within the single-gender Academies. Although the segregated academies often led to generalizations in students' perceptions of the other gender, the single-sex environment had the opposite effect on students' perceptions of same-sex peers. Within the boys' classes, the single-sex organization actually allowed for an increased recognition of intragender differences. Without girls in the classroom, boys saw themselves beyond simply a uniform group in opposition to girls. Instead, distinctions among boys were heightened, as they began to appreciate that not all boys are the same:

> ST: They try to say that all guys are a certain way and you might not be or whatever.

> ST: Yeah. There's a lot of guys that are a lot more feminine than regular guys. Like there's some kids that I see walk around and talk to girls and like they kind of like bounce around kind of like a girl would. And they're a lot more shy or something like a girl.

In response to the institutional categorization of boys as a uniform group (often with negative associations), these boys insisted on a more complex understanding of masculinity. Gender, once a useful category of social organization in coed situations, was now replaced by more subtle descriptors, such as "rowdy" or "shy" or "big," to mark distinctions among peers in the single-sex classroom.

In some ways, the size and intensity of the academies, with small groups of students together for the entire day, allowed for a loosening of gendered restrictions among boys. The close bonds forged in the single-sex classes brought a greater tolerance of those boys who did not fit the norms of masculinity:

> I: So you think single-gender is more comfortable for guys who are not - who don't act like a "guy" guy?

> ST: Well kind of.

> ST: Because if there's a bunch of guys in the class you can act the way you want really. Because last year it was like that because we stayed together for so long. We stayed together for so long we knew what people were like. Which people were rowdy and which people were quiet.

The intimacy of the single-sex classrooms allowed students to develop a knowledge and understanding of one another that moved beyond stereotypical expectations of how boys should act.

Similarly, the all-boys classrooms provided some relief from boys' efforts to "act hard" in front of girls:

> ST: In a way it's easier just to be with a guy cause you don't have to impress the girl. All the time guys like in football have to try their hardest and I'm getting hurt try-

ing to impress the girl and not look like a moron. But instead now that girls aren't watching you can do whatever you want and not have to.

ST: Me neither.

ST: I agree with him. You don't have to impress the girls or show off but at recess you show off.

ST: Yeah. You show your stuff.

With less pressure to "impress the girls," boys noted the positive impact of the single-sex environment on their academic performance:

I: Do you guys feel you learn more without girls in the class?

ST: Yeah cause we're not trying to be macho macho kind of guys.

Many boys spoke of trying to hide their intelligence in a coed classroom, for fear of being labeled a "nerd" or a "school boy." As one boy explained, "If you want to be known as a popular dude [in the coed classroom] you don't do your homework. You get bad grades." The underlying assumption was that boys who did well academically were less masculine. Without girls in the classroom, boys were less likely to hide intelligence in an effort to assert a hegemonic masculinity.

NEGOTIATING THE RULES OF MASCULINITY: "LIKE THEY SHOULD ACT LIKE BOYS, LIKE BE INTO SPORTS."

Despite certain freedoms within the context of the single-sex classrooms, students ultimately maintained strict rules for the expression of masculinity. Acceptance of individual differences among boys came with a set of limitations; boys were still expected to behave within the confines of "appropriate" masculinity. Indeed, both boys and girls agreed that girls had fewer restrictions than boys in their expressions of gender identity. They essentially believed that girls could do anything, and most importantly, anything that boys did. Boys, however, were not equally free to blur the lines of masculinity and femininity, as this girl explained:

I: So you want to be able to do anything but you don't want the boys to be able to do anything they want?

ST: Uh huh. Well, they can do anything, it's just that some things they should leave alone, like girl things. Don't ask me what those things are because I don't know. But some things boys shouldn't do because they're for girls.

Student definitions of appropriate gendered behavior reflected clear restrictions for boys, most notably, that they could not act like girls:

I: Isn't there more than one way for a guy to act? Or are you saying there's just one way that all guys have to act?

ST: Oh no. There's more than one way, but not the girl way.

Times when boys did do "girl things" were either kept secret or justified as just "playing around." When boys spoke of playing with their sisters' dolls, for example, they insisted that it was "not for real." During a conversation about playing with dolls, one boy affirmed his masculinity by stating, "I play with dolls, but then I decapitate them." Similarly, this boy who took ballet made sure to distinguish himself from the "kind of feminine" boys who actually wanted to be there:

> Yeah. I took ballet actually. I took it because I used to play basketball and I had bad balance. So I signed up for ballet. I took it for three months. And when I was there, there were a few other guys there that weren't as manly as I was. They were kind of feminine. But that's because they liked to do ballet. I took it because I was trying to—I didn't really like to do that but I needed to get better balance. Because I'd always trip and fall and stuff like that.

Participation in what was perceived to be a feminine activity was risky for boys. If they were unable to offer a reasonable justification, then the activity was kept secret, as this girl told us, "Yeah, actually, I have a lot of [boy] friends that are in ballet with me, but, I mean, they keep it a very well known secret. Very big secret."

Students often offered the examples of boys doing ballet and girls playing football to illustrate the different rules of masculinity and femininity. They unequivocally agreed that girls be allowed to participate in a traditionally male sport. Yet, when asked whether boys should be able to take ballet, both boys and girls typically responded with nervous laughter:

> *I*: Ok, so now do you think that women should be able to do these things that the men do?
>
> *ST*: Do what the men do, yes, duh!
>
> *ST*: Yes, I think there's . . . like football, they should have a football . . . like a women's football team . . .
>
> *I*: But now what if this, what if this . . . let's have this scenario. What if Sandra comes in to school and she's got football gear on, and what if Hector, whoever, some boy, comes in with his dance costume on . . .
>
> *ST*: (Laughter) a ballerina.
>
> *I*: Why do you guys laugh at that?
>
> *ST*: We're just imagining him in his tights (laughter). It's so funny because boys [inaudible].
>
> *ST*: 'Cause they look strange.

I: Because it's different, it's out of the ordinary?

ST: Yeah, and 'cause it's . . .

ST: Because it look like . . . it looks different.

The idea of a girl breaking stereotypes of femininity was far less disturbing than a boy acting outside the norms of masculinity. Within the academies, the original intentions to provide discipline for boys and empowerment for girls had repercussions for students' definitions of masculinity and femininity. As we heard in their discussions of career goals, for example, girls were well-versed in the notion that they could "do anything." Yet boys expressed stricter expectations to be strong and support a family, upheld in part by institutional messages that boys should be more disciplined. Institutional efforts to control boys' behavior mirrored students' own efforts to enforce the rules of masculinity.

MASCULINITY AS CONTEXTUAL PERFORMANCE
Despite a lessening of restrictions in certain contexts, for the most part, students in the single-gendera academies consistently reinforced a hegemonic masculinity. Boys understood that masculinity, in a sense, was a performance, and more importantly, a role that was not easily challenged yet might shift according to context. A group of boys told us, "it's kind of like everyone's kind of playing a part. But like it's not really the way they want to act." Boys were well aware of societal expectations to perform a certain masculinity: "Because when a guy grows up that's how he thinks a man should act. So he's going to act that way. He's going to act strong and big and tough."

Significantly, boys felt pressures to "act" among both girls and boys, albeit in different ways:

I: Why go along with it?

ST: Put on a show.

I: For who?

ST: For the girls. For the other guys.

Boys generally noted more restrictions on their gendered behaviors around other boys: "You can act as feminine as you want but you just don't want to show it around other guys." In their analysis of masculinities in schools, Haywood and Mac an Ghaill (1996) write, "Male peer group networks are one of the most oppressive arenas for the production and regulation of masculinities. . . . Language can express such definitions of appropriate masculinities which in effect regulate and actively police male behavior" (1996, pp. 54–55). Our interviews with boys revealed a similar use of language in constraining nontraditional expressions of masculinity. Boys set the rules of masculinity through the use of insults such as "sissy" or "fag" to describe peers who did not fit their norm of boyhood. Crossing the lines of gender, as in "acting like a girl," or sexuality were considered suspect. Students used homophobic teasing as a means to enforce the rules of masculinity and femininity. Those students who did not meet the norms of gender were labeled "gay" (Woody, 2001).

For many boys, relationships with girls provided a relief from the pressures to fulfill traditional expectations of masculinity: "I admit it. I've cried in front of my girlfriend. But I wouldn't cry in front of a bunch of guys." Yet that freedom, which many boys found in individual relationships with girls, did not necessarily translate into group relations. In group situations, boys persisted in enacting hegemonic masculinities around girls:

> *ST*: When you're around girls you . . .
>
> *ST*: Some like to like act like they're hard, they try and act hard, like . . . like if there's girls right here . . . like, then just say, I'll try to act hard and try to get him to like . . .
>
> *ST*: We'd just start arguing and all that.
>
> *ST*: Trying to make him look like he's bad, like . . . what do you call it.
>
> *ST*: Yeah, trying to act all hard.

Boys understood masculinity as a context-dependent performance. The ability to challenge a hegemonic masculinity was limited to instances of intimate relations, whether in the tight-knit group of the single-sex classrooms or in relationships with individual girls. Outside such contexts, the pressures of peer groups served to enforce traditional notions of gender. Connell (1996) writes of the "collective dimension of masculinity," explaining:

> The peer groups, not individuals, are the bearers of gender definitions. This is presumably the explanation for a familiar observation by parents and teachers, that boys who create trouble in a group by aggression, disruption, and harassment, that is, an exaggerated performance of hegemonic masculinity, can be cooperative and peaceable on their own (1996, p. 220).

Students confirmed the group dynamic of masculinity, with girls often complaining about the tendency for an otherwise "nice" boy to "act hard" when in a group of his male peers.

Ironically, boys recognized that girls did not necessarily want boys to play the part of the dominant male:

> *I*: Okay, but go back to the idea of playing the game thing right? So guys are trying to act like guys to impress who?
>
> *ST*: Girls.

ST: Anybody that they think they should impress.

I: I mean do you really think that girls really go for big, loud—macho?

ST: I don't think so.

I: No?

ST: Not really.

I: So what's all this posturing going on?

ST: I don't know.

ST: It's probably immaturity. They need to mature a little more probably.

Yet despite their acknowledgment of its absurdity, boys continued to play the "game," in part because they felt that their ability to move beyond the restrictions of masculinity could only go so far:

I: What kind of guys do you think girls are interested in?

ST: Guys that aren't assholes.

ST: Sentimental.

ST: Probably honest.

ST: Open.

ST: And have some kind of way of showing yourself that you're yourself. You're the kind of person—but at the same time the girl's going to see that is a man so he has to have some kind of ground—some kind of like—some kind of way of showing that he is a man. That he has like a strong [?] or something like that.

I: So you can be honest and open and sensitive but there still has to be some level of—?

ST: Macho-ness.

ST: Yeah. To show that yes I am a man.

ST: Yeah. Not to show that you're weak and everything.

These boys reveal the complexities and contradictions within their performance of masculinity. On the one hand, they believed that girls welcome a show of nontraditional masculinity ("sentimental . . . a way showing yourself"). Yet, on the other hand, boys felt that girls would still want some confirmation of hegemonic masculinity, an enactment of strength and "macho-ness." Indeed, girls held contradictory expectations for boys; on the one hand, they complained about boys' immaturity and "tough guy" posturing, yet they also wanted a boy who would buy them dinner and "show that yes I am a man." When asked, for example, to describe her ideal boyfriend, this girl replied, "He'd have to be nice, but then not a wimp. He'd have to be nice to me, but then kind of gangsterish. I don't know, it's crazy." Any efforts to challenge expectations of masculinity were constrained by students' adherence to a strict set of rules for boys' behavior and expression.

ACKNOWLEDGING PRIVILEGES OF MASCULINITY

Among students in the single-gender academies, gender was seen as a source of more restrictions for boys than for girls. In other words, being a boy carried with it a stricter set of rules in terms of appropriate behavior. Within the context of the single-sex classroom, girls were told that they could do or be anything, following efforts to empower girls. Across the hallways, the all-boys' classrooms employed a pedagogy of discipline, following efforts to restrict boys' behavior, and in turn, gendered expression. It is important to note, however, that the rules and limitations of gender play out very differently in girls' and boys' lives.

The restrictions boys face do not necessarily limit their opportunities; likewise, girls' apparent freedom of expression does not necessarily translate into limitless opportunities. As Mills reminds us, "The important thing here though is that whilst most men experience oppression of some form or another, they do not experience it because they are men, but because they are particular types of men" (2000, p. 232). A masculine identity is less likely to result in a loss of privilege for men; more likely, it is an identity such as race or socioeconomic class, which may restrict men's opportunities. For example, Weis heard an articulation of privilege among working-class boys in their discussions of domestic issues, specifically in their presumption of male-dominated households. Although the sense of power in relations with girls and women is offset by "the real loss of privilege in the new economy" (1993, p. 258), nonetheless, by virtue of their masculine identity, working class boys and men maintain certain privileges over women. Any "oppression" that working-class men experience comes as a result of their economic status, not so much because of their gendered position. Likewise, many boys are limited in the sense that they do not meet the criteria of a hegemonic masculinity, often because of locations of race or class, or as the single-gender Academy students noted, an inability to fit the norms of physicality, academic performance, or sexuality.

Ultimately, boys' experiences in the single-gender Academies need to be understood amid the complex interplay of limited definitions of masculinity and the inevitable privileges of being a boy. Our interviews with students revealed an awareness of what McIntosh (1988) calls the "invisible system of male privilege." For example, when asked whether they would prefer to be a boy or girl in this world, without hesitation, boys chose to remain a boy, whereas girls weighed both options, aware that their current status was not ideal. Students recognized that being a boy carried greater advantages:

ST: I just say I'd rather be a guy. A guy in the world right now. I think a guy is a lot more—a lot more—not a lot more advantage than a girl does in the world right now but he probably has some sort of advantage than a girl does.

ST: Yeah.

ST: It shouldn't be. It's not the right way but that's the way it is.

Within their immediate lives, students saw how the physical differences between boys and girls led to differences in privilege. Physicality was seen as a marker of masculinity, and in turn, a source of power. For example, students recognized how boys' presumed physical strength and ability to defend themselves translated into greater personal freedoms, as this girl explains:

ST: Like my brother . . . like he can go out more and he's gonna have less chances of being, you know, endangered, but if I'm the same age as he is, I don't think I'll have the opportunity because like, oh well, you know, you might get raped or something 'cause, you know, you're our teenage girl. And . . . well, I tell them that I'm not gonna go anywhere by myself, I'm gonna go in big groups, but like, you know, it still could happen.

I: So they're very much more protective?

ST: Yeah, and they're more protective of me having a boyfriend, you know, I might get pregnant or something. But my brother, since he's a guy, he can't get pregnant, so he's allowed to have a girlfriend.

Both girls and boys were aware of the power associated with boys' physical strength, which allows them to pass through the world with fewer fears of violence. This awareness came in part from messages heard from teachers in the single-gender academies. In several cases, teachers used the single-sex classrooms to discuss issues of gender, such as sexual harassment or the risks of intimate relationships. More often than not, students came away from discussions about sexual violence with the understanding that girls, not boys, were at risk of being victims:

I: And how about boys . . . boys don't need protection from anything?

ST: I think it's easier to hit a girl because she's more like . . . she's not weaker, but like I guess she's just scared . . . 'cause mostly guys who take girls in cars, or they grab her and they're stronger than the girls, so it's harder to get away, but boys, some boys can be stronger and . . .

I: So where do you all hear about all this?

ST: Like in school they show the news about it, about, yeah, how to get away and what to do.

I: And those videos are always just about girls getting away?

ST: And boys, but most of the time they show these small boys, or like, you know, ten-year-olds, not really teenagers.

ST: Most of the kidnappers are men, so they show kind of like . . . men mostly . . . most of the men go after a girl, I've been hearing a lot about that on the news, and like if they go after a boy they [inaudible] small boys, so that the boys don't have to get away.

The girls in the preceding understood that the physical strength of adolescent boys and men precluded them from being victims. Instead, men were seen in a position of power, as the primary perpetrators of violence. Only younger boys or boys who did not fit the masculine norm of physicality (i.e., "small boys") were at risk of violence. In her study of boys' and girls' experiences of puberty, Martin (1996) found the majority of boys interviewed, across race and class, enjoyed a sense of agency and pride in their bodies, unlike the insecurity and shame often heard from girls (Brooks-Gunn and Petersen, 1983). For boys in particular, the effects of puberty bring increased status. Indeed, boys at the single-gender Academies recognized that their taller, more muscular peers were less likely to be teased and more likely to attract girls.

Just as Martin documents boys' sense of power during puberty, academy students recognized the privilege associated with boys' physical maturation. Although in reality, not all boys benefit from the experience of puberty, they may benefit from the presumption of power associated with becoming a man. The restrictions boys face in their gendered expressions may not be seen as a source of limited opportunity, but instead as a source of power. With the enactment of hegemonic masculinity comes privilege, thus making it all the more risky for boys to challenge traditional notions of gender.

Issues of privilege are important to consider as educators turn their attention to the experiences of boys in schools. The recent focus on boys and masculinity can offer significant contributions to the study of gender and education. However, asking the popular question, "What about the boys?" is an all-too-simplistic approach. The issue at stake is not whether boys or girls are more shortchanged by current gendered practices and assumptions in schools. Indeed, this approach relies on a limited, dichotomous view of gender, failing to consider the relational aspects of masculinity and femininity. We need to consider the experiences of both girls and boys simultaneously and in relation to each other. The challenge is not a question of boys versus girls, or even how to make schools friendly to boys and/or girls. Instead, we need to consider what we mean by "boys' needs" or "girls' needs" and ask which boys or which girls are included. As this chapter has done, we need to consider the use of gender as a category of identity, including the assumptions and definitions of masculinity and femininity that inform institutional practices and individual relations.

CONCLUSION

In the case of the single-gender academies, the goal of segregated schooling was to meet "the differing needs and learning styles of boys as a group and girls as a group" (CA Education Code 58521). Subsequent classroom practices and peer relations were informed by the presumption of boys' need for discipline. Administrators and teachers employed a stricter approach to security and classroom management for boys. Students, in turn, understood that boys were typically the troublemakers in both academic and social contexts. Institutional assumptions about boys' need for discipline went largely unchallenged in classroom discussions and practices. Likewise, both girls and boys reinforced a collective definition of masculinity grounded in "bad" behavior.

Within certain contexts of the academies, however, students did articulate an awareness of complexities among boys. Advocates of single-sex education argue that the segregated environment allows for a loosening of restrictions on gendered behavior (Streitmatter, 1999). Boys, for example, expressed a greater appreciation of intragroup differences as a result of the close bonds forged in their smaller, single-sex classes, recognizing that not all boys act the same. Yet, despite certain freedoms in the all-boys classrooms, students continued to uphold hegemonic notions of masculinity. Ultimately, separating boys and girls did little to challenge students' beliefs about how boys should act.

Students articulated limited definitions of masculinity, with few opportunities to challenge traditional gender expectations. The structure of the single-gender Academies, with students organized first and foremost by gender, was grounded in simplistic notions of masculinity and femininity. By separating girls and boys, gender became the primary marker of identity. Teachers and students were forced to think of boys as a singular group and girls as a singular group, homogenous and different from the other. Within the segregated school structure, any individual contradictions or complexities among boys or girls were lost under a dichotomous theory of gender.

Students recognized the limitations of gendered expression, particularly for boys. In many instances, students struggled to advocate for a loosening of restrictions in the face of pressures to uphold a hegemonic masculinity. Yet despite an awareness of constraints, both girls and boys recognized the inevitable privileges that came with maintaining a traditional masculine identity, with continuing to put on the "show."

Students remained caught in the dualistic framework of gender put forth by the academies, seeing limited opportunities for the expression of a masculine identity. Indeed, without a more complex model of gender available to them, embedded within institutional assumptions and practices, it is unlikely that students would risk challenging traditional notions of masculinity.

NOTES

1. Legal restrictions to single-sex education in the public sector are largely based on Title IX. The law states: "No person in the U.S. shall, on the basis of sex, be excluded from participation in, be denied the benefits of, or be subjected to discrimination under any education program or activity receiving Federal financial assistance."

2. The last decades' work on girls focused heavily on the lack of girls and women in advanced science and math courses, as well as in science and technology-related careers. It is significant, then, that the focus has shifted to examine boys' lower enrollments and test scores in reading classes. The concern is that boys will be shortchanged in a new economy that privileges communication skills.

3. The influence of biology versus society on the construction of masculinity is an ongoing debate in both popular and academic discussions. Certainly, boys' physical characteristics play a role in the formation of gendered identity (Martin, 1996). Yet, a singularly biological assessment of masculinity provides an incomplete analysis of boys' behavior and experiences.

4. In his 1996 "State of the State" address, Wilson proposed all-male academies as magnet schools for at-risk boys and all-female schools focused on math and science. Legal advisors quickly recognized that differential single-sex offerings would violate Title IX legislation, and the academies were reconceived as identical in purpose and resources. However, initial assumptions about boys needing discipline and girls needing educational empowerment pervaded practices in the single-gender academies.

REFERENCES

American Association of University Women (AAUW). (1998). *Gender Gaps: Where Schools Still Fail Our Children*. Washington, D.C.

Biddulph, S. (1998). *Raising Boys*. Berkeley, CA: Celestial Arts.

Brooks-Gunn, J., and Petersen, A. (1983). *Girls at Puberty: Biological and Psychosocial Perspectives*. New York: Plenum Press.

Connell, R. W. (1995). *Masculinities*. St. Leonards, NSW, Australia: Allen and Unwin.

Connell, R. W. (1996). "Teaching the Boys: New Research on Masculinity, and Gender Strategies for Schools." *Teachers College Record* 98 (2): 206–235.

Datnow, A., Hubbard, L., and Woody, E. L. (2001). *Assumptions and Realities of California's Single-Gender Public Schools*. Final Report submitted to the Ford and Spencer Foundations.

Dyson, A. H. (1994). "The Ninjas, the X-Men, and the Ladies: Playing with Power and Identity in an Urban Primary School." *Teachers College Record 96*: 219–239.

Ferguson, A. A. (2000). *Bad Boys: Public Schools in the Making of Black Masculinity*. Ann Arbor: University of Michigan Press.

Gilbert, R., and Gilbert, P. (1998). *Masculinity Goes to School*. London: Routledge.

Grant-Thomas, A. (1996). "Male Oriented Black Academies and the Politics of Gender." Unpublished paper.

Gurian, M. (1997). *The Wonder of Boys*. New York: Putnam.

Hawley, R. (1991). "About Boys' Schools: A Progressive Case for an Ancient Form." *Teachers College Record 92* (3): 433–444.

Haywood, C., and Mac an Ghaill, M. (1996). "Schooling Masculinities." In M. Mac an Ghaill (ed.). *Understanding Masculinities: Social Relations and Cultural Arenas*. Buckingham, UK: Open University Press.

Hudley, C. (1997). "Issues of Race and Gender in the Educational Achievement of African American Children." In B. Bank and P. Hall (eds.), *Gender, Equity, and Schooling: Policy and Practice*. New York: Garland Publishing, 113–133.

Kenway, J., and Willis, S. (1998). *Answering Back: Girls, Boys, and Feminism in Schools*. New York: Routledge.

Kimmel, M., (October/November 1999). "What Are Little Boys Made Of?" *Ms.*

Kimmel, M., and Messner, M. (2000). *Men's Lives*. Boston: Allyn and Bacon.

Kindlon, D., and Thompson, M. (1999). *Raising Cain: Protecting the Emotional Life of Boys*. New York: Ballantine Books.

Kleinfeld, J., (1998). *The Myth that Schools Shortchange Girls: Social Science in the Service of Deception*. Washington, D.C.: The Women's Freedom Network.

Leake, D., and Leake, B. (1992). "Islands of Hope: Milwaukee's African American Immersion Schools." *Journal of Negro Education 61* (1): 24–29.

Lee, V., and Bryk, A. S. (1986). "Effects of single-sex schools on student achievement and attitudes." *Journal of Educational Psychology*, 78, 381–395.

LePore, P. C., and Warren, J. R. (1997). "A Comparison of Single-Sex and Coeducational Catholic Secondary Schooling: Evidence from the National Educational Longitudinal Study of 1988." *American Educational Research Journal 34*(3): 485–511.

Levit, N. (1999). "Separating Equals: Educational Research and the Long-Term Consequences of Sex Segregation." *George Washington Law Review* 67: 451–526.

Mael, F. (1998). "Single Sex and Coeducational Schooling: Relationships to Socioemotional and Academic Development." *Review of Educational Research*, 68: 101–129.

Martin, K. (1996). "Puberty, Sexuality, and the Self: Boys and Girls at Adolescence." New York: Routledge.

McIntosh, P. (1988). "White Privilege and Male Privilege: A Personal Account of Coming to See Correspondences through Work in Women's Studies." Wellesley College Center for Research on Women, Working Paper No. 189.

Messner, M. (1990). "Boyhood, Organized Sports, and the Construction of Masculinities." *Journal of Contemporary Ethnography* 18 (4): 416–444.

Mills, M. (2000). "Issues in Implementing Boys' Programme in schools: Male Teachers and Empowerment." *Gender and Education* 12 (2): 221–238.

Noguera, P. (1997). "Reconsidering the 'Crisis' of the Black Male in America." *Social Justice* 24 (2): 147–164.

Orenstein, P. (1994). *School Girls: Young Women, Self-Esteem, and the Confidence Gap*. New York: Doubleday.

Paley, V. (1984). *Boys and Girls: Superheroes in the Doll Corner*. Chicago: University of Chicago Press.

Pipher, M. (1994). *Reviving Ophelia: Saving the Selves of Adolescent Girls*. New York: Putnam.

Pollack, W. (2000). *Real Boys' Voices*. New York: Random House.

Ruhlman, M. (1996). *Boys Themselves: A Return to Single-Sex Education*. New York: Henry Holt and Company.

Streitmatter, J. L. (1999). *For Girls Only: Making a Case for Single-Sex Schooling*. Albany, NY: SUNY Press.

Thorne, B. (1993). *Gender Play: Girls and Boys in School*. Brunswick, NJ: Rutgers University Press.

Titus, J. (2000). "Boy Trouble: Underachievement, Moral Panic, and the Social Order." Paper presented at the Annual Meeting of the American Educational Research Association, New Orleans.

Watson, C., and Smitherman, G. (1996). *Educating African American Males: Detroit's Malcolm X Academy*. Chicago: Third World Press.

Weis, L. (1993). "White Male Working-Class Youth: An Exploration of Relative Privilege and Loss." In L. Weis, and M. Fine (Eds.). *Beyond Silenced Voices: Class, Race, and Gender in United States Schools*. Albany, NY: SUNY Press.

Woody, E .L. (2001). "Public School Reform: Student experiences in California Single-Gender Academies." Unpublished Doctoral Dissertation. University of California, Berkeley.

Yates, L. (1993). *The Education of Girls*. Victoria: Australian Council for Educational Research.

CHAPTER 17

Constructions of Gender in Parents' Choice of a Single-Sex School for Their Daughters

Barbara Heather

INTRODUCTION

In 1993 and 1996 two schools for girls opened in a western Canadian province, one private and the other a publicly funded junior high program. The province is one that had been dominated by its rural population politically and demographically until the 1960s. Consequently, although in the forefront of economic growth and scientific and technological development in its cities, rural and generally conservative values remained common. This gave rise to questions about motivation in the opening of the schools. It seemed equally likely that the schools could be based on conservative or feminist values. Further, the schools opened at a time when school choice had become provincial policy. Parents could select a public school, and because the private school offered relatively low fees, more families could include it in their selection possibilities as well. The combination of two new girls-only schools and school choice created a unique opportunity for researching the role of gender in the decision-making processes of parents and their daughters.

This chapter is based on research conducted at those two schools and focuses on the process of school selection by the parents. Most studies of school choice include single-sex schools as one factor taken into consideration, but when gender is considered, it is not problematized. How parents or their daughters construct gender for themselves generally is taken for granted. Consequently, the distance of the school from the home is seldom a concern in selecting a school for boys, but is considered important when selecting for girls. This chapter examines how parents in particular responded to concerns for the safety and future success of their daughters by cloistering, building character, and gender-proofing the girls. However, their ideas about gender and its relationship to education, occupation, and marriage created contradictions that have implications for school administrators and policymakers.

THE SCHOOLS

In 1993 an ecumenical Christian community opened a girls' school for grades seven through twelve in a rural area about forty-five minutes' drive from River City in a western Canadian province.[1] The headmaster had taught for sixteen years in Christian boys' school that featured a curriculum emphasizing an independent spirit, a willingness to push physical and mental limits, discipline and hard work, respect for the individual, and responsibility to the community. He believed that girls could also benefit from such a program; after finding the boys' school unwilling to accept girls, he founded a separate school. The curriculum, in addition to that required by the Provincial Department of Education, incorporated religious studies, entrepreneurial skills, and a rigorous outdoor exercise program. This was designed to challenge the students, build their confidence, teach them leadership skills, and bring them to a level of health and fitness that would contribute positively to their academic performance. Each school year, for example, began with a week-long hike in the mountains, during which the girls carried all needed supplies on their backs, used tarpaulins to create a shelter every night, dug their own toilets, cooked their own meals, and learned survival skills.

The girls were expected to work and exercise as hard as boys at the brother school. They were pushed to never give up, for example, by a rule that disqualified the whole team in the various cross-country races if one member dropped out for any reason, including injury. The headmaster called this "giving the girls spine." The school was built on relatively authoritarian, hierarchical structures in the belief that imposed discipline leads to self-discipline.

Three years later a group of parents in River City, influenced in part by the private school program, succeeded in establishing a girls' junior high school within the city's public school system. They received much publicity, including editorials in the press. Public opinion seemed to be evenly divided between the dire warnings of correspondents in the local newspaper that the school would turn all of its students into man-hating lesbians, to those writers and parents who thought that the removal of girls from boys and the temptations of adolescence would lead to much better grades and higher self-confidence. The school incorporated women's studies into all aspects of the curriculum and offered science fairs, travel programs, and encouragement to participate in physical fitness and sports. Entrepreneurial skills were also emphasized. The stated goal was to produce independent, confident, and high-achieving girls through encouragement in every sphere from sports to academic studies and entrepreneurial skills. For parents in this province, the two schools added gender to their list of considerations when choosing a secondary school for their daughters.

SCHOOL CHOICE

As a result of neoliberal policies introduced into educational administration in the United Kingdom and the United States in the early 1990s, most studies of school choice have been carried out in those two countries. In Canada, few provinces have allowed school choice up to now and consequently the political and social issues have not attracted a great deal of attention. (See Gaskell, 1992, for a discussion of class and gender.) British and American researchers have focused on the accuracy of casting school choice as a way of making schools better through competition for students (Ball and Gerwirtz, 1997).

Watson (1997) argues that two challenges have been made to "policy-makers of a neoliberal persuasion" who argue that school choice will be based on instrumental rationality by parents. The first challenge comes from the inclusion of social class in research on school choice. Social class structures the educational market as well as the decision-making process of parents, undermining the concept of instrumental rationality. Second, Watson argues that the integration of gender into research also challenges neoliberal assumptions. "In this area, however, there has been very little research which specifically explores why some girls and their parents choose single-sex secondary schools" (p. 172). To what extent do gendered considerations undermine or contribute to instrumental rationality?

Parental choices of secondary school have been found to prioritize certain factors more than others, such as location, sibling or family member attendance, reputation, academic results, facilities, religious affiliation, or restriction to one sex. Also included in the "top ten" choices are factors such as the behavior of students who go to the school, whether the child wants to go, or whether it has been recommended by someone whose reputation is valued (David, West, and Ribbens, 1994; Hunter, 1991; Thomas and Dennison, 1991; West et al., 1995; West and Hunter, 1993; West and Vaarlam, 1991). Several researchers found that working-class and immigrant parents' priorities differed from those of middle-class parents, and that fathers played an active role in school selection more often when a private school was contemplated, possibly because that affected how family income was distributed. Immigrant families were more likely to favor a single-sex school, whereas working-class parents placed more emphasis on the child's preferences and community values, such as choosing a local school or one that other family members had attended.

Although these studies place "single-sex school" in the top ten factors considered by parents, research has not examined the role of gender itself in school choice. David writes, "What is surprising, however, given the focus on issues of 'equity' within much of this [school choice] research, is how little of it concerns the impact and effects of educational reforms on issues of gender for parents and pupils" (1977, p. 77). The role of gender occasionally emerges in the research, for example, when parents express the perception girls need a single-sex school environment more than boys. West, David, Hailes, and Ribbens (1995) give the following typical quotes about girls' and boys' schools from two participants:

I think that to go to an all-boys' school you've got to be quite tough. It's the stereotype I have and I don't want James to be in that situation. I don't see him as a real boys' boy.

She'd be better off with no boys around. She'd be better getting on with her schoolwork and then she could cope with boys when she's a bit older. (1995, p. 32)

David's (1997) research focuses on the role of mothers in decision making. However, the way in which gender roles are played out is only one facet of gender. Little has been done on how constructions of gender inform and shape the process of school selection by parents and their daughters. Few researchers have questioned the ways in which gender affects the choice of a single-sex over a coeducational school, much less examined how ideas about gender may permeate other areas of the decision-making process.

First, questions arising from this have to do with parents' assumptions about their daughters' performance in school. To what extent are girls performing differently than boys and is their performance of less quality overall? Do parents think that girls get lower grades than boys in some subjects, such as science and mathematics, and does this contribute to their choice of school? When they prioritize school performance, what terms do they use? Are their concerns for daughters generic or specific to their sex?

Second, what support is there for the beliefs expressed by parents in British and American research on school choice? The first question is addressed in this research. The second is addressed by research already carried out, which suggests that the assertion that boys do better in a coeducational environment, and girls in a single-sex environment may not be supportable (Mael, 1998). It is not clear that girls suffer more than boys from the school environment. For example, there is clear evidence that more boys than girls drop out of high school (Statistics Canada, 1995), and that more than half of all Canadian women hold a postsecondary degree, diploma, or certificate of some kind (Statistics Canada, 1999). In fact, women are more likely than men to hold a degree. Further, if there is a career disadvantage caused by femininity it may be more that an assumption that they will have a family in the future leads some girls to prioritize family over career by limiting their choice of occupation (McLaren, 1996).

It would appear that at least some assumptions about gender are not in accord with research on school performance, but continue to be used in school selection, and lead to prioritizing different factors for each sex in school choice. It might also be that those same assumptions are shaping the meanings that parents attach to education for their children. Lorber (1994) argues that gender permeates social structures to such an extent that it should be seen as a social institution in itself. That is, the assumptions about gender, the expectations about gender, and the ways in which individuals are socialized and policed into gender suggest that gender permeates our thinking, and is so taken for granted that it appears to us as natural and inevitable. Given this, gender would seem to be an inevitable part of the decision-making process when parents select schools—specifically single-sex as opposed to coeducational schools—but also when they think about a future for their children.

When a single-sex school is selected for girls, Watson (1996) argues that there are two opposing possibilities as to the intent of separating girls out. It can be interpreted as a means of silencing their resistance to the harassment of boys by refocusing them on academic achievement. In other words, by removal from the distractions of boys they do not learn to resist male dominance but only to get on with their work. On the other hand, a single-sex school may be a safe environment for the voicing of resistance, and analysis of how gender and heterosexual relations are produced (Watson, 1996). When parents select a single-sex school, do they do so, she asks, to enable girls to "get on with their work," or is the choice intended to encourage resistance? If so, of what kind and to what extent? The focus of my question for this research, therefore, was to ask, "What role has gender played in the choice of a single-sex school and to what extent are parents aware of any role that gender might be playing in their decisions?" This could have implications for educational policy makers and administrators.

RESEARCH METHODS

To answer these questions I conducted a case study of the two girls' schools described in the preceding. The study was carried out between 1996 and 1997, during the first year of the public junior high school program and the third year of operation for the private school. Having obtained permission to enter the schools, I drew up a description of my research project, together with a statement outlining how participants, some of them high-profile people in their communities, would have their confidentiality and anonymity protected. I spoke with and gained the support of most teachers and principals. Letters were sent home with the students at the public school, and I telephoned parents at the private school, explaining the research and inviting them to participate. With those letters were consent forms for the participation of their daughters. The research design was intended to enable an in-depth study of the decision-making process by all parents, teachers, and students who became involved in the schools. I spent time observing in the schools, and conducted a textual analysis of literature by and about the two schools. In total I conducted some sixty interviews, of which about half were with parents. Most couples spoke with me together, but when only one talked with me, it was always the mother. On two occasions I spoke with the mother and father separately. There were three single mothers in the group.

A list of questions was used as a flexible framework within which participants were encouraged to discuss the process of choice and their hopes for their teaching, children, or futures. In other words, not all of the questions were asked of each participant, nor were they asked in any particular order, but they were used to initiate and keep a conversation going and as probes to understand more clearly the assumptions being made.

The process of interviewing, transcribing, and topic identification continued until a point of saturation was reached. When no new ideas were emerging, analytical codes were established from the original substantive codes, at which point patterns began to appear. Toward the end of this process I sent out a rough draft of my findings to all participants and invited them to focus group meetings to discuss their reactions. This helped to ensure that I had accurately represented all of their perspectives. This chapter focuses on the responses of parent participants in the research.

It is important to remember that this was not a representative sample of parents generally. These were parents who had selected a single-sex school for their daughters. In other words, they were a self-selected sample who had a particular way of thinking that led them to their decision. Because their choice was based on gender, it seemed likely that gender played a relatively large part in their decision making, which might reveal more generalizable ideas. A much more comprehensive sample is needed to determine to what extent their views are representative of all parents. What this study offers is insight into the preferences for a single-sex school that should be of concern to policymakers considering any kind of sex-segregated schooling.

The parents who participated in this research came from a range of socioeconomic backgrounds, but were mostly white and of European extraction. This was partly a result of there being few students from other ethnic or racial backgrounds in the schools during the year in which I carried out the research, and also that of those few who were at the public school, none came forward to participate. As the public school grew in popularity I noticed more minority group members among the students. At the private school I interviewed one student from Mexico, but was unable to interview her parents because they did not visit the school that year. A Native student from the Yukon left before the year was over. The absence of ethnic cultural variation could be an important issue in these schools and needs to be addressed in future research.

Occupational differences in both schools ranged from a couple who were working four jobs between them to pay the fees at the private school to a lawyer from the public school. There were single mothers and dual-income parents as well as one-income parents at both schools. Parents at the private Christian school were no more likely to be practicing Christians than those at the public school. The responses and ideas that the parents expressed showed no class differences other than that professional parents were more apt to say that their daughter must either do as well as they had, or must do better by getting where they were without wasting so much time first, whereas blue collar workers, farmers, and tradespeople more often said they wanted their daughters to have a more secure lifestyle than they themselves had. They had far more concerns in common than any differences, but where there were differences they related strongly to the questions raised by Watson (1996) as to the underlying goal of a single-sex school for girls. Was it to raise resistance, or simply to ensure the girls got on with their work? The content of parents' concerns fell into several larger themes, which are outlined in the following. Because there were no significant differences between the responses of parents from each school, the data were analyzed together.

HOW PARENTS SELECTED A SCHOOL FOR THEIR DAUGHTERS

In the sections that follow I discuss the factors that led to parents' choice of a single-sex school for their daughters. As I will explain, parents had read news stories and heard accounts about the high school years, often from their daughters, that included the distractions of male behavior, discrimination, and harassment, with a resultant loss of confidence and decline in grades. Further, they looked back on their own school years and argued that they had wasted them in part for the same reasons. They wanted their daughters to do better in school because their common sense told them that would give them a better chance at having a safe and secure life in the future. More important to the parents than any successes was the hope that their daughters would be safe, secure, and happy.

Parents assumed that adolescence and gender would play a role in undermining their daughters' achievements in school. They also believed that such behavior was "natural" but dangerous to the safety and security of their daughters. The "natural" dominance and greater power of the boys could work against their daughters' school performance. They reflected on what they knew about the distractions of boys, the discrimination and harassment experienced by girls, the impact of adolescent sexuality, and on their own school behaviors, and concluded that they had to find a way to bypass adolescent masculinity and femininity at least until their daughters could handle it more appropriately.

DISCRIMINATION, SEXUAL DISTRACTIONS, AND HARASSMENT

Discrimination, sexual distraction, and harassment at school were key concerns for parents in their decisions to send their daughters to single-sex schools. Both the parents and their daughters had experiences of discrimination and harassment, and in several instances, fathers talked about being the perpetrators when they were young. Although much of that discrimination focused on appearances, some also included a girls' intellectual, sport, or other achievements or limitations. It was common for boys to "rank" girls and to pick on those who did not meet their standards of attractiveness. However, other types of harassment were also common. A mother talked about her daughter's requested transfer to another school (prior to legislation allowing school choice) that was disallowed, although it would have furthered her athletic career, whereas a boy at the same school was given the necessary permission. Several daughters had been left out of school sports activities by teachers or taunted by the boys for their athletic abilities. Some had been physically bullied, including being kicked, slapped, or punched, in one instance for refusing to do a boy's homework for him. A father commented that the girls became "afraid to be who they are." Boys determined popularity and acceptance or rejection from their particular group. Popular girls were those who took their teasing, giggled at their jokes, and were good looking. Girls had to conform to the demands of fads and fashions without which they could not fit in or be popular with boys. A teacher who was also a mother said, "girls are groupies around male cliques." Those cliques demand a conformity that works against good school performance.

Parents believed that girls became less confident when they moved to secondary school. They talked about reports in the media that girls who had done well in elementary school were getting much lower grades in junior and senior high. Removal from distractions by the opposite sex was believed to provide girls with the freedom to develop intellectually and to experiment with other activities, such as sports and athletics, without having to compete with boys. Physical activities, and the sciences, traditionally the preserve of boys, were considered valuable to girls' development, and the presence of distractions in school meant that the girls would not gain skills in those areas. Distraction led to poor school performance and in turn to lower self-confidence and self-esteem, jeopardizing careers and therefore the safety and security of their daughters.

SEXUALITY

Parents viewed adolescence as a time when interest in sexuality was predominant and dangerous to school performance. One father joked that he would prefer his daughter not have sex "until she's twenty-seven." When daughters were focused on boys and sex, seen as natural desires for their age, pregnancy became "a parent's worst nightmare . . . well almost the worst" as one parent said. Sexuality was considered a natural adolescent preoccupation, a normal developmental stage, but the timing was wrong because it came when young people needed to be focused on school. Girls, parents thought, were more vulnerable because it is girls who get pregnant. Parents' main concern was that their daughters not marry or especially have children until they had established their safety nets—their careers. They argued that to have an egalitarian and satisfying relationship, young women needed the independence and sense of self gained by being successful outside of that relationship.

MY DAUGHTER WILL NOT MAKE MY MISTAKES

Parents saw themselves as having been distracted by the opposite sex from schoolwork or continuing their education. They did not want this to happen to their daughters. Girls, they said, were distracted by the competition to gain a boy's attention and approval, and by watching the boys and laughing at their antics in class. That distraction also led to the silencing of many girls. Afraid of the disapproval of boys, they stopped speaking out in class. One mother said of her own experience in a junior high school math class that one boy "would turn around and look at you [if you said anything]. I was so scared that he would say something [denigrating] to me, I never spoke."

Parents drew on their own experiences in school, at work, and in their family life to arrive at a set of beliefs or truths about what their daughters needed to do in order to be safe and secure. Those perceptions were often linked to parents' memories of how they had handled their own school years. One of the phrases that, worded in various ways, I heard frequently was "my daughter will not make my mistakes." Fathers and mothers had different reasons for making the assertion, however. For fathers, it was usually framed in terms of school performance. They said that for them it had been more important to be popular both with other boys and with girls than to perform well academically. They saw this as the reason that they had either not done very well since leaving high school, or that they had taken twice as long to reach their goals because they had performed poorly.

Mothers, on the other hand, most often said that they had done well in school but married as soon as they graduated rather than going on to further education. "I do hope she won't do what I did," they would say. As a result of beliefs about the consequences of parents' own behavior, daughters were perceived as both likely to "play around" or be distracted and not get on with their schoolwork, but also as likely to throw away their good grades by marrying too soon. Consequently, daughters were removed from the distractions and dangers of being around boys so they would focus on their schoolwork (unlike their fathers), get good marks, and go on to get further qualifications (unlike their mothers). There was a strong element of control in these comments. As a student told me:

> She [mother] signed me up for both schools . . . the public [coeducational] one and this one, and then she said, "O.K. you don't have to go" and then two days before I went she goes "You're going to that all-girls' school."

Persuading or even forcing a daughter to attend a single-sex school was justified in terms of her future safety and security. The extent to which this control was exercised appeared to underscore the strength of parental desire to protect the young women from the perceived dangers of both adolescence and gender. Parents looked back at their own past performance, what they knew about their daughters, and reports on girls' performance in high school, and formed not only goals for their daughters but also a particular image of how they should be as young women in order to achieve those goals and be safe and secure.

Safety and security included economic, emotional, and physical safety. All of the parents agreed that a "good education" was key to a good job and to the safety and security they wanted for their daughters in the future. A good education meant a high school diploma and some form of postsecondary training, although many said that university was not essential. Parents were insistent that it was not the type of occupation that mattered. The following comments are evidence of these beliefs:

> I just want these girls to know that they can do anything they want to—whatever makes them happy. I tell my kids—go to [local technology institute], learn carpentry, I don't care as long as you get an education and you can support yourself. (Marianne, mother at public school)
>
> Yeah, as long as they have got some kind of training other than high school education they'll be able to get work of some type—it may not be in their kind of field but because they've got a piece of paper from college or university it just may help them. Pam added "with Grade 12 you may get a job but you don't advance much." (Ed and Pam, parents, public school)
>
> My hope for them [daughters] is that they'll be doing something that can support them no matter what. (Britta, mother at private school)
>
> My daughter, by God, one way or another, is going to start her life as an adult knowing she can do anything she wants to do and who she wants to take into her life . . . and it will be an informed choice—the kind I never made. (Sonja, private school mother)

Parents insisted gender was not an issue in their goals for their sons and daughters. They wanted the same for their daughters as they did for their sons. What was different was not the outcome but the means of getting there. Pam, a public school mother, said:

> The most important thing for me for my kids is that they *are* able to think for themselves, and I don't mean just financially but, um, maybe Sara [daughter] comes to mind for me more than anything else but I don't want her to think, um, that in order to succeed in her life that she'd finish school, get married and have to have a family, that she'd have to have a man to make her a complete person, and I guess I haven't thought that far ahead for Mark [son] but it would be my thought too that I want them to be a whole person in themselves before they become somebody else, a partner, that's really important to me.

Their daughters could be anything they wanted to be as long as that occupation gave them safety, job security, a good income and benefits, along with the happiness parents also wanted for their daughters. One mother said, "I hope they'll be happy in whatever they're doing, whether it's being a mum, or a business, or a career." Happiness and self-confidence were seen as ingredients of safety and security in fact, because they meant that the daughters were successful. The parents believed that without that "piece of paper" their daughters would be more vulnerable to poverty.

Success in a relationship meant an egalitarian marriage, including either shared care of children or mother at home, in which case it was his job to earn income to support the family. This period of time was seen as temporary, however, with a return to work when the children were old enough (variously defined). A good job and income were seen as ways of ensuring an egalitarian marriage but also as insurance should the marriage fail. Parents accepted without question that mothers are the primary caregivers for their children, and would be the ones who had custody should they divorce.

From their selection of a single-sex school close to home by public school parents, to the choice of a residential program by private school parents, from wanting uniforms to end a focus on fashion and from an emphasis on achievement by both sets of parents, parents attempted to protect and control their daughters. In the private school this tended to stand out more, because the isolated setting allowed for the physical removal of daughters from their previous friends. In the public school it was less evident, except when listening to students themselves who claimed they had been "forced" to go or in discussions of the uniforms, generally hated by the students and approved of by the parents. Aware of women's more vulnerable position in society, the solution parents turned to for the protection of their daughters was to cloister them away from the distractions of sex, and build character as a way of "gender proofing" them against the more negative aspects of femininity. Gender proofing was to be a kind of insurance policy against vulnerability to poverty, poor relationships, and failure. Parents were controlling their daughters now so that their daughters could control their futures.

CLOISTERING, BUILDING CHARACTER, AND GENDER PROOFING

The heart of the problem, as parents described it to me, was that adolescent boys and girls had a negative impact on each other's school performance. Girls in particular were easily distracted by sexual attraction and by the peer hierarchy that was headed by boys and that determined popularity and membership of cliques. Further, they were intimidated by the boys, especially in athletics or science, and would not compete with them. Coeducational schools allowed boys to be "disrespectful" to girls and distract them from their work, and they failed to assist the girls to get good marks or value education. The solution was to remove the girls from the boys, either for junior high or for the entire high school years. Cloistering removed girls from the company of boys so that they would focus on their work and not be distracted. Parents sent their daughters to a single-sex school so they could "build character." This was also a phrase used in publicity about the schools. Building character, said one parent, is "what takes [place] on the inside." According to school literature, building character included learning to make good decisions, becoming a leader, being independent and motivated, and working hard while being caring and responsible for the community. Building character was acquiring characteristics needed to be safe and successful. Girls were not safe or successful in coeducational schools. Building character would ensure that they could cope with coeducational environments later on.

In a world where characteristics are divided into two sets, one masculine and the other feminine, any deficiency in one sex can only be addressed by deleting the offending characteristics and/or by adding characteristics from the other. Parents wanted their daughters to shed their passivity and devotion to boys, and take on some male characteristics, such as leadership, decisiveness, independence, competitiveness, and ambitiousness. But they were definitely not to take on other male characteristics, such as competitiveness at the expense of others. What had to be done, as a teacher said, was to "give the girls spine." Girls had to learn how to stand up to boys and demand respect. It was the girls, therefore, who were deficient and needed to learn how to be stronger. If boys could not be changed, girls could. They could be made less vulnerable by being removed from the boys and building character. They could learn to focus on their work, get good grades, do well in science, math, and athletics, and then they would not be intimidated or silenced when they were again with boys.

Parents were choosing a single-sex school to build character so that their daughters could take care of themselves. They did not want them to remain ultrafeminine, but neither did they want them to be masculine. The daughters were to retain the best feminine characteristics such as caring for others, but not to remain passive, not to be followers. They were to be a hybrid that could move from family to employment easily, demanding shared family work roles and fair treatment at work. They were to be superwomen, something I term *gender missionaries*, converting boys to equality individually, one by one. . . . In other words, parents regarded gender as natural and unchangeable and yet at the same time believed that they could change the behavior of their daughters. They were proofing them against the weaknesses of femininity by teaching them some male characteristics.

Parents might express egalitarian views of their children's future but they also held strong views about masculinity and femininity. They regarded it as more socially produced than biological, and yet at the same time talked about it as "natural." It was as if the social aspect was imbibed rather than taught, something that happened inevitably. They also insisted that boys and girls *were* different. Girls were more compliant, cooperative, and caring, easier to discipline, less independent, and less willing to take risks. It was not the physical differences of body build or strength that parents saw as a major factor, but the reproductive role. It was the reproductive role that justified the female role as givers of care and nurturance. When I asked what femininity meant to parents, there was a range of responses from the private school mother who argued that women were naturally suited to mothering and the father who said that he wanted his daughter to remain feminine because "the woman is the glue in a marriage," to the mother who said, "But I think for my kids I just want them to choose for themselves. . . . I think I'd be thrilled if my son stayed home with his child because he'd be good at it . . . and if my daughter chose not to, that would be good, too. (Janine, public school)."

Parents' assumption was that the world outside was dominated by businesses and business ways of behaving, so that many of the characteristics they thought important were those associated with business such as drive, ambition, and taking risks. They saw the business world as male-dominated, competitive, and tough. To achieve their goals, girls would have to learn to make good decisions, stick to their career plan, and stay motivated. They needed to be self-sufficient, confident, and determined, people who achieved their goals, and were leaders in their field. To do this, parents agreed that girls needed to take on some of the characteristics, such as risk-taking, that are usually attributed to boys. But they were not to *become* masculine. Although they did not want them sexually active, they did want them eventually to enter relationships in which the girls would offer the feminine element—the glue. There was a sense that the parents thought society or social life would be unbalanced if girls or boys changed too much.

Thus the concerns parents had about discrimination, distraction, and harassment, the interpretation that they placed on their own experiences, their understanding of gender as natural, and of the prerequisites for safety and success, led them to believe that although boys could not be changed very much, their more compliant daughters could, and that through cloistering and building character, a single-sex school would help them to accomplish that change, becoming safe without losing femininity.

Parents' decision to send their daughters to a single-sex school therefore was to end distraction, control sexual interest in boys, and build character, all of which would lead to better school performance. They were doing what I term *"gender proofing."* They were inoculating their daughters against the worst effects of being female, while keeping them feminine. Gender proofing is the process by which parents attempted to keep their daughters feminine but tried to ensure that they did not suffer for their femininity. They wanted the girls to grow up able to compete with men for jobs and success, as well as be able to have and hold on to a heterosexual relationship. The girls were to educate men to respect them, and through this would come equality. Gender proofing required the building of character but not the breaking down of gender difference. Given that perspective, I wondered to what extent parents wanted their daughters to learn about, understand, and respond to systemic discrimination. How would they feel about feminism and women's studies?

ATTITUDES TOWARD FEMINISM

Approximately one-third of the parents thought it would be great for their daughters to embrace feminism, explaining that was why they had sent them to a single-sex school. One father's response was, "she damn well better be!" Another thought that, "The feminist revolution has been 90 percent positive . . . now the focus needs to be on changing men. [That men] think they ought to be in charge of things is so stupid (Peter, private school).

> I think feminism's fantastic. I think the movement's past roots are good and sincere and I'm behind it 100 percent. We needed a bomb to shock us . . . everyone has their own idea of what feminism means, and then they don't like it. . . . If Ann [daughter] is a feminist, that's what I'm paying for (Phil, private school).

Many said, however, that girls should be equal to but not the same as boys. There was support for equal rights and respect toward women. However, there was still an emphasis on difference, and this came from both supporters and opponents of feminism. Some supporters also attached qualifiers such as she not be a *radical* feminist.

The majority of parents were either wary of feminism or antagonistic to it. They were not sending their daughters to a single-sex school to learn to be feminist but to get on with their work and learn to be independent. The wary parents said that it was all right for their daughters to be feminist as long as they did not become confrontational. They did not like aggression. One mother said "I'm not really feminist, because I just want everybody to be treated equally." She thought that feminists wanted women to be the superior sex. Antagonistic parents seemed to have taken up the stereotypes of feminism.

> I don't buy into that equity stuff . . . feminists get the business of equity mixed up. The sexes are different from the very beginning. (Tonia, public school)

> I think feminists are, er, I don't know, maybe it's a negative connotation, the word does, in that, er, it's a female only, you know, point of view, and I don't like that, I mean, it's not women alone that live in the world. (Marianne, public school)

> [School staff] try very hard to tell these girls that you have strengths you can use and you should use, [but they] also try . . . to tell them that you do not have to do that at the expense of anyone else, male or female. (Arlene, private school)

This group saw feminism as antimotherhood, as prioritizing career over family, as hating men but also—in an apparent contradiction—as wanting to *be* men. These parents often used breastfeeding as absolute justification of the essential difference between women and men. They thought feminists were exclusionary toward men and saw women as the superior sex, but parents would also say that men "have got to learn to treat women better." However, women should not descend to men's level and act like them in order to gain respect. This meant not getting aggressive. Militant feminists gave the movement its bad name they said. Women are the nurturers and men need the nurturing.

I asked parents how they felt about the women's studies component incorporated into the curriculum at both schools. Generally their attitude was that it was fine as long as it did not interfere with the *real* curriculum. Education was about such things as history, social studies, and science, not about women.

> I like it as long as it's not overdone to the point that, hey, if it's male it's no good. Why shouldn't they see what women can do, you know, it's a good incentive for them. (Arlene, private school)

> And at the public school, Celia, in a surprised tone of voice, commented: and the interesting thing about that is that it was done, I think, without in any way deflecting from what was happening in that period in history . . . it's very complementary to it.

Parents did not consider women's studies to be an important part of the study of history or other subjects. Rather, it was an "optional extra" of value as an incentive to girls. Curriculum was not perceived as male dominated or what O'Brien (1981) called "malestream knowledge." Rather, it was factual and necessary information. It seems then that parents accepted the curriculum as objective or unbiased and as important in achieving occupational success. The issue was not curriculum or educational practices so much as the social interactions of boys and girls. They were not focused on training their daughters to see the structural causes of inequality or to become agents of social change. They were cloistering their daughters to ensure that they "get on with their work." Aware of women's more vulnerable position in society, their solution was to protect their daughters through gender proofing—a kind of insurance policy against vulnerability to poverty and failure. They were controlling them now so that the girls could control their futures.

THE CHOICE OF A SINGLE-SEX SCHOOL

Understandings of gender, interpretations by parents of their own experiences, their daughters' present behavior, and the future life for which they wanted their daughters made safe and secure are far from being sufficient ideas to determine the choice of a single-sex school. Even having considered their views on feminism, parents can still be seen to have had several ways in which they could make the decision. They could have selected a coeducational school, giving their daughters support to stay clear of peer pressures, keep their interest in boys under control, and remain focused on their work. Some might also have opted to teach their daughters about feminism. They could have shown them how to recognize systemic discrimination and respond to it not alone, but collectively, and if a school were available that supported that choice they could have selected it for their daughters, whether it was single-sex or coeducational. Or they could remove their daughters from the distractions of boys through cloistering, choosing a single-sex school that might or might not be feminist. They could remove the source of the problem with or without analysis of its causes. Future research needs to focus on parents who did not make the decision to cloister. Here the focus has been on those parents who chose to do so.

CONCLUSION AND IMPLICATIONS OF THE RESEARCH FINDINGS

Parents were concerned for the future safety and security of their daughters. They believed them to be more in need of protection than boys. The parents' own experiences and their assumptions about gender told them that young women were vulnerable to poverty because of such things as lack of postsecondary education or training, poor employment prospects and the likelihood of single parenting should they divorce. Only a good education would shield girls from their own vulnerability. At the same time daughters were presumed to be heterosexual, with marriage and children in their future. The question then was how to protect them from poverty and insecurity, making them safe and successful while maintaining femininity and their ability to get along with men, and eventually marry.

The answer was to cloister or remove the girls from the distractions of boys, placing them in a single-sex school. The school's role was to foster in the girls the characteristics needed for success so that they would be able to go on and get further qualifications, find a good occupation, and make an egalitarian and safe marriage. They would always have a safety net of savings and/or of a good job behind them should anything go wrong.

The parents understood the safety of their daughters in both individualist and gendered terms. The daughters had to take care of themselves by taking on characteristics suited to the businesslike structures of the economy. It was not a question of changing society or doing away with ideas about gender as natural and dichotomous. There was a hope that strong and independent young women would affect change by gaining the respect of men, but structural change was not addressed, and the gendering of social structures was rarely acknowledged. Gender proofing required the building of character but not the breaking down of gender difference.

Parents wanted strong daughters, but many were uncomfortable with feminism and few were aware of its complexity. Most of their ideas appeared to be based on popular stereotypes. They saw feminists as aggressive attention getters out to denigrate men and they did not want their daughters to be like that. In fact they wanted their daughters to foster their "social skills" (Watson, 1996), to get along well with men and to marry one. They did not want their daughters to work toward changes in social structures or be in the public eye fighting for women's rights. Rather, they were to work for change on a piecemeal basis, one action at a time. They were to be able to take care of themselves.

The issues that arise from this perspective stem from a general understanding of gender as dichotomous and oppositional; that the sexes are naturally and unchangeably different in their behaviors and attributes. There is a widespread belief, for example, that women are better at parenting, particularly of young children, and that men are more aggressive than women. As Kokopeli and Lakey (1995) argued, this leads to an assumption that men will naturally be dominant and aggressive in their relationships with women. Connell argues that: "In our culture the reproductive dichotomy is assumed to be the absolute basis of gender and sexuality in everyday life . . . For many people the notion of natural sex difference forms a limit beyond which thought cannot go." (1987, p. 66).

Parents accept the naturalness of sex difference, and combine it with validation of individualism and an understanding of the necessity for a good education for safety and security in adult life, to produce a model of the feminine superwoman who can take care of herself. Gender was not seen as a structural problem but as one of individual character traits. That in turn created new problems.

First, the only characteristics in a dichotomous gender system that are available to improve femininity are masculine. It appears that women cannot be equal to men without being masculinized, and therefore rendered less feminine, equated with feminist (an imperfect woman). However, the parents are trying to make girls more like boys without them becoming masculine. They are to be competitive without doing so at the expense of others, and to remain feminine and nurturing while also being ambitious, career-focused, and assertive. Gender is muddying the waters so that the only solution is to create a superwoman—the woman who can have it all. Second, most of the parents would prefer that their daughter not be a part of the feminist movement, or at least not publicly demonstrating for change. However, in expecting the girls to deal with systemic discrimination on an ad hoc basis they make it likely that the girls will not succeed in their efforts to defend themselves. They may well fail as superwoman too. As the dictum of W. I. and Dorothy Thomas (1928) states, if we treat gender as real, then it becomes real in its consequences. By definition, single-sex schools treat gender as real. Their very existence may operate to perpetuate hegemonic truths about gender. The heart of the problem is that parents are responding to the symptoms and not addressing the social construction of gender as dichotomous and oppositional. This in turn sets up contradictions because femininity cannot be challenged without changing this definition.

These contradictions suggest problems for school administrators and policymakers. The basis for separating students by sex needs to be questioned. First, research on school performance suggests that the concerns of this group of parents about their daughters may be overstated. Second, should single-sex schooling become a more general practice, school administrators face a difficult set of decisions as to the extent to which they take a feminist stance. First they will have to decide to what extent they are trying to change male-female relationships. To what extent is this to be part of the education system's responsibilities and therefore integrated into school curricula? Further, what impact will segregation have on boys? Might it not increase the pressures to be masculine and possibly even antagonistic to femininity? Second, policymakers could find themselves up against their own guidelines on inclusivity, which are likely to point toward treating girls and boys as the same, or at least as to be given the same opportunities. No matter where policymakers take a stand they could face vocal parental objections from parents who see gender as natural and inevitable. Further, the extent to which their policies reflect anything resembling feminist values will be controversial no matter where the "line" is drawn.

A further problem arises out of the first two. Unless gender awareness is included in the curriculum girls will not gain experience in dealing with boys' dominance and the discrimination that permeates education, and later, family and work, undermining the very strengths that the school is aimed to provide (Watson, 1996). Schools need to include women's studies (including the raising of awareness about the practices of discrimination) in their curriculum, because without it, no matter how strong the girls might become, they are unlikely to be able to recognize and respond effectively to systemic discrimination, especially on their own. Trained to cope by themselves and yet to remain feminine, the girls could become additionally vulnerable through self-blame and a sense of their own inferiority. However, should a girls' school be overtly feminist, it appears from this research it could have trouble with recruitment.

The school system, like the parents, can either insist on the "different but equal" stance, which will lead to attempts to create a better feminine, or it can base policies on a "as similar as different and all equal" stance, leading to inclusive and feminist-based curricula likely to stir controversy at least from those parents who favor cloistering, building character, and gender proofing. Finally, if school policies are to go beyond addressing symptoms, and address the cause of gender problems in the education system, they will have to engage in sweeping changes throughout the school system. To address the problems caused by gender requires an overhaul of school practices so that conceptions of gender as natural are themselves challenged—a commitment that might give pause to many administrators given the probable time and money, not to mention controversy, involved. However, not to do so might commit school systems to spending money on segregated programs that do not address the real problem and which perpetuate inequality.

NOTE

1. All names have been changed to protect anonymity and confidentiality of participants.

REFERENCES

Ball, S. and Gerwitz, S. (1997). "Girls in the Education Market: Competition and Complexity." *Gender and Education* 9(2): 207–222.

Connell, R. W. (1987). *Gender and Power*. Stanford, CA: Stanford University Press.

David, M., West A., and Ribbens, J. (1994). *Mother's Intuition? Choosing Secondary Schools*. London: Falmer Press.

David, M. (1997). "Diversity, Choice, and Gender." *Oxford Review of Education* 23(1): 77–87.

Gaskell, J. (1992). *Gender Matters from School to Work*. Toronto: OISE.

Hunter, J. B (1991). "Which School? A Study of Parents' Choice of Secondary School." *Educational Research* 33(1): 31–41.

Kokopeli, B., and Lakey, G. (1995). "More Power Than We Want: Masculine Sexuality and Violence." In M. Anderson and P. H. Collins (Eds.), *Race, Class, and Gender: An Anthology*. (2nd ed.), Belmont, CA: Wadsworth, 450–455.

Lorber, J. (1994). *The Paradoxes of Gender*. New Haven: Yale University Press.

Mael, F. A. (1998). "Single-Sex and Coeducational Schooling: Relationships to Socioeconomic and Academic Development." *Review of Educational Research* 68(2): 101–129

McLaren, A. T. (1996). "Coercive Invitations: How Young Women in School Make Sense of Mothering and Waged Labour." *British Journal of Sociology* 17(3): 229–297.

O'Brien, M. (1981). *The Politics of Reproduction*. Boston: Routledge and Kegan Paul.

Statistics Canada. (1995). *High School May Not Be Enough: An Analysis of Results from the School Leavers Follow-up Survey 1995*. Statistics Canada Catalogue 81–585–XPE.

——. (1999). *Education Indicators in Canada 1999*. Statistics Canada Catalogue 81–582–XPE.

Thomas, A., and Dennison, B. (1991). "Parental or Pupil Choice—Who Really Decides in Urban Schools?" *Educational Management and Administration* 19(4): 243–249.

Thomas, W.I., and Thomas, D. (1928). *The Child in America: Behaviour Problems and Programs*. New York: Knopf.

Watson, S. (1996). "Hetero-sexing Girls: 'Distraction' and Single-Sex School Choice." *Women's Studies Journal* 12(2): 115–127

Watson, S. (1997). "Single-Sex Education for Girls: Heterosexuality, Gendered Subjectivity, and School Choice." *British Journal of Sociology of Education* 18(3): 371–383.

West, A., David, M., Hailes, J., and Ribbens, J. (1995). "Parents and the Process of Choosing Secondary Schools: Implications for Schools." *Educational Management and Administration* 23(1): 23–38.

West, A., and Hunter, J. (1993). "Parents' Views on Mixed and Single-Sex Secondary Schools." *British Educational Research Journal* 19(4) 369–380.

West, A. and Varlaam, A. (1991). "Choice of High Schools: Pupils' Perceptions." *Educational Research* 33(3): 205–215

AUTHOR BIOGRAPHIES

John Ainley is Deputy Director of the Australian Council for Educational Research (ACER) and Head of its Policy Research Division. He has expertise in the investigation of school influences on student progress through high school and beyond and his reports have been widely used by education authorities in the review and development of Australian educational policy and practice. Dr. Ainley has directed national studies of subject choice in senior secondary school (*Subject Choice in Years 11 and 12*), conducted a longitudinal study of the progress of students through the senior secondary years (*Progress through High School*) and is the principal author of a report (*Schools and the Social Development of Young Australians*) that provides a national picture of the affective development of young people.

Emily Arms is a doctoral candidate at the University of California, Los Angeles. Her research interests include educational reform, gender studies, and teacher education.

Heather Blair is an associate professor in Language Arts and Reading in the Department of Elementary Education at the University of Alberta, Canada. She is interested in the intersections of language, gender, and schooling for early adolescents.

Celeste Brody is an instructional dean at Central Oregon Community College in Bend, Oregon. She specializes in instructional theory and classroom practices that enhance inquiry, group problem solving, and student diversity. She is copresident of the International Association for the Study of Cooperation in Education, and has published (with Neil Davidson) *Professional Development for Cooperative Learning* (SUNY, 1998). Her interest in gender studies spans thirty years of work in public schools and higher education curriculum, and includes the book, *Gender Consciousness and Privilege* (Falmer, 2000) with Schmuck and Nagel, also in this volume.

Patricia B. Campbell, the president of Campbell-Kibler Associates, Inc., has been involved in educational research and evaluation with a focus on gender and race, since the mid 1970s. An expert witness in the Citadel sex-discrimination case, Dr. Campbell's publications include *The AAUW Report: How Schools Shortchange Girls,* and *Of Two Minds: Single-Sex Education, Coeducation, and the Search for Gender Equity in K–12 Public Schooling* (New York Law School Journal of Human Rights).

Peter Daly is an associate dean (postgraduate studies), Faculty of Legal, Social and Educational Sciences, Queens University, Belfast. He teaches in the Graduate School of Education. His published work reflects research interests in comparative educational effectiveness, featuring the use of multilevel statistical models in the analysis of hierarchical social data. He has a particular interest in school gender studies.

Amanda Datnow is an assistant professor in the Department of Theory and Policy Studies at the Ontario Institute for Studies in Education of the University of Toronto. Her research focuses on school reform policy and politics, particularly with regard to the professional lives of educators and issues of equity. Within this broader research agenda, one of her areas of focus is the intersection of gender and school reform.

Diane Diamond is a doctoral candidate in sociology at the State University of New York at Stony Brook. Her research interests include gender integration; masculinity; gender equity in education and work; and the impact of social, cultural, and economic changes on family life.

Kathleen Gallagher is an assistant professor in the Department of Curriculum, Teaching, and Learning at the Ontario Institute for Studies in Education of the University of Toronto. Her recent book, *Drama Education in the Lives of Girls: Imagining Possibilities,* is based on an ethnographic study of drama practices in a public, single-sex school. Her research continues to examine questions of equity in theater/drama education in urban contexts.

Judith Gilson is an instructor in teacher education at the University of San Francisco. After teaching in coeducational and all-girls independent schools for fifteen years, she has focused her research on the effects of single-gender education, specifically in mathematics, in the independent school sector. Dr. Gilson has presented the results of her research on situational interest in mathematics classrooms, middle-school girls' achievement in mathematics, and middle-school students' attitudes toward technology at annual meetings of the American Educational Research Association (AERA) and Research on Women in Education.

Barbara Heather is a professor at Grant MacEwan College in Edmonton, Alberta. She is interested in the impacts of constructions of gender and has conducted studies of parental, teacher, and student choice of single-sex school and small town and rural women.

Kathryn Herr is on the faculty in the College of Education at the University of New Mexico. Her particular interests include youth studies, qualitative and practitioner research, and social justice issues.

Lea Hubbard is an assistant research scientist in the Sociology Department at the University of California, San Diego. Her work focuses on educational inequities as they exist across ethnicity, class, and gender.

Michael Kimmel is a professor of sociology at SUNY at Stony Brook. His books include *Changing Men* (1987), *Men Confront Pornography* (1990), *Men's Lives* (5th ed., 2000) *Against the Tide: Profeminist Men in the United States, 1776–1990* (1992), *The Politics of Manhood* (1996), *Manhood: A Cultural History* (1996), and *The Gendered Society* (2000). He edits *Men and Masculinities*, an interdisciplinary scholarly journal, a book series on men and masculinity at the University of California Press, and the Sage series on men and masculinities. He is the spokesperson for the National Organization for Men Against Sexism (NOMAS) and lectures extensively on campuses in the United States and abroad.

Leslie Miller-Bernal is a professor of sociology at Wells College, a women's college in Aurora, New York. Her research interests focus on the significance of single-sex versus coeducation for women students, and on the implications for women of recent transitions to coeducation of formerly men's and formerly women's colleges. She is the author of *Separate by Degree: Women Students' Experiences in Single-Sex and Coeducational Colleges* (Peter Lang, 2000).

Nancy G. Nagel is an associate professor at Lewis and Clark College in Portland, Oregon, where she coordinates the elementary intern program and teaches courses in mathematics and real-world problem solving. Her research interests include students' construction of understanding in mathematics, gender issues in schooling, and empowering students to become active citizens. Recent publications include: *Early Childhood Education, Birth–8: The World of Children, Families, and Educators* (coauthor with Amy Driscoll, Allyn and Bacon, 2002), *Gender Consciousness and Privilege* (coauthor,

Falmer Press, 2000), and *Learning Through Real-World Problem Solving* (Corwin Press, 1996).

Cornelius Riordan is a professor of sociology at Providence College. He has studied the effects of single-sex and mixed-sex education at all levels of schooling for the past two decades and is the author of *Girls and Boys in School: Together or Separate?* and numerous papers on this subject. His areas of specialization are the social organization of schools and the educational outcomes related to various types of school organization. He is the author of a textbook in the sociology of education entitled *Equality and Achievement*, 2nd ed.

Alan R. Sadovnik is a professor of education and sociology at Rutgers University-Newark and chair of its Department of Education and Academic Foundations. His publications include *Equity and Excellence in Higher Education* (1995), *Exploring Education: An Introduction to the Foundations of Education* (1994, 2000), *Knowledge and Pedagogy: The Sociology of Basil Bernstein* (1995); "*Schools of Tomorrow," Schools of Today: What Happened to Progressive Education* (1999), and *Founding Mothers and Others: Women Educational Leaders During the Progressive Era* (2002).

Rosemary Salomone is a professor of law at St. John's University and a former faculty member of the Harvard Graduate School of Education. She is the author of *Equal Education under Law* (St. Martin's Press, 1986) and *Visions of Schooling: Conscience, Community, and Common Education* (Yale University Press, 2000). As a fellow of the Open Society Institute, she has completed a book on single-sex schooling to be published spring 2003 by Yale University Press entitled *Same, Different, Equal: Rethinking Single-Sex Schooling*.

Jo Sanders is the director of the Center for Gender Equity at Washington Research Institute in Seattle, Washington. She has specialized for many years in gender equity in mathematics, science, and technology, and is the author of ten books and dozens of articles and book chapters.

Kathy Sanford is an assistant professor at the University of Victoria in western Canada, working in the areas of literacy curriculum and teacher education. Her research interests focus on the intersections between gender and literacy, teacher education, and assessment.

Patricia Schmuck is a retired professor of education at Lewis and Clark College in Portland, Oregon. Her work on gender has spanned thirty years and focused on women in administration. In 2000 she received the Willystine Goodsell award for "scholarship, activism, and community building on behalf of women" from the Research on Women and Education of the American Educational Research Association. She continues to teach, consults on gender issues in schools, serves on the Hood River District School Board, hikes Mount Hood, and is a master gardener and active grandmother.

Susan F. Semel is an associate professor of education at the City College of New York, CUNY. Her publications include *The Dalton School: The Transformation of a Progressive School* (1992), *Exploring Education: An Introduction to the Foundations of Education* (1994, 2000), *"Schools of Tomorrow," Schools of Today: What Happened to Progressive Education* (1999), and *Founding Mothers and Others: Women Educational Leaders during the Progressive Era* (2002).

Janice Streitmatter is Professor of Educational Psychology at the University of Arizona. Her primary area of research is in the field of gender issues related to adolescent females and schooling.

Elisabeth L. Woody recently completed her Ph.D. at the University of California, Berkeley, where she studied gender and diversity issues, adolescent development, and critical and feminist pedagogy. Her dissertation, "Student Articulations of Gender in California's Public Single-Gender Academies," explored student constructions of gender and sexuality within the context of public single-sex schooling. She recently received the Outstanding Graduate Student Instructor award for her work in two courses: Current Issues in Education and Gender Issues in Education.

INDEX